THE AMERICAN POET

Weedpatch Gazette
For 1995-1996

Samuel D. G. Heath, Ph. D.

iUniverse, Inc.
New York Bloomington

The American Poet
Weedpatch Gazette For 1995-1996

iUniverse books may be ordered through booksellers or by contacting:

iUniverse
1663 Liberty Drive
Bloomington, IN 47403
www.iuniverse.com
1-800-Authors (1-800-288-4677)

ISBN: 978-1-4401-5656-4 (sc)
ISBN: 978-1-4401-5657-1 (ebook)

Printed in the United States of America

iUniverse rev. date: 06/29/2009

CONTENTS

CHAPTER ONE

My initial essay of December 1994 calling for a meeting of good men to address the need of a New Systematic Theology has met with positive response. Most church leaders agree that the need for a Council to discuss issues of the role of the churches in our contemporary society and questions of presently accepted dogmatic theology is necessary. The major problem that presents itself is the manner in which such a thing is to take place.

I've started the New Year, 1995, with a visit to a community church here locally in Bakersfield. I had met with the pastor previously, a very good man with the heart of a real shepherd. We had an extended conversation about some of the issues I have raised; we shared our concerns about the inability of the churches to deal with many of the realities of life which face people in the world and our dysfunctional society.

This good man has been the pastor of this church for over twenty years. He is an expert in churchology. My heart went out to him as he shared much of the helplessness he faced in trying to deal with real life issues to those who are so insistent on insulating themselves from those realities. People want church; they don't want to be made to feel responsible for the conditions out in the real world.

As I sat through the service, however, I made the following notes:

People will never advance, spiritually, beyond infancy as long as their teachers constantly re-hash, endlessly, the milk of the Word every Sunday. Hebrews 5:11 - 6:2.

Do pastors bear the responsibility and the blame for keeping infant congregations or are the people at fault for not demanding more of their leaders? Or do they share equally in the tragedy of a hopeless world that Christ said should be the mission field of the churches, a world to which Christians are to be salt and light?

A further thought came to me as it has in so many churches I have visited. Thoreau claimed the churches of his time actually blasphemed God by their pious concern for each other while accepting none of the responsibility for conditions outside their comfortable pews and contenting themselves with comfortable sermons and songs.

After the service I wandered about. There were probably about one-hundred people yet, knowing I was a stranger, knowing this was my first visit to this church, not one single person even said "Hello," introduced themselves or offered a hand in greeting to me. As my mother used to say; "If the churches were as friendly as the bars they would be packed." The truth of her criticism came to me once more at this church. Good Shepherd, good people, but....

Like all human beings, perverse thoughts often come to my mind. It occurred to me, standing in the courtyard of the church, that if I suddenly lit a cigarette I would most certainly get the attention of these brethren. And in my considerable experience with such people, I could reasonably expect some soldier of the cross to see an opportunity to show a sinner the error of his way or try to convert someone who obviously needed to be shown the way and saved from my obvious path to perdition.

Having been properly tenured in the way of Phariseeism myself, I thoroughly understand the mind-set of such people who so easily judge from the outside of the cup. But I shrugged off temptation and left unnoticed and unwelcomed by all but the pastor himself.

This was New Year's Day. It came on a Sunday for 1995. I had many invitations for New Year's Eve but had spent the night quietly with friends and had gone to bed early in anticipation of visiting this church early the next morning.

One of the places I was invited was a tavern in Lake Isabella. I would have known many of the people and they would all have made me feel very welcome. I would have danced with some of the women I know and the atmosphere would have been one of friendliness and camaraderie, the music and atmosphere would have been lively and real, no pretense or hypocrisy. I would have been right at home among the sinners, many of them drunkards and harlots, who have become more of a family to me than those righteous calling themselves God's people.

But I chose not to go to the tavern up at the Lake. I was a good boy, stayed home and went to church early the next morning. With the result I have just described. No, I'm not going to say I made a mistake in this. As a Christian, I belong among the family of believers, my brethren in Christ. But my ministry, more and more, seems to be among the great unwashed, the unchurched that have failed to find the caring love and compassion they so desperately need among those same brethren.

Because of the very humanity of the problems we face in our society, I often feel constrained to point out my own frailties before I can find the courage to make suggestions to others. It's a case of examining the beam in my own eye before I attempt to remove the speck in another's.

In just that spirit, I sometimes intrude stories, telling on myself that give the reader an opportunity to examine the extent of the truth of myself as a badly flawed man.

Not a little of the embarrassment I cause good Christian friends is my weakness in mixing with and reaching out to those sinners with whom I often find more in common than with so many of the righteous. For this reason I intrude another excerpt from my book "Birds With Broken Wings" at this point:

Now that I'm in the big city, and being a Christian, I am checking out the local churches (and the local bars). More war stories ahead. One large church advertised a Singles Ministry. I certainly qualify so I went.

Well, the people were all exceptionally nice and friendly and certainly made me feel welcome; but... As I sat and endured the sermonette I couldn't shake the impulse to cry out: "Where's the reality of what Jesus is all about here?" In other words, a nice group of people was sitting listening to the same old thing you hear virtually every Sunday in both Sunday school and Church. The word *dynamic* did not exactly come to mind. The word *boring* most certainly did.

I had to comment to one of the nice fellows after surviving the meeting that it only confirmed my own theological (and heretical) observation that if the churches could only make Heaven half as exciting as Hell, they would be doing a thriving business. He was not amused. I confess I don't make many converts of good church people with such views.

But as I sat there I remembered that I too was once one of these people, satisfied with comfortable religious beliefs, dogmas, that allowed an easy mind if you didn't ask the hard questions. Unhappily, I did begin, finally, to ask such questions of God and others and I haven't had an easy time of it since.

There was a moment during the harangue from the speaker where I found myself fervently wishing that I had opted to go to the Cadillac Ranch out at Marin instead. Well, I thought, if this finishes in time I could still make it out to a place where the people were actually alive, some actually enjoying themselves rather than pretending to as a religious exercise. But, it wasn't to be.

The time was redeemed in some fashion by my being able to actually discuss some of my views with a few people before I left. These are nice people. Nothing I have said should be construed otherwise. They are caring, concerned and trying to find answers to their own loneliness in a manner that fits their own beliefs and faith. I heartily commend them for this.

It is I suppose the, to me, oppressive, insular attitude I meet with in the churches. These folks just don't seem to know there is a war going on for the hearts and minds of our children, our future as a nation. And, if they are

Samuel D. G. Heath, Ph. D.

aware of it, they seem ill suited to do battle in the Devil's arena. Religion is the protective shield they have built to insulate themselves from all the ugliness about them. God help such warriors if I were allowed another pulpit from which to tell them of the realities outside their comfortable pews.

Harsh as such criticism is, let me be the first to confess that I would willingly re-join them in shutting out all that ugliness if I only could. How fervently I wish I had never intruded myself into the World, how I wish the questions had never begun to be asked that led to my alienation from my brethren. I feel like Paul who could have wished himself accursed for the sake of his own brethren according to the flesh, the Jews, if they could only be made to see the light.

But all the wishing in the world won't change what I know and what I have learned and experienced in my own pilgrimage through this vale of tears. How I wish I could get those brethren to listen and understand. But I'm damaged goods and, like the Publican, no matter how low I bow my head and beat my breast crying out to God: "Be merciful to me, a sinner," the wicked, the seducers, the liars still prosper and those with a tender conscience still grieve alone. And I can't shake the belief that if the churches were really doing the job God called them to, it wouldn't be this way.

Well, I'll be going to the Cadillac Ranch and mixing it up with the rest of the sinners. The music will play, I'll dance with the ladies and some will provide me the stories I love to tell. I'll find the real poetry of life in an accurate recounting of real people and real events. At least it will be lacking the stench of hypocrisy (mine, at least).

As a sinner saved by grace alone, I'll be with those that certainly understand the subject of sin and often show a more sincere sensitivity to their own sins than many of those I know in the churches. Could this be the reason Jesus said the prostitutes and tax collectors stood a better chance of Heaven than the professional religionists of His time?

Now the reader has a pretty fair idea of how far I have removed myself from accepted orthodoxy. Is this condition terminal? I often ask myself. Not a few have judged me so. Have I plunged too far into the Glory of Evil and the Dark Side of love and romance to be extricated to the realm of those more enlightened? Or do I see, as a poet, the difference between the diabolical and the divine because of such in-depth exposure?

Those among the brethren that have read my Birds book are justifiably concerned about me. Those that still love me warts and all is more to their credit than any cooperation on my part to be more circumspect in sharing my own dark thoughts and adventures for the whole world to see and judge.

It may be that I am so badly flawed in my associations with such people as the tax collectors and prostitutes that I can no longer discriminate. Yet, it was

4

Jesus who said these would enter Heaven before the righteous of His time. I can't help thinking there is a message here for my brethren in the churches.

So, as a Christian my message seems to be for the benefit of those whose love has grown cold, those who Thoreau claimed blasphemed God by pious attending of church while uncaring of those outside and not belonging to their own; a very nice club whose membership is restricted to those only who fit a proper mold of behavior and the traditions of the elders.

And I'm sure Jesus weeps for such children who claim His name and shame that name because of their refusing to accept responsibility for the millions without hope outside the doors of the churches and missing the ominous message in Cain's words: "Am I my brother's keeper?" Not to mention Jesus' caution about failing to help those hungry, thirsty, naked and in need of human compassion of Matthew 25:31-40.

This small example of the many failures of the churches to address the needs for which God called them into being should serve to bring attention to the pressing need of making God more real, more relevant, more human if you will in order to understand the Great Commission, to understand the desperate need people have for love and compassion which is supposed to be the identifying characteristic of The Lord's disciples and yet is so tragically, abysmally missing among those that claim to know and follow Him.

So it is that I have taken it upon myself to face the problem out of genuine concern for the lost and concern for my own brethren. And no small part of my concern is for the honor and integrity of The Lord Himself, my concern that He is shamed and dishonored, not by the world, but by those that profess to be the teachers and leaders of His Gospel and Church.

Nor do I sleep content in the knowledge of the sureness of my own cause and mission. I am filled with doubt and anxiety and come before The Lord often in fear that I may be doing, speaking, asking or writing something that might be of offense to Him. I often find myself clutching my Bible to me and, like the Psalmist, communing with The Lord on my bed, trying to find sleep but going over these plaguing questions which will not leave my mind, will not leave me to the peace and rest I so desperately seek.

My own weaknesses and failures give the enemy plenty of ammunition with which to rob me of any peace of mind and even knowing that God is greater than a heart that condemns, greater than our Accuser, I continue without the peace of certainty along this path that is so treacherous to those more sure-footed than I.

But feeling keenly the abject failure of the churches to be a relevant force for good in our own nation, it has become a burden to me that I feel must be shared with those who must surely, I tell myself, genuinely care about this and want to do something about it. I don't flatter myself that I am sufficient in and of myself to carry such a burden or to be the voice of the prophet in calling the churches to repentance. I need, myself, too much forgiveness of sin and failure in my own life to think such a thing. But I am compelled to write of such things regardless my own sins and weaknesses and, perhaps, it is just such an awareness of such things that gives the impetus to do it.

Maybe I am seeking absolution in bringing such things to the attention of others who are undoubtedly better suited to do so. If such an unfit instrument, such a badly flawed man as myself can see these things; surely better men than me do as well. It may be that I can shame them into action just because of my obvious unsuitableness for the task I believe they should be taking on themselves.

With these thoughts in mind, I take up the questions that I feel would promote action by the churches in redeeming themselves in the sight of God and the world. Please believe I do so in all due humility and concern for the honor of God Himself, never supposing that as a man, I am sufficient for any of these things. My call is really as I have said a plea to better men than myself to take up the task.

Please, don't become hardened in your own view because I touch some of your sacred cows, because questions I raise get your back up and as a result cause you to defend the indefensible. Who are you Paul might have said to become angry with me just because I have made you defend a point of view that is only thinly, veiled prejudice? Too many times have I had to face friends who became unfriendly because I have questioned their prejudices and interpretations when I only sought dialogue; not controversy. With this in mind, I continue with the hope that good men will yet respond in openness and earnest seeking of truth in spite of the character of the questioner.

The supreme question of the relationship between men and God that weighs so heavily in human affairs and is the basic cause of the way people treat each other admits of no ready or easy consensus. The very complexity of the ideas of men throughout the centuries concerning this relationship bears testimony to the confusion that reigns over the subject. Yet the need of definition is ever more critical as the world becomes an ever more chaotic and dangerous place. The irreligious may think the question does not impinge on them but such a thought is foolish in the extreme. Whole societies function, and come into conflict, on the basis of the moralities of their religious taboos and commands.

Therefore, it becomes ever more critical to have a consensus among peoples and nations as to the nature of God and His relationship with men. It is the answer to this question, more than any other that foretells the future of our own nation and the world.

As a Christian, my own view of this relationship is obviously colored by that belief system described as Christianity. I don't delude myself that my perception of other belief systems, no matter how well studied academically, precludes elements of prejudice in my own thinking or conclusions. Such a thing would be, obviously, ignorant and a damning indictment of the very objectivity I seek as an essential ingredient of coming to a consensus of understanding of others and their diverse cultural and religious distinctives.

To consider one's self objective without the necessary examination, acceptance and recognition of your own biases are prejudicial ignorance that cries out: I'm ignorant and proud of it! Not much hope of any useful contributions toward understanding and compassion for others in such a case.

Yet, with that admission in mind, an examination of humanity in general admits of common concerns and beliefs that should be the building blocks of community among all peoples. For example, parents love their children whether Christian, Moslem or Jew, whether black, brown, white or yellow. Commonalities of human behavior do exist and should be the focus of attempts to understand the relationship with God and with one another.

Conflict invariably occurs where an ideology, a belief system, demands obedience and acquiescence from all others, particularly when such an ideology chooses force of arms to enforce acceptance. But with understanding and compassion as goals in dialogue with others, many of the questions concerning Christians become legitimate questions of all people regardless of their own belief systems.

I would call the attention of the brethren to Hebrews 5:8: "Although he was a son, he learned obedience from what he suffered and once made perfect, he became the source of eternal salvation for all who obey him and was designated by God to be high priest in the order of Melchizedek."

Several things immediately suggest themselves in this passage. That Christ was ignorant of some things and had to learn them. Also, that God means something else by the word perfect than religious people ascribe to it. I asked a friend whether he thought God was still learning things. He gave me the party line that God knows everything and has no need of learning. I responded that I would consider it really hell if I thought I already knew it all and had nothing else to ever explore, to learn.

He accused me of casting God in a human mold, the old argument that I was making a god after my own image rather than God making me in His. He then showed me a picture and pointed out the obvious that the picture was only an image of the real thing. I think he missed something in his illustration. God didn't claim to make us dead pictures but living images of

Him and made us live by breathing His Spirit into us and the *Adam* became a living soul.

Yet, if Jesus Himself had things to learn about love and compassion, of suffering in order to represent us as our Savior, Mediator and High Priest, I'm inclined to suppose that God is still learning and so is His Son. The apostle John in his First Epistle makes the point that there are children of God and children of the Devil. But the interesting thing to me is the fact that just as human wisdom at its best acknowledges those that are compassionate, forgiving and loving are children of God, that those that do righteously are righteous. Conversely, those that do evil and harm to others are of the devil are unrighteous. Makes imminently good sense but comes into conflict with orthodox, dogmatic theology.

For example, the serial killer, those who inflict torture on children surely cannot be human by any definition but that of a monster without conscience. Such might very well be called children of the Devil. But an Albert Schweitzer whose views were so very much in conflict with accepted orthodoxy? How consign such a man to the pit together with those cruel monsters that abuse and kill children? I find I cannot.

Will a good man, who by the definition of the apostle John is righteous, go to hell because he doesn't subscribe to my personal creed of faith? I have always had trouble here. Will those Jesus described as giving only a cup of cold water when needed be cast out into darkness because they don't know what I do of the Bible?

I admit of a good deal of confusion in my own mind when considering such things. In all the chaos surrounding so many questions of the Faith, I find I have to resort to the wise counsel of others. But too many of these others are far removed from the acceptable company of orthodox believers. Many are long gone and their thoughts on these subjects survive only in their writings.

Things like my writing once that if I were to supply another pulpit I might choose my sermon theme from the Broadway play "South Pacific" rather than Moses in the bulrushes have caused a cold reception among the brethren. And, I must add, understandably so.

But my confusion is lessened when I consider common humanity, when I think about my ministry to the down-and-out, people so like myself that moved The Lord's heart of compassion and caused Him to be sorrowful because they were like sheep without a shepherd. But my own orthodoxy comes in and causes me to doubt, to suffer anxiety and confusion. It is too easy to fall back on comfortable dogma rather than ask questions that admit of no easy answers, questions like what does God do with dead babies and why do the wicked prosper? Asaph (Psalm 73) might have found his answer when he entered the sanctuary of the Lord but I'm still having the same difficulties as the writer of Psalm 71 and so many others.

I mentioned the manner of baptism and celebrating the Lord's Supper as an on-going battleground between the churches in my December essay. Just recently I confronted the monster again with a friend who believes immersion the only way of proper baptism.

He said, with the usual undisguised disdain for the unenlightened to which I have become so accustomed because of my numerous heresies, that sprinkling was only a symbol of a symbol. And he may very well be right. Now I believe that immersion is the meaning of *baptizmo* and gives a beautiful picture, symbol, of being buried by being immersed and raised coming up out of the water.

Now, as I said, perhaps my old friend is right. Maybe immersion is the only proper way of being baptized and those who are sprinkled haven't really had a proper baptism and have to suffer the Lord's displeasure accordingly, but his animated frustration with my not agreeing with him only served to make my point for me. If my close friend, like my old friend Gary North, could become angry with me on such an issue it only serves to point out the reason the churches lack so much credibility in dealing with reality, real life.

If the mode of baptism or the manner in which we take communion is such a life and death thing that it brings some to the point of anger, and as with abortion, even murder in some cases, something is definitely wrong with this picture. Is the anger properly directed at me if I don't become a convert to another man's interpretation (naturally this is not an interpretation to such people. They are dead right and I am dead wrong)?

It might help, in examination of the writings of those earliest fathers of the Church, to find that the mode of Baptism, as with Communion, was a mixed bag at best. Whether immersion was the only form of New Testament time's baptism, sprinkling (laving) was quickly in vogue as acceptable from the earliest recorded history of the churches.

I have taken the view that the Lord has allowed some to be dunked and some to be sprinkled. To me, it isn't a question of tremendous magnitude. If I become spiritually inferior to those who hold opposing views of something God has not made explicitly clear, and He hasn't in these two cases, I can't help thinking that those who are angry with my lack of agreement with them are missing the larger picture.

I have become ever more sensitive to such things because I have seen the evil that separates brother from brother on such issues. Of one thing I am certain; God never intended such things to be a battleground but expected us to show the world we are His by the love we have for one another. And a love that condescends or patronizes is not the kind of love of First Corinthians 13 and First John that God demands of those that claim His Name. I therefore make that love of those great epistles the criteria of fellowship rather than the keeping of ordinances. And, as a result, become the spiritual inferior of those that have better doctrinal views and adopt, at best, a foul spirit of condescension toward those lacking their spiritual superiority in such matters.

Still, it is those who continue to love and accept me in spite of disagreement on some particulars that gives me continued hope that the spirit of Christ still reigns supreme in real believer's hearts and minds. It is this that motivates me to continue to keep trying in spite of all the obstacles.

I guess I have been exposed to too much of the Glory of Evil and the Dark Side of love to make a proper theologian. I don't find the easy dogmas comfortable to me any longer that consign those better than I am to the outer reaches. It is questions like these that keep me from the comfort of fellowship with those with whom I share, for the most part, a common belief and background. But I am, seemingly perversely, compelled to keep asking the questions; hopefully without having to share a Hemlock cocktail with Socrates.

Questions concerning our contemporary society such as abortion, homosexuality, euthanasia, suicide, etc. make a meeting of church leadership a critical demand. The tyranny of Caesar's laws which increasingly pervert the cause of justice make a further demand for Christian, political activism as never before in history. It is agreed that unless the churches are able to play a crucial and realistic role in our government, Caesar will make the decisions that will dictate our way of life and the concomitant loss of freedoms that we have taken for granted for too long.

A very difficult part of the problem is the fact that too many fundamental believers have a prejudicial mind-set that closes the door to a realistic evaluation of the questions and answers needed. It's as though they have made up their minds, shut the door and, as a consequence, no further light on the subject is allowed to enter. The obvious comparison to those Pharisees of old immediately comes to mind in this respect.

An example of what I am speaking of is the issue of abortion. As a Christian, I believe abortion to be the murder of an innocent child. But when those calling themselves Christian gun down pro-abortionists there is an obvious problem to be resolved here.

Euthanasia- assisted suicide? What should be the stand of the Christian in this case? But if Christians are divided on these issues, clearly a Council is needed to come to a consensus between The Holy Spirit and church leaders just as in that earliest Council of Jerusalem.

Disagreement should be the herald of the need of wise counsel. We may all hold different opinions but where is the leadership needed to come to conclusions about these matters that would be binding on all believers? No one believes in personal freedom and responsibility more than I. Yet, one of the evils that plague the churches is the fragmentation caused by the lack of proper, organized leadership. The small community churches, numbering in the thousands that have no denominational ties or are not bound to a hierarchy of organizational creeds and discipline are cases in point.

Many of these small churches, and not a few larger ones, are very proud of their independence. All well and good except for the fact that so many are opposed to any discipline of creed or organization and most, consequently, are of no impact to a society. More grievously, many are subject to the vanity of the egos of individual pastors and the vanity of *They are right and all others are wrong in their interpretations of God, His nature, His Word*, etc.

I have attended so many of these smaller churches that the words of an Episcopalian friend often come to mind. He said he was an Episcopalian because his church didn't require his checking his brains at the door before he entered the sanctuary. His blunt criticism has all too often been justified in my dealings with so many of these independent and virtually all the charismatic churches.

As Philip Schaff pointed out in his "History of The Christian Church," organization proved of crucial success in the history of the church. It was the corruption of the organization that led to the Reformation and the schism that exists even today. But the need still remains of such organization even as evidenced by the earliest example of that headquarters church in Jerusalem.

I'll take the opportunity to intrude a personal bias concerning the music of the churches. The choir and choir director are a historical problem in all churches, large and small. But nowhere is this in more evidence than in the small churches of today.

It seems the music director of today's churches is out to make a name for himself rather than glorifying God in song. I have had to endure so much of this kind of music lately all because someone fancies him or herself with musical genius or gifted with the muse of lyrics that it has become wearisome to me.

Gone are the hymns of Wesley and White. Now, a screen and projector warn me that I am going to suffer through a session of what someone thinks is his or her gift for music and lyrics. I've yet to find inspiration or the lifting of my own soul in response to such shabby attempts to be a church version of George Gershwin or Glen Campbell.

One of the worst sessions I ever endured was a fellow who claimed his ability with a clarinet was his ministry. His imitation of Pete Fountain and

Benny Goodman was, at best, only the most thinly veiled attempt to impress all of us with his own virtuosity. He would intrude a religious comment once in a while in order to justify the travesty. One lady sharing my sentiment and I walked out together in the middle of his egotistical jam session.

But I learned many years ago to deal with the fact that The Lord is usually the beneficiary of the shabbiest and most tawdry attempts to offer religious entertainment in competition with Broadway, Hollywood and Tin Pan Alley that do such a superior job of it by comparison. T.V. religious broadcasting abundantly evidences the basis of my criticism. And I ask myself for the thousandth time: When are God's people ever going to get the message that they were never called to compete with those things better left outside the churches?

No one loves music more than I do. As a musician myself, music has always played an important role in my life and it always will. But, like the marches of Sousa, the music sets a mood and should be appropriate to the occasion. Too many churches have lost their way in this regard in a vain spirit of competition with the world.

As a professional writer, I have had to deal with the problem of those who thought they could write but never disciplined themselves to the craft. How many poets I have met whom, like the complaint of Sam Clemens said of one such: "He claimed to be a poet. His problem was convincing others of this."

So it is with the juvenile so-called lyrics of so-called contemporary Christian music. If you say Lord or Jesus or Glory or Hallelujah enough times, it constitutes a song (I won't dignify such with the term hymn). Now if you are going to have a sing-along just for fun, that's fine; but to carry such a thing into the worship service? I don't think so. And the smaller, independent churches are the worst offenders in this regard.

I would also intrude the criticism of the charismatic churches which are filled with members and clergy that see visions of angels, engage in gibberish called *tongues*, hear the audible voice of God, receive angelic messages and prophecies, etc. That such religious quackery could ever contribute to sensible and reasonable discussion of the paramount questions facing a society is beyond anyone with a reasonable and rational mind. And too much of the mysticism of even mainline denominations, and especially Roman Catholicism, falls into this category and can't possibly make a contribution to a proper dialogue of the issues facing our society.

The Roman Church has a further problem in its doctrine of Papal Infallibility, of a man speaking *ex cathedra*, concerning questions of the faith. While the Pope can do much good in his counsel due to his far-reaching influence over such a large segment of professing Christianity and the kinds of information to which he is privy politically, this particular tenet of Romanism is deadly to working in concert with leaders of other denominations and belief systems.

Romanism is bound to traditions and superstitions in such a dogmatic fashion that it limits itself tremendously in being able to deal with real life issues sensibly. No one wants to believe more than I do that my departed loved ones, my daughter, my brother, my grandparents and my great-grandmother are able to see and hear me. I believe I will see them when I go to be with The Lord. A large part of my lack of fear of death is the fact, to me, that these precious ones have gone on before me and will be there to greet me.

I talk to these loved ones but I do not pray to them nor do I hear any audible response when I hold converse with them. But I find a kind of peace of mind and soul in doing so. I would never, however, pray to Mary, the Apostles or any patron saints. I believe in prayer to the Father and the Son; that Jesus is our mediator and we have no need of a priest to hear confession or that such a person has power to remit sins through repetitious chants of the rosary.

But in examination of my own opinions, I most certainly find the latitude to accept those into fellowship whose criteria is the love for one another and the actual works that evidence righteousness no matter our doctrinal differences. And if you believe counting beads and prayers to the saints is efficacious and pleasing to God, so be it as long as you don't hold my disagreement with you against me.

One thing the Roman Church certainly has in its favor is its historicity and its ability to discipline its membership; would that Protestantism had these things in its favor. It must be admitted that the Protestant churches, even the largest denominations, suffer from the lack of ability to discipline members and clergy. And the mainline denominations are most certainly not excluded in regard to my criticism concerning their music. They further suffer from a lack of agreement on vital issues effecting our society and government. But the mainline denominations do, unlike the smaller independents, have necessary structure and are able, consequently, to do much more and have a larger voice in important affairs.

But it is to be admitted that even these have little credibility in the face of the mounting chaos and demands for answers to real life issues. The inability of even the largest denominations to be the force for good they could be is an indictment of their failure to deal with realities.

Yet, if the larger mainline denominations could come together in concert to address these issues and make rational decisions concerning them, much good could be accomplished. Here too, however, the problems of individual egos often circumvent the needed coalescing and agreement on issues and courses of action. But the essential point is valid, that is if the larger denominations could find fundamental agreement on the issues that divide them and act in concert, they would be a considerable force for good.

A very disturbing element has recently arisen, however, in particular regard to the largest segment of professing Christianity: Roman Catholicism. The very real prospect of a jihad, a Holy War against abortionists promulgated by the Catholic churches has become a genuine and legitimate concern of mine.

The history of the Roman Catholic Church would indicate that such a possibility most certainly exists. When its priests begin to foment the concept that the killing of abortionists is a righteous act against the murderers of babies, that God approves of such action and given the many superstitions of the religion it doesn't take much insight to see where the unstable among Catholics just might see the justification for such a thing.

Early in childhood, I was properly catechized and sprinkled into the Roman Church. I am more than a little aware, certainly more so than any Baptist, of the tremendous power of the ancient history and liturgical methodologies of Roman Catholicism. For those with a natural bent toward mysticism and superstition, the magnetism of the Roman Church is a given. Input an unstable personality with a natural inclination to obey the voice of God, even to the point of killing in the name of God, and you have the potential for escalating violence against the ungodly.

Obviously it isn't just the Roman Church that has such potential. It is simply the largest one and, as a consequence, with such monumental organization throughout the world, poses the greatest threat if its power is misdirected or corrupted. But there are many so-called *churches*, especially those independents I have mentioned, which promote hatred and violence against those with whom they disagree.

As to abortion as a means of contraception as a specific, in counsel with various friends it is easy to see that this issue is a most profound one and desperately needs the attention of the churches and our whole society. When my best friends, good men and women, are disturbed and even inclined toward sympathy for those who are killing abortionists, we begin to understand the magnitude of the problem. Only duly constituted authority has the right, according to God's own Word, to exercise capital punishment.

Yet, to underscore the magnitude of the problem in all its ethical and moral dimensions, I look into my own heart and realize how easy it would be for me to execute, personally, those who would molest, torture and kill children. By extension, would my own belief system allow me, in spite of my knowing God's Word on the subject, to take on myself the role of Prophet Vigilante and gun down those who are murdering the innocent, the unborn?

This is a very dark area and demands the wisest counsel of the best of men in arriving at a consensus of agreement.

I am suggesting that a New Systematic Theology is both needed and could have an ameliorating influence if the hard, but legitimate, questions I am raising could be addressed without that Blind Orthodoxy and egos getting in the way. Now if, as with Luther, my own 95 theses cause the churches to act, even if they act against me, at least they will be doing something together. I'll settle for that for the time being.

In my political writings I have often made the point that unless the difficult choices we face in our nation are not addressed and dealt with the choices will be made for us by force of circumstances. I have called these forced choices *Hitlerian* because just as nature abhors a vacuum, so do these things demand finding a place.

We are presently facing the hard questions of welfare reform, immigration reform, and dealing with the homeless, questions of ethics in the areas of abortion and euthanasia and so much more. The most obvious bottom line in many cases is a dollar sign. Our society is coming to grips with dire economic necessities that must be faced and won't go away.

I have said, and say again, that no nation that fails to cherish its young has a future as a nation. Nor does it deserve one! But we have squandered our children's inheritance and must now find a way out of our financial disaster for the sake of our posterity.

Thus, those Hitlerian solutions like sterilization, mass euthanasia, selective breeding, weeding out the incapables (*human weeds* if you will); the unproductive mouths that drain the resources of the productive or stand in the way of needed reforms suggest themselves. The unthinkable becomes thinkable as history so well records in all civilizations that have had to come to grips with grim realities.

It is in such a climate of impending disasters that the need of the churches to provide moral leadership becomes increasingly, urgently needed. I contend that if the leadership of the churches will open the door to dialogue between men of good will and encourage a spirit of cooperation, God would bless and provide the wisdom and guidance we so desperately need in these times.

In my essay of last December I raised the point that the very nature of God Himself is an essential need of further investigation before there can be any hope of solutions of many of the questions plaguing our present age. But questions of such a fundamental nature as whether God is capable of error or has made mistakes of judgment immediately meet with cries of heresy or blasphemy and thus preclude the most elemental discussion of the nature of God Himself. And, without such discussion, no further light is sought or allowed.

The honest seeking of wisdom and light in our present dysfunctional society where the threat of actual anarchy, which already exists in all our major cities, is becoming a real possibility in our nation would seem to demand that God's people get their priorities straight. My suggestion that His people are badly in need of asking the right questions and being of a mind to explore hitherto excluded areas of examination into the nature of God has been rebuffed by most. Yet, simply telling me to shut up, go away and quit bothering us isn't going to solve the problems.

I just asked a close friend his opinion on the question of euthanasia. He immediately began to equivocate. Did I mean the assisted suicide of the elderly or those on expensive life-support systems, or those who were the incapables like those in insane asylums, etc.? In other words, euthanasia might be acceptable to him in one instance but not in another. Having studied and written extensively on this subject, I was not surprised at his inability to come to a ready conclusion concerning such a complex issue. He is an intelligent man and we have discussed many things including this in the past. It is nothing against him that he finds himself in a moral quagmire and dilemma trying to come to terms with such a critical question; most sensitive and thinking people do.

So, with these things in mind, I bring up another question concerning the nature of God. As with the question of whether God is capable of error, particularly whether a decision made on the basis of the purest motive of love which is betrayed can honestly be called an error on the part of the lover, I now bring forth the question of errors of judgment.

Of course, as human beings, albeit made in the image of God Himself, even called gods by Him, we all make errors of judgment. But is God capable of such a thing? The fundamental statement in Scripture by God Himself that He was pained in His heart that He had created man and determined to destroy him would seem to admit of no other interpretation but that God was admitting an error and, possibly, an error of judgment.

But, I bring up the point again of whether the purity of love as the motive for action makes that action an error, a mistake, when that love is betrayed? If God did not know what the outcome would be, and I bring up the point again that I don't believe He would have done as He did if He had known how much misery would ensue as a result or that He, any more than we, would choose a betrayer as the object of His love, can we properly blame God for making a mistake, an error of judgment?

God paid the penalty for sin in the sacrifice of His own Son. No higher price can be imagined. To pay for one's own mistakes is a tenet of humanity; but of God? As to the humanity of Jesus, the picture of Him in the garden praying three times that if it were possible He might not have to go to the cross comes to mind.

Yet Jesus had repeatedly told His disciples that this would have to take place. And now that the time had come, He pleads with His Father that the cup, if possible, might pass from him? How very human, I tell myself. There is a question here that, if pursued, might shed light on the relationship between God the Son and God the Father and the character of Jesus himself during his tenure in the flesh.

But to continue: That God, when deciding to destroy mankind, changed His mind and risked another try with Noah demands an answer that the churches refuse to acknowledge. And why did God have to come down to earth in order to find out if He had been told the truth about conditions in Sodom and Gomorrah? Further, why was He willing to bargain with Abraham concerning this issue?

There are, to me, many fascinating things about this unique meeting of God and Abraham. This man, called the Friend of God, seemed quite concerned that his friend, God, might be making a mistake in destroying these cities. His remark about the Righteous Judge destroying the righteous along with the unrighteous would indicate the genuine concern of one friend for another that his friend might be doing something wrong and out of character. I've often wondered if Abraham knew something of the nature and character of his friend God that we have lost?

But there is so much to the story of the relationship between The Lord and Abraham that I haven't even been able to start to grasp; the fact that God dealt with this man on such a human level in so many cases for example. The seemingly cruel demand that he take Isaac to offer as a sacrifice- what a living hell that must have been for Abraham until the moment God stayed his hand.

And this man, Abraham, was to become the progenitor of Jews, Christians, and Moslems, three religions that would be historical enemies! Why? Did God, indeed, foresee the continual conflict of such a thing, the bloodshed and hatreds engendered by such a thing as blessing Abraham with a son in his old age? Yet Hagar didn't restrain Abraham in having Ishmael. God even answered Abraham's request to bless the boy and cause him to be the father of a nation as well. God even saved the boy when he and his mother had been driven away from their home.

Granted this prevented any contention concerning problems of inheritance from Abraham but look at the history of conflict that was to come about as a result, a conflict which keeps the Middle East in constant foment and crisis to this day. If God blessed Abraham and Sarah with a son out of love for His friend, the price of such love in friendship has been an exceeding dear one.

Yet, there is the point of view concerning what is called the "Unfolding Drama of Redemption." It may be that God, doing what was necessary to save a peculiar people from an evil system, the world, did what He had to do in order to accomplish such a purpose. In the eyes of men, seeing through a glass darkly, what may appear an error of judgment in love might very well have been essential in the long view.

"In understanding be men!" The Biblical injunction is still the impetus of asking questions and seeking reasonable and rational answers. So it is that an examination of God's dealing with men throughout recorded history bears the closest scrutiny though sacred cows must be slain in the process. There is far too much suffering in the world that demands an accounting, a seeking of answers to accountability and responsibility for such a thing.

Do I, as a mere man, seek such an accounting from God Himself? I believe that if I am a child of God, a joint heir with Christ, I not only have a right to do so, I have the obligation as well. To search for knowledge and wisdom, to seek out answers from my Heavenly Father seems to be the most natural thing to do in view of the relationship.

If we are to trust the Biblical record, and I do, there are a host of questions that the churches have refused to acknowledge and deal with. Perhaps they don't hold the view I do that there is a responsibility and a right to do so. Some, I am confident, haven't even been recognized because of that *Blind Orthodoxy* I continue having to confront. Yet, dealing with these questions is one of the purposes of the organized Church, the very body of Christ.

Granting that we may be under tutors and governors until the time of our full inheritance, if I am bought with the price of the blood of God's own Son, and, as a consequence, have become a joint heir with him, a brother to him, a child of God myself, why shouldn't such a personal relationship admit of personal cares, concerns and questions which properly should be a part of that family relationship? But to be condemned by those who purport to know better, by those who say such a relationship exists but deny it by censuring me for acting like one of the family; doesn't make much sense.

Sensibly, no earthly child with a proper upbringing is going to dishonor his father or mother. I was taught respect for my elders and reverence for The Lord and His Word. But I'm no longer a child and the world has become an ever more dangerous place for our children. There is no lack of respect in my questions of The Lord and His Word, of His dealings with humanity. But there is an ever-increasing need for sensible answers to legitimate questions that I believe The Lord has an obligation to answer. I even believe He wants and expects such questions to be asked of Him.

I have the greatest pleasure in my children coming to me for advice, for answers to their questions. That our Heavenly Father is less pleased by our coming to Him in such a manner is, to me, unthinkable. And, as my children would never ask a question of me out the desire to cause me shame or embarrassment, neither would such a thought ever enter my mind in reference to God.

But we are desperately in need of answers to increasingly difficult questions. If God is to be our ultimate source of wisdom in these dangerous times, His people better begin asking the hard questions which demand an answer; and quickly. He commands, in fact, that we do so.

The Bible, as I have often said, should be viewed as an essential Primer, the foundational knowledge that points us in the right direction of asking the right questions and in the pursuit of answers. It does not answer all our questions but provides the foundational knowledge that provides a path of learning and acquiring the necessary study skills to search for answers and develop wisdom in the searching. God is to be worshiped, not the Bible (Bibliolatry), as much as I love it and essential as it is to our faith and spiritual health.

God's Holy Word is, as He says, profitable for instruction, building us up in the faith, comforting us in sorrow and grief (and how many times it has done that in my own life), for reproof, for answering those who attack our beliefs, for so many things. It is, indeed, The Living Word of God, that sharp sword that He has given as the only offensive weapon in our dealing with our enemies. And not one jot or tittle will pass away. God's Word saves and it condemns. It is indeed without parallel in our lives and nothing I say should ever be construed as taking anything from its supreme importance in the Christian's life.

Yet, I view it as a Primer because God expects us to build upon its foundation. Not adding to it, but understanding it. And, in understanding, go beyond to the kind of maturity it encourages in learning and wisdom. "Study to show yourself approved" is not confined to the Bible alone. It is my absolute trust in God's Word that has led me into other areas of study in order to vindicate that Word, that Living Water, that Bread of life, living in me as a Christian. Born again by that very Word which is settled forever in Heaven; nothing can take its place and I am a committed defender of it to the death.

It in no way detracts from the supreme importance of God's Word to point out the fact that God has given us, in that very Word, the needed tools to carry on the building of the Church, to carry out the Great Commission, to know the history of our salvation to call it a Primer. No study of any kind can begin without a basic text. And that basic text will never be supplanted by any further learning since further learning would be impossible without it. Just so, as Jesus said, we would do greater works than he because he was leaving to go to be with the Father. We remain to do those greater works but who would dare minimize the work of Christ as the foundation of those greater works?

The Spirit of the Word is superior to the literal word. God Himself makes this clear. The letter kills but the Spirit gives life. So it is that so many spiritual things transcend the letter of the law. David, for example, went into the tabernacle and took the Showbread of the priests in order to feed his men. Jesus gave approval to this breaking of the letter of the law. When the Pharisees reproved Jesus and the disciples for breaking the Sabbath his reply was that the Sabbath was made for man and not man for the Sabbath; further, the Son of Man was Lord of the Sabbath.

In many ways Jesus declared such things as a way of showing us the truth of the Spirit's transcending the formal, written word. That we are to have mercy, as with God, rather than pass judgment is clearly superior. It is in mercy and truth meeting together that we find the overcoming elements that answer to the letter of the law which judges, condemns and kills. And we must always remember that love covers a multitude of sins.

It is the answer of a clear conscience before God and men that we must ever seek. Not that the conscience does not require development. We must do those things, the righteous works that encourage a tender conscience in order to rely on that as guide to behavior. And even at that, only a fool would declare his conscience an infallible guide. Yet, it remains superior to the calculated coldness of judgment without mercy.

It is in the Spirit of the Word that I find an infallible guide. Just so I find forgiveness of wrongs in others by adhering to the principle of the Spirit rather than keeping score. How many times must I forgive my brother? Love keeps on forgiving and doesn't keep score.

If this were truly the guiding principle, as the Lord's people acknowledge it should be, of the way in which the churches do business how much more encouraged I would be in looking to them for answers. But when they continue to say and do not, there is too much of our Lord's righteous condemnation of honoring Him with the lips while denying Him by the works.

To wax anecdotal for a moment, I was at my daughter Karen's house Christmas Eve when I got word by my grapevine of a desperate situation in Lake Isabella. A young mother was sitting alone with her two-year-old son, a bare, donated tree without any ornaments, not a single gift for the child and needed gas money to get to Bakersfield if the child was to have any Christmas at all.

Knowing the young woman and knowing of suicidal tendencies, I immediately set about trying to help her. But I was in Modesto and needed someone to respond to her need in Lake Isabella. Now I knew a number of people who would help but it was Christmas Eve and many were not available.

Finally, I called a friend who owns a bar at the Lake. Her only question was how much I wanted her to give the girl. I arranged for enough to buy simple gifts and gas to get her to Bakersfield where other friends would be able to help her.

Now I know that there must have been a number of churches and church people who would have been willing to help, but they were busy with religious celebrations or their own families. The incongruity of the situation wasn't lost to me. In how many cases I have found more help through such people as my friend who owns a bar rather than the righteous.

My good and trusted friend, State Senator Don Rogers, later shared with me a similar situation that came to him Christmas Eve. I can only say, brother Don, the Lord richly blessed us in being able to help others when the need arose; it more than pointed out the true spirit of this special night in celebration of God's great gift.

It certainly isn't a case of a lack of good people, people in the churches who sincerely do their best to meet the needs of people like this girl and her little boy. But they seldom know or associate with the kinds of people like this girl. Hence, these good people do not know the desperation of too many cases like this. And some die as a consequence of this lack of missionary sensitivity and awareness.

Christmas day my grandchildren were inundated with so many gifts they didn't know what to open or play with first. It was almost a vulgar display of opulence. How could I not be grateful for the abundance of my own grandchildren? Yet the picture in my mind of that young mother and her little boy, the bare tree and not even enough money for gas to get to town haunted my mind; that and the fact of a saloonkeeper friend of mine coming to her aid.

As we sat at dinner that evening, a magnificent Christmas feast amid all the trappings of the good life, it was all quite surreal. In the midst of so much want and misery, we were drowning in comparative, vulgar opulence. But I would commend my hosts for that Christmas dinner and gifts, for the efforts at helping those in need of which they made me aware. We all need to do what we can to assuage the suffering of the truly needy else we should choke on our own bounty.

Ok, I know all the rules of the game. I know how foolish it can be to let the needs of others rob you of the relief and gratitude that you are not among those in need. Yes, I am acutely aware of the problem of taking on a load of undeserved guilt for those things over which you have no control and for which you are not responsible.

But as a nation, as churches and church people in such a nation as ours, where is the legitimate line of responsibility, caring and doing? I can't shake the feeling that the case of the girl and her little boy should have been the attention and help of the church, not a saloon keeper and myself, that the rich abundance of my grandchildren couldn't in some fashion be shared with those children who have nothing and go to bed abused and hungry in this country.

There it is: This country. No, I do not subscribe to taking from those who work and earn their way and giving to the indolent, those who will not work and want a free ride on the backs of responsible working people. But there must be a mechanism of providing honorable employment to those who do want to work but can't find jobs. Now that is a reality the churches should face and quit blaming government. And certainly we should not expect Caesar to fix things at the expense of our freedom and liberty for which so many noble have given their lives. To feed at Caesar's table is still to be Caesar's dog and I'll never bark to his tune. I'm far too much a soul brother of Paine, Emerson, and Thoreau to ever do so.

In my political work and writing, I confront the situation constantly of the relationship between religion and politics. I have already pointed out the fact that the two are, historically and contemporaneously, inextricably entwined. As goes the one, so goes the other throughout the world.

Having recently sent the G.O.P. to Congress, I am asked whether I see this as a ray of hope that things in our own nation might be on the mend. I certainly see it as an opportunity to deal with conditions in a more pragmatic manner than the history of a failed, social welfare experiment for which the nation has been plunged into possibly terminal bankruptcy, as in California. But unless good men of vision, statesmen, are overseeing government I don't hold much hope of any long-term benefit.

I do believe it falls to the churches to be a moral voice in the midst of so much moral confusion. We have recently, in Kern County, a school district that has passed a resolution to teach morals in the classrooms. It is easy to see both sides of the argument, pro and con, to such a thing. Something that has been, historically, the purview of the church and home, is now thrust upon the schools. Having worked in the state schools at every level from elementary to graduate school, I easily commiserate with the schools being asked to take on any additional, social burdens. *In loco parentis* was never intended to make schools take the actual place of parents in all respects.

But in a morally failed society something must be done. If the churches fail in the role to which God called them, something else will surely take their place and what better institution than one that impacts our whole society as profoundly as our schools? I've written reams on this subject but will only treat of it here in its moral dimension as relating to my call for that New Systematic Theology.

A paramount question raises itself in this regard of making the schools the arbiters of morality. My own tenure in the state schools presents an unpleasant situation of their being amoral at best and downright immoral at worst. Not a little of this immoral atmosphere has been generated by the teaching of evolution as fact instead of theory. At a time when reputable scientists are leaving the field in droves saying it is a thoroughly untenable hypothesis, the schools still treat the subject as fact in their curriculum. Not the only subject, of course, where the schools are woefully behind the realities of the times. In fact, the schools, in much the same way as the churches, are only able to function on a status quo basis. Change is definitely not a part of the curriculum or innovative designs in learning.

I'd best depart that subject for the time being since I could easily go on, and have done so, for hundreds of pages. If we ever meet at a social gathering, just ask me a question concerning the schools and you'll learn more than you ever wanted to know about the subject. It didn't have a little to do with Phil Wyman's failure to be elected to the State Senate in California. He wouldn't listen to me when I offered to educate him.

It was in retaliation to a failed state school system that led me to starting three, private schools- two in California and one in Colorado. I would often tell parents concerning the state schools: Things aren't as bad as you think; they are far worse! But no one believed me.

My doctoral dissertation was on the subject of accountability in the state schools. It was such a damning indictment of the way the schools functioned that no publisher would touch it. My statement that we couldn't have designed a system for failure any better if we had done so intentionally didn't commend me to many of the educational hierarchy. Suffice it to say that the worst class of students I ever had to deal with was a class of adults, fresh BAs in hand who were in training to become teachers! The system had graduated them from college and told them they were prepared for graduate study in order to teach others. And not a one of them could write a paper worthy of a college freshman!

I had to prove my criticism of them in a most painful manner by critiquing their first efforts. They cried out for me to stop before I had finished the second paper in front of them. The shameful thing was the fact that I was the first instructor that had confronted their deficiency in this manner.

Now before you accuse me of losing my train of thought and subject, I need to make you acquainted with the fact that the schools have become, for better or worse, the dumping ground for failed families, churches and government. It is the schools to which we now look for redemption from a failed society. That such a fact is unpalatable won't make it go away.

Whether we agree on school prayer or not, I have made the point many times that it was the fault of the churches that one woman, Ms. O'Hare, could have prayer declared unconstitutional in our schools. That is a damning

23

indictment of the lack of cooperation, consensus and effectiveness of the churches in our society.

I don't think anyone would reasonably disagree that the Ten Commandments are a pretty good basis of morality and moral teaching. Yet where was the effective voice of the churches in confronting the removal of these hoary precepts from the classrooms of America?

You simply cannot put one segment of our society in a box and say: This does not impact on any other. The family, the church, the schools, industry and government either work as a cohesive whole or the entire structure of society eventually fails. History only allows of three choices for any nation: Anarchy, Slavery or the course of our founding fathers.

In my political work, I have called for a New Continental Congress. Not a few have been alarmed at such a thing. But considering the alternatives, it isn't really such a far-fetched thing. What was done once can most certainly be done again. And when the long train of abuses reaches a flashpoint?

Now that I have introduced ever more complexities to an already extremely complex equation, I hope the reader is getting a better idea of the enormity of the task before us. Yet it all comes back to that most fundamental question of all: The nature of God, Man's relationship to God and, depending on the answer, Man's relationship to his fellows. And, of course, I have made my point of how critical the relationship between men and women, as the two halves of humanity, factor into this most complex study.

I once wrote of the need of an army of scholars to address these questions. I hope the reader can now see the necessity of such an army. Yet, as with those few that turned the whole world upside down with their itinerate preaching about one named Jesus who raised from the dead, as with one man who changed the course of history by calling the teachings of his church into question, one man who changed the course of history by his pamphleteering against a crowned tyrant who would not listen to the voices of men who thirsted for freedom and liberty, one woman who caused the subject of slavery to become a household concern and, as a result, caused an entire nation to war against itself, setting brother against brother and, again, changed the course of history, one man with his manifesto that caused world upheaval, one man with his dream of a pure and superior race of beings destined to rule the world for a thousand years and the resulting world-wide conflict and destruction, and so on. One man or woman- and to say it couldn't happen? How very foolish.

CHAPTER TWO

THE OKIE INTELLECTUAL

JULY 1995

I don't know about all of you but I have had to confront many mysteries in my life such as why do you wind up with a bunch of single socks? What really happens to the missing mates? Do washing machines, indeed, eat socks?

Oh, I know; this is an old story but I use it to lead to a mystery that isn't much thought or wrote about; why towels have a rough and a smooth side?

Now before you consign me to that group of tiny brained folks, I have, like you I suppose, always assumed it was due to the manufacturing process where, unknown decades past in a galaxy far, far away, it was decided to make towels in this fashion. It took a fellow, professional and perennial bachelor (married eight times at last count) to acquaint me with the real facts of the case.

By virtue of hard, diligent research on things of such esoteric and consuming interest to inquiring minds, I was already cognizant of the hot rivet syndrome of Levis, of the fact that the original Levis had a rivet at the stitch-point at the bottom of the fly of those venerable trousers. But the complaint, verified by Strauss himself, of those Westerners who had to wear the things, was that the copper rivet would get extremely hot when crouching next to a campfire causing some very real and exciting discomfort in a most private part of the anatomy when you arose. Now you have, undoubtedly, never been treated to the kind of dance such a thing leads to, I imagine one not unlike an Irish jig-master with a pocketful of bees. This led Mr. Strauss to discontinue placing a rivet at that point in his pants thereafter.

So, as with towels, there is probably a story connected with why they have a rough and smooth side (not unlike a lot of us). Ok, we know the story about Levis; but about the towels.

My friend's explanation, one only a devoted and well-entrenched bachelor could fathom or come up with is this: Seems that laundry is a dirty word to inveterate bachelors; like dishes; why have four different bowels, plates, cups or glasses when one or two is all that is needed for the microwave or cold cereal?

As with cooking utensils and silverware, a few do the job when you eat out of the pan or can and only have to rinse the spoon off.

If, as my friend explained, you use one side of the towel only after showering, you simply have to remember rough or smooth. The next shower, you use the other side of the towel. Simple; this enables you to get two showers with a single towel use. Now if households followed this obvious and eminently sensible format across the nation, just think of the enormous savings potential in towels, water and soap! Why it would amount to multiplied millions of dollars and thousands of acre-feet of water! We could reduce the National Debt and send millions to starving orphans in Appalachia!

Because of the kind of information covered in this essay, I am publishing it under the Okie Intellectual heading rather than Christian Perspective. I know the brethren will appreciate this, particularly since many grouse about some of the things I write about as a Christian.

And since this edition of OI has to deal with some very somber, political subject material, I decided I should try to introduce it with some degree of humor. Part of the serious aspect has to do with my friend and bachelor buddy who is a research scientist in a skunk works facility.

I had made his acquaintance during a brief hiatus in his life between jobs and wives. It happened he came into one of the bars I was frequenting while doing research on my Birds book. We took to one another quickly when we got onto the subject of women and physics, women and music, women and computers, women and writing, women and hydroponics, women and religion, women and so on.

My friend was living in a tent on the river at one point. Out of work and down on his luck, he lacked much motivation to get on with living. His genius, as with my own, didn't include an ability to suffer fools gladly. But you have to suffer some fools if you are going to find work. Now if he had had my experience in the schools, he could have been a most successful embezzler. But that's a different story; one that goes with the reason the GAO couldn't audit the IRS. When you are dealing with a system like the IRS or the schools, systems without any accountability and, as a consequence, systems which lend themselves to stealing, wholesale, so easily, if the money is just lying there, why not take it? As I learned of the schools and municipal construction projects, if you keep three different sets of books, you simply cook them to order. And there is usually enough to find a little something for everyone. But I digress; to continue about my buddy.

Lest you get the wrong impression, he is nearly as romantic and poetic as I am. He even likes my Birds book. At our last get-together we were in a bar owned by one of my good friends, a tough lady with a heart of gold. She is the one I was able to call from Modesto last Christmas Eve and helped me divert a young woman with a two-year-old from suicide. When I asked this lady to please give the young girl some money on my account, her only question to me was: "How much do you want me to give her, Don?" That's good people.

Anyhow, my buddy was downing greyhounds and I was having my usual cup of coffee and chatting with my good friend and bar owner. Then, to my surprise, there appeared my Lady in Red! And I'm not going to explain that. You'll have to read my book for the details.

She came up to me and throwing her arms around me, gave me a kiss and said: "Don, where have you been? I've been worried about you!"

I had to explain somewhat of my actions and movements since I had last seen her. Due to her own unusual circumstances, she won't have a phone and I had been unable to call her. She understood. I have shared a great deal about my work with this extraordinarily beautiful and intelligent lady, enough so that I will never forget the night she said she loved me and prayed for my safety. And she knows I love her as well.

Since it was a Saturday night and drawing near 9 p.m., the dance band was warming up. My Lady wanted to dance. So did I. As the band played one of the slower melodies we both loved to dance to, we looked at each other and wondered once more why things never came together for us.

There are reasons of course, reasons we understand and don't need to talk about. But the ache of "What might have been" still haunted both of us as we held each other tightly and moved to the music in each other's arms. It was then that she said one of two things I will always remember from that night: "Don, we have never danced like this before."

Oh, we had danced together many times. But she was right; this night was somehow different and we both knew it. And it made the way we held each other and danced together this time different as well. I wrote in my Birds book that maybe there was a chance for My Lady in Red and me. Maybe this night would bring that chance for the two of us.

She had been drinking and I suppose it was the freeing influence of the alcohol that caused the following to happen. After finishing the dance, instead of going back to sit at the bar, I led her to a table wanting to have a chance to speak to her away from the others. But she didn't take the offered chair. She asked me to sit first.

Strange, I thought, but I did as she asked. Then, with a sad look in her eyes, such beautiful hazel eyes that showed the moisture of soft and quiet tears, she sat on my lap burying her head in my chest and put her arms around me. She had never done such a thing before. I was so taken aback by her actions that all I could think of was my description of her and our relationship in my book. It was then that I said: "Sweetheart, we're a funny story."

Her next words pierced my heart: "Not funny." She said this so softly I could barely make out her words. But there they were and there was no use denying the truth of them. We would never be and we both knew it. She knew full well, of course, I hadn't meant the word in any humorous way. We both knew our relationship was a tragedy. But she had the courage to say it.

My buddy saw all this happen as did my friend, the bar owner. They didn't know, of course, what was really going on between my Lady and me. They probably had their own hopes up about the two of us. I'm glad, for their sakes, they didn't know what had happened. They both care deeply about my Lady and me and they didn't need to share in the pain of the moment.

Like the song says: "Why Can't God Make An Unbreakable Heart!" I'll never sing or play that song again without it piercing my own heart at the thought of my Lady and me. But it helps steel my resolve in the battle against Caesar and his cohorts, not only for the sake of our children, our nation, this America, but for young women like my Lady and against the kind of evil that destroys the chance of happiness for the two of us together. I know that statement is ambiguous but I have to let it stand as is.

I tell the story in part to let the reader know that this many-times divorced friend of mine, this genius has, like myself, the soul of the poet and understood, completely, my explanation of what happened. Now you can better understand why I'm proud to be able to call him a friend.

One of his specialties is antennas and their effects. Now this doesn't have much to do with your radio or TV. But this particular specialty enabled him to design the night radar for the F16 that was used with such efficient and deadly results in Desert Storm.

This man is an electronics and computer genius. This has not had a little to do with his problem with women, problems similar to my own. We share a good deal, without trying I say in our defense, in succeeding at making women feel ignored. This, as I have written about in the past, is one thing a woman cannot tolerate.

Given our peculiar traits, it isn't any wonder that we have been the bane of many women. They cannot figure us out and, finally, give up on us. This has led to my making the point several times that while I have met many women who love poetry I have yet to find one who can abide living with a poet.

But my eccentric buddy and I have developed a fast friendship, respecting each other's areas of expertise with common ground not only on the basis of constant disappointment in the affairs of the heart, but our mutual love of esoteric physics and music. That's right, music! In fact, we have done a few gigs together. He plays Congo drums and trumpet. We make pretty fair music since I contribute clarinet, tenor sax and guitar. But apart from our having so many things in common which seals our friendship, he contributes somewhat to my understanding of what is happening in some areas of science of which little is known to the general public.

For example, he just had to go to Utah to babysit a Universal Black Box of his design. He has been working in fiber optics most recently and most people, as with his antenna research, would never connect these things to Germ Warfare!

Yes, that's right, Germ Warfare. Now the Utah test was supposed to be an antiseptic one. And if you believe that, I have a bridge for sale. Nevertheless, the military gave it a nice label and got what they wanted.

I would never betray my friend by giving any details of the test. Yet, I can't help wondering just what the leadership of Utah and the military used to betray the people of that state in selling them on the idea that such a test was antiseptic?

As we continue to read of the experiments done by the military and our government on human beings in this country in the 50s, things that have caused such tragedy in so many lives, I cannot help wondering just how far they are now willing to go in sacrificing people to their ideas of what is expedient for national security? Given the likes of a Janet Reno, one doesn't have to wonder too far!

Believe it or not, there are some real human beings employed by the F.B.I. and the B.A.T.F. I freely admit to knowing a few personally. One of them shared his own concerns with me along these lines recently. And, in view of some of the things I am doing and writing about, advance warnings when possible are a nice thing to have from such contacts.

Seems ever since I got involved with Roy Kendall and the Radisson Hotel scam, things have warmed up a bit for this poor, old Okie Intellectual and Weedpatcher. Not that I haven't gone out of my way in keeping things interesting in my life and making things a little more surreal for my friends, but this latest episode has really generated a lot of heat.

A few things I didn't share with my readers in last month's essay. One in particular had to do with our California Attorney General, Dan Lundgren.

I apologize for practicing a subterfuge in my last essay in regard to my brief tenure with Child Protective Services in Tulare County. In answer to the worker who asked if I were a spy or plant in the organization, I have to plead guilty with an explanation. It was an opening gambit to determine the facts of certain allegations that had come to me about corruption and nearly criminal ineptitude in Tulare County government, a thread I have been following throughout California and our nation.

And, there was the remote possibility that I just might get close enough to certain material and individuals to verify a connection to the pedophile and homosexual elements I have been tracking for a very long time involving certain judges, officers of law enforcement and government officials. If there were any chance at all to flush such unmentionable, slimy creatures out from under their respective rocks, I accepted the obligation to give it my best effort.

To put the best face on my actions, I even went to the expense of buying a very nice home in an exceptionally nice neighborhood giving the appearance, at least, of my resolve to stick with the job and stay in Visalia. I had placed this before the Lord and friends in this manner, if the Lord should open the door for me to take such a position, I would go. Granted I did so knowing the odds were very slim that the hierarchy of Tulare County would hire a man with my over-qualifications for the position. Yet, as He has done in the past, The Lord did make the position available and I went.

Several good friends like Dick Palmquist, the owner of radio station KDNO in Delano, and others were concerned for me but knew of my motives for taking such a job, especially in a county and an organization which is so rife with such corruption, chicanery and abuse of authority. That I lasted a full two months is nothing short of extraordinary. It shouldn't have taken them that long to determine who I am. Yet, in that short time, I was able to uncover so much that this organization, CPS, wants to keep hidden from everyone.

And at that, I would undoubtedly still be there if it hadn't been for the material Roy Kendall gave me and I passed on to State Senator Don Rogers concerning the Radisson Hotel scam. Knowing the Senator both as a friend and an honorable man, one of the few in our state legislature, I was confident he would know what to do with the material and act on it.

As an aside, and a very important one, I certainly applaud Don's being a keynote speaker at the forthcoming Constitutionist Convention in Missouri and will not be surprised if there is growing support among patriots for his presidential nomination. People are mistaken, thank God, when they say an honorable man doesn't have a chance to make a difference in politics.

Roy had been unsuccessful, even after spending over $70,000 of his own money, in getting the courts to act on this matter of corruption surrounding the Radisson project; it was evident that some of the same people, straw men and organizations were involved with this project that were involved with the bankruptcy of Orange County.

Yet, even after going to the grand jury in Tulare County, in spite of the report by Scott of Intravest International Investigations, in spite of the efforts by a couple of honorable Visalia attorneys, the proof that Roy presented the grand jury was rejected. Not only rejected, but resulted in a warning (reading the material, I call it a threat) to Roy by county officials and county attorneys not to pursue the matter any further.

When I finally made my way through all the material Roy had gathered and before I handed it to Don Rogers, I made the same statement to Roy that investigator Scott did: "Be very careful about speaking on the phone and to whom you speak in person!" I had given, due to my considerable experience in this kind of white collar gorilla warfare, the same advice to Roy once I knew what was at stake and who some of the players were.

Before I go further, while I have become, by force of circumstances, quite expert in how our shadow government operates, how to look for the clues and material that lead to which rocks the worms are hiding under, Roy was very naive and innocent in such affairs in which he now found himself embroiled.

I immediately tried to educate him to the fact that this kind of thing he was pursuing is only a minute part of the overall, the tip of a colossal, dirty, black iceberg if you will. My own research, still on-going into the pedophile, homosexual connection to the Lords of Bakersfield and the Kern Fag Mafia with certain men in high positions in the courts and various government positions leaves no doubt in my mind of the extreme seriousness of the situation.

It was no coincidence that shortly after my giving this material to Senator Rogers, Attorney General Dan Lundgren paid a personal visit to the sleepy little community of Visalia where I was working. And, that shortly after the Attorney General's visit, I was immediately dismissed from my position with CPS, given only five minutes to clean out my desk and leave now! My sincere apologies to my co-workers for not being allowed to say good-bye.

Roy has become a household word in Tulare County because of his intrusion into this sordid affair. His business has suffered dramatically and personal threats have been made against him. In spite of precautions, because Visalia is still a small place- it was only a matter of time, I knew, before the authorities would know my association with him and they would take action against me.

I have often made the point that this kind of work ultimately requires men with nothing to lose, men without family and small children they have the responsibility for, men of such principle that they will try to work within the system, using the ballot box and reason, rather than advocating anarchy. In spite of the fact that it is a dirty war, a war against totally unscrupulous men and women and a system of monumental evil, an Evil Empire if you will, it still requires civilized men and women to prosecute it honorably. I freely admit I paid little attention to my debt in this cause until I saw the way this evil war impacted our children, the innocent victims of it.

It was during my tenure with the schools that the pledge of our founding fathers began to take root in my soul. To pledge material possessions, sacred honor and one's life to the cause of liberty and freedom were no longer historical, high-sounding rhetoric to me. The future of our nation, of my children and the children of our nation demanded such a pledge. The blood of countless martyrs of attaining and keeping the precepts of those hoary documents, the Constitution and Bill of Rights invaded my very soul and cried out for responsible commitment and action by people like myself.

Now I find myself reading the comments by the city attorney and city manager of Visalia that there ...is no basis of impropriety in the proof Roy gathered against city and county officials and the same words of Orange County officials come immediately to mind.

Here in Kern County, because of the unusual history of the county which resulted in the dark stories surrounding the Lords, I fully expected the results of our own Taj Mahal (the convention center fiasco) and other things like our own Radisson Hotel (yes, Kern County has one) to lead to the media headline of the County's sudden loss of favor with Standard and Poor calling the County's own investments questionable and risky.

One of our county supervisors, Roy Ashburn, is trying to promote a County Charter government for Kern. Excellent idea, Roy; however: I don't know how knowledgeable Mr. Ashburn is about some of the things in his way like the attack on our own District Attorney, one Ed Jagels, by Dick Palmquist.

Because of legitimate questions raised concerning the actual cause of the D.A.'s divorce, Dick Palmquist is being threatened with a libel suit by Mr. Jagels, but if the facts support the accusations against Mr. Jagels, will he then be ordered by his people to stand down? Mr. Hoffa comes immediately to mind. I await the outcome of this with the greatest interest and curiosity.

And, I can't help wondering how the de-briefing I am to undergo on KDNO will contribute to the whole affair? But those that know me well also know I am interested in the truth, not making Film at Eleven! As I tell folks, my self-preservation index is well in place and while I've learned to handle physical pain extraordinarily well, it isn't something I look forward to enjoying. I am not the stuff of martyrs and the Lord surely knows I usually go out of my way to avoid ugly situations and people.

Now I became conversant with the Jagels' case over a year ago when I was researching those dark stories about the Lords of Bakersfield. But the sources of information were somewhat circuitous and questionable at best. Some involved testimony by ex-cons who claimed to have been persecuted (not just prosecuted) by Mr. Jagels. Some even professed knowledge of murders being committed in order to cover up such things and protect the names and influence of powerful people.

Things were told to me such as Mr. Jagels' ex-wife and her son being threatened if testimony were given against the D.A. But lacking hard evidence together with questionable witnesses, it is extremely difficult to prosecute such a case. And most especially against those who hold powerful office and may be involved with the Lords and the Fag Mafia.

Just recently, Tim Palmquist, Dick's son, was arrested and accused of attacking a Kern Deputy Sheriff with a pen! Tim had gone to the Sheriff's office in an attempt to get material in the department's possession that had to do with Tim's leading a recent anti-abortion protest. Tim claimed someone in a crowd of pro-abortionists had pointed a gun at Tim's group. Tim claims the Sheriff's department had video of the act and refused to act on a complaint of the threat.

Whatever happened at the Sheriff's office, the Bakersfield Californian reported that Tim attacked a Sheriff's Deputy with a pen when he was refused any cooperation by the department. Now I know Tim and I know he can be confrontational. I don't think he has issued any Wanted posters against abortion doctors but I know his fervor in the righteousness of his cause, a cause I support whole-heartedly.

In speaking with Terry, Tim's wife, I'm given an all-together different scenario of what happened at the Sheriff's office. And if Tim hasn't yet joined the Whatever It Takes group in attempting to stop abortion murderers, this could well push him over. Yet, given the local climate of hatred and fear, especially in his dad's taking after the D.A. on his radio station, KDNO, it does seem somewhat fortuitous for the D.A. for Tim to be suddenly jailed, and especially when dad, Dick Palmquist, is out of state. Now because of the obvious conflict of interest, the case against Tim is being kicked upstairs to the state level for prosecution; too much publicity in this case for Mr. Jagels to risk trying a personal, local solution. My question is how Mr. Lundgren, if he gets involved, will handle this one?

The greatest difficulty I have faced in the battle I have enjoined for the Soul of America, in attempting to put a Human Face on the Politics of Patriotism, is trying to convince people that the lust of the flesh plays such a prominent role in the whole scheme of such things, that pedophiles, homosexuals, perverts wield such clout in our nation that leaders are in fear of them.

As I have written in time past, no amount of money or power compares with sex when it comes to blinding men and women to reason. Now I'm as normal a man as you're ever going to find when it comes to sex. But in this case, it is the perversion of sex to lust that is the point. This *Power of Perversion* has destroyed powerful leaders, even nations. Sodom and Gomorrah stand as the historical lesson of this.

And when the ruling passion becomes such as Paul describes in his epistle to the Romans, the destruction of a culture, a society, a nation is assured. For those with no interest in any religious application, the facts of history alone speak for themselves in this regard.

Mr. Dole is right about Hollywood (the so-called entertainment industry in general). But so were Dan Quayle and Dolly Parton. And just where was Mr. Dole when the liberals were having so much fun with Dan Quayle ala Murphy Brown? Newt? Just look at the double-speak he resorts to because of the family connection with lesbians. Never, Never underestimate the power such perversion wields in history or our nation! And to have our Top Cop, Janet Reno with her personal associations calling the shots, literally! Unless something is done quickly about such a stench and abomination in the nostrils of God Almighty, we most surely will reap the whirlwind of His wrath!

Karen Gentry, a leader of the patriotic group GOLD, knows the truth of Melville's words "The truth? It don't pay!" But I have always hearkened to his addendum of this dour pronouncement: "...but to write all together different, I find I cannot!" And because I cannot write all together different, I am writing this current essay in unbelievably difficult circumstances. It is 110 degrees out here in the backyard of the friends with whom I am presently staying. My computer is set up outside here but the patio cover has a tin roof.

I have a fan blowing the hot air over me in an attempt to keep the computer and printer cool enough to function. If the constant dust doesn't cause the equipment to fail, I think I'll make it; so far, so good. As I tell my kids, I'm a tough old bird but computers and printers are a different matter.

Being a desert rat by nature has its advantages under these circumstances. I've learned many tricks of the trade in my desert travels such as keeping a wet towel around my neck. I worry about the equipment but please don't think I am complaining about my personal circumstances. I am more than a little grateful for the friends who supply me a place of any kind to carry on the work as I look to the Lord for my next move. And as a second-class citizen, a smoker, I have learned to accommodate myself to being on the outside looking in. I've done the work in far less favorable circumstances and, like the Apostle Paul; I know both how to be abased and how to abound. And I've learned to never take the luxury of being able to close a door for privacy for granted.

Yes, there is a price to be paid for doing this kind of work and I don't recommend it to anyone else. Friends, patriots in Arizona, Nevada, Idaho, Wyoming, Montana, Colorado, Arkansas, Nebraska, Missouri, North Carolina, Virginia, Michigan and all over the country share the same message with me: The truth? It don't pay! As a consequence, some try to take a short cut to financing their message to Americans. Some I know have resorted to selling drugs, guns, even burglary and robbery in the perverted doctrine of the end justifies the means. This will never fly among honorable men and women. Providing things honest in the sight of both God and men is a criterion for the Truth. And it has to be admitted, though it is too obvious in many cases, that, as with our enemy, Caesar, the ranks of many patriot groups have their fair share of those who seek profit and position at the expense of others, of those that like to carry guns and thump heads, of kooks and kranks, even some that I have met who enjoy killing.

However, as with Hitler's thoroughly phallic Third Reich, such people invariably prove counter-productive to the cause of justice and liberty. The men and women who fight this war must, like our founding fathers and those who followed them, be the reluctant heroes, men and women who believe in exhausting every civilized means possible before resorting to force of arms.

But knowing that writings like my essays have to be self-supporting, I long ago reconciled myself to the fact that I would have to continue to make tents so as to both support myself and the work of this kind of writing. On the plus side, it removes you from the constraints of the petty minds and egos of those who seek self-aggrandizement at the expense of others, not to mention sacrificing the real message in the process.

So, to those my compatriots in the cause of freedom and liberty I have this to say: No Whining! If you put your hand to the plow, don't look back and don't blame others for the lack of support. The words of Jesus are clear in this respect: "Many are called but few are chosen; the fields are white unto harvest but the laborers are few."

There is a price to be paid for telling the truth. There always has been. Diogenes had a tough row to hoe. But it's funny how many drop out when they begin to learn they aren't going to make a living at it! This is one of the reasons for so many gospel-peddlers behind most of the pulpits of this nation: The truth? It don't pay! They should read, and believe Paul's words on this: Unlike so many, we do not peddle the word of God for profit! II Corinthians 2:17 NIV. And as far as the price of liberty being eternal vigilance; I could say from my considerable experience in the battle, in meeting so many sunshine patriots in both the churches and the bars: Don't make me laugh! But I won't.

Suffice it to say; harking back to my justifiable complaints against my brethren in the Lord, and especially against those false shepherds who peddle their perverted gospels for a paycheck, I can only say paraphrasing Peter, admittedly redundantly: Go To Hell! You have no part in this ministry, your money perish with you!

Knowing Peter, I'm not so sure he didn't preface his remarks to Simon the so-called Sorcerer with this justifiable command of a needed direction to the pit. But if he didn't, I'm positive he thought it when he substituted the word perish. And looking at what passes for evangelism on TV, I'm equally sure some of these charlatans have made the deal Simon attempted.

These scurrilous, conscienceless scoundrels haven't had to face Peter in the process but they, like their ignoble predecessors in the religion business, will face the Righteous Judge of the Universe someday. It is still a fearful thing to fall into the hands of the living God! Especially for those that shame His name for ego and profit.

To pledge wealth, sacred honor and your life in either the cause of Christ or the freedom of our nation and posterity, our children, still requires you possess all three attributes. And while, as that old disciple so well pointed out in scathing sarcasm: "No longer can the church say 'Silver and gold have I none,' " that item of sacred honor still remains to mock such hypocrites as fill our pulpits and pews, those hypocrites that in too many cases find the title *American* sticking in their throats. As for those who stand in pulpits to promote perversion as love, the words fail me in my contempt and revulsion for such. But God and far better men than me have said it anyway.

In respect to the politics that rule the way the churches do business, I'm reminded of the corruption of the Mexican government. Now why, do you suppose, is Clinton and his ilk so gung ho on supporting such corruption? Why should these unspeakably vile people support things like NAFTA and the giving of billions of our dollars to a bloatedly corrupt regime like Mexico's?

Now silly me; I think I just answered my own question. But it would be amusing if not so tragic in its effect to watch how our would-be masters try to manipulate Americans. I'm a pretty fair psychologist; even have the degree and a life credential to teach the subject in college. But it doesn't take a rocket scientist (or a Ph. D.) to figure out where people like Clinton are coming from.

Given his pedigree as a lying swindler, coward and womanizer with a hick background trying to mix it up with the moneylenders and the Big Boys it isn't any wonder he often looks the fool. I don't sell him short on native intelligence by accident of birth nor do I take from any of his educational accomplishments. However, as the old saying goes: "You can't make a silk purse out of a sow's ear." I would, however, not compare Clinton to a sow's ear. I would compare him to a mule's anatomical nether relief port.

More than that, if a man sells out his country we have a word for that—Treason! If, as it appears, Clinton and his cohorts have made the deal for their idea of a New World Order, if he wants to push for One World Government, count me out.

A beautiful blonde recently asked me: "Don, do you play?" Now why in the name of heaven do I suddenly bounce from such a serious subject like calling Clinton what he is; and you have to admit that's a serious thing, to beautiful blondes?

Allow me to explain. As I have mentioned many times in both my writing and in speaking to individuals and patriot groups, people may appreciate lengthy, well-researched, well-documented educational essays and books. But they don't read them. I have been guilty of contributing my fair share of such material as an academic with that alphabet after my name. You ought to browse through my Confessions book, all 650 pp.

But somehow along the way over the years as a professional writer I discovered a marvelous fact that changed much of my writing style. It was a fact that caused me to start publishing various materials under titles like The Weedpatcher, The Okie Intellectual and the Okie Poet.

What was this marvelous secret of the universe, this wonderfully liberating thing, this hook that makes people, just plain, ordinary Joe and Jane Citizen read my writing while George Will and what's his name, oh yeah, you know, that guy that loves yachts and sailing, decorate the tables in doctor's and dentist's offices or go into the circular file? Simple: Beautiful Blondes! Gotcha!

We can only take so much of bad news, we can only read tables of statistics and facts for so long before our attention wanders away and our brains say *Whoa, Enough*! But beautiful blondes; handsome men, SEX! Ah, the perversity of our minds and natures. "Give me more, more" as Tom Lehrer says in his little ditty on "Smut!" Even my good Baptist friends are still reading at this point.

Seriously folks, we are no longer a nation of readers. Because of King Sports and Queen Entertainment, the tube and videos have largely supplanted books. And sustained thought through complicated sentence structures and lengthy paragraphs is no longer the long suit of most.

My second language is German. Now you can't beat these folks for long, complicated passages. Clemens cursed, imaginatively of course and with good cause, the declension of the German Verb. And those of us who submitted to the torturous process of learning to read and write the old German script must really be into self-abuse.

Nevertheless, (one of our longer English words compared to which the Germans make us look like pikers. I've always thought one of the reasons the Germans lost the war was because of the length of some of their words and complicated paragraph structure) the learning of this language was one of the most difficult and important disciplines I ever undertook in college.

Now as a Litt. Major (my other major was vocational education. Figure that one out), no one appreciates good writing, literature more than I do. But I've had to come to terms with an immutable fact; did I want people to read what I write? And, if I did, was it also important to communicate at the same time?

Of course, you say. Well, here was the conundrum. I can dance with the best in exercising the power of obfuscation, of taking a page, even several pages, to say something that could be said in a single sentence; but why? Unless, like too many educated fools, I just wanted to show off and write a book of a thousand pages which could be nicely condensed to about, oh, say, something like two pages. I could do that. But like the man said: Why?

Now I haven't forgotten the Blonde. Neither have you. Get the point? You're still reading because you want to hear about that blonde and me. And I'm not going to disappoint you.

Many of you know, especially if you have a copy of my Birds book, that I sing and play professionally. Music has been the other half of my life since I was a child, writing being the other.

This beautiful, petite blonde was a choreographer for a Western Dance team. She had been in Mexico on vacation and on returning home, called me to ask if I would accompany her to Reno for the weekend where a national contest was being held for Western Dance Teams.

She asked me if she could pick me up Friday and we would be returning late Sunday night. She explained she needed to take her vehicle that was specially set up for traveling with the costumes and other things necessary for such events like this national competition. Knowing of my C&W involvement, my singing and playing in some of the groups, she thought it would be a natural thing for me to want to go. She had heard me sing and play and knew of my hope in encouraging my daughter Karen's involvement in music using her extraordinary beauty and voice professionally. She assumed it would be a good thing for me to experience what was involved in this aspect of the C&W movement, an aspect of which I had little first-hand knowledge.

Now I have raised several anticipatory questions in you, the reader's mind by telling you all this. All of you, Christian and non-Christian, churched and non-churched share one commonality with Hindus, Buddhists, Moslems and Jews; you're all human. With that admitted common frailty, there will be a bunch of you who will entertain the most titillating, libido-enhancing even, *gasp*, puerile thoughts of my enjoying a wicked weekend in Reno with a little, bewitching, blue-eyed blonde. Some of you, knowing my background, and me will say; Nah, he wouldn't go. Wrong! I went. And it was a most educational weekend. Now at this point I could engage in a very convoluted and torturous effort to defend my honor (to say nothing of the little blonde's) and my motives. But I won't.

I will say, however, that I still live with the specter of the *Infamous 30 pages*, as they came to be called, from my first book hanging over my head.

It led one lady friend (with whom I was keeping company, to use the old euphemism) at the time, when she started reading them to suddenly bolt straight up in bed and say with fire in her eyes: "We'll talk!"

In her case I did have a chance to defend myself. However for the women out there who got the idea from that first book that I didn't like women, nothing could be further from the truth. Why, some of my best friends.... No, I don't think that will fly. But I have made the point in my defense in my Birds book that: If I didn't like women, I wouldn't have married so many.

Let me start over. At this point, I guess I'd better.

Since I have been heavily involved in the Country Western phenomenon in this country and having written quite a bit about it I couldn't miss the opportunity to get into the act on this scale of a national competition with some real pros in the business. And, I might add, the little blonde won second place for her choreography of her team's dances. Not too shabby especially when I was able to see how good the competition was from a front row seat (next to the little blonde). When we returned that Sunday night....

What happened? If I failed to tell you anything more than what I have about the weekend with the little blonde most of you would be shredding this paper and calling my ancestry into question; and with all due justification. "Details, we want details" I hear you all saying (and shame on all you good folks for thinking such things).

I have often made the point that I would gladly give my life over to writing of the softer and gentler things between men and women, of the love and romance possible in ordinary lives. I would, given the liberty to do so if I could turn my back on other responsibilities, live for singing and making music, live for the writing of the poetry I find in love and romance, of children and their marvelous capacity to overcome evil and love without pretense or reservation. And I do a lot of such writing and making music just to get the bad taste of the other job, the job I am compelled to do, out of my mouth. So I went to Reno. But there was a dark side to the story.

Now some people are born to dance just as some are to make the music others dance to. But when that man or woman looks like a hippopotamus in a tutu, something is lost in the magic of the moment. I saw too many whom, grossly overweight, thought that by putting on colorful costumes and performing the steps correctly made them beautiful people. Wrong!

These people remind me of the guy Sam Clemens told of who claimed to be a poet. His problem, Clemens said, was convincing anyone else. I have nothing against fat or skinny people. They can love things totally unsuited to their physical characteristics. But if you are going to perform for the public, if you are going to try to offer something of value that requires the talent and physical attributes appropriate to the thing you're trying to present publicly, you better be careful. Illusions of ourselves are all right to a point. Beyond that point they are in poor taste at best and psychotic at worst.

I've seen some who couldn't smile while dancing. Not much fun you think when you see these. I don't much care for line dancing. It is too stilted and mechanical for my taste. Now the kind of dancing performed at the competition in Reno was something all together different. It was more what I would call a kind of ballet set to Western music. Much of it was quite beautiful. But there were too many who were terribly overweight and too many who took the business too seriously to be having any fun at it.

But a kind of dichotomy was in place. While I could appreciate the whole scene and love to sing and play all kinds of music including much of C&W, this kind of dancing wasn't my thing. And the little blonde quickly determined this. But it was her life.

We had beautiful accommodations at one of the finest hotel casinos just a short walk from the Convention Center where the competitions were being held. The food was terrific and there was the excitement such an environment always provides in cities which never watch a clock and the action is 24 hours without let.

But, while I have spent time in Las Vegas, Reno and Tahoe due to a variety of circumstances, as with the kind of dancing the little blonde lived for, they aren't really my thing. I seldom drink and never gamble. I thoroughly enjoy mixing it up with people in every kind of environment but these towns are made for a lifestyle and a kind of fun that doesn't particularly appeal to me. And never has.

For example: the zombies at the slots. This is having fun I always ask myself? Now gambling is a very serious business to many people and I don't make light of it. It is even tragic in some cases. I watched the little blonde pump silver dollars into various games and my heart broke for her. It was very serious for her. Between this and my not being able to share her complete enthusiasm for the kind of dancing which was her life, a love affair died a'borning. It was a very quiet drive back that Sunday evening. And I started ... workin' on my next broken heart.

A recent tongue-in-cheek book, "The Book of Members", by Robert J. Versteeg, a Methodist pastor, deals with Paul's analogy and commentary on the body of Christ, the Church, in I Corinthians. It reminded me of a man with whom, as with the Apostle Peter, I share a lot in common: Martin Luther. The Apostle, Luther and I are pretty rough elements in the Body. At times, we prove an embarrassment to many of the more orthodox and saintlier members thereof. For example, Luther compared himself, in this context, to the bowels of the Body. This essential but dirty job of the body is something only a Luther, in absolute honesty and understanding of his rough edges and responsibility would admit to; as the saying goes: It's a dirty job but somebody's got to do it.

In my case, a friend said he thought I fit the description of the bladder of the Body! Why? Because as with Luther, there is a need in the body to eliminate poisons, waste. In order to do so, the body needs the bowel and bladder to get rid of the toxins, the waste material, or the body would die.

Now my friend was wrong in consigning me the role of the bladder alone. I could be justly compared with the kidneys and bladder working together. That would be an appropriate analogy. I suspect, knowing me as well as he does, having read much of my writing, he wasn't willing to assign me the role of filtering the poisons, the toxins which accumulate in the bladder. Had he really thought the thing through, he would have realized that it is only in the filtering process that I am able to remove the waste, to recognize and deal with the evil in the churches and prepare the body to eliminate these poisons.

But, humble as I am, I will carry along the analogy as the bladder of the Body and not make too much of the necessity of my function as the kidneys in the process. I'm sure Luther knew what he was talking about in reference to his being the bowel of the Body and I'm sure that while the pope might have assigned him only one role in the alimentary system, the bowel is much more than the final orifice of waste disposal.

As to the function of this bladder, waste allowed to accumulate for too long the progression goes rapidly from a hint, to mild discomfort to urgency then Emergency! I fear the Body today is in the emergency phase of this process. And we better get rid of the poisons infecting it; and quickly before it is beyond our control! The results in the case of the churches are not going to be simple embarrassment, but an incontinence not of our choosing but the Lord's.

In the process of gathering these poisons in preparation for evacuation from the body, these essential organs make absolute demands that simply cannot be ignored. You can ignore virtually every other part of the body, you can live without many of its parts, but let's face it folks, When you gotta go, you gotta go! (You all knew that one had to be coming didn't you. My readers are a quick lot).

Now as irritating and often inconvenient as it is, this is a fact of life and living for all of us. The friend who made this comparison to me knows me as well as any in the world. We have been friends for over thirty years. He knows of my love of the Church, of God's Word and God's people. But he also knows that my ministry has become one of confrontation with the way the churches operate. And, just as with Luther, there is a need for cleansing of the poisons, the waste that is infecting the body.

This Bladder, then, might not care for its position in the body, it might wish it had a nobler and more attractive place, but it is, nevertheless, an essential one and due to my own rough edges one I am preeminently well-qualified to carry out. Like Peter and Luther, I'm a rough man at times (except when around ladies and children) who sometimes uses such plainness of speech it proves offensive to many of the members of the body. But the bladder, like the bowel, will not be ignored! And it sometimes requires a story about a little blonde to get the members' attention.

By telling embarrassingly personal stories about me, the reader will read and remember the important points such as my calling for a New Continental Congress, New Systematic Theology and a New Council of Jerusalem. Luther and I are not noble parts of the Body. But if I am faithful to the part I have been assigned, the Body has a chance to dispense the toxins, and the poisons with which it is so obviously infected and live rather than die. And if my friend is right in his assessment of my position, I hope the brethren will not curse the necessity of getting rid of the poisons that are infecting the body.

However, if the brethren refuse to listen, just as their counterparts throughout Scripture, the bowels and bladder will perform their essential functions with or without the cooperation of the rest of the body. That is a fact of life. It might be my wish that the elimination process of getting rid of the poisons could be done in a civilized fashion surrounded by the services which make it the most comfortable, like a padded toilet seat (Pew or pulpit) and least distasteful.

But the body will expel waste whether or not in a comfortable and civilized manner and setting; of that we are all aware. So, folks, as the Bladder of the Body, I strongly suggest you heed the call and let's get the necessary and dirty job done with cooperation. Otherwise...!

Now we all know it is the kidneys that process waste. But the bladder is the organ that, when filled, makes the demand that must be met. And, as a bladder, when that point is reached, when I cannot hold it any longer I respond with the kind of writing and speaking I do concerning the poisons infecting the churches, our families, schools, government. And for those of you who want to be the brains of the operation, you are still at the mercy of the bowel and bladder, the Luther's and Heath's. Never forget that. You don't have to like it but there it is in plain, good old Okie Homiletics.

In exercising my responsibility for such a seemingly ignominious position in the body, I provide a further example of religious heterodoxy (mine, of course). I write a good deal about the pew-warmers being so insulated and out of touch with reality (like the schools and government in general) that I draw on my own pedigree as a well-qualified Pharisee.

A friend recently commented on how wonderful it is that the Lord's people are instant saints. Well, I knew what he was talking about. It is a tenet of Fundamentalism that with the new birth, instant sainthood is bestowed on the new child of God; that with a decision for Christ comes this exalted position both on earth and in the heavenlies.

Now, as a good bladder, as with many perplexing questions I raise with the brethren, I pose the following: What does God mean when He says: "The righteous enter into life through much tribulation?" What does he mean when He tells us to "... strive to enter into the straight gate, that ... he that endures unto the end, the same shall be saved" and so on?

So it is that when I innocently and inadvertently took on (was assigned?) the role of a bladder, I was forced to honestly deal with so many questions of accepted orthodoxy and begin the most painful process of separating what I believed from what I knew. Now I know God's Word. And that is the root of the problem. I know what God has said: From cover to cover. And what He has said doesn't always fit into a neat framework or box of established, dogmatic orthodoxy or theology. So I coined the phrase in my case: *Blind Orthodoxy*! That had been my previous problem. Now, I faced a new one.

Departing from a comfortable position of unquestioning loyalty to a belief system that didn't address the hard questions that began to plague me was far from easy. I recently wrote a lovely lady and explained to her the manner in which I hoped to get the message of what we are facing in our nation in a format I am sure people will read and take heed to. It will also enable me to get those disquieting questions I have been asking before the general public for consideration.

How's that, you ask? Well, some of you know of my work on a novel. It is a dark comedy in a way. In another, it addresses love and romance together with humor and the darkest thoughts that plague all human beings, those things that, as I have described them in the past, tear at the fabric of sleep and cause you to awake terrified and drenched in sweat. But you, mercifully, can't remember the nightmare. I live that nightmare for all of you in the novel. By force of circumstances not of my choosing I am eminently well qualified and, I believe, responsible for doing so.

In spite of our becoming a largely illiterate nation, people will read if you get their interest. Those who have previewed the opening chapters of the book are agreed that it certainly keeps you interested. I wouldn't be human as a writer and not be susceptible to a commercial success as a writer. Money certainly has its place. It's a great motivator; and if the book can both make money and move hearts, all well and good. There are a lot of people, readers of mine for years, who are saying of me in this respect: "It's about time!"

Before I go further, let me explain some of the facts of life about writing and publishing. Very few writers make a living at the craft. The average income is about $5,000 a year for those that consider themselves professional writers. Now I don't include most journalists or those that have their own columns, etc.

But for those of us who are compelled to write, it is a most difficult thing to break into the big time, most especially in areas like poetry. Simply put, poetry is not a big moneymaker in today's market. But there are many who feel compelled to write poetry and are satisfied to make little or no money at their craft.

Many specialty writers like the writers of technical works or religious books make very little from their writing. As with the music, it's a tough racket and the competition is fierce. Some will go to the Vanity Presses because they think they need to say something and can't get a publisher or agent. Some do this, admittedly, just out of ego, to see their name on a book in spite of the huge cost of doing so. Some will self-publish for any number of reasons, not the least of which is the fact that you get to keep most of the money going this route. But it's a grim task in order to be successful and requires a good deal of time and money to make it work.

I have published several books knowing they were not going to be popular or successful moneymakers. But they have been successful in a number of ways, not the least of which has been the honing of my own skills in the craft and learning the publishing and book selling business.

The books I have written which show promise of commercial success, provided I am diligent in promoting them, are "The Lord and the Weedpatcher" and "Birds With Broken Wings." The "Confessions" book is largely political and theological. It was written as a specialty book and I knew it would not have general appeal.

But, as with Melville, while it might be said that I have written books like Confessions which fail, they are not failures in so far as my getting the message out to the few who appreciate the book. That, in some cases, is its own reward for those who feel compelled to write such books.

But a book of such vast scope as I have undertaken is enormously difficult to write. I am not a writer of fiction. I am an essayist. This is the first work where I have literally put all my professional and academic qualifications and training, all my experience and knowledge of life itself to the test.

I had told friends who asked why I hadn't given myself to completing a book with such potential for success that it would take the inspiration of the right woman in my life to do so. Dealing with the dark side, I told them, was easy. I have become so experienced in that area that it comes naturally knowing what I do, tragically, of human nature. But the joy of life and living, of loving and being loved in return in faithfulness was missing. I still haven't found that woman who can live with a poet.

It was only after completing the Birds book that I realized I had not been fair to either myself or my children and others, that I was demanding something of myself that was not reasonable or fair. And I had been using that as an excuse for not writing the book.

A close friend is writing a book in which he discusses his own thoughts of suicide. But after introducing the subject, he dealt with it in such a cursory manner that it left too much unsaid. I was able, after reviewing the chapter in which he brought this up, to tell him he had an obligation to the reader to treat the subject with all the seriousness and depth it deserved. Either that or don't mention it at all.

I have become expert in the psychosis of grief. I could have written the chapter for him; I know both him and the subject that well. I realized, as a trained professional, that he had never really dealt with the pathology of the thing in his own life. Now he was going to bring it up in his book. But at this late stage of his life, how go back and, with great emotional pain; deal with such a sober issue? But if he doesn't, the book lacks credibility; he lacks credibility.

I don't know if he is going to be able to accomplish such a feat. I know it will be enormously difficult for him to face things in his life that he has successfully masked for so many years. And will it be ultimately worthwhile for him to do so? These are questions he must resolve for himself and I wish him the very best in doing so.

After finishing the Birds book, I faced somewhat the same task. I have loved, and been loved, by many women. The fact that my love for them has suffered so many betrayals didn't diminish the fact of that love being real at the time.

My love for my children has brought me through many a midnight of the soul. My love for children and others has sustained me when all else has failed. But only the love of a woman can give a man some of the things he needs to be a complete man, to motivate and inspire him to the best he can do as a man.

I love several women now. And a few love me. That love is real, just as it is with my Lady in Red. What I had to do was go back and recapture those past loves and, together with present loves, let that be the guiding principle, the motivation and inspiration for making that element of the novel live and breathe reality.

No easy task. The betrayal of love and trust through infidelity, especially, is the murder of the innocent. This is why God says: "I hate divorce!" Adultery breaks something that simply cannot be mended. And where children are involved, they suffer the most. I have experienced too much of this ugly, vile destroying thing in my life. I had convinced myself that I could never re-capture those things with these women that made my life with them worthwhile at the time before the betrayal.

I would have to go back in each instance and relive the first moments of attraction, the giving of the flowers, the things that led up to the first date, the first holding of hands, the first kiss, the things that had brought us together in the beginning and the falling in love with each other.

I've said it many times; the problems of our society involve two classes of people: men and women. It is the relationship between the two sexes that predicts the future of a nation. So I write a great deal about the relationship. The Birds book is a book of relationships. But like my friend, if I could not recall the softer and gentler aspects of a woman's love that made my life at the time worthwhile, I could never make it real for the characters in the novel.

So I did what my friend must do. I turned inward and began to deal with my own black pathology of the psychosis of grief in respect to these women and those dark and brooding issues that rob us, too many times, of any joy or happiness in our lives. I realized that in spite of Solomon's jaundiced pronouncement that a virtuous woman was impossible to find, the romantic and poet, me, had never given up the hope of such. I realized this had a great deal to do with my love of children, of family, and compelled me to write as I did in the Birds book. So I had a lot to build on if I gave myself a chance to do so. And while not giving up the search, while unwilling to forego the warmth and softness of a woman in my life, that lover, friend and companion without which a man is never really complete I came to terms with those things that were preventing me from getting on with the work of the novel.

Being in the September of my life with December too quickly ahead, I at least have gained the maturity to deal with the issues the book raises. Also, by accident of birth and the choice of education, I have the essential background to use the historical setting of the antebellum South. I was raised with the Southerners and Negroes that gave me the single, most essential tool for the book: Dialect. Sam Clemens called dialect the single, most difficult thing to master in writing. And he would have known. He said he considered Bret Harte the only writer to have mastered the craft.

Writers and publishers hate dialect. It is not only most difficult and terribly time-consuming to write but the editing process is pure hell. And, of course, your spellchecker goes out the window. However, having been gifted by circumstances with a mastery of the white and black dialect of the South, and that language in many cases so rich and colorful, to my mind it would be nearly criminal not to use it. And the significance of it to the success of the book cannot be overestimated. For example: *Y'all* may be two words in reality but to the Southerner, white and black, it is one word.

Bottom line: I have plunged into the novel with a vengeance. And the story is beginning to flow, to live and breathe. Even realizing I have taken on Ye Damn'ed Whale, the book has taken on a life of it's own as it must, ultimately, do. I think I feared this as much as anything else in setting myself to the task.

But I have to guard against the book becoming a vampire that would suck up my own life's blood in the process of birthing the thing. Now why am I telling you all this, especially in an essay which includes so much sobering material of a political nature? Because I want to alert the reader to what lies ahead in future essays. As I deal with the evil that men and women do, as I continue the battle for the soul of America and for our children and families, for Americans, I will need your understanding of myself as a man. As I told my friend, the story, in order to be real, to be credible, to inform and move hearts to action against the tyranny of Caesar, the man must be real and credible as well.

Given a full plate in regards to the writing and activities for which I have accepted responsibility in dealing with our battle with Caesar, trying to give counsel to the churches, trying to deal with personal issues in my own life and the lives of others, where, you might well ask, am I going to find the time to write this book? I don't know. Nor do I know where I am going to do so. That is going to be up to the Lord and His leading.

In closing, the more astute of my readers know I haven't answered several plaguey questions. For example, when the little blonde asked me: "Don, do you play?" an immediate question must have been raised in the reader's mind. What did she mean by that and what prompted the question? I use this to go on to attempt to answer another obvious question the reader must have. Can the physician, indeed, heal himself?

The little lady knew me pretty well by the time she asked the question. As I wrote, she had heard me play and sing, she had read quite a bit of my writings, we had shared many things together at dinner dates, etc. And while she knew I love music and literature, she recognized me as a solitary and introspective, meditative man who dealt with a host of very somber issues; hence her question. And, given her perception of me, it was a legitimate one. Since she played a great deal, it seemed to her that I just didn't give much of my time to having her version of fun.

Having answered that question, I address the other. Can the physician heal himself? In an attempt to deal with the issue of suicide in his book, is it possible for my friend to do so without the wise and professional counsel of another? Not likely.

Analysis is a tedious, time-consuming process; even self-analysis. The psychosis that results in thoughts of taking our lives is extremely complex. I have made this point in other writings and won't belabor it here.

In having to face and deal with the psychosis of grief in the death of a child, in the betraying of love and trust which ends in divorce or the death of a love affair, I have had to live through these two most common aspects of this particular psychosis, and in the case of the betrayal of love and trust, several times.

That professional part of my mind and training tells me that in my own case I will need help in resolving some of the issues I have mentioned when I have to confront them in the book. But I'm fortunate to have such help close at hand. First, as a Christian, I trust the Lord and the Holy Spirit to work in my life, especially through His Word.

Secondly, I have many friends who care about me, some who pray for me. Because of the Lord and these friends, I am not without hope and I am not consumed by the loneliness and despair that usually results in the kind of despondency that precedes suicide. But I do not delude myself that I can deal with the demons that plague and hinder me without the help of others, and, hopefully, that significant other to use the current euphemism.

In any event, this month of July should find me making some changes. Hopefully, they will include more permanent and amenable quarters in which to carry on the work and the novel. In the meantime my sincere thanks for the continued encouragement from so many of you; please keep your calls, your letters coming. They are most appreciated. And don't forget that the books, The Lord and the Weedpatcher and Birds With Broken Wings are available in local bookstores here in Bakersfield.

CHAPTER THREE

THE OKIE INTELLECTUAL

AUGUST 1995

One of the first things I did after getting back to Bakersfield was contact a really fantastic, beautiful little blonde lady. And no, it's not what you think. Shame on all of you good folks!

This lady, Karen Gentry, has done so much for the Patriot Movement it boggles the mind. I, among others, have told her repeatedly: Slow down! You can't do it all yourself! But she tries.

As I mentioned in my last essay, Karen is one of those who, like me, has learned the wisdom of Melville's caustic remark: "The Truth? It don't pay!"

Why do I bring this up? Because of someone who has taken advantage of the trust of Karen and many other good people who are fighting the battle for the Soul of America; because of Johnny Lee Clary. Let's talk about Johnny Lee Clary Ministries.

A lot of us first heard about Johnny Lee when he made a media splash by setting fire to a Black minister's house in the name of White Supremacy and the Ku Klux Klan. Then, when the Black minister returned love for Johnny's hate, Johnny was supposed to have had a conversion experience and wound up loving everybody. Nice story.

So nice, it created a bit of a media frenzy resulting in Johnny's finding the spotlight ala Montel Williams, etc. Johnny really liked the attention (and who of us wouldn't?) and made the most of it, as did the media. Good vs. Evil, the Evil White Man converted by the love of a Good Black Man. Good press in that.

You may wonder at the mocking tone in what I have written so far. I'll explain.

A few month's ago I got a call from a Hispanic man who said he and Johnny wanted to meet with me. Then he said a very curious thing. "Dr. Heath, he said, I'll understand if you might find it objectionable to meet with me, a Hispanic, but I would still like you and Johnny to meet and discuss some things."

49

It was obvious that this man had me confused with the persona some have tried to tar me with involving White Supremacy and hate mongering. Granted my political writing where I have called for closing our borders and abortion clinics, welfare reform, English as the national language, repeal of gun control laws, voter reform, my having associations with questionable organizations like the Aryan Nations, Christian Identity, Posse Comitatus, The Order, the various Klan's and publications like The Spotlight, The Jubilee and others have made me a prejudiced, bigoted hater of minorities and a psychotic gun nut!

Whew! I sometimes even amaze myself trying to keep up with the various stories about my reputation as a dangerous man and a racist! Not so (at least about being a racist), as I try to make clear in my writing to all these groups and publications, in my speaking to the churches etc. But, this man had me in that category of racists.

Good thing they don't know about my corresponding with Louis Farrakhan and a few other politically incorrect minority people and organizations or I might really be in trouble!

Now I've had more than my share of notoriety via newspapers and TV due to running for Supervisor and the State Senate, letters to the editor and publishing of books and essays and speaking to various organizations. In fact, when I was leaving the Lake Isabella area for another of my torpedo runs, some wit asked me what the local paper was going to do for news now that I was leaving?

But the media, in some cases, put their own spin on many of my statements and writings. They really had fun, I remember well, with my comments concerning voter qualification reform for example. And Enlightened Self Interest? What's that? I still wonder how many reporters even know where that came from?

As a result, I still encounter people at various functions who come up to me and say: "Say, aren't you that guy...?" And then I have to spend time disabusing them of their distorted views. Some of them think I recruit for Soldier of Fortune!

My attempts, so far, extreme as they have been in some cases to make the Patriot Movement coalesce into a force against Caesar has lent some credibility to the stories circulating in certain circles about me. The C.I.A., F.B.I., J.D.L., A.D.L., even people like Louis Farrakhan and others could straighten these folks out but even these organizations find me confusing to them at times.

I'll never forget the history teacher who confronted me one time with these words: "Just what in the hell is a shop teacher doing with a Ph. D.?" It was terribly degrading to this poor man. Why everyone knows Ph. D.'s don't belong in a shop class teaching the rejects! It's just poor form old fellow, just isn't done, I say!

(Now I'm getting to Johnny Lee the long way around. Okies have a way of doing this. Please bear with me as I continue to set the scene with these prefatory remarks. I'll get it together yet).

Well, I still mix my Levis and three-piece suits. It makes my day to make things a little more surreal for folks. And it usually brings out their prejudices and biases as well. Maybe it's that Cherokee and English blood, the conflict between the wild and untamed and the civilized man who knows how to discriminate between the silver service at a formal dinner and how to fend for himself in both the asphalt jungle and the natural wilderness.

I just don't fit neat and tidy labeling. And given my childhood background, my work in the Ghetto of L.A. and the Barrio of East San Jose with those families and children, well, it's just awfully difficult to paint me with that racist brush if you really do your homework.

But Tom Paine, as I try to tell people, didn't fit a neat and tidy mold either. Yet, as Washington himself said, without this man there would never have been a War for Independence, an America! Yet, as with Tom and Thoreau, no one had any difficulty discerning their (or my) hatred of Caesar and his Big Brotherism form of government. And I write and speak, sometimes indiscreetly, as those men did, very plainly in this regard. As with those two Patriots, the battle is against an Evil System, not against people regardless of color or background.

Evil men and women, as with the good and noble, come in all colors and I've met their representatives in every ethnic and cultural setting. Wickedness, as with drugs, alcohol and perversion is non-discriminatory. It cuts across all national and religious boundaries and station of life. But, fortunately, so does goodness and virtue.

Well, I managed to assure my caller that I wouldn't be upset if he accompanied Mr. Clary and we set a day and time to meet at a restaurant in Bakersfield. You can imagine my curiosity being aroused by the request but since many of us, on all sides, don't trust our telephones, not even my Ultima line, I didn't press for any substantial details of why they wanted to meet with me. While I hadn't given any thought to Mr. Clary other than what the media had made of him, in anticipation of the meeting I fired up my network and got quite a bit of information on him; none of it complimentary.

At the appointed time, we got together at Fresh Choice, a place with an abundance of food items to suit any palate. Johnny and his Hispanic friend were very cordial and we sat together to enjoy the meal and get to the issues. I admit being somewhat curious to meet this man who had created such a stir in the media. And, more than a little curious as to what he might want of me?

Well, it seems they were both misdirected. They thought because of some literature and stories that had been distorted and circulated by some groups using my name that I was someone who would use his influence to introduce Mr. Clary to some of these people, particularly among the Patriot groups.

Granted the work I had tried to do in the past lent credibility to their misperception of me. For example, many people know of my efforts, thanks to the media, at the request of the Constitutional Attorney Terrence Shannon of Atlanta, Georgia to, in his words: Bring the Klan into the 21st Century.

But this debacle precipitated by Morris Dees of the Southern Poverty Law Center (a real money-maker for Dees, you know, the guy that prosecuted the case against Tom Metzger in Oregon?) and J.W. Farrands the Imperial Wizard of the International Ku Klux Klan (then called the Invisible Empire) died a sudden death due to the ego of Mr. Farrands and his betraying so many who trusted him.

However, due to my, some call, inflammatory writing, my acquaintance with Supremacist leaders like Richard Butler, Carl Franklin, J.W. Farrands and others Mr. Clary saw me as someone useful to his ministry. They say politics (and I add, religion) makes strange bedfellows. Mr. Clary most definitely wanted me in bed with him.

Being a natural Cracker, Johnny Lee was born to his trade as an evangelist for the love everybody religion. An orphan (according to him, though this story changes from time to time), horribly abused physically and emotionally as a child (he claims) a loner and a drifter who was easily taken in by White Supremacists (he claims), he was a natural for induction into the Klan. Or so it would seem. And his miraculous conversion due to the ministrations of a Black Man! God most certainly had great and mighty plans for Johnny Lee Clary! After all, just look at his testimony of what God had done in his life through a Black Man; and Johnny having been a qualified, card-carrying, nigger-hating Kluxer of the first order! (He claims).

And my, what a testimony he had at lunch! I'll tell you folks the truth; if I hadn't had so much experience with the flim flam artists like the Johnny Lee's of this world I would have been his convert on the spot! This guy has charisma. But he doesn't have any education and that was a real weakness in his attempts to flim flam me. Like one of the characters in my novel, Johnny Lee was blessed at birth with a native intelligence and cunning that, together with that charisma makes such men inordinately successful in gulling the ignorant.

But that lack of education beats people like Johnny Lee every time. His ignorance shows. Educated people are not easily taken in by the Johnny Lee's. It's a case of Breeding Tells. Educated people generally get taken by their own kind. The same motives prevail of course irrespective of education, the same human nature is susceptible to the greed, envy, lust, etc. to which all flesh is heir, those human characteristics that don't discriminate by accident of birth or breeding.

It was immediately apparent to me that I had better keep my own counsel during this meeting. I purposely did not let on to what I had learned of Johnny Lee from my own sources, sources not available to Montel, Sally, Phil, Geraldo, etc. I did learn, however, that Johnny Lee had tried to join various Klan's and tried to insinuate himself into leadership positions in some of them without success.

My sources verified his proclivity to embellish to a great extent, claiming connections he didn't have, memberships he never had, knowing people who didn't know him. I wasn't surprised. Such a thing is a commonplace with people like Johnny Lee; and for some in prison, a mechanism of protection and survival if nothing else. But I encouraged him to do the talking which required little encouragement at all from me. Johnny Lee is a talker. And I know how to listen.

Johnny had a good shtick going and it wasn't surprising, given his humble origins that he would have kissed the backside of any Arab, Jew, Chinese, African, Troglodyte or Space Alien to get where he wanted to go. We are all knowledgeable of how cheaply many people, even those of great power, like Judges and Congressmen, sell out. So common is this that even in the time of Sam Clemens he could call Judas Iscariot a premature Congressman.

He reminds me of so many beautiful women who sell out to get their pictures in Playboy or that part in the movie or rent their bodies to avoid having to earn an honorable living. But, as I've said in other writings, I don't always blame women for turning to prostitution when so-called men have left them with babies and no other means of support. And in Johnny's case, prostitution of the body is nobler than prostituting the Gospel. Johnny Lee is a religious whore, a gospel-peddler!

But poor Johnny; ignorant, white trash background, so in need of a way to express his natural talents and ability, how could he not take advantage of such a god-given opportunity, an opportunity made feverish by the media which had made him? Johnny Lee is a short, chubby, blond and fair - complexioned young man. He's obviously strong, strong enough that I wouldn't want to go to fist city with him unless I had to. He has robust good health and a strong voice; professional Preacher material.

He said something of his supposed bodyguard duties to David Duke. Then he threw in some comments about Mr. Duke's womanizing; a scandalous thing to Johnny Lee in his new capacity as a minister of the Gospel. But Mr. Duke told me he knew virtually nothing of Johnny Lee but what he had seen in the papers and on TV. Somehow, I'm inclined to believe Mr. Duke, especially in view of the fact that no one else in Mr. Duke's organization knew anything of him either apart from the brief splash in the media; and no pictures or written corroboration of course. We just take Johnny Lee's word for it?

In fact, I learned the fire he set was an attempt to get the attention of those who wouldn't allow him in where he wanted to be. Seems Johnny was always kept at a distance, a street grunt, by these groups, the leaders of which, I know by experience, are better judges of men than much of the media usually credit them.

But remember, much of the media isn't in the business of presenting the truth; only what sells their version of it! And when your guiding principles lead you to blindly accept only those proofs that reinforce your own bias or prejudice, the results are easily predictable. So, left on the outside, knocking to get in, Johnny lit a fire. To get attention! And he got it! Who says a little terrorism (or a lot) doesn't pay off? Not me!

When it was opportune, I did ask a few leading questions of Johnny Lee, questions about some other organizations and leaders I knew he could only answer if he was truthful in his claims concerning them. He failed in every instance. But I had couched the questions in such a way that I successfully left him thinking he had answered or evaded them satisfactorily.

But the fact that he knew nothing of J.W. Farrands, Tom Robb, Richard Butler, Carl Franklin among Supremacist leaders or Sheriff Mack and other prominent people in the Patriot movement, his ignorance of the Turner Diaries, Vampire 2000, The Anarchist's Cookbook, Mark Wachtler and the American Research Institute and similar items gave the lie to his having ever been privy to any insider information in any of the major Supremacist or Patriot organizations.

He was totally ignorant of even the most prominent literature of the groups with which he was supposed to have been involved. He knew nothing of material like the Protocols, which has been around since the time of Marx or the Fort Smith sedition trial in the 80's. He didn't even know of Richard Butler's sedition trial! Maybe, I thought, Johnny Lee didn't even know about a program called 60 Minutes!

In fact, he knew nothing of the Holocaust literature or General Ernst Roemer, knew nothing of any of the English, Canadian and European groups, leaders or literature. As to the anti-abortion movement of which so many of these groups belong, he didn't even know who Randall Terry was! Just what and who did this man really know? In the over two hours we spent together, I learned Johnny Lee didn't really know very much about any of the literature, the organizations and people he was supposed to have been saved out of and from!

Letting him and his poor, misguided Hispanic convert think they had my interest, letting Johnny think he had been successful in conning me, we left the restaurant in seeming good fellowship, with firm handshakes all around. I'll dance with the Devil if that is what it takes for me to get close enough to him to get the noose around his neck or cut off his family jewels! At least Satan and I take the war seriously, unlike most of the churches.

Speaking of which, Johnny Lee was going to bring the message that coming Sunday at the church the Hispanic man attended. They asked me if I could possibly be there as a special favor so I could get the full benefit of Johnny's powerful testimony and preaching. I assured them I would be there. And you gotta know I wasn't going to miss it!

But I could have written the script for the whole affair- been there, done that, many times. It was a Holy Roller Meetin' of the first water. A real entertainment extravaganza suited to the most discriminatin' conna sewer of Pentecostalism. There was a garn'teed movin' 'a the spirit 'n' 'a holy ghost 'nointin' 'n' blessin' on the menu shur nuff!

Seems Johnny Lee is an Elvis wannabe. A full one-third of the program was given to his renditions of so-called *gospel* lyrics set to Elvis tunes, the actual Elvis music being used! And Johnny really threw himself into the act. He told his captives (the congregation): "Why should the Devil have all the good music? Why, all we Christians have to do is steal the music (my interpretation) and put religious words to it and voila! Instant Gospel with an Elvis beat!" Again my interpretation; makes sense to some. In any event, Johnny had a goodly supply of tapes and videos of his Elvis impersonations with religious lyrics for sale to the faithful wherever he went. The entrance of the church had a table stacked with them.

The performance began with the usual hand waving, body-swaying songfest of homegrown lyrics and the charismatic church version of 99 bottles of beer on the wall. These are seemingly endless repetition of a single stanza that always includes the words Love, Glory, Hallelujah, Jesus or Zion in order to sanctify the gibberish.

But, as I have written so much about this kind of thing in a couple of my books and several essays on the subject, I won't belabor it here. Suffice it to say Johnny Lee was in his element. More might have been given to the musical part of the worship service because of my being in attendance. Why; because he knew something of my contacts in the music business. But there was a much more important reason for his reluctance to do much talking.

Johnny Lee didn't know much about me and he certainly showed his ignorance in not doing his homework (Like CPS in Tulare County), but what he did know, or thought he knew, caused him to be very cautious in his message. So he kept it fairly short. He has enough intelligence to be wary of those letters Ph. D. and he surely knew I could not be easily fooled by his typical methods of flim flam.

But I got the distinct impression that since he really believes he is the church version of Elvis resurrected and personified, he would rather devote himself to being a song and dance man than a preacher, that he would rather be a performer than a cleric. I know what the reader is thinking; it's often difficult to distinguish between the two and, of course, you're right. And I will say; it's a tragedy that Jimmy Swaggart didn't stick to his marvelous gift of music instead of meddlin' in preachin'. Oh, well.

As with our luncheon get together, Johnny Lee avoided specific information during his harangue from the pulpit and said just enough, like a fortuneteller, to make his audience think he was really telling them something specific. They don't call then *Confidence Men* for nothing.

Names, dates, places and actual events except for the fact of his setting fire to the Black Man's house and the Black Man's reaction to the act were conspicuous by their absence. He tried to drop a few names but he was at least aware that I knew some of these men personally so he was very cautious during the service. At the altar call, people began to line up across the front of the church three deep. Johnny Lee really had his hands full. With much shouting and chanting of Hallelujahs, Amens, Glory, Jesus and the usual tongues gibberish, people were being slain of the spirit right and left.

Johnny would mutter his incantations, place his hand on the forehead of the penitent or sufferer of everything from PMS and gout to demon possession and at the persuasive push of Johnny Lee the relieved soul would swoon into the faithful arms of a couple of grabbers strategically positioned behind him or her. The ushers were kept busy hauling the fallen faithful off out of the way until the fit passed.

It was at the end of the show that I simply couldn't handle any more of the hypocrisy of it all. It was one thing to be entertained by Johnny Lee's Elvis impersonations, it was ok to submit to his ranting about how he and God loved everybody no matter what their skin color was, but when it came to the miracles, tongues, visions and healing part at the end, I took my leave.

I consoled myself with not contributing to the love gift taken up by the sheep for this false shepherd. But he was doing well, I understand, through his tapes and videos and didn't need my money. Failing to get my help in his so-called ministry? Now that, I'm sure, hurt him; couldn't happen to a nicer guy as they say.

Yes, Johnny Lee has a calling all right, and one imminently well-suited to those who seek to be deceived, who want to enjoy their religion without asking any of the hard questions of either God or themselves. He has perfected the lingo and mannerisms of such churches and blends in perfectly. But he's still a charlatan, a fake and hypocrite!

And please don't take offense, folks. As I wrote in my Okie Intellectual book: "I don't mind people having fun with their religion just please don't blame and shame the Lord and the Holy Spirit for such foolishness and shenanigans!

It ill serves Tulsa, Oklahoma to be the base of such a so-called ministry. I may only be an Honorary Okie by virtue of my birth in Weedpatch, California and raisin' among all those good Dust Bowl Okies, Arkies and Texans that settled the area but I still take offense at the likes of a Johnny Lee besmirching that good State and those good people!

And since the honor of us Okies is at stake, I've sharpened my acerbic and vitriolic pen and taken after good ol' boy Clary and I certainly am well schooled in cleanin' the clock of these flim flam artists and feather merchants. Y'

all can tell when this here ol' Okie boy is riled! Don't get on his bad side! And a whole lot of folks who know him pretty well say: "Even his good side sports a Randal and a 9mm.!" I don't disabuse them of the notion.

WANTED! FOR HYPOCRISY!

There's a postscript already to the above article. Because of a situation that existed with the daughter of a wonderful lady I know, I sent her an advance copy. She phoned to tell me she had her daughter read it because of a young man, a very religious young man that was courting her daughter.

I used Clary as an example of religious charlatanism. I had only met the young suitor in question once. But he had all the earmarks of one of those enthusiastic, well-intentioned Bible Believers who use (misuse and abuse) the Scriptures as a theological club to beat others into submission to their brand of Christian. I ought to know; I was a card-carrying Pharisee of the Pharisees once myself (just like Saul, later the Apostle Paul) until the Lord took me to the woodshed and cleaned my clock on the issue!

Anyhow, this lovely lady called to thank me for the article and to express the thought that it might have helped her daughter deal with the young man. I sincerely hope so. That's when my writing is rewarding beyond my expectations; when it pays off in helping people like this lady's daughter. I hope the young man might listen, take to heart and learn something from my comments on Mr. Clary.

It helps tremendously that I have beautiful daughters as well and have the same hopes and dreams for them as this lovely lady for hers. I thank you so much V—for your taking the time and effort of sharing this with me. It was so characteristically thoughtful of you.

***

Had an interesting talk with a psychiatrist the other day; and to anticipate the chorus I know a lot of you folks are saying: "It's about time!" And I reply: Shame on Y 'all, twarn't that way 'tall.

It was, in fact, an interview for a job. Seems the good doctor is thinking of opening a branch office and my name came up. Since she wasn't looking for an M.D. but needed someone of my qualifications, I agreed to meet with her. I never earned my Ph. D. in Human Behavior with the intention of hanging out my shingle in full time practice. And I'm still far too busy to entertain the notion but the good doctor wanted someone to staff the branch facility on a part time basis. Good enough; a chance to help people and earn some money; good combination. Ulterior motive number three-hundred and sixty-three coming up: It would give me a chance to jump through the hoops of another system of government which determines who is mentally ill and what to do about it!

Well, we all know how many psychiatrists/psychologists it takes to change a light bulb: Just one. But the light bulb must really want to be changed! Old joke. And I'm certain to hear them all before the dust settles on this chapter of my life no matter what the outcome.

But we're still in the talking stage of the game (comes with the territory) and I'll let you know what transpires. Things just keep a' changin' for the ol' Weedpatcher. But as I say in the Birds book, no one has ever accused me of leading a boring life!

***

According to some folks at the American Research Institute, one of the good old boys, Harry Lamplugh, has had his training session with the BATF. They held him and his wife without showing a search warrant while they confiscated his gun collection in Pennsylvania.

But that wasn't the worst of it. According to the periodical, "Gun Show Calendar," they took all of Harry's records of the membership of his organization, "Borderline Gun Collectors Association," some 70,000 names and addresses. Now we all know what Caesar wants with this information.

Well, Harry, consider yourself lucky as opposed to a lot of others like Randy Weaver's wife and son and the women and children of Waco! But I have a hunch I know what you and your wife will do now. And I want you to know I don't blame you! In the words of Thomas Jefferson: "The strongest reason for the people to retain the right to keep and bear arms is, at last resort, to protect themselves against tyranny in government."

And I would add that the arms of the people should be at least the equal of the government's just as they were at the time of Jefferson! At least the

Minutemen weren't reduced to throwing rocks at the Lobster Backs. Nuff said.

When I was in the business, I warned people to never trust that smiling face behind the table at the gun shows that wanted to sell you a lower case for your tamed M16. He was probably a Treasury agent bent on entrapment.

Because of my family and increasing political activity, I could read the writing on the wall and I divested myself of my collection and got out of the business. And it proved to be a wise decision. If the Feds wanted me, they were going to have to lay one on me. They would never find me with any contraband.

Harry has not been charged with any crime! Yet all documents on the incident have been sealed in Caesar's court! The Feds got what they wanted and 70,000 people have cause to worry as a consequence! And how many of these belonged to underground militias and were involved in clandestine publications? And I have to wonder further in the light of this, how many converts to anarchy may be the result? It took less than a dozen to get the ball rolling in Russia resulting in 1917!

But as with Rousseau, Paine, Stowe, Marx, Darwin and Hitler, one man or woman, one book or pamphlet can change the course of history. Never underestimate the power of the pen for good or evil, TV and videos notwithstanding! Pictures fade and pass; the written word remains!

If government leaders have to stump behind bulletproof glass, if the cry of Soap! Soap! is accompanied by the increasing sound of cocking pistols in their audiences, who is to blame? Not Americans, of that I'm certain.

***

In a lighter and positive vein, Birds With Broken Wings and The Lord and the Weedpatcher are selling well. Both books have great potential for commercial success. One good reason for self-publishing is the fact that you retain all rights including creative. And while I would certainly entertain an offer from a major publishing house, much is lost to a writer in the process of the typical contract with such houses.

Since I brought up the subject in my last essay and since so many have asked, I publish under several names and companies. The parent company for most of my publishing is: S.D.G. HEATH PUBLISHING. The subsidiaries or divisions are: BitterSweet Publishing, WEEDPATCHER PRESS and OKIE PRESS.

Why so many different divisions of publishing? Because, as with most publishers, of the broad areas in which I write and publish. While self-publishing is a hard way to go because of the difficulties of promotion, I am beginning to see some success. Our Writer's Conference here in Bakersfield on September 16th will attract writers, publishers and agents from all around the country. As a publisher, I am allowed a display table at the conference. This will be an outstanding opportunity to promote the books. Wish I could have the novel ready but hopefully, next year.

Just recently, the library bought a copy of the Weedpatcher and the local museum even displays and sells copies. I guess I'm one of the few people who get a check from the Museum; this primarily because of the old pictures and anecdotes of the past in the book.

But the alter ego and persona of yours truly on the cover in good ol' boy boots, Levis and Western hat with his old pickup (I courteously left the Randal and 9mm. in the truck for the picture)? I declare some folks have bought the dad-blamed thing just for the picture on the cover! There just purely ain't no accountin' for taste at times!

My daughter Karen's picture on the cover of the Birds book I knew, would sell the book. She is the most beautiful woman in the world and I want the world to see that her dad is telling the truth! When I say beautiful, I want everyone to see that I know what I'm talking about! And the bookstores love to display it, as I knew they would.

But as I have shared with her, how in the ever-lovin', blue-eyed world did a man like me have such an extraordinarily beautiful daughter?

***

Seems researchers in the Netherlands claim to have found a genetic defect in one family that causes outbreaks of periodic, seemingly unprovoked, violent outbursts. I quote: "The men lack a gene for the production of monoamine oxidase, an enzyme that breaks down several of the brain's important transmitters. Without MAO, one researcher believes, a surge of excess chemical messengers could flood the victim's brains, causing their furies."

MAO, I know from my own studies of abnormal psychology, releases serotonin that usually has a calming effect on the firing of neurons. The researchers feel the lack of this gene may account for a Jekyll-and-Hyde personality.

The report states that the family in this case involves men who have an I.Q. of only 85, mildly retarded. The obvious implication is that if violent behavior has a genetic basis, and if a fetus is determined to be missing that gene, abortion would be a solution to the problem.

Just what we need, another Pandora's Box, another ethical conundrum; Hitler wouldn't have had the problem. If his scientists had the information we have today, they would know exactly what to recommend. They had already determined what to do with the retarded. Now if such a genetic defect were proven as the basis of unpredictable, violent behavior, it would become a national health problem to be studied as a disease.

Please don't misunderstand me. I'm fully supportive of good science. Ignorance, as I've often said, is a real killer. But as with theological questions I raise that the churches don't want to deal with, it does no good to take positions without looking at all sides of the question.

The world itself is considering, in some cases actually practicing, those Hitlerian Solutions I have long warned our own nation is facing. But now that we have faced the *disease* of Alcoholism, will we have to, increasingly, face the possibilities of the *diseases* of rape, murder, theft, molestation, etc.?

Much as I admire so many church people, so many involved with the Patriot Movement, I have to make a very sobering point. It is a point that could lead to my carrying out something I have shared with my children.

I've told them that if I should ever come up missing (apart from the results of my writing or some of the interesting situations and people in which and with whom I involve myself) they could look for my bones in a wilderness area next to a pristine trout stream far removed from any vestiges of civilization.

There are times when I want to go to that area I know so well, tell the world to go to hell, shut the door and just go fishing. I have a little sign that says: I Don't Want To Know! I look at that once in a while and wistfully think to myself, I don't want to know. Why; because I have always been a man who believed in the responsibility of knowledge. If you know something, you are required to act on that knowing. The somber point: Too many good people don't seem to want to know. It's as though they want to evade the responsibility of knowing.

I may begin calling it the Johnny Lee syndrome (JLS). If it doesn't suit your agenda, your bias or prejudice, if it doesn't stroke your ego or contribute to your pocketbook, it isn't something you want to know. Or do anything about.

In spite of the many good people I know in the churches and the Patriot groups, seldom do I ever find anyone, let alone an organization, that is able to transcend the JLS. The Radisson Hotel scam in Visalia is an excellent case in point. If nothing comes of this, it will be the fault of the JLS. And the enemies of America count on this.

These evil men and women are usually good judges of human nature. After all, they were all human once themselves! They depend on the JLS to kick in when little people suddenly get involved in something that will make them big in their own eyes, will suddenly make them *Somebody*!

The Unabomber may not have wanted notoriety in the beginning of his crusade, but now that he has learned how easy it is to disrupt the lives of a whole nation? The psychology of the thing is easily predictable. Give a nobody some recognition and he wants more, given a taste of power he wants more; big frogs in a little pond? Certainly: better than a little frog in a big pond.

How about the song, "You can put your makeup on and drive the men insane." Or, "Baby's got her blue jeans on." Now I don't want to seem to be picking on the ladies but the point is pretty obvious. If you want attention, there are ways to get it. And we all want to be noticed. No one wants to be a *Nobody*, a cipher, a supernumerary, a nonentity.

There is an old Hollywood saying: "Be careful who you step on, on your way up. You may meet them on your way down!" I believe firmly in another old saying: "Give credit where credit is due." There are a number of little people involved in trying to get the Orange County bankruptcy and things like the Visalia/Tulare County corruption before the attention of the American people. If these little people fail, it will be, primarily, because of the JLS. A name and picture in the newspaper! A TV interview! Heady stuff to most little people; a moment of fame! Ah, now how to get more than just a taste!

Things like the Radisson Hotel scandal in Visalia have all the necessary ingredients to make stars out of a lot of little people. If we were to pursue this thing ala O.J. Simpson, it has amazing opportunities! First, we'll crank up the archival reports of the Kansas City Star concerning Metro North State Bank. Bingo! Here it is; "The lying, conniving, duplicity and thieving trail is a mile broad already that will lead from Kansas City to Orange and Tulare counties among others; and the connection to construction in Oxnard and Baldwin Park in California? It begins here also."

I just might have my friends in K.C. make a little friendly visit to Matt Whitworth, the U.S. Attorney concerning the situation. Or you might give him a call at: (816) 426-4122; could be interesting.

Now the F.B.I. in both L.A. and Fresno counties has the necessary materials to give chase but guess what? They and the state of California are treating it as a political issue! When, I asked my deep throat, will the Feds decide these are crimes; and crimes that are contributing to the bankruptcy not only of California, but the whole nation?

I'm sure only insiders are aware that the state of California has an open file on the failure of Tulare County and the city of Visalia to demand a water test of the Radisson Hotel site. Why, because a proper test would have revealed, from public records, that the ground would fail the LUFT (Leaking Underground Fuel Tanks) test!

Now we all know The Power to Tax is the Power to Destroy! Would you hazard a guess where all these things are headed? Visalia passed its tax in order to repay the money the scoundrels already stole with the assistance of the city and county officials.

How many official people lined their pockets in the process of helping the professional thieves, the moneylenders and their straw men rob the folks in Orange County and in Kansas City? Now the leaders have the unmitigated gall to go to the same people they stole the money from and ask them to pay for the stolen money! They don't call it a Racket for nothing. Where's RICO in all of this? Conspicuous by its absence!

Now all you good folks in Orange, Tulare and counties statewide, keep your ropes handy and your muskets well cleaned and oiled. Remember the words of Jefferson. And you have to know he meant what he said. So do I! And I'm as sure as he was that if the power of the ballot which all civilized people try to use for change should fail, constituted authority, just as in the time of our founding fathers, will rise to the occasion and today's Minutemen will be needed as they were then.

To that end I would ask every governor of every state to encourage their militias and give them the honorable leadership of honorable offices. Caesar would then have cause to tremble and tremble he must! He will not listen to the voice of reason and his hordes of sycophants, unearned bread masses and incapables grows daily.

***

Well, as I told you folks last month, July promised some changes. The most arduous was my move back to the little house in Bodfish in the Lake Isabella area. It has been a lot of work to restore the place due to a very bad tenant but now that I'm once more in the place, the work has all been worth it.

Some of the work required a complete re-painting inside and out; a new front door due to some of the tenant's unsavory friends who kicked the door out. Lots of patching, plastering, some masonry work and new flooring was also required due in part to a number of dogs being allowed to remain in the house.

I've been a landlord over 30 years and this has been one of the worst jobs I've had to do to refinish a house after it has served as a rental. But, as I said, it's been worth it.

Once finished inside, I could start on the outside. I cleaned out the small pond in the rear and have my small waterfall going again. The critters are glad to have me back in the place. The quail, especially, sing to me in gratitude of the water source, something really critical to all the critters due to the extremely dry conditions.

I finally got to the point where I could actually think about cooking. Now I don't usually think much about this. I'm not really into food as my wiry frame testifies. But someone mentioned Okie beans some while back.

The only Okie beans I know about is boiling the tar out of the things and serving them with homemade cornbread, one of my specialties.

So it was that the first home cooking in the joint was beans and cornbread. And just so you don't get the idea that the friend who told me about the towels that I mentioned in last month's essay is the only bachelor with genius, I'll tell you about my method of cooking cornbread.

I combine all the dry ingredients first in my cast iron frying pan. Then, adding milk, eggs and shortening, I mix it thoroughly. After this, I simply pop the mess in the oven and bake it. No bowel to clean; simple Okie cooking. I quit heating hominy in the can by placing it on the stove in a pan of water the day the phone rang during the process and during the conversation I forgot I had left it cooking.

Lacking the needed vent hole I forgot to punch, the resulting explosion left me a stove to repair and an entire kitchen to clean with a putty knife and repaint. I learned years ago to avoid natural disasters like hurricanes, using a knife to pry out a piece of recalcitrant toast from the toaster and asking a lady her age. But new disasters keep coming at me and keeping me on my toes.

Another advantage of being a desert rat is my ability to drink coffee, warm lemonade, and beer just like the Aussies no matter if it is 110 degrees outside and 98 in the shade or house. Since my rehab of the house does not, at present, accommodate my refrigerator with icemaker, it's a good thing my physiognomy favors the heat.

It has been good to be back here with so many friends. As I write this it is Sunday evening. My old music teacher, Willard Swadburg, and I made the rounds of Kern County playing classical music to all kinds of crowds and organizations. We did duets with Mr. Swadburg on the piano or organ.

I know that dear man must turn in his grave to hear some of the music I took up later, especially C&W. Lo, how the mighty have fallen! But I believe he would understand my love of making music no matter the genre and despite my failure to remain pure and true to the classics.

But "Begin the Beguine" or "Swan Lake" and "Clair de Lune," my clarinet still does the job and it is all beautiful music. My debt to that old music teacher remains for his having taken such an interest in me as a child prodigy.

Byron McKaig tracked me down at one of the local pubs recently and came in and joined me for a cup of coffee. He made a comment concerning last month's essay comparing some of my writing with that of Soren Kierkegaard's. Byron isn't the only one to make that connection between the Dark Dane philosopher and me.

In matters of the faith, I often join forces with those whose minds are too restless to accept easy answers to complex questions. In plumbing those vast, dark frontiers of thought, I find good company with men like Kierkegaard, Melville and Thoreau.

My friend Byron, the Episcopal Priest, shared some of his thoughts about last month's Okie Intellectual, remarking my affinity to the Dark Dane. This led to my telling him the following story:

Just recently a lovely book store owner and I were chatting when she asked me: "Don, how do you manage to keep from getting totally depressed writing about the things you do, involving yourself in the lives of some of the people and organizations you do?"

I pointed to the rack at the front of the store where the Birds book was prominently displayed and said, pointing to the book: "J--, the answer to that question is the little lady on the cover of that book! It is a picture of my daughter, Karen."

I had to leave somewhat abruptly because the tears were in my voice and in her eyes at my emotional admission of the truth of the matter. In speaking with Byron about such things, I related the story of the hangman who, when he was asked if his job didn't cause him to awaken screaming and drenched with sweat from the nightmares that surely must accompany his job replied: "Doesn't everyone?" At least I'm blessed with the music, my friends, my children and these keep the nightmares in some perspective.

Byron is a well-educated and sensitive man, and he continues to love me warts and all. Even knowing of my heterodox views, these men credit me as an honorable man. Men like these and my friend Senator Rogers know that a good name is to be prized above gold. That I continue to have a good name among such honorable men and many honorable women is nothing short of miraculous and certainly an evidence of the best sense of that thing called Christian Charity on their part.

***

As long as I'm back in the Valley, it was only natural for me to get together with the folks at the various taverns where so many stories came from for the Birds book. And the music is still here.

I have given complimentary copies of the book to the local Alano Club and some of the bar owners here in the Valley, in Bakersfield and Oildale who were so helpful and friendly to me during the time I was doing the research for the book. Several of them have become close friends.

When I walked into Slugger's Saloon after my long absence from the Valley I was greeted with a big hug and a kiss from this marvelous lady, Slugger herself. It was a genuine pleasure to be able to give her, her own special copy of the book. Another copy went to two wonderful people, Bill and Bev of Shady Lane Saloon.

Now I have been writing professionally for many years. Most of it has been of a political and theological nature. The Birds book and The Lord and the Weedpatcher were the aberrations of a generally somber man.

I've had enough notoriety in Kern County, Sacramento and even in Foggy Bottom (D.C) to be known to a few of these kinds of folks as well. The media has treated me, for the most part, kindly. But I wasn't prepared for the statement made to me by a lovely, young lady the other night in one of the taverns.

We all know the story of parochialism so well illustrated by the fellow who, in addressing a group of Rotarians in some little burg ala Babbitt, said: "You know folks, I've been as far South as Mule Corner, North to Hog Center, West to Whiskey Gulch and East to Broken Knee and I've learned that people are pretty much the same the whole world over."

Now my little corner of the world is sometimes reduced to just such a laughable size here in the Valley or Bakersfield and Oildale, Taft, Arvin, Lamont, Pumpkin Center, Ridgecrest and, oh yes, Weedpatch. And you know folks, people are pretty much the same the whole world over (ok, the Devil, not Sinclair Lewis, made me do it).

Seriously, this young lady had been looking at me for some time while I was enjoying the local band and having the usual cup of coffee. Finally, she came over to where I was sitting at a table and asked if she could take a chair next to me. Being that Southern Gentleman of the Old School how could I refuse?

Naturally I wondered what her interest in me might be. She then asked if I really usually only drank coffee or whether the bartender and I had an understanding and the coffee were spiked with something more substantial than caffeine? I assured her it was only coffee. She pondered that a moment then she got up and, standing near she put her arm around me and said: "You're a famous writer aren't you!"

I put my arm about her and drew her head down to me. Since the noise of the band made conversation difficult, I put my face in her marvelously soft, deliciously scented, long auburn hair and spoke into her ear saying: "Not famous, Sweetheart, but I'm sure working on it."

She laughed and exchanging a quick kiss, she left to talk with some of the other girls at the bar. Eventually they were all looking in my direction and talking animatedly; about me? I suppose so. There are a lot of stories about me in this small area.

However, since the Birds book is a hot topic of conversation locally I hasten to point something out. The last chapter, as I said in the book, was added to prevent any hint of hypocrisy. I expose some of the various affairs I have had with a number of women in this final chapter. I also mentioned two girls with Electric Skin, a very rare quality not unlike the static electricity of silk that certainly, as I said, make the sparks fly in lovemaking! But being a true romantic, a true poet, I did not, as some suggested I should have done, refer to these two girls as Electric Wenches (winches)!

Which reminds me of one of the major difficulties I am having with my novel; it is a truism to writers that: The difference between Reality and Fiction is that fiction has to make sense! God knows how little sense I make of the realities of my own life at times.

Those who know me well aren't about to think I would put this little lady thinking me a famous writer down for parochialism. But it is true that in certain areas of our lives, we do tend to make much of things that are outside our own sphere of knowledge and experience. And some do find themselves, on occasion, the big frog in the little pond.

Many years ago I held doctors in awe until I knew some well enough to realize they were as human (well, almost) as I was. I'm a good auto mechanic. I've run shops and used to teach the subject in high school. I learned to equate doctors with mechanics. Both say: "Well, we'll try this and see if it works." But I've made the point in time past that mechanics have to be better at their trade than doctors since doctors get to bury their mistakes!

And what do you call a hundred lawyer/congressmen at the bottom of the ocean? A Start! The honorable ones like Senator Rogers know I don't include them in this category. Besides, he wasn't a lawyer but earned an honest living in another profession. Men like Senator Rogers are the only real hope I have in the system.

Now while I have friends, like the song says, In Low Places, I have been known to socialize with some who really know and prefer champagne to beer and can afford the difference. But Rosie and her daughters, as I described them in my book, victims of Welfare Slavery might not know much about writing but even they knew that in some mysterious way, my being a writer was somehow very important. The power of the pen to mold people's hearts and minds, to move them to action can never be underestimated.

I don't know how much or what the little lady at the pub reads. But she knew I was a writer and she knew that was a very important job. I credit her with the good sense to realize this.

Recently, I received a most encouraging note from a beautiful lady friend who made the statement: "Your writing is very important; you're having an impact on lives." What greater, and humbling, testimonial could any writer have or wish for?

Another lady friend recently told me: "Your book (The Lord and the Weedpatcher in this case) made me laugh so much. You have a way of keeping the narrative flowing and I have to keep picking up the book and reading."

Thanks M—for those encouraging words. And I promise to try to keep as much humor in my writing as possible. We all know how important this is.

***

Junkie Jerry just came by for coffee and conversation. Jerry owns a local antique shop and, being a fellow bachelor, waxes lyrical on occasion about women. Personally, I don't think any woman would be crazy enough to put up with him and have told him so. Of all the men I have known who have a jaundiced view of the fair sex Jerry is one of the worst.

On rare occasions, however, even Jerry makes some sense crazy as he is; especially when the subject is politics. Jerry is of the same mind as Peter Grace. What to do about the problems in Foggy Bottom? Fire 435 Clowns and start over!

I'm looking at the picture I was sent by Jerry Falwell of some of the 150 perverts that Al and Tipper Gore hosted at a party recently. All of these are part of the Clinton administration. That our VP and his wife could have these people in their home was no surprise. I know enough of the Gores not to be surprised.

I noted the power of perversion in my last essay. I also said no nation has ever been able to survive this kind of an abomination. I also said it explains why so many government leaders are fearful of confronting it. When your own dark sins of greed, envy, avarice, lust for flesh and power rule your life, how condemn others?

The whole world watched in shocked disbelief as Storm Troopers of Kern County shot down, in cold blood, a 23-year-old mother of three on Highway 99 near Bakersfield. To think that this young mother with her little popgun was a threat to all these men surrounding her with their heavy artillery? Come on now, just who is kidding who!

But knowing as I do, professionally, that fully one-third of those in police work are psychologically unfit to carry a gun, I'm only surprised there aren't more such incidents. If you want a license to kill, legally, what more appealing job than one under color of law that will let you do a boy and a mother holding her infant as at Round Mountain or a distraught, young mother! Or even 82 women and children at one time as in Waco!

Mass Murderer Janet Reno may yet, I fervently pray, get hers from the hearings presently being held. As to Vincent Foster and Whitewater Gate, I can only hope the lying swindlers and traitors, Mr. and Mrs. Clinton, will get theirs as well!

There has been a rash of police shootings in Kern County lately. One cop shot an unarmed man in Bakersfield for simply running away from him. The cop said he thought the man matched the description of a wanted suspect.

But going back to the Gore's pervert party for a moment; there is a relationship between this and the Lords of Bakersfield and the Fag Mafia. With the pressure building to expose the homosexual influence, the abuse of power and authority like police and judicial rottenness in this county (as with others), it has to find release in some fashion. I find a connection between the two when such an abomination is given the sanction and approval of high, government officials like the Reno's, Gore's and Clinton's.

For example, when men like Tim Palmquist are arrested and jailed for threatening a deputy with a pen (talk about the Power of the Pen!), when a young mother is shot down in cold blood and a man is shot for simply running from police, when women and children can be slaughtered wholesale with Caesar's approval and sanction, you know things are out of control. Granting that the wicked flee when no one pursues them, the wicked in this case know that, like the Devil, their time is short when I and others like myself begin to pursue them.

As hard as it is to believe, such corruption does exist. I'm reminded of the fascinating story in the 19th chapter of the Acts of the Apostles concerning the fuss at Ephesus. I have to quote a politician of the times, the city clerk:

"Men of Ephesus, doesn't all the world know that the city of Ephesus is the guardian of the temple of the great Artemis and of her image, which fell from heaven? Therefore, since these facts are undeniable, you ought to be quiet and not do anything rash."

Now I've often wondered if that ancient politician wasn't like the Roman Senator who, when asked by a close friend if he believed in the gods replied: "Publicly, I believe in all of them; privately, none of them." Now there was an honest politician.

But I admit of the possibility that the city clerk really believed what he said. We can all be sincerely wrong. However, it must also be admitted that sincerity can be bred of deception.

Elmer Gantry finally began to believe in his own lies. As they grew with the telling and the sincerity of his own illusions and delusions of himself, and having the benefit of captive audiences it is hard not to fall into such a trap of believing your own press.

Most preachers and politicians ham it up and too often begin to believe in their own self-promotion. When this begins to happen, when they begin to gain any kind of following, they commonly begin to mistake self-promotion and enthusiasm for a message or divine calling and anointing! The so-called *special anointing* of many religious charlatans, and politicians, fall into this category. Those Pharisees and Sadducees of old were incensed, enraged by being caught out of Jesus in their self-deceptions and promotions. And, eventually, they would kill God Himself to keep their vaunted lies and nation.

I meet many who believe the image of the goddess actually fell from heaven, many that believe the whole world knows this is actual fact! And God help those who disagree! The time has always been ripe for such to kill others in the name of their gods and goddesses and in the killing claim they do God a service. Such godly killing is a commonplace throughout history and we read about it and see it on TV everyday throughout the world.

Just recently a man decapitated his son in our own country because he said the boy was demon possessed! There has to be a hotter place in hell for such people!

Low Frequency Electro-magnetic emissions may pose far less of a threat than driving a car but we feel in control of our cars. That's the primary difference in attitudes. We fear and are suspicious of the unknown, that (or those) which is different. Consequently, we will often make gods and goddesses to fit our needs of worship. If Baal, Bacchus, Moloch or Mammon then have gods accordingly; even the most devout Christian or Moslem will often have a distorted view of his God because of the need of mysteries in religion.

By mysticizing, by spiritualizing, God is conveniently removed from humanity and people convince themselves that He not only can be worshiped from afar after a fashion of our choosing, they can also believe that He will only see us from that position far removed from the reality of actual life. In short, have a god who is blind to our humanity and doesn't enter into our lives on an actual basis of realities.

Superstition? Of course. To say that we are so removed from the obvious superstitions of that city clerk's time is nonsense. How far removed are we, really, from the events that led to the Salem Witch Trials? Or, for that matter, the superstitions and lust for flesh, wealth and power, the superstitions that lead to conversion by the sword between Moslems and Jews, Protestants and Catholics as in Ireland or those that lead to the Round Mountain's, Waco's or Oklahoma City's of our own nation that continue to plague the world as throughout the recorded history of humankind?

If some of you wonder at my continued insistence on bringing religion into the picture, please keep in mind that the greatest crimes against humanity have been, and continue to be, committed in the name of ideologies and those ideologies invariably have a fanatical, religious basis. If you wonder at my persistent call for a New Council of Jerusalem, of a New Systematic Theology, of a New Continental Congress, just look at what is happening in our nation and the world at present and try to tell me such things are not needed! In condemning me for such heterodox views as those I expose publicly, both religious and political, the churches, government leaders have first to address the sicknesses infecting them before they condemn me out of hand.

While I usually reserve my theological writing to other publications I want the reader of OI to get some idea of what I am talking about in this context. A good friend and scholar of history and religion came by to visit and, as usual, the topic was some of my heterodox (heretical?) views. In the course of conversation the topic of a young vs. old earth came up.

Barney and Jurassic Park (much over-hyped in my opinion) have created a surge in interest in those ancient reptiles. Most of us have wondered, from time to time, about dinosaurs and their place in the whole scheme of things.

Being a Christian and a Creationist, I could never quite see God creating such creatures unless as a divine experiment; but to what purpose? To provide Coal and Oil for humans as some suppose? Maybe. But I proposed an alternative. Suppose Satan created the dinosaurs? As a Christian, I have the latitude to intrude thoughts about such things that are mentioned in Scripture and since Satan is given such a prominent role in the scheme of things, why limit him to the usual role the churches have assigned him? Even the most cursory examination of Satan in the Scriptures cannot help but present a picture of a most intriguing and powerful creature, one so powerful and influential that he thought he could rise above God Himself!

The single most devastating concept I have advanced in theology is the idea that God is capable of error. This called down on me the most damning indictments of heresy by my friends and colleagues in the churches. And not a few of the unchurched took the attitude of those who horsewhipped that poor fellow in Elmer Gantry. Now while I am adamantly opposed to the obvious fraud of evolution, it being wholly untenable scientifically, I am not opposed to rational examination of all that God has said and created. And this gets me in a lot of trouble.

The very evil exemplified by those living horrors, monsters of the Jurassic Period, lead me to believe them to be a creation of a malevolent mind, not of God Who, we are told and believe, is motivated by a heart of love, mercy and kindness. That God's love has been betrayed by both Satan and mankind is a given in Scripture. As I have written in the past, is an error of love to be construed as a mistake? And if so, who, ultimately, bears the responsibility of the blasting result and consequences of the betrayal of love?

Since we are led to accept the precept that God, as creator and ultimate power and authority, is ultimately responsible for both all good and evil, it makes sense of His accepting His responsibility and paying the ultimate price of His own errors of creation in the sacrifice of His own Son as the consequence. As to what God has in store for those, His children, who live according to His guiding precepts of an equally loving, forgiving and merciful heart, I have said many times: If the churches could make heaven half as exciting as hell, they would be filled to overflowing!

In that ideal world where a man and woman come together in love and make the decision to create a child, they take on the responsibility for the messes that little one is guaranteed to make. The loving heart of the parent is prepared to clean up after that little one from the changing of diapers to even, as in the story of the prodigal, keep on loving no matter what mistakes are made by the child in later life.

But a child can commit acts of atrocity even the most loving parent cannot forgive, acts beyond the redemptive power of love. The parent may not stop loving the child, but Hitler's and Stalin's own parents would have had a hard time forgiving some of the acts of these children. And the results of such acts of atrocity live on long after the initiators have passed away.

What if God, in cleaning up the mess Satan made, had to leave a few things hanging? I'm reminded of the imperfections of our own world as I try to keep on top of the ants in my kitchen. And flies? Gophers? Ground Squirrels? Rattlesnakes and Black Widows?

Speaking of gophers, my daughter has a pet gopher. I know; there ain't no such thing. Well, Karrie, like her brother Michael and their dad is a critter person. We love birds and animals. But a gopher? Heresy!

Seems Karrie and my son-in-law John had a major gopher problem in their backyard in Modesto. They gained the upper hand with poisons, traps and flooding the varmints. One by one, they managed to subdue the voracious creatures; all but one. This one particular gopher knew every game. He actually buried one of the traps after gnawing through the cord attaching it above ground.

But one day, after copious amounts of water were forced into the remaining burrow, the little varmint finally exposed himself. Karrie, grabbing a large towel, captured the critter. He was amazingly docile, probably completely tuckered out from toxins, traps and water.

When I last visited the kids, I was treated to their pet gopher. He was safely ensconced in an extra terrarium they had. He was about the size of a small guinea pig and could be handled as easily as a pet rat. Amazing! I still wanted to shoot the critter. In my mind, the only good gopher is still a dead gopher. But, what could I say? The critter had certainly earned his place of safety; a genuine survivor of admirable skill and courage.

Trying to get out of my own trap in mentioning some of the things I have in this essay, I relievedly see I am running out of space in this edition of OI. I can now take a well-earned breather in preparation for the battle of finishing the kitchen floor and moving my washer, dryer and refrigerator up here from Bakersfield. Anyone with a strong back and weak mind is invited to assist.

CHAPTER FOUR

THE OKIE INTELLECTUAL

SEPTEMBER 1995

One of the real treats for me in returning to Kern County is the people I know in the music business. Buck Owens is still seen at the old studio in Oildale, Trout's is thriving nearby, my friend and genius at piano and keyboard, Don Hinton, is still making the rounds, Oscar still plays at Arlie's Club and Steve and John hold forth at Ewings on the Kern.

Last Saturday evening I returned to Sorella's in the Stockdale area of Bakersfield. A magnificent Italian restaurant/lounge owned by Nancy Sorella. It was old home week as Nancy and her most beautiful daughters greeted me like a long lost friend of the family and plied me with their fantastic and unsurpassed cuisine in this upscale, fashionable establishment.

I was here once more by request to contribute my clarinet in accompaniment with Mark to the mellower songs of the 50s and 60s. Good music to dine by; and, for romance in a thoroughly romantic atmosphere. How very good it is to make music of this kind and in such a gracious and friendly environment.

But poor Nancy, I'm such a disappointment to her in the food department. Much as she tries, she can't put any weight on my wiry frame. And I know this is frustrating to her. I can only say in sympathy, many others have tried to no effect as well. I just move too fast and am too physically busy to occupy myself with the routine of meals.

Mark and I did a benefit for a group of oldsters at a convalescent home a while back. He did the Frank Sinatra style songs with my clarinet backup and then I sang requests like Funny Valentine, Deep Purple and, of course, September Song. The old folks loved it; and so did we. I didn't do Sleepin' With a Drifter. Didn't know how many weak hearts were in our audience.

But it reminded me of the time I first made a stage appearance when I was a child and student at old Mt. Vernon Elementary and the temptation was on me to sing my favorite at the time, Cocaine Blues circa 1942, rather than my teacher's selection. She never knew how close came disaster- bad enough I decided to sing Cold Icy Fingers rather than Red River Valley. Should have known I was warped from the beginning. Oh well.

Oscar always insists on doing Cool Water when I'm in attendance; goes back to our sharing so much of the music of Old Bakersfield and my book, The Lord and the Weedpatcher. The song is his idea of humor. But I'll grab some gal and we'll dance while I sing it. And we all get a laugh out of the show.

But I'm haunted, at times, by the opening statement in the prologue to the Birds book that probably explained the quiet tears in the eyes of so many of those oldsters when I sang to them:

"Why can't life be more like the music?" I asked.

He replied, "Because people don't listen to the music anymore."

***

I'm back to shooting ground squirrels. In my absence from the little house at the lake, a colony had moved into the rocks of my backyard. So, in addition to doing battle with the repairs on the house, I had to rid the premises of these verminous rodents together with the gophers and black widows.

I have a really fine German .177 mounted with a Bushnell 4x that has excellent killing power and accuracy well past 100 yards. It does a fine job on the rats, ground squirrels and gophers. Because of nearby houses, it wouldn't do to haul out any heavier artillery in this case.

The blood lust of my hunting days (at least in the case of four-legged animals) is well past. When I used to boondock in the outback with my .357 Colt Single Action Army and fast draw rig it had already come down to 100 rounds, hip shooting, and one jackrabbit.

I was a charter member of the Redondo Fast draw Club years ago. And the time came when the fun had become the shooting and hiking those vast, desert wildernesses with that beautiful Single Action strapped to my leg; not the killing.

But I still know how to do the job and am familiar with the proper equipment to take care of pests and vermin. Now why do the images of some crooked judges, politicians and moneylenders come so readily to mind in this context? Just wishful thinking, I suppose.

In answer to so many that have asked if I sleep with a loaded pistol I reply: Sleeping with an unloaded one would be kind of silly. And I still prefer women.

My mind has taken this dark path due to a conversation I had recently with an acquaintance. This man used to play major league baseball until an injury took him out of the game.

He has a boat in one of the marinas down South. He likes to play with the younger women (and girls) and has money to do it. Since he rubs shoulders with some of the wealthy and powerful, he always has some interesting tidbits of information about such people and their lifestyles.

I happened to be in one of the pubs he frequents when he came in and, spying me, took a seat next to me.

"Still drinking coffee Don," he asked? Well, I couldn't deny it. The cup was right there.

"Guilty!" I replied.

"Stuff 'll kill you" he said with a laugh.

"Sure thing something or someone will get all of us eventually" I replied; normal repartee for him and me.

"Yeah," he said, "but you sure seem to go out of your way asking for it sometimes."

He was right; I came home the other day to find a couple of bullet holes in my shed door. They matched the ones in a couple of my windows. Better the shed than the house or another window I thought. Kind of silly, shooting the shed door though: and cowardly. But sensible since such people know I'd take a thing like this personal and return fire had I been at home.

My local network works well and threats like shooting me or burning me out are usually cowardly bluster or Booze talk for the most part and are invariably turned in to me by friends. I am fortunate to have so many good people watching my back.

This explains the remark in last month's essay about still being above ground when my friends ask how I'm doing. It has a serious edge.

I've become insensitive to such warnings like bullet holes in a shed door. Now, had they punched a hole in the Maserati (or me) you can be sure I wouldn't be nearly as blasé about the matter.

But it reminded me of the fellow who offered his services during the Supervisor's race in Oildale. He wanted to shoot a few holes in my car so I could claim risk to my life in the politics of Bakersfield/Oildale. I thanked him for the sincere offer but assured him that I was perfectly capable of shooting up my own vehicle if I were after that kind of publicity.

Not long ago a big, drunk half-breed invited me into the men's room of one of the taverns. I knew him and, in order not to disturb the patrons, I went in with him.

He wanted to cut me because he was under the same misperception as Johnny Lee Clary (OI, 7/95) that I was prejudiced. I put my arm up to his and said, "I'm part Cherokee and my skin's at least as dark as yours! Besides, if you start anything here, you know they are going to 86 you from this place and the barmaid would have to clean up the mess in here." That part of the argument penetrated his drunken mind and persuaded him.

Why is it important to know and mix your life with such people; because of the drugs and high unemployment among other things; I'll give you a couple of examples. Some time ago I had to call on one of my crazy acquaintances for help. A young man was being pursued by a couple of drug dealers. He called me for help. He couldn't stay in the house he was calling from. He didn't know how long it would be before they kicked the door down and took him. He desperately needed someone to pick him up immediately!

I knew the cry for help was legitimate. And, even if the young man in question had brought this on himself, I felt I had to help. But I was in Bakersfield dealing with another emergency which precluded my going to his aid in time myself. I made a call and had my friend take his gun and go to the rescue of the young man. This guy is well enough known that just the sight of his vehicle at the scene was enough to accomplish the rescue. But they also knew this fellow was a friend of mine and that wouldn't be forgotten. They know my hatred of the drug traffic. Hence, in all probability, the bullet holes since my return.

Because of the lack of minorities in the area, there is little, really violent crime. Why? Racist remark? Not at all. Since there is no ethnic battle over drug turf as in the major cities, there is no killing. For example, on another occasion I let a young man take a beating. He had made the mistake of taking some drugs on consignment and when his friends didn't pay off, he couldn't pay the dealers. I knew they wouldn't kill him; the killing is done in Bakersfield, not in the Valley, so I let him take the beating in the hope it would save him from any further such business.

Back to the conversation with my ex-jock acquaintance; he ordered a beer and began to regale me with his recent trip to the marina. Mixed with the tales of nubile and willing young women he told me of a retired, federal judge he had been partying with on the judge's boat.

He described the typical scene of the judge boozing and smoking pot with the young women and partying hardy. The conversation with the judge had turned on the simple-mindedness of the great unwashed, the sheep, those who pay the price in their taxes for the lifestyle of this debauched old lecher.

Of course, like many such so-called men (and women), the laws and taxes are for the little people ala Helmsley. Now a few words to those who think they are doing the job: To you folks and my friends with the New American, the Spectator, the Chronicles, Rush and so many more I could go on naming, I have a short story for you.

Yesterday, I was pulling the radiator out of my pickup so I could take it in for a core job. It's 99 degrees in the shade of the tree I'm blessed to be working under but it's still a hard, dirty, greasy job. I'm doing it in order to save fifty bucks from the shop.

But I just gave my CPA $300 to prove to the state and the feds I don't owe any taxes for 1994. Like millions of other Americans, I work hard to save money only to have it stolen by Caesar in one way or another.

Now with the heat, grease and bloody knuckles, I wonder how Americans are going to survive when a system of government rewards greed, sloth, incompetence and corruption while it steals from those who are willing to work and earn their way?

Officer Laurence Powell still waits in prison, despite the flagrant disregard of double jeopardy supposedly protecting him, through an iniquitous system that allowed Caesar to tell the serfs (a jury) to go to hell! And LaRouche; still a political prisoner of Caesar in a psychiatric ward! By the way, for a very informative message concerning juries, please call: 1-800-TEL-JURY.

The American Gestapo in the form of the infamous IRS still grinds the little people to powder under its iron heel! Ruby Ridge, Waco, Oklahoma City, Vincent Foster and Wastewater Gate, the cops and feds shooting and imprisoning at will, CPS with authority to destroy families without any checks and balances, without, like the schools and government in general, any viable accountability!

M-, a lovely lady friend, has sent me the information concerning Forbes Magazine's refusal to print one of it's own editor's stories about Vincent Foster selling U.S. secrets to Israel! No one dares talk about the Israeli connection to our national, economic disasters! But as an FBI agent told me: "Money always leaves a trail!"

Media Bypass Magazine had the guts to tell the story. When quizzed, Michael D. McCurry, Press Secretary to the Clinton traitors called the material outrageous!

No, Mr. McCurry; what is outrageous is what you and the Clintons continue to try to hide from Americans!

A Quote from Spotlight: "The fatal shooting of the 50-year-old chaplain of an Ohio militia group by a policeman in central Ohio has angered militia and patriot groups across America and caused the FBI to issue a nationwide alert for possible civil disobedience."

Possible civil disobedience? It has already started! And the FBI, CIA et al. know this.

Michael Hill, a militia chaplain, was stopped on June 28 for not having a proper license plate according to the police report. Ohio officials at first refused to accept the testimony of three, eyewitnesses to the murder of Hill. But Nancy Lord, a well-known civil libertarian lawyer demanded that the testimony be accepted by Ohio Attorney General Betty Montgomery.

The witnesses state that officer Matthew May had followed the chaplain knowing who he was. The officer shot Hill as he got out of his car and approached the officer. At no time was there any threat to the officer except the chaplain's license plate that read: "Militia Chaplain 13-3". As with the Vincent Foster subterfuge, you have to read the whole story to get the real import of this. The FBI is trying, desperately, to cover its backside regarding the murder of Randy Weaver's wife and son. Mass murderer Janet Reno is running scared.

When I began almost fifteen years ago to write about such things, when I put my signs up on my property here at the lake almost three years ago, I knew they would bear fruit. But don't do such things if you have a wife and family to protect! The responsibility for being a man, a husband and father, begins with your responsibility to that wife and those little ones! And don't ever think otherwise! There are more than enough of those like myself to get the job done.

Now, Newt et al., tell me you supposed conservatives, what substantial difference for good have you made? Oh, my! Massacre in Courtroom 425! And you want to sell me a book about a single incident of which I could give you dozens of examples by personal experience? I don't belittle the tragedy of the Winner family but let's get real! It's by far no exceptional case!

Jack McLamb, Bo Gritz, Lawrence Pratt, Lindsey Williams, Don McAlvany are not (yet), any more than I, telling people to start shooting so many who definitely need killing! I have said, following Alice Vachs' statement about rapists to its logical conclusion: "You cannot reform a rattlesnake. All you can do is kill it." In its own environment, it might well be left alone. But when such snakes don long black robes and hold high political office that is another matter!

And so my good, conservative brethren, when the killing starts, and Caesar has already fired the first shots, where will Americans find you? Are you advocating the needed New Continental Congress we so desperately require? Or are you, like so many pew warmers in the churches, trying to play it safe or simply make a name for yourselves by your rhetoric? Talk has always been cheap unless followed by action. It is never enough to discern evil; action is required!

Now a lot of politicians are jumping on the Welfare Reform bandwagon. Do-nothing Wilson in California is trying to make presidential material of his little self, like ridiculous and unbelievable Ross Perot whose ego is even bigger than his pocketbook, by proclaiming his conservative stance. Where were you, Mr. Wilson, when I made the point to you and wannabes like Ed Davis and Willie Brown of the plight of our families, children and our schools? I know; you passed the information to committees! Then, like Pilate you washed your hands, like the whore of the Apocalypse, Mother of Harlots and Abominations, you tell Americans you have done no wrong!

Go ahead and cut welfare, stop funding abortion, make the poor find work where no work is to be found thanks to the deals you have already made with foreign powers to strip our industries and sell out to the UN and profits from abroad! Then wonder if you can, when the killing starts in earnest- not in Watts, East San Jose or Harlem but in Beverly Hills, Georgetown and Scarsdale! I have to give even the Devil his due when you so-called leaders have the courage, more likely the bald-faced arrogance, to gather in D.C., surrounded by the hoards of vandals and barbarians, so many who want to kill you!

You can truly believe you are only alive so far because it's against the law to kill you. But thanks to your laws which pervert the cause of justice, thanks in large part to your own hypocrisy, even religion is fast losing its power in this country to keep the poor from killing the rich!

And when the law can no longer protect because people are hungry and hurting, when families fall apart because dad and mom can no longer provide for their children? When loss of hope for a future for our children, our posterity is confronted?

My fellow Americans; Newt, Rush, Bo, the GOP are not the answer. Neither is the Spectator, the New American or Chronicles. They never have been. The answer will come from YOU when YOU have had enough, when YOU are hurting enough, angry enough and like our founding fathers and those Minutemen and those who kept the faith at Valley Forge are ready to lay it all on the line in the cause of the liberty and freedom that evil, wicked men and women have stolen from us and our children!

Some wonder how many people read these essays. I want Caesar to know this! Don't delude yourself that just because they are mailed with a first class stamp that the readership is represented by a lack of bulk mailing.

In Canada, a copy of the essay is duplicated and portions are sent to over 300 other publications! In England, Germany and France the process is repeated! Hundreds of publications in this country use some of my material; many of them clandestine, underground publications many with which I do not agree. But they still publish my material. Naturally, much that I write of the softer and gentler things, like the relationships between men and women, are edited out in these other publications. I wish the focus could be on these things. And in a kinder and saner world where poets could flourish, it would be.

I have to admit that this use, and often abuse, of my writings sometimes proves embarrassing to me when my views are distorted to suit some racist or anarchical organization. Or, where the media seem intent on making me something I am not. But there is little I can do to keep others, including mainline media, from using, or misusing, what they want of my writing. This creates, as you can well imagine, some uncomfortable situations for me.

I'm constantly being caught unawares by letters or calls accusing me of belonging to some organization I have never heard of. I even get checks and requests for applications from people who want to join one of the Klan's, Aryan Nations and NAAWP! It isn't only the media and our shadow government that misinterprets my statements about such things as the need for voter qualification reform and sealing our borders, anti-abortion, etc. The truth suffices without embellishment and causes me enough grief as it is! I belong to the N.R.A. and, as a matter of form, the G.O.P.! That's It! No others. Not even the Triple A!

But my warning of long time still stands; When Americans have had enough of the corruption and abuses of Caesar and his hordes of sycophants, incapables, thieves and murderers they will take action. I can only pray such action will be led of men of the stature of those founding fathers, men who will not tolerate Hitlerian Solutions but will honor the blood shed for a nation dedicated to liberty, justice and personal responsibility.

Now, in case some new readers have wondered about my reputation as a dangerous man whose writings have been called inflammatory, wonder no longer! Damned Straight!

***

At this point, I go out back and meditate on my little pond with its waterfall. The birds love it and at night a skunk and a raccoon make nocturnal visits. I have even seen a bobcat on rare occasions. This helps take the bad taste of things like I have just written out of my mouth.

The raccoon precluded my putting goldfish in the pond. I did that when I first built it. The next morning all twelve goldfish were gone! Coons are superb fishermen.

A momma quail has a nest of ten eggs next to the house. I didn't even see her until I inadvertently nearly dumped a pail of water on her. I hope the chicks hatch successfully. A big, beautiful, gray tree squirrel and a cottontail grace my backyard once in a while as well.

Like Thoreau, I welcome the occasional visitor and treat them to stories of this little corner of my world. Everyone needs such things to remind him or her of what is important and of real value.

On the nights when the moon is full, it is wonderful to sit out back by the little pond with the crystal tinkling of its waterfall and bask in the brilliant glow of the moon or the Milky Way listening to the soft music of the slight breeze through the old pine overhead.

As a child living on the mining claim nearby (now Boulder Gulch Campground), I would always move my bed out under the pines in the Summer and go to sleep with that soft, soughing sound of the wind through the pine needles and watching the stars overhead, considering the heavens.

I'm thankful that, by God's grace, I have never lost that best part of the man, the child within, who still finds wonder, joy and magic in such things.

***

Locally, housecleaning is popular with some of the younger women. Let me explain.

Some of the old men have young girls come in to their homes and pay them $20 to clean house for a half hour. They dust tables in the nude. Hence, cleaning house in Welfare Valley is quite popular. And in case you're wondering, I do my own house cleaning such as it is. Not so much a matter of nobility as the fact that I'm not into being a spectator (voyeur).

So when a young woman recently told me she cleaned houses for a living, I knew what she meant. At least, as she later shared with me, there was no risk of disease and if you had a couple of houses a week, it made for a good welfare supplement.

It has taken a few years, due to the circumstances of a painful love affair, for me to watch Dr. Zhivago again. I could read Pasternak's marvelous book but the movie had most painful memories attached.

A spectacular and beautiful film, I realized as I got into the picture why I couldn't stand to see it for so long a time. It wasn't just the betrayal of love and trust I had to confront.

I'm a poet and a romantic. It was painful to see the doctor uninspired by his adoring and faithful wife, Tonya. Why, I asked myself, did he have to have the inspiration of Lara in order to write? Why wasn't a good woman, his wife Tonya, inspiration enough?

He married the wrong woman. She married the wrong man. It was that simple.

I can sympathize with both. I always married the wrong women and they married the wrong man. But I never betrayed any of them for the sake of inspiration! Yet I realize that there are other kinds of betrayal of which I may well have been guilty by simply marrying the wrong women. As to their betrayal of me; the answers are both common and legion. Granted, it wasn't until I was without a wife for a long while that I began to be able to confront the muse and my responsibility to the writing I have done these past years.

My good friend, Nelson, has come by to visit. He has worked for some of the major studios and, like myself, is an artist with the soul of the poet. It causes him a lot of trouble with the business end of the entertainment industry that is really dog-eat-dog.

In discussing Zhivago, Nelson asked the question I had asked myself: "What if the doctor had married Lara? Would he have found her as inspiring as his wife as he did as his mistress?"

I've written a lot about the fact that once the thrill of the chase is consummated in marriage, the romance begins to pale and the honeymoon is too soon over. Are men and women the Christmas packages I mention in the Birds book that once the lovely wrapping is removed and the toy played with for a while, it soon loses its desirability and attractiveness, even becoming tiresome?

For example, I had a beautiful, petite lady tell me not long ago that I was the only man she had ever met whose intellect surpassed her own, that she had been searching for a man she could respect for his mind. Quite flattering but I discovered she had a rather distorted point of view in regard to what she thought she wanted in a man. And it wasn't an intellectual, a poet.

I've recently had two supposed Libbers break down and tell me in tears that they had discovered that all they have ever wanted is a man who could take care of them the way a woman is supposed to be cared for. But our perverted society has blurred the distinctions between men and women and neither seems to know what their distinctive roles are any longer.

It certainly doesn't help when a society considers the value of women solely on the basis of youth and beauty. Yet, it cannot be denied that women in our society grow old and wrinkled, of no value, but a man is considered to grow mature and seasoned! What's wrong with this picture and how do you correct it? In view of the history of nations and their cultures, is it possible to correct? Small wonder so many of the women I have known are resentful of men.

I told Nelson that I believed my mission in my writing is to reestablish those parameters of genuine love and romance, the proper roles of men and women in their relationships; quite a challenge. But the politics of a nation must allow of the fertile soil from which artists, poets and philosophers can emerge and gain ascendancy once more.

In addressing the needs between men and women, I ask the question in my book: Why, in fact, does sex itself, this most profound act between a man and a woman, soon become stale between husband and wife in too many cases? In my discussion of love letters and the giving of flowers in the book, I ask: Why do they stop (if, in fact, they ever began) so soon after marriage?

I think it is a valid statement that it takes a leisure class and a strong middle class, to build a society in which the arts and the finer, gentler sentiments of love and romance, of poetry to flourish. As the pendulum has swung back to grubbing in the soil or welfare for daily sustenance in our own country, the arts and those gentler sentiments begin to suffer proportionately.

What is the loss of this in our own society? One single fact helps to understand. The largest selling genre of books sold in bookstores is romance novels. And eighty per cent of the buyers of books are women! As I point out in my book, women are hungering and thirsting for romance. But I also point out the ways in which they betray themselves in searching for this elusive thing called romance.

My daughters were the primary inspiration for the Birds book. When the book was finally completed, I wrote my youngest daughter, Karen, the following: "Everyone wants to know who this extraordinarily beautiful, young mystery woman is on the cover of the book. I take the greatest pride in telling them she is my daughter, Karen Heath!"

Karen's older sister, my daughter Diana, was killed in a motorcycle accident; so it fell to Karen to be her father's choice for the cover. And had she known what her dad was going to do with the picture, I'm sure I would still be nagging her to get it taken.

But inspiration came, at times, from my relationships with several women however none has worked out to be that *One* who could inspire me to do my best work. I never found and married Lara! The difference between being in love and being in lust is well known as are the degrees of both. Inspiration involves passion. If there is no burning passion of love or hatred, inspiration suffers accordingly. I have passed on many women in fairness to both them and myself where I knew the igniting spark of genuine passion for inspiration was lacking. But loneliness is a real killer and mistakes commonly are made accordingly due to this as well.

And it must be admitted that not everyone requires such passion in a successful match between a man and a woman. But for those whose hearts burn for release due to some gift of artistry or whatever, it will find release in one fashion or another. In this I commiserate with the doctor. Perhaps he sold his own soul in order to exorcise the fire in his bones, to trade it all for the release from the greater agony of that cursed gift.

It is my considered opinion that every man has the divine right to be a fool over a woman. Perhaps I believe this because of my proven proclivity to exercise that right on more occasions than most. I mean it when I say: I don't know how one man, in one lifetime, can have made as many mistakes as I have! But, of course, they haven't all been made in respect to the fair sex. Just the most painful and disastrous ones!

And to respond to the lovely brunette who, like many, was a little miffed by my association with, and comments about so many blondes and redheads I will say that brunettes have come in for a great deal of my attention as well.

Now at last count.... No, I'd better leave that one alone.

Instead, I'll tell you about my friend Ben's visit the other day.

Those of you who have read the Birds book will recall my friend Ben, a man much like me who has suffered so much from broken romances. The chapter in my book entitled: "Alcohol, a Common Tragedy," is the story of Ben and J-, a beautiful, petite blonde Ben fell in love with. The problem was that Ben, like me, isn't much of a drinker. Blessed with the lack of a predisposition to addiction, Ben and I can take the stuff or leave it, generally preferring to leave it as a matter of choice. But J- was an alcoholic. Loneliness, the need of the warmth and softness of a woman in his life, the list is a common one that made this unlikely match come about between Ben and J-.

At her best, J- was all a man could wish for; beautiful, loving, kind and thoughtful. But she never had a dry day in all the time they were together. Hers was one of the most tragic cases of addiction I have ever known. And I've known a lot of them. I was one of the co-founders of an Alcohol and Drug Abuse Center in Lancaster, California.

The relationship only lasted a few months before J- left Ben for a boozing bum she could party with. Her short time with Ben had to be difficult for J- since Ben didn't drink. At least she found someone with whom she didn't have to feel guilty about drinking though Ben never once said a critical word to her about her addiction. He was, if anything, an enabler.

But Ben learned the bitter lesson of Alcoholism; no one can help the alcoholic except him or herself. All the love in the world, and Ben truly loved J-, won't cure the disease. When Ben came by, he was in tears. I had seen Ben weep over J- before. But a year had passed since J- had left him. Why the tears now? As I did in the book, I'll let Ben tell the story in his own words:

"Don, please let me tell you what just happened! You know about my little place in the country. You remember when J- and I were together and I built her a little pond with a waterfall just like yours. You know how we used to sit out in the yard and just enjoy watching the birds, the quail and the squirrels playing in the water, the place J- and I had provided for them, all the beautiful flowers and things J- planted around the yard."

I remembered; it was one of the places I loved to visit when I was in the area.

"Don, it's been over a year since I have seen J-. But the other day I was driving the boulevard and saw her walking alongside the road. The pain of seeing her stabbed my heart. It was just past noon and extremely hot. Why was she walking this road in the heat of the day? I didn't stop. I didn't dare. I still don't trust myself with her. I loved her, love her too much still."

I thoroughly understood Ben. Been there, done that.

Ben continued.

"Don, I didn't sleep that night. The sight of her walking that road in such heat plagued my mind. I knew something was dreadfully wrong with her."

I didn't need to point out to Ben that the local prostitutes were the only ones seen doing what Ben had seen J- doing. He knew though he wouldn't admit it. And there could be another explanation.

"But that isn't why I'm here and so upset, Don. Yesterday afternoon I saw her again! In my backyard!"

Ben waited for me to respond. But what could I say? Everyone who knew about him and J- had warned him that she would probably return. They had also warned him not to have anything further to do with her for his sake.

"Don, I didn't know what to do! She would walk up to the road, look back at the house and walk back to the yard. She must have known I was home but she never came to the door. It was obvious she was very drunk but she knew where she was. But why was she here? I kept asking myself. I longed to go out to her and take her in my arms once again. She must have been going through hell thinking about her life with me in the place, a place she loved and worked hard to make better for the two of us. And then to throw it all away like her marriage, for booze and a drunken bum! It had to be torment for her to come back to a place where she was loved and secure!"

I knew Ben was in real torment himself, just thinking about such things. Yes, it was obvious Ben still loved J-.

"Don, much as I wanted to run out to her, I decided against it. If she came to the door, I told myself, I'd let her in. I wouldn't have been able to refuse her. But she never did. She must have been there for two hours. She had a bag with her and I would watch her take out a beer. She would sit on a rock and drink and just look at the place. And Don, it had to be a hundred degrees out there in that heat! The whole thing tortured me. Yet, I found myself wishing so badly that she would come to the door, I wanted so much to comfort her from the nightmare she must be suffering. I thought about the times I would hold her when the nightmares used to cause her such torment in her sleep! Had things become so bad for her that she had come back to a place where she had known love and security? If so, what was going on in her tormented mind that had brought her here and yet unable to come to the door unable to face me?"

I didn't need to reply to Ben's tortured questions. They didn't require an answer. Ben had answered these questions before he came over. I knew the pathology of J-; I knew the monstrous grip of her addiction. As recovering alcoholics say of their lives as addicts: "It's an insane life; don't try to make rational sense of it!"

Ben wasn't looking to me for answers to questions that make no rational sense. He knew better. He had lived the nightmare with J-.

"Well, Don, she finally left without ever coming to the door. But I just know she is in desperate trouble and my heart is breaking for her. I can't help wanting to try to help her, even knowing that as long as she is drinking there is nothing I can do to help!"

"Ben," I said, "if you think she is ready to enter re-hab, if you firmly believe she wants to quit drinking, she might have a chance with your love to carry her through. But as a friend, I have to tell you this. It's a most dangerous game and only real professionals are able to deal with it. Don't, under any circumstances, delude yourself that you can simply take her back and do the job yourself. You should know better by now."

Ben understood. He knew I was right. We talked a while longer and Ben left.

***

The on-going story of Ben's struggle with his grief, his broken heart for J- reminds me of so many people who talk and behave as though they had a license for ignorance, as though it were something of which to be proud!

Too many are so very quick to judge the motives of the heart and too often lack the necessary compassion to enter into the sufferings of those like Ben and J-. Granted, who would really choose to be able, through suffering themselves, to do so?

Yet, through ignorance or sheer hardness of heart Ben and J- are surrounded by those that would call either or both damned fools! I know too many people who know both of these sufferers that fall into this category.

Yes, J- betrayed Ben for a drunken bum who would party and drink with her. But what of the tormented, hellish state of mind that would drive J- back to Ben's place? And, in respect to Ben, as I have said, men have a divine right to be fools over women! Even though the wheel is often crooked, it remains the only game in town.

I had a beautiful, lady bar owner, Bev, respond to this story in this fashion: She said she knew that as a wife and mother she was playing a significant role as a human being. But we live in a society where such a role is no longer given the honor it is due. "How much of this kind of thing contributed," she said, "to J-'s destroyed marriage, to her leaving Ben?" I couldn't answer her specifically in J-'s case but I knew she had put her finger on one of the possibilities.

My beautiful daughter Karen should be on the cover of magazines. With her marvelous voice she should be singing professionally; she would be the ticket to any group's success. And, like her dad, she has a gift for writing. But she is a loving, faithful wife and mother. Much as I would like to see her succeed in using her extraordinary beauty and talents in other areas of her life, I tell her, as her father: "Sweetheart, you have the highest, most exalted position anyone could ask for in your role as a faithful wife and mother!"

I can think of no greater success for any man or woman than a successful, faithful, loving family. On this foundation the whole success and future of a nation rests.

The pain and misery of a nation is the pain and misery of individuals. When this same lovely bar owner asked me for more specifics in regard to my writing about the battle against an evil system of government, against Caesar, I can only say it comes down to the roles men and women play in a society. When the purity of womanhood is treated lightly, even despised in respect to being a faithful wife and mother, one can easily predict the outcome in any society.

Yet, we are still, as human beings, so very quick to judge the fallen woman but too forgiving of the despicable bums who are the cause of such a fallen state! Men are still the responsible parties in the matter of seduction, of the lack of moral standards in a society. Men lead and women have to follow. That is the true nature of the beast and there is no changing it. Not all the laws of a society will change this immutable fact of humanity, the hellish double standard between men and women that seems to prevail in history notwithstanding!

I've made the point in the past that the first thing God did when confronted by the betrayal of Adam and Eve was to say to Adam: "What have you done!" God held Adam responsible for the betrayal, not Eve. Then Adam tried to blame both God and Eve for his miserable failure as a man and it's been hell on earth ever since. Hence the expression: Take it like a man; blame it on your wife!

Granted that since the laws of men and women make divorce as easy as buying a bottle of shampoo, and in some cases taken about as seriously, there is little a real man can do to keep a woman if she decides to go to someone else; or vice versa. This is a prominent problem that has made the destruction of family and family values so easy for our enemies.

As I've said many times, the problems we face as human beings involve two classes of people: Men and Women. It is the relationship between the sexes that predicts the future of a nation. We will honor what is best and noble that is peculiar to each or we will not. Men cease to be men at their best, leaders, when women try to dictate to them. Women cease to be women at their best when men try to treat them as objects rather than human beings, persons in their own right.

Needless to say, when women de-value themselves by catering to the lust of men through things like pornography, they become their own worst enemies. When women sell themselves to the role of objects of the unholy lust of men, they betray themselves. In respect to the betrayers of America, I and others can name individuals that, in fact, need killing, evil men and women who are destroying everything of value in our America, destroying our freedom and liberty, destroying the hope of a future based on personal responsibility that should be the birthright of our children.

Few would dispute the fact that we have become an ignorant nation, an illiterate nation thanks in large part to our becoming so busy running to stay in place, thanks to the kind of leadership that has betrayed us to the point that it takes two paychecks to take care of a family, thanks to the kind of leadership that bows to the pervert lobby and One World Order that few have time, even given the inclination, to read and try to stay informed.

When running for public office, I campaigned on the following issues: Re-structure our schools; a massive and absolutely essential job. Change voter qualifications to eliminate those from voting who, like welfare recipients, have a vested interest in voting a free ride on the backs of the workers and taxpayers. Eliminate salaries and retirement benefits for Congressmen, the President and Supreme Court Judges.

Effectively implement border patrols and vigorously prosecute illegal aliens denying them any benefits and eliminate the automatic citizenship of babies born in this country to illegals. Make English the national language and refuse to print political material including ballots in any language but English. Eliminate so-called *gun control laws* and vigorously prosecute those who have or use guns for the purpose of committing crimes. Make child molestation a crime punishable life in prison. Return to the Constitutional intent of making states and their governors the power of government rather than a Federal Caesar. Make the governors of the several states provide for state militias and give them the honorable leadership of honorable offices. Abolish the present system of the American Gestapo, the IRS and establish an equity-based, earnings only system of taxation. Make it illegal to operate a business outside the U.S. that has only a profit motive.

As to the last, all the talk in the world about Welfare Reform will go nowhere except to contribute to more crime and violence unless there are jobs, and I mean real jobs, in this country, not just flipping hamburgers! This would go a long way to getting mom back into the home with the children and this would do a world of good in healing the growing hurt to our nation of children without real homes.

The above short list should give you some idea of why some folks find me somewhat controversial as to my political views and writing. But who can deny such things need to be done? And, unless things like this are done, we will have no choice but those Hitlerian Solutions I keep mentioning; we will have to kill the elderly and other incapables like the retarded, etc. through escalating euthanasia for example.

Social Security and Welfare will be eliminated together with all medical attention for those who cannot pay. We will become ever more dependent on other nations hence hastening One World Order. There will be an increase in Federal Power via the military and Federal Police and so on.

Hitler and his Germany, Stalin and his Russia were not aberrations; they were the natural result of the circumstances of evil and wicked, greedy, perverted men and women who ruled. And a greater evil overcame them because, little by little, the good choices became impossible. As our own choices become, increasingly, not between good and bad but bad and worse, we face the inevitable and immutable dictate of history and human nature, those same Hitlerian and Stalinist Solutions! I mentioned the fact in my last essay that my political and religious heterodoxy keeps me in trouble. You can now easily understand why.

In respect to the churches and their failure to be a force for good in our nation, I repeat the one thing that has caused me more grief in respect to the brethren than even my statement that God has made errors, the thing that many want to horse whip me for. What is this dreadful, heretical thing? It is my contention that the churches should abandon their emasculating taxes exempt status! I repeat the justification for this horrifying, dangerous and dreadful position I have taken: He who feeds at Caesar's table is Caesar's dog!

And when an organization abandons even the most fundamental rights good men and women have died for, has traded it's effectiveness for Caesar's largess, it needs to be called to accountability! Did you know that the churches cannot advocate a good man, by name, for political office without losing their tax exemption? Even the lowliest citizen, the most despicable organization or lobby retains this right. But not the churches! Talk about selling out for a mess of potage, of becoming religious whores!

With King Sports and Queen Entertainment ruling, with Caesar's encouragement, the great unwashed, including most church members, our society will glue itself to comfortable chairs and couches being spoon-fed our information (and, increasingly, misinformation) and vicarious living of dreams and fantasies through the ubiquitous tube: Bread and Circuses; déjà vu all over again. Well, this ought to be enough to encourage the wrath of a goodly number of people.

It took a generation of Americans finally relieved of constant grubbing in the ground for sustenance to give us the poetry, literature, art, music, charity, philanthropy, inventiveness, liberty and freedom which put us at the front of world history in these noble things. But the best of our ideals was betrayed for the things promised by the world, the flesh and the Devil. Now, to borrow the words of Scripture: "Evil men and seducers wax worse and worse and because iniquity abounds, the love of many will wax cold!" And, as a result, too many now say: "Who will show us any good!"

And now, as I pointed out earlier, we are being betrayed to once more grubbing in the ground (flipping hamburgers or welfare) for daily sustenance. The two-paycheck syndrome dooms children to growing up without a mother's attention and care in a home thereby betraying a child's right to a childhood.

The blurred distinction of the roles of men and women, of husband and wife, of mother and father in our society is dooming a future generation that cannot produce the needed artists and philosophers who would encourage the softer and gentler things, the finer sensibilities toward things of eternal value that we so desperately need for a viable civilization.

My answer to beautiful Bev and so many others: I, and those like myself, will fight for our children and their birthright as Americans. My part is, largely, the Power of the Pen. Your part may only be prayer if that is all you can contribute. But I believe God hears and answers the prayers of the righteous; those whose hearts are obedient to the love of children and others who have no voice or choice who cannot do battle with Caesar and his master, the Devil.

***

Still moving stuff to the house in Bodfish. I was in Bakersfield and decided to load a large metal cabinet I needed for storage. I had moved it full of books including my sets of The Harvard Classics, Great Books of the Western World and my Encyclopedia Britannica.

Since I was going to load this thing by myself, I had the foresight to remove the first two sets but decided I could leave the encyclopedia in the cabinet. It was a 102 degrees and I wasn't into moving that large and heavy set of books separately if I could help it.

The driveway I had to back into was quite steep and I couldn't back all the way up and have room to load. I managed to use my dolly to get the cabinet to the back of the truck; now, for the loading operation. The problem was that I had to lay the cabinet down on the tailgate and slide it into the truck. The steep incline caused the dolly to have a mind of its own.

So it was that I found myself under the heavy cabinet with its 150 pounds of encyclopedia pressing on my back. By gaining leverage through grabbing the edge of the tailgate and using my shoulders and legs, I managed to heave the thing forward off the dolly (and my back) and into the truck.

Now I knew that metal tailgate was awfully hot when I grabbed onto it. But with the purchase point of the cabinet on my back, my knees already on the driveway under it, certain disaster was ahead if I had let go. How hot was that tailgate? Once the cabinet was loaded, I watched in wonder as a blister the size of a quarter formed on the palm of my hand. Talk about hot enough to fry eggs!

It was then that I had one of my briefer conversations with myself: Heath, I said, you're getting too old for this! And I know I was right no matter how my mind continually tries to convince my body it's still only 20! And I still had the refrigerator, washer and dryer to load!

***

I have a few, favorite stories gleaned over the years. One of my all-time best is about the guy who, while drunk of course, demonstrated detonating a dynamite blasting cap using his teeth! I still have the news clipping of this attention-getting little prank. Talk about shooting off your mouth literally!

And when it comes to attention-getting news leads few compare with one I have which reads "Footbone, sock found." This after the tragedy of the Challenger accident.

Things like this come close to making sense of the lyrics: "I'm married to a waitress and I don't even know her name." If you make the C&W scene you've heard the song. Kind of cute; as one woman in a bar told me: "The problem wasn't going to bed with a man she didn't know after meeting in the bar; it was getting rid of him in the morning." But, of course, a few men I have met have had the same problem with a woman.

Now since I'm not much of a drinker, I've never had to worry about waking up one morning after a particularly interesting night out and finding a wife in bed whose name I didn't know. Came close enough sober a couple of times; I shudder to think what might have happened in my life if I were a boozer!

But once upon a time in the West ... This is about my Lady in Red and me. Because so many have expressed an interest in this one lady above most others in my book, I have gotten her permission to say a few things in regard to us.

Many wonder, first of all, why the relationship didn't pursue a natural course for a couple in love? I'll begin by saying that hers was not the most usual childhood. Her father was a well-known racecar driver. But he was an alcoholic. These were factors. But my Lady shared with me a most poignant story once when I was telling her of my daughters. "Don," she said, "my father never once took me on his lap and hugged me, he never showed me any of the expressions of love that you showed your most fortunate daughters."

Just how much this had to do with her attitude toward men in general, her own self esteem, her attitude toward herself as a woman one can only guess. But, like me, she has never entered into a successful relationship with a significant other.

She told me once that she knew she should be my girl. Then she bowed her head and said in a very quiet voice: "But you're too nice a man, Don."

She couldn't have been more wrong from my point of view. You can't imagine how her quiet statement pierced my heart. I tried to tell her of my own deficiencies, my own failures to no avail. I was too nice a man and that was that. I consider myself to have been one of the poorest fathers and husbands imaginable. I disciplined my children in anger on occasion. My son Michael was so self-willed and rebellious as a child that it is a wonder I didn't go to jail as a result of my disciplining him. Talk about losing it! I made countless mistakes that all the child-rearing and husbanding books warn against.

Yet, through it all, due to their mother running off with another man and not even wanting the children, only her "freedom" as she put it I wound up single-parenting Karen and Michael unexpectedly. How we survived I'll never know. In retrospect, I think it was this period of time that drew me to my oft repeated conclusion: I don't know how one man, in one lifetime, could have made as many mistakes as I have! The countless things I did wrong, the mistakes I made still give me nightmares. When pressed to the wall, I tried to practice tough love. It wasn't enough on occasion.

Yes, I know it takes both a mother and a father to do the job. And I failed miserably alone. The pressures were extreme at times due to a lack of resources, financial and emotional. I will never forget the night I boiled spaghetti noodles and fried them for a dinner for Michael and me. The children got in trouble at school; there were friendships that resulted in break-ins and burglaries, thefts of all kinds to contend with; and the all-pervasive drugs.

All three of us were looking for love in all the wrong places; trying to put together shattered lives. A good deal of this was the result of the time it took for me to come out of the psychosis of grief that resulted from an unexpectedly shattered marriage. Strictly speaking, I wasn't able to function on a rational level for some time. And by the time I was, much damage had been done.

A single incident of child abuse does not make a child-abuser any more than a single act of homosexuality makes a homosexual. It took a lot of failure on my part for me to enter into the kind of love and compassion for children that I now have. It took my daughters and so many Birds With Broken Wings to make me an understanding champion of a woman's needs for love and romance.

My years in the schools, my failures as a husband and father, the tragedies in so many lives I began to confront and try to do something about, these are the kinds of things that made me a man to confront Caesar and all bullies who would mistreat and abuse those who are weaker, those who have no voice or choice.

An old friend, D-, is sitting next to me at one of the clubs. He and I are really together when it comes to music and romance. At one point he turns to me and says: "Don, my hat is really off to you. How I wish I had your education and talents and gifts, how I wish I were able to do the things you do! I wish I was a man like you!"

I was stunned. A man like me! My God in Heaven, I wanted to shout at him; you don't begin to know what you're talking about! A man like me; God forbid! That's what I wanted to shout at him.

And my Lady in Red thinks I'm too nice a man for her! What a warped perception we often have of others when we think our own sins are so heinous, when we refuse to forgive our own mistakes and think we have committed the unpardonable sin!

Granted I am talking about honest mistakes, honest failures. Not those that result from greed and avarice, those that result from wanting to harm others to our own advantage. Hell is indeed for such of the Devil's spawn. But if we do not learn compassion for others, if we are unable to enter into their own sufferings and help carry their burdens, we will never be effective in helping ourselves.

So it is that I am qualified as a psychologist, a counselor, not just because of the academic disciplines of the subject and the hard-earned degrees and credentials but by the mistakes and failures of a lifetime, the experiences of life itself. Only the loss of a child or the betrayal of love and trust such as that of a shattered marriage or love affair can teach the necessary compassion and understanding of the resulting psychosis of grief attached to such things.

Only the recovering alcoholic or drug addict can relate, knowledgeably, to the living hell of those suffering such affliction in the grip of such a fiendish prison of the mind, body and soul. And don't try to tell me or anyone else who has had to work with such people: "Well, that's their choice!" You don't know what you're talking about! It wasn't a choice. It was, like Hitler's Germany and Stalin's Russia a series of choices, little by little where the circumstances became such that the choices for good were impossible of attaining.

Who, as I've often said, would choose to be a drunkard or drug addict? Who, humanly speaking, would choose despots like Hitler and Stalin to rule nations? Only when a person finds himself in the grip of such things that lead to not having choices for good does a person or a nation confront anarchy or slavery as the only possible solutions! Bottom line: It is not enough to discern evil; action is required. Do you think Jefferson was making a bad joke when he said the price of liberty is eternal vigilance?

Speaking of Hitler's Germany, everyone has heard by now the stories of the atrocities and mass killings practiced by the Jews during the 1956 and 1967 Middle East wars. But the heavily propagandized media blitz of the atrocities of the Nazis precluded anyone from speaking out against the Jews. The term Anti-Semitism was a killing pejorative to anyone who dared speak the truth about either the propaganda following WWII or the Jewish atrocities following this period.

But as Dolly Parton found out, the Jews controlled the entertainment industry so a Christian based TV series didn't have a chance. Now she knows the propaganda agenda and value of films like "Exodus" and a host of others that glorify the Jew and denigrate Christians and others; and as to Pat Buchanan calling Congress "Israeli Occupied Territory?" Whew!

Needless to say, it doesn't matter what ideology or ethnicity is involved, when a minuscule number of people whether they be homosexuals, Jews, Moslems, Nazis or left-handed buggy whip makers make the great majority dance to their tune, something is horribly amiss! And let go too far, such things invariably lead to those Hitlerian and Stalinist Solutions!

***

My propensity for opening Pandora's boxes evidenced itself once more by my reference to Satan and the Jurassic period last month. I have a couple of lizards in the house. Good thing, in this case, there is no little lady (at the moment) in attendance. Not all of them are kindly disposed to these small reminders of that ancient time.

I just opened a lower cupboard door where I have some pots and pans and there one of the little fellows was, curled up against the side of the cupboard. Well I could have probably grabbed and dispossessed him but I thought maybe he would keep the spider and other insect population down so I left him alone.

The other night, as I was reading in the living room, I caught sight of one of the little guys as he moved along the baseboard. Again, I elected to leave him alone and for the same reason. Let 'm catch the bugs. Better lizards than insecticides. Nature's way; and, as I said, as long as there is no woman of the house I don't mind the occasional lizard.

Lizards and the evolution myth aside, I long ago came to the conclusion that the opening chapters of Genesis allowed of much broader speculations concerning the origins of the universe, earth and mankind than fighting fundies permit.

I have mentioned those who attempt to make ignorance and prejudice a virtue, those who talk and behave as though they had a license for ignorance and prejudice, men like those who whipped that poor fellow in Elmer Gantry. As a Christian, I know God does not require me to check my brains at the door of the Sanctuary, that He does not place a premium on ignorance no matter how many TV so-called evangelists try to make it appear so.

For example, a Christian Racist is an oxymoron; there ain't no such animal! But it is not racist to deal truthfully with facts. It is in dealing with such facts that some have tried to tar me with the racist brush. It doesn't stick, however.

In calling attention to some of the tenets of the blind orthodoxy of those whose loyalty is to a belief system as opposed to the truth, I have often found myself consigned to the pit and the outer reaches beyond the pale of redemption. But I have found myself in better company with Emerson, Kierkegaard and Thoreau than many of these ignorant, prejudiced believers who mistakenly think they uphold the honor of God and His integrity by adhering to their own peculiar doctrines in respect to holy days and touch not, taste not interpretations of His Word.

To love God and others is still the summation of all the Law and the Prophets according to Jesus Christ Himself. I'll take His word over that of my detractors. I have said many times that it does God no dishonor to use the brains He has given us as long as we continue to fulfill His Royal Law. In this respect, I find there are no illegitimate questions we may ask of God. And I find no dishonor to Him in pursuing answers to these questions that the churches refuse to acknowledge. Even speculation is allowed if it is honest and has a purpose in pursuing the truth. And we all speculate and have questions of God that I believe He is pleased to have us ask.

We are now being told that man walked upright over 4 million years ago! The new finds have a name, of course: Ardipithecus ramidus. Since Latin was their native tongue, I've often wondered what language the Romans used to bamboozle the gullible? Oh well, since I brought it up, I'll continue to hang myself by offering some further speculation vis-à-vis those earliest ages and, in particular, the time of The Fall.

In the midst of the chaos (Without form and void, the Hebrew definition) God made things. That God used the instrumentation of beings like angels to do the actual work is something I considered.

Then God said: "Let us make man in our image and after our likeness" etc. I've done a lot of writing about this us thing and won't go into that here. God planted a special garden for Adam and Eve. It was a place of beauty and required the maintenance of the gardener, Adam. Sounds like the kind of place Thoreau and I would have enjoyed. But it seems the Serpent was allowed access as well; so much for Utopia.

If God was cleaning up the mess after Satan and his followers as I have suggested, Adam and Eve might well have required a special environment in order to have a chance. Then Adam blew it by his betrayal of God and Eve, by failing to be a real man and blaming both God and Eve for his miserable failure as a man!

Now this month's brainteaser for all you Sunday school dropouts: Just what kind of world did Adam and Eve face outside this special garden? We're told that God's Creation was blasted by sin, that death came about through Adam's rebellious betrayal of God, but just what does this thing blasted by sin mean? Nature Red in tooth and claw seems to have already been in full swing during the horror of that Jurassic Period. Now we have lions and tigers but back then? Wow!

Man was going to drudge in the soil for sustenance, waging war against weeds and who knows what else in that time before the Deluge, and Eve was going to go through the curse of child bearing with its attendant life-threatening pain and most unpleasant, cyclical, physical reminder of her part in the betrayal. Worse, Adam was to rule over her. It was going to be a man's world and Eve would have to play the role of the weaker vessel.

I've pointed out in my very first book, the irony of God's judgment in giving Adam a most recalcitrant and unwilling subject for his rulership. And as I've said, it's been hell in far too many cases for both ever since! To be continued; I hope.

***

A most interesting and recent development involving my intrusion into the mental health field where I occasionally have to prove my credentials. Nelson, my director/producer friend and I have just returned from making a videotape with Alice Hill of A. Hill & Associates.

The goal of A. Hill & Associates: To have numerous departments such as music, education, law, political, medical and others, all working throughout the world to find ways to better understanding, sharing and caring among people from all races and creeds. A most ambitious and noble concept with which I am in absolute agreement. Alice, whose concerns about the children of the world match my own, invited me to take part in taping a film about the research being done by a French doctor, Philippe Bottero, in the area of Rickettsiae.

Few seem to be aware of the worldwide spreading and impact of the rickettsiae (and related Chlamydiae). But Epidemic Typhus, Lyme disease, Spotted, Q and Trench Fevers are but a few of the diseases caused by the bacteria. My especial interest was in the suggestion of Doctor Bottero's research concerning the psychopathological results of the bacteria such as schizophrenia and various mental disorders attendant on the infections. Hence important vectors suggest themselves in relation to many psychiatric and neurological pathologies- there are even suggestive pejorative links to Mycoplasma and AIDS, Hepatitis B, Chronic Fatigue Syndrome and considerable evidence of the role of rickettsiae in the origin of multiple sclerosis.

The doctor handed Alice a copy of his research on the plane while she was returning from Australia where she was in charge of the Leadership Chair for the International Congress for Communications and the Arts held in Sydney in July. The doctor asked Alice's help in disseminating his research among American doctors and those in the mental health professions; and therefore my involvement in the project.

Alice and I met through a mutual friend, Mary, who told her of my qualifications and interest in the subject and had shared some of my writings with Alice. In making the film that is to go to France for final editing before being distributed, I stressed the fact that Doctor Bottero pointed out the need of regrouping the epidemiological, clinical, serological, evolutive and therapeutic concepts of rickettsiae.

There will be much more to say about this most important issue and its relationship to mental health treatments in the next issue of OI. Another part of the story involves an associate of Alice, Loretta, investigator for the Civil Rights Task Force (CRTF) who accompanied her for the filming; should prove to be a most interesting story for the next issue.

CHAPTER FIVE

THE OKIE INTELLECTUAL

OCTOBER 1995

This month's essay is going to be considerably different because it will be, literally, a global mailing due to the kind of information it contains and the diverse population in other countries that will receive copies.

In July, an International Congress on Communications and the Arts was held in Sydney, Australia. The American Biographical Institute jointly hosted it with headquarters in Raleigh, North Carolina and the International Biographical Center headquartered in Cambridge, England.

I mentioned Alice Hill of A. Hill & Associates in last month's essay. Because Alice and I share common concerns about the future of America and the rest of the world, this month's issue will address things of international interest.

Alice was in charge of the Leadership Chair for this meeting in Sydney and I will begin with some comments by Alice herself: "To all of the participants of this International Congress, I say: Wasn't it marvelous! People from all races, religions and creeds reaching out to each other with respect and caring! For that period of time we held The Keys To World Freedom In Our Hands for there can be no lasting freedom anywhere until All People Are Free!

"After returning to the United States, I traveled more than 8,000 miles in my own country and also took part in the International Platform Association's activities held in Washington D.C. When I made it back to my home in Oxnard, California I had a wonderful honor and thrill awaiting me.

"Elizabeth Wong from Hong Kong whom I had met at the Congress had written an article about me that was published in the Eastern Weekly Magazine. She quoted a verse from my poem, 'Come Listen To The Music' which I had written for use in the music department at the Congress. She also quoted what I had said to her: 'world governments will never achieve True world peace. It will only come through people like you and me working together with love and caring.'

" My dear friend, Elizabeth Wong made this humbling appeal for me: 'So, I ask all people from all nations who care about world peace to join A. Hill &

Associates and to help in whatever ways you can. All things are possible if we only believe that we can build a better tomorrow for all people everywhere. Let us 'Come and listen to the music' with Alice Hill.

"And the people are coming from all walks of life and all nations. Together, we hold The Keys To World Freedom In Our Hands by loving and caring about all people. I, too, ask everyone to come and join all of us who are listening to this music.

"Listen to the music from the world's throbbing heartbeat. Commanding its people to live in true harmony by hearing the voices of heavenly angels Singing love, joy and peace can be earth's destiny."

While there are many who would accuse both Alice and me of altruism in having hope that the world's peoples can work together in harmony toward world peace, the alternative is the dark prospect that such a thing is not possible. Both Alice and I refuse to subscribe to such a thing.

I ask at the beginning of my book; Birds With Broken Wings: "Why can't life be more like the music?"

He replied: "Because people don't listen to the music anymore!"

The Dark Side of the relationships between men and women of the world, those things that make us lose hope that the world's peoples can live in harmony is promoted by the loss of such music in our lives. But to sing, to listen to the music requires some joy and happiness in people's lives. My part, in cooperation with Alice and her organization, is in bringing some of that joy and happiness to people by using my gifts as a writer, poet and philosopher to explain some of those things that rob us of joy and happiness and cheat us of hope of a future for our children.

Through such an educational process of explanation, I work on the principle that if good people know better, they will do better. In exploring the reasons that people do the things they do, my studies in Human Behavior, in history, the arts and sciences, the experiences of a lifetime, especially my mistakes, working with people from all walks of life in every conceivable circumstance have led me to certain conclusions.

Alice and I hope that all of you will listen and contribute what you can to help us in our efforts to reach out to a hurting world filled with hurting children, the innocent victims of the evil that men and women do in the name of their peculiar ideologies that selfishly have no concern for others not of their own kind!

If you find our efforts worthy of your support, please let us know so we can continue this work on a global scale. While Alice and I are Americans, we know that the freedom of the people of all nations is the only answer to world peace. Our efforts to provide hope for a future for all children of the world must have your support to be effective.

My own peculiar contribution to this effort is the emphasis I place on the importance of the two, respective halves of humanity, men and women, working in harmony before there can be any hope for world harmony. The major part of this introductory essay is dedicated to bringing this issue to the forefront of people's attention. It is my earnest hope that once the issue is confronted and its importance understood, we can begin to have hope and begin to *Listen To The Music*!

In respect to any accusations of Altruism, I want to make it clear from the beginning that Alice and I are fully aware that evil must be confronted. It is not enough to discern evil, however, action is required! As I have written in time past: It is an evil system, led of evil men and women that have destroyed the poetic connection between men and women.

Much of my time and effort, my writing has been directed at confronting such evil. I have dealt with the human tragedy, the Dark Side of Human Behavior for so many years that I have become a most unwilling expert in such things. But it takes just this kind of expertise to deal with the problems we face in a pragmatic and realistic manner.

So, while known as a romantic, a poet and philosopher, you will quickly discover for yourself that I can separate the diabolical from the divine because of my experiences of both. Because of this, I become not only the Tom Paine for freedom in America; I lend my pen to the larger issue of freedom for all people throughout the world as well.

My responsibility to my country, the future of my children in America requires my writing in many cases as an American for Americans. But I do so with the realization that there are larger issues to be addressed, issues of worldwide significance that impact on the future of America that must be confronted.

To that end, the ideologies of nations must be understood, especially those ideologies which result in ignorance and prejudice towards others. For example, as a Christian, I place the emphasis on God's Royal Law that we are to love one another.

The ideological Christian would have me believe God allows David Livingston into heaven but Albert Schweitzer goes to hell. But both men gave their lives in sacrificial love to serving all mankind, not just those of their own kind! Thus, I place the emphasis as a Christian on love for all people, not just those of my own kind.

I believe that God so loved the world that He gave His Son. Not for just those who subscribe to a doctrine that would consign good men and women to hell but for the whole world! To quote the Apostle John: "God is love. Whoever lives in love lives in God, and God in him!"

The universal absolute of love should be the criteria of fellowship with all people, not just those who are of our kind. I believe the story of the Good Samaritan teaches this. There will always be fundamental differences between the peoples of the world based on things like cultural distinctives, of language, etc. But love for one another should always be the criteria of fellowship and understanding, the basis of hope that we can work together in harmony for the sake of a future for our children. And if we are successful, you and I, there will be a world, once more, where the artists, poets, philosophers, musicians and composers in the embryonic stage of our children will find fertile soil to make the world a lovelier and safer place, a kinder and gentler place for their future and their children.

Most of the following material is an attempt at a degree of global understanding and harmony through a discussion of the various aspects of the actual, fundamental basis of such things: The relationship between the two, respective halves of humanity- Men and Women. This is a subject about which I have written at great length. I know it will be of interest to all of you.

Last month's essay ended with reference to Alice Hill and Associates and the video tape that was made in particular regard to Dr. Philippe Bottero's research in the field of Rickettsiae, the bacteria responsible for so much tragedy world-wide. The tape has been sent to Dr. Bottero in France for final editing in preparation for global distribution. It is Alice's and my hope that we will be able to gather the necessary funds to bring the good doctor to this country where many in the legislatures, the media and professional organizations are intensely interested in learning of the doctor's research in this field, particularly it's impact in the area of mental health.

The worldwide epidemic of diseases caused by this bacterium has enormous implications for all peoples in all nations. There is a very real urgency that the health professions become knowledgeable of the treatments being implemented by Dr. Bottero and learn to recognize and deal with the psychopathology of these diseases.

We are awaiting the final, edited tape and further information before more details can be shared with all you folks. In the meantime, it has fallen to me to pave the way in the hope that when the material is available, readers and others will be properly prepared.

My readers of some years understand my interest in such things from my writings. But there will be many who will not make the connection between my writing as a poet and philosopher and scientific material such as Dr. Bottero's research.

As with Alice, my training and experience covers several fields. As a poet, I work with people from every conceivable background. As a teacher of many years, I found myself teaching so many different subjects that it kept my own interest alive in the classrooms.

It takes the breadth of such experience and training to appreciate the impact of Dr. Bottero's work. Therefore it shouldn't be too surprising that Alice, who is known as the Oklahoma Poetess and I (The Okie Poet) find common ground in scientific material as well as the softer and gentler things we love to write of. It always takes the poets and philosophers to make such research intelligible, comprehensible to the world community. The great, Russian poets are prime examples of this. It is on this basis that Alice and I hope to reach out to that global community and make such material of interest to others. Without that interest, people will not learn of it. And children and adults by the score will suffer as a consequence.

I also understand the time constraints we all are working under. It is difficult to set priorities when so many things are crying out for attention. Reading, as a consequence, is often neglected and the material begins to pile up on our desks. A virtual sea of information threatens to overwhelm us at times.

As a professional writer of many years experience I know how essential it is to get the reader's interest. And I have learned that nothing gets reader interest as quickly as SEX!

No, I am not using the word as a tasteless gimmick to get your attention and will come quickly to the point. The problems of the world involve two classes of people: Men and woman. And that equals sex. I repeat what I have said so many times: The relationship between the two sexes determines the course of nations and the course of history.

The fact that our waking thoughts are oriented to sex in some fashion roughly eighty per cent of the time should give the reader some appreciation of the gravity and importance of the subject to all people of the world. To make the point even clearer to the reader, I will take a quote from the introduction to my book; Birds With Broken Wings:

"Another of the many How To books on the market, this one written by a woman, Marianne Williamson, includes this statement: 'Some men know that a light touch of the tongue, running from a woman's toes to her ears, lingering in the softest way possible in various places in between, given often enough and sincerely enough, would add immeasurably to world peace.'"

Two things: This may not, in fact, be overdrawn, and, removed from erotica to the purpose of God in men cherishing their wives it is a valid statement. It is at least a shade ironic to find a woman making my point for me in this respect. The point being that if men and women would give attention to those things which bring out the best in each, undoubtedly the world would be a lovelier and safer place, especially in the cherishing of children and family. How could it be otherwise when, in fact, a man and woman cherish each other? Compatibility, as God intended, not Competition, is the antidote to the plagues of divorce, adultery and the destruction of family and family values.

Unfortunately, men and women are too busy in tongue lashing each other rather than love making. It is an evil system, led of evil men and women that has betrayed the poetic connection between men and women. I hope the reader will take the foregoing to heart. I re-emphasize the point: It is the relationship between men and women that orders the destiny of nations. Therefore, this relationship cannot be over-emphasized in its importance to world peace and world order. And I believe that is the preeminent importance of the work I am called to as a poet and philosopher.

The Birds book is about relationships between men and women. I treat the subject, among others, of how women betray themselves in the matter of romance. But I make a point in justification of girls and women in respect to something men call the calculating, cunning mind of the fair sex.

Men are generally of the opinion that women can be far more cold-blooded in respect to relationships than men. This is one factor that contributes to men being in the majority of the great poets and artists of history rather than women. Men are far more prone to the idealization of love and romance than women. You could say that men find women more inspirational rather than the obverse in the affairs of the heart.

There is a patently good reason for this as I point out in my book. Women have to learn early on to trade their sex for love, family and security. Having only that one option severely limits them in so very many areas of life and a natural resentment is born of it. To add further to the resentment, many cultures continue to treat women as chattel and, often, little different than children.

I'll never forget the scene in The Quiet Man where John Wayne is handed a switch to use on Maureen O'Hara. This is not a reflection on the Irish, but a comment on attitudes that prevail in many societies.

Yet it cannot be denied that men, especially in retaliation to a woman's most dangerous weapon, her mouth, often meet the deeply ingrained resentment of so many women with physical abuse. But the physical abuse of a woman by a man is never to be excused under any circumstances.

It still remains one of the facts that have to be confronted in any discussion of the relationships between men and women. And using facts to reach understanding may bring about necessary changes of behavior and attitudes on the part of both.

In reference to the kind of information that material like Dr. Bottero's research represents, if it is to be read, if the goal is educational, the interest of people must first be captured and then, once done, must be kept. That is the challenge of all educational pursuits.

The work and the message of the poet take many forms. It is the hugely complex study of human behavior, my academic specialty, the study of what makes people do the things they do, of how they treat one another, what each expects of the other that makes it such a monumentally complex undertaking.

For example Solomon himself, reputed for his great wisdom, was of two minds, confused about women. Allow me to give you an example of the dichotomy of this man's thinking. In his Proverbs we read: "A virtuous woman who can find, for her price far above rubies." Yet, in another place concerning the proper role of the husband in relationship to his wife we read: "Let her be as the loving hind and pleasant roe; let her breasts satisfy thee at all times and be thou ravished always with her love."

The following verse shows the real Wisdom of Solomon in the rhetorical question: "Why be captivated, my son, by an adulteress? Why embrace the bosom of another man's wife? For a man's ways are in full view of the Lord, and he examines all his paths. The evil deeds of a wicked man ensnare him; the cords of his sin hold him fast. He will die for lack of discipline, led astray by his own great folly." (NIV).

In respect to the last, I will always maintain the position that there would be better women if there were better men to accept responsibility for the standards of morality and leadership. In other words, you men quit blaming women for things for which you are responsible! And for the women, quit intruding yourselves into areas where you attempt to emasculate men by pursuing an insane course in the name of some kind of ephemeral and thoroughly counterproductive equality!

Because of the relationship between men and women being not only monumentally complex but also so very crucial to any kind of harmony and understanding throughout the world, I write about the relationship in many different ways. And some of the writing as my Birds book evidences is from considerable personal experience with many women in my own life.

As to confusion, I'll never forget an ex-wife telling me that the reason I was so shattered, physically and emotionally crippled by her betrayal of my love and trust was because a woman had done it to me! She said it like it was something of which to be proud! Why didn't she realize that only a woman can so profoundly cause such pain and grief in a man's life, could destroy his very heart and soul?

In respect to the betrayal of love and trust, the accompanying psychosis of grief is perfectly understandable. The one betrayed has no rational basis from which to deal with such pain and grief. Like any unexpected loss of a loved one, whether the burying of a child or the loss of a spouse, it is incomprehensible to the rational part of our minds. It simply isn't supposed to happen!

When the marriage bed is defiled, the victim of such treachery and betrayal has no rational frame of reference. The resulting psychosis leaves the victim unable to deal with the ordinary affairs of life while he or she struggles, uncomprehendingly, with the pain and grief. The victim cannot understand such a thing happening, cannot accept such action on the part of the one loved and trusted and the mind goes into the various stages of grief.

A large part of the agony and grief is based on the fact that the victim of betrayal is alone in his grief; he doesn't have someone else as in the case of adultery where the adulterer, obviously, has found another. The very knowledge, the dreadful mental pictures of the one loved and trusted in the bed and arms of another causes pain and grief beyond words.

The betrayed, the victim of such a thing has to work through the pain and grief alone while the Judas has someone else. The obvious injustice of such a thing contributes so much to the torment, agony and grief. The resulting agony is usually of long duration. I compare it with that of a wounded animal that cannot understand why such a thing has happened and seeks, mindlessly, some way out of its misery.

In time, usually a great deal of time, the reality of the loss begins to present itself and the person goes on with life. But it is a life that has experienced such selfish cruelty and injustice from another that it will never be the same. You might love and trust again (some, tragically, never do) but never, any longer, unreservedly.

That grim specter of remembrance of the betrayal remains to haunt all future relationships. Thus the damage done by the selfishness of one goes on to affect others for the rest of that life and the lives of others. And, far too often, children are made to pay the price of such betrayal as well! Small wonder that God equates the adulterer with a murderer!

Yet, from Solomon to Freud and Kinsey, confusion seems to reign in the thinking of men and women when it comes to the universal absolutes of love and sex. And I have discovered it is those who selfishly refuse to accept any standards of morality, honor, integrity, and fidelity in their own lives that causes the confusion. Where evil reigns, whether in the individual or in nations, confusion and chaos are the natural handmaidens.

Some of my writing, of necessity, is political and theological in nature due to the fact that the relationship between men and women determines the very politics and religious structure, the ideology of a nation. And that ideological evolution mirrors the relationship.

When what is best and noble that is distinctive to each sex is recognized and honored, when the compatibility of differences is emphasized, we have the best of all possible worlds. When the relationship is selfish, when the differences become a battleground or are used and abused, we have hell on earth. What should be the compatibility of differences then becomes competitive and combative.

I often become embarrassingly personal to make points in my anecdotal style of writing, telling stories on myself. To paraphrase Thoreau: If I knew anyone as well as myself, I would use them as the foil for the stories. But since I don't: Here am I, warts and all. And now, to get on with it:

I criticize and castigate the schools, universities, churches and professional religionists because of their ivory tower, insular attitude among other things. Safe in comfortable, protected classrooms or pews and hiding behind comfortable sermon and song, such people lose sight of the larger picture of a suffering humanity.

But another picture is emerging from the patriot groups with which I have worked over the years as well which I find disturbing. It is another kind of insular attitude that too often ignores reality as well.

As a poet, I interact with all different kinds of people in order to, as a beautiful woman said of me, write The American Epic of the lives of ordinary Americans, to put a Human Face on the Politics of Patriotism. And this is of interest to the rest of the world because all nations look to America for leadership. This nation still holds a preeminent position as a beacon of hope for the world.

One of the nicest things my friend Senator Don Rogers says of me is that I mix with people from all walks of life. But a poet does just that if he is to do the job of his calling.

However there is a deadly tendency in the churches and patriot groups to forget or neglect the larger picture of America and the global community by mixing with only those of your own kind! I call this deadly because it leads to just that kind of insular, prejudicial, parochial thinking that limits the usefulness of people and groups. In its most deadly form, it becomes paranoid, judgmental and, finally, a mind-set that your kind is the only right kind!

I have caused myself a lot of grief by mixing with some people and organizations in order to get the facts, the rest of the story if you will. I have suffered the harsh judgment of many who did not understand the task of the poet in striving to get at the truth.

For example, just recently I received a nasty, threatening phone call from Mr. Johnny Lee Clary because of my exposing him as a religious fraud in the August issue of OI. Now I invite Mr. Clary to make good on his threats if he can disprove anything I said about him. I await further developments and will share them with my readers. If anything further develops. And since the loss to Mr. Clary amounts to a very considerable sum of money, I take the threat seriously.

And, Mr. Clary, while I didn't take the space to mention it in that August essay, I knew full well why you didn't dare respond to my questions concerning the likes of Jimmy Swaggart, Jim and Tammy Baker, et al. and the whole disgusting, charismatic heresy. In condemning such obvious, religious frauds and doctrine, you would have condemned yourself!

You have successfully gulled Negroes and Hispanics into believing you are some kind of Blond Massa or Moses with the holy anointing of a prophet that will lead them out of darkness but you do it for a paycheck and your own ego, not their welfare. You tried to infiltrate into the patriot and militia groups in order to use and betray them for your own self-aggrandizement and financial gain but you were found out!

And to the ignorant and self-righteous out there who like to pop off with Judge not lest ye be judged nonsense, and this to justify your own hypocrisy, I would remind you that God still requires His people to judge evil and wicked people. That so many such wicked call themselves godly doesn't change this requirement that God Himself set. It was just such godly people who crucified the Son of God! Evil and wickedness must be confronted. Try doing so without judging who the bad guys (and women) are! It was righteous Lot the perverted citizens of Sodom were going to kill because he had become judgmental of their perversion!

Now I most certainly do not enjoy the kind of writing that results in such confrontations, exposing corruption wherever I find it. Yet, when people betray and take advantage, others deserve to be warned of such predators. The poet often finds himself doing this kind of dirty work for the sake of the truth and others. As everyone knows, Russia has an ignoble recent history of mistreating that nation's poets because of this duty of the poet.

I attend and am invited to attend all kinds of functions, to join many different groups and organizations. My desk is piled with such material. The American Center For Law And Justice is doing a noble job. I'm looking at a flyer for the Stand Up For America Freedom Rally in Anaheim. I wish I could attend but time constraints and other priorities prevent my going. As good as these things are, as with fellowshipping with my brethren in the churches, it is too easy to lose sight of the larger picture by insulating yourself through association only with those of your own kind.

Travel is, indeed, broadening. In time past, one was not equipped for certain occupations unless travel outside the continent had been accomplished. Henry James had to visit the Louvre to write with understanding. Our world has shrunk due to modern technology. Satellites bring instant news of world events. No longer do doctoral candidates spend years in the stacks to accomplish the task of that dread monster, The Doctoral Dissertation. The computer changed that.

Yet, it still takes mixing with other cultures to gain understanding of our world as a whole. It takes travel and association with many diverse groups in all kinds of environments to speak and write with understanding about the problems we face in this country and throughout the world.

The study of cultural anthropology is a fascinating one. To learn of the different ways people live and interact throughout the world gives us valuable insights and appreciation for others. But the emphasis should be, for the purposes of world harmony, on the universal absolutes that exist in all cultures, absolutes such as the love for children and between men and women.

In association with Alice Hill and her organization, we have just put together a mailing list of artists, philosophers and professional people worldwide. We will soon be making a global mailing of information to share with a broad cross section of people who share our concerns for world peace and harmony, those who share our concerns for the future of children throughout the world.

It is essential to the task to form groups and organizations in order to do the required work. But my task is to remind people that there is a larger picture of Americans, of the world of which we must not lose sight. That is the job of the poet. And few are called or suited to that kind of work. And it is a job I wouldn't wish on anyone else! It is very lonely work.

In the job description you find the requirement to not only be able to describe and promote what is pure and beautiful, soft and gentle but to be able to deal with the truth and enter into the sufferings of others, to understand the grief and pain, the diabolical ugliness of betrayal of love and trust. Not many takers qualified for this job.

Jesus, as a result, was called the Suffering Savior. He has been named the greatest poet who ever lived, and rightfully so. If anyone ever understood the compulsion that drives the poet, who understood the mechanisms of the work, it is Jesus.

Poets forever face Pilate's rhetorical question: What is truth? It is the constant facing of this question and seeking answers that makes the work so hard and filled with heartache and pitfalls. In trying to find answers to so many facets of the truth, the job becomes monumentally complex. And the answers come from the whole of humanity, not some select group.

In last month's essay I mentioned a conversation with a friend during which I said that I felt my mission in my writing was to reestablish the romantic, poetic, softer and gentler connection in the relationships between men and women. I repeat that the problems of our society, of the world itself involve two classes of people- men and women. And I repeat: It is the relationship between these two halves of humanity that predicts the future of a nation.

A good friend recently came by and told me he was beginning to think in terms of a monastery due to his continuing disappointments in the affairs of the heart. I tried to tell him I'm simply not wired the same way. In spite of the many betrayals of love and trust in my own life, I have never become bitter toward women. He couldn't understand it. "If anyone has a right to be bitter about women Don, he said, it's you!"

His own disappointments in the romance department had led him, like many men and women I know, to this sorry state of mind. But he didn't have daughters. This might have helped soften his views. It certainly helped me.

As my little girls grew, I would look at them and think to myself: There is something about these precious and adorable little creatures, something that gets down deep in the heart of a man unlike anything else in the world, a something of infinite value. I just can't figure out what it is? They are going to grow up to be women. And women are the most perverse of God's creatures (typical man thinking)! Women have caused the greatest pain in my life. Yet these aren't women. But they will be. Just exactly what is going on here?

The romantic, poetic part of me, the responding softness and gentleness I learned from my daughters, knows that goodness is the only investment of eternal value. But it must be, at least most of the time, a goodness tempered by the ability to separate the diabolical from the divine. And this can only be done, especially in the subtlest cases, by experiencing both.

I love music. Drop Kick Me Jesus Through The Goal Posts Of Life might have its place but when you have heard Moonlight Sonata there is quite a contrast. There's A Tear In My Beer When I Think Of You Dear or I Stepped In A Pile'a You And Got A Mess'a Love All Over Me isn't intended to compete with Red Sails In The Sunset. I know this. Nor am I implying such lyrics are diabolical. But they serve to make a point. I love satire and irony. Such things are not necessarily diabolical. But they can be.

When I exercise my acerbic wit toward religious or political charlatans, I often use satire and irony. When it comes to women, however, I am loath to do so; and this because of my daughters.

Every woman is some man's daughter. I never lose sight of this fact. It doesn't matter what kind of father she has or had, I like to think she has a father who loves her with the kind of love that automatically separates the diabolical from the divine. And in spite of the many tragic exceptions I know of personally, like my Lady in Red, I hold on to the hope that the women I meet have a father that loves them and man enough to not be afraid to show that love.

I tried to explain to my friend why I couldn't tolerate a male roommate that I preferred living alone rather than with another man no matter how close a friend he might be. I told him that I have always been the kind of man who would need a woman to care for, a man who needs the warmth and softness of a woman in his life to be a complete man. My home will remain a solitary abode otherwise. Without the softening influence of a woman, I become hard-edged and morose; not very good company.

I deal with so much of the evil that men and women do, the harsh and cruel elements of life in confronting the betrayers of America and humanity that without that softening influence, I can easily become too hard, too grim in the battle for the soul of America and lose the softer and gentler perspective, unable to put that human face on the Politics of Patriotism.

But there is a catch 22 here. As a writer, I need a great deal of solitude to think and gather my thoughts, to meditate and consider the things I write about. Even as a child and adolescent I was known as the quiet type and I grew up to be a quiet man. And if there is anything I have learned about the female psyche, it is the fact that a woman cannot tolerate feeling ignored. As a writer, as a quiet man, I have had to contend with this in my relationships with many different women.

I try to do the thoughtful things every woman needs from a man. But when I drift off into my meditative, contemplative, introspective mode, the resident other half of the proposition feels ignored. And, eventually, she has always sought and found attention elsewhere.

But my book about love and romance, Birds With Broken Wings, is the proof of my lack of bitterness against women and has generated a lot of discussion, as I knew it would. The highest praise and justification for the book has come from other fathers of daughters like me. Recently, a man came up to me and asked to shake my hand. Like me, he has three daughters. He had received a copy of the book through a mutual friend. Seeking me out, he introduced himself and taking my hand firmly in his, said with tears: "Dr. Heath, you really love women! I read your book and now I am having my daughters read it as well. I pray they will listen to what you have said about the things that women should value themselves for, that my girls will take these things to heart and not let men use and abuse them like so many you describe in your book. God bless you for what you have done. All fathers and their daughters owe you a huge debt of gratitude!"

The emotional, tearful sincerity of the man left me with a lump in my throat. I could hardly respond with the thanks that welled up in my heart for his remarks.

I haven't shared this man's comments to flatter myself. I do so to make a painful point. Far too many who should profit from the research and real life experiences that went into the book have become critical of me because of some of the facts I lay bare in it. One especially sore point among men is my statement that men are the responsible parties in the matter of seduction, that there would be better women if there were better men to set the standards of morality! Men don't like this- understandably.

Concerning the hypocrisy and ignorance so rife among the churches and so-called *Christians*, I really call a spade a spade in the book thus incurring the wrath of the brethren. Yet, it is God Himself, who calls men the responsible parties; it is men who God holds responsible for leadership! Thus I quickly tire of the women are no damned good argument of so many so-called *men*! It was such so-called *men* who had to sneak in the back door to my ex-wives rather than being man enough to find a woman of their own!

The world would, undoubtedly, be a kinder and gentler place if men would accept the responsibility Adam tried to cop out of. Those so-called *men* that seduce other men's wives are, obviously, beneath the contempt of good, civilized men and women. And nothing needs saying about the so-called *women* who cooperate in the betraying seduction by such animals. The contempt for them is equal and according to their selfish, betraying actions.

Because of my work in the churches over the years, my Christian background, training and orientation, I often write things of a theological nature and use illustrations from Scripture. The Bible remains The Good Book despite the abuse and distortions of its teachings by the ignorant and unscrupulous.

Among the things of which so many are ignorant, even those who should know better in the churches, is the matter of the Ten Commandments, the Decalogue, being directed toward men, not women. Few seem to realize that God, from the very beginning in The Garden, placed the responsibility for leadership directly on men. The Buck Stops with men, not women.

As proof of this, in The Decalogue of the Old Testament and the elaboration on this theme in the New Testament, you have only to look at the last Commandment: "You shall not covet your neighbor's wife!"

Now all the Commandments were to be binding on men, women and children. But they are peculiarly worded and directed at men, the last Commandment being the proof of this.

God did not say to women: Don't covet your neighbor's husband! And, while this is a common enough problem, especially in our godless society, The Lord still considers men the responsible parties in the matter of coveting and seducing and makes His meaning very clear in the wording of this last Commandment.

And to anticipate you men, I am not excusing women for their part or responsibility before God and others in respect to faithfulness and fidelity. Nor would I ever attempt excuses for them in the matter of betrayal of love and trust. A betraying woman is the greatest and most painful curse of any man's life! It wasn't without foundation that Solomon wrote: "A virtuous woman who can find, for her price is far above rubies!" God knows I have had more than the average man's experience with the other kind, the unfaithful ones!

Yet the responsibility of men in the matter of leadership, for standards of morality still stands. Men are without excuse when they fail in these things and they cannot get away, any more than Adam could, with blaming women and/or God with their own failures. But this brings me to the antidote for such things, the antithesis of those things which cause such hurt and pain in people's lives: Love.

Love, as Jesus and the Apostle Paul make abundantly and indelibly plain, is the fulfillment of The Law. It is preeminently sensible in its application. Obviously, if love is the motivating factor in behavior a person is not going to betray another. Where selfishness, lust, covetousness, greed and envy are the motivating factors, love is absent.

One of the supreme attributes of the kind of love God means for us to have in our relationships with others is that kind of love (as in I Corinthians 13) which never betrays. As a Christian, I believe God's own heart of love is peculiarly sensitive to the pain of betrayal and this is why I believe He places so much emphasis on His hatred of those evil and wicked people (the Judases) who cause so much pain in others (as in God's statement: I hate divorce!) by their acts of betrayal of love and trust.

It is a given among all peoples of the world that the betrayers of love and trust, whether it be the molester who destroys the innocence of a child or the adulterer who murders love are the very scum of the earth. And only the guilty, those who attempt to justify their own perversion will disagree with that statement! And they can go to hell where they will find suitable company among their own kind, the Devil and his servants, who share their *values*!

I gave a copy of the Birds book to the pastor of the Fruitvale Community Church, one of the largest independent churches in Bakersfield, with the request that he read it and tell me how he would go about making it a Christian Book. I never heard another word from this good man. Nor did I really expect to. The Christian Community, as a whole, is caught with its pants down as a result of the hypocrisy I expose in the book. I, like Peter, Paul and Luther, use great plainness of speech in regard to this hypocrisy.

And I distinguish between hypocrisy and plain ignorance. I have found, in some cases, good men and women will do better if they know better. But the churches fail, abysmally, to deal with the realities of life, choosing rather, to talk about pie in the sky by and by and have the temerity to call this garbage teaching, repeating the same tiresome things endlessly Sunday after Sunday rather than doing battle here in the real world where God requires we get dirt under our fingernails in the work.

In respect to organizations that are doing the job, I point to Alcoholics and Narcotics Anonymous, the Alano Clubs and Al Anon. If any organizations deserved the support of the churches and society at large it is these. Recovering addicts of drugs and alcohol are the only ones qualified to enter into the sufferings of those who seek help concerning addiction. Yes, there is the desperate need of qualified, academically trained personnel as well, many of the local clubs suffer in their effectiveness from the lack of such personnel. Yet, only someone who has suffered through to recovery is able to relate on the most elemental, human level with those seeking help. I thought I knew something of alcoholism until I loved, and lived with, an alcoholic. I found I knew nothing of the realities of such a thing! But the pompous assess in the churches who, generally, know nothing of such addiction personally, will pontificate on Jesus will help you as though incantations approaching witchcraft will substitute for actual knowledge and experience!

So it is that my book gets a very cool reception among the brethren. They don't like having their faces rubbed in the dirt of their ignorance and hypocrisy, their failure to deal with the realities of life itself in the raw. Jesus certainly saw things differently as even the most cursory examination of the Scriptures prove. The Lord is the preeminent realist and has a great deal more sense and humanity about him than the churches usually give Him credit for or exhibit themselves.

I am very plain spoken regarding sex, drugs and alcohol in my book. I take a very human approach to things that include both the strengths and weaknesses of us poor mortals. But I take the point of view that God has made us thus and trying to religionize, sublimate, ignore or refuse to acknowledge our own humanity ties God's hands in respect to His help.

On my ever-growing list of things to do, I am going to have to publish my commentary on the Psalms. Here, as nowhere else, we find that very humanity of which I am speaking. Here is where men get confrontational with God, pouring out the legitimate complaints of the heart that we human beings face every day of our lives.

But the churches refuse to acknowledge these legitimate complaints and attempt to spiritualize them away to some nether region far removed from the actual realities of life itself. And, in so doing, they become ineffectual in the battle against the very evil they are supposed to confront! And people by the millions suffer accordingly.

As a consequence, I seldom go to the churches anymore; I go to the bars and taverns, I mix with people from businesses and professions, waitresses and truck drivers, workers in every area of life for the honesty, truth and realities of a suffering humanity. It is in these environments I find friends who lack the stench of hypocrisy, people who are open and honest about themselves.

Yet I am blessed with knowing some good, religious men. My good friend Byron, the Episcopal priest comes by frequently and we have many a good discussion. We discussed some of the things I have just written and I got some good input from my friend.

I was looking at that intriguing sixth chapter in Genesis concerning the period just before the flood. And, as per the introduction to this edition of OI, Sex is the prominent subject. Many Biblical commentators have missed the point that it was the lust of the flesh that caused God such pain that: "The Lord was grieved that he had made man on the earth, and his heart was filled with pain." We read in this same place: "The Lord saw how great man's wickedness on the earth had become, and that every inclination of the thoughts of his heart was only evil all the time."

The result of this, God's determination to destroy man, whom God had created, through a great flood, the Deluge, is a common story of antiquity in the histories of nations in one form or another. But my point is the prominent role sex (actually the perversion of sex) played in God's decision to destroy mankind and, later, the cities of Sodom and Gomorrah. The point is elaborated on extensively in Paul's epistle to the Romans and several other places in the New Testament.

When I mentioned the fact that the waking thoughts of people are sexually oriented in one form or another roughly eighty per cent of the time that should have given the reader a good indication of the extreme importance of the subject. So, to use the question women often ask of men: Is that all you ever think about? The answer is roughly Yes! But we must not ignore the fact that women are equally occupied with such thinking as well.

And this is only to be expected in view of the fact that one of the earliest lessons women learn is that their sex is the one thing they have to offer in return for love, family and security. It is, and has always been, a man's world. Men lead and women have to follow.

But a culture such as ours in America has blurred the distinctive roles of men and women through insane laws that have attempted by force of law to make men and women equal. The point is missed that the problem is one of equal value. Such attempts at legislating morality and fairness have only resulted in making both sexes resentful of each other, much like the Equal Opportunity and Affirmative Action laws that have bred such resentment toward minorities in our society.

In attempts at fairness, we have simply gone too far. The result has been a thoroughgoing perversion of the legislative process in order to fix inequities. But such laws have flown in the face of immutable facts of the differences between men and women. These differences will not change in spite of all the laws passed by legislators that fly in the face of God's own creative powers that established those differences.

Through the prideful and ignorant attempts by men and women to make such changes, by the resulting chaos where the proper roles of men and women have been thoroughly obfuscated, we have evolved a society that places the emphasis on youth and beauty, on sex over love and fidelity. As a consequence, women in our culture grow old and wrinkled, of no value whereas men grow mature and seasoned! Women have to contend with jealousy and envy of younger women who attract men. Men, on the other hand, worry little about such things. And more resentment is encouraged and fostered on the part of women.

Yet, without a basis of love, with divorce so easy and the role of mother and homemaker denigrated, with a government that betrays it's citizens and forces women into the workforce through insane policies and laws which eliminate the industry and jobs which enabled men to support a family on a single paycheck, women have been forced into roles for which they were never intended, roles that devalue themselves as women in their proper roles as wives and mothers, homemakers. And the home is the very backbone and foundation of America and all viable civilizations!

A nation that fails to cherish its young has no future as a nation; nor does it deserve one! And that cherishing is characterized by providing a home with a mother and father in their distinctive, proper roles, each providing for each other and children those things necessary for family, for hope of a future.

And what of the resentment of many women who come to the realization that they must trade sex for security while men have so many other options available to them? This has led to the misconception so common among men that women are naturally manipulative and cunning, calculating. When your options are as severely limited as in the case of women, you must keep your wits about you.

I have written about the problem women have with other women as friends. A large part of the distrust among women has to do with the fact that women steal the boyfriends and husbands of other women. How often has that best friend turned out to be the betrayer in this regard.

As a singer and musician virtually all my life, I deal with a lot of music. But one song always comes to mind in regard to the pain and grief of the betrayal of love and trust: "Why Can't God Make An Unbreakable Heart?" How often many of us have wished He could; but it is the love and trust we are capable of that enables us to practice the kind of divine humanity that makes us vulnerable both to betrayal and the suffering of others as well as the joy of loving and being loved that makes us capable of being human in the very best sense of that word.

This sixth chapter of Genesis together with Paul's commentary, not to mention the voluminous attention it has always received, the thousands of books written and being written on the subject, should be enough to make the matter of sex clear in it's importance to the decision making processes of all mankind that effect virtually every aspect of our lives throughout the world and throughout history.

As cynical as it appears, I subscribe to the Christian doctrine that people are inherently selfish- the fallen nature if you will. Perhaps it was God's intention that through children, through parenting, sacrificial, unselfish love could be learned by us mortals.

Certainly the total dependence of a baby should evoke the tenderest care and emotions of mother and father. But doesn't always work that way, does it? Especially when insane laws encourage the having of babies simply to receive a larger welfare check! When babies become commodities to be bartered for unearned money what becomes of a home or hope of a future for such children? Another rhetorical question.

But where are the fathers of these babies? It is to the shame of so-called *men* that, failing to maintain that standard of leadership and morality for which men, not women are held accountable, girls find themselves with babies and no husband, no man worthy of the name.

Again, you men, we lead and women have to follow. Don't you dare try to make girls and women equally responsible for this evil system, this double standard for which men are responsible! And it took an evil system, led of evil men and women, to evolve such a system that has led to these conditions in our nation, conditions that leave only those three, inevitable and immutable choices of history: Slavery, Anarchy or the course of our founding fathers; and until the leadership faces the hard facts, the hard choices and acts accordingly, nothing will get any better.

A New Continental Congress is needed. A return to those foundational precepts of the founding fathers and the clear intent of our Constitution must be re-instituted. Enlightened Self Interest resulting in freedom and liberty with corresponding personal responsibility is the only way out of our national bankruptcy, morally and economically.

As America and the rest of the nations of the world face very hard questions that resist simple solutions, the potential grows for slavery to those Hitlerian and Stalinist Solutions I fear. It doesn't help my own state of mind to find myself alienated from so many with whom I wish I could find common ground. The problem consistently presents itself, however, when you deal with the whole truth. Invariably I find myself in a confrontational mode with so many who should listen to the message rather than kill the messenger.

For example, my heterodox views of Christianity keep me in trouble with the churches. My exposing the abuses and fraud in the schools and government keeps me at odds with these people. The rewards come from my exposing the Johnny Lee Clary's, seeing the rats run for cover when I keep the heat on those that murdered Randy Weaver's son and wife, those who murdered those women and children in Waco, the arrogant cowards responsible for running roughshod over our freedom and liberty under color of law like the IRS, FBI, BATF, the Clintons and Janet Reno.

The rewards come from those fathers and women who say my Birds book made a difference in their lives or the lovely lady who said my writing was having an impact on others and changing lives. But that kind of writing is so intensely personal in order to be effective that I often cringe when I look at some of the things I say about myself and my relationships with others.

Yet, I know this kind of personal approach is essential to, as a friend stated, put the passion in the writing that gets and keeps the reader's attention and makes it of value. It is that compulsive passion, like the moth to the flame that separates the poet from other writers.

And I keep the pictures of my children and grandchildren, especially the one of Karen, my youngest daughter, that I used for the cover of my book ever in front of me to remind me of what the battle is all about; and to also help me not lose sight of those softer and gentler things I would so much rather devote all my time, all my life to writing of.

***

My book, The Lord and the Weedpatcher, contains a satirical piece on political and business charlatanism. I have just learned I have won a writer's award specifically for the piece entitled: "An Apologetic to my Critics Regarding the Iguana Ranches."

To be honored by my peers as a humorist will come as quite a surprise to many people. But I deal with the Dark Side so much of the time I find it essential, as with devoting time to music and singing, to give vent to humor on occasion. And it must be admitted that the human condition in politics, religion and business yields a good deal of humor, particularly in a satirical mode. Nor do I fail to appreciate the irony of my being honored as a humorist. My whole life seems dedicated to irony and satire, the Divine Comedy in its many manifestations.

The book contains some old pictures of mining claims, Old Bakersfield and is filled with anecdotes about my idyllic life in the Sequoia National

Forest as a mountain man. There are also stories of my early experiences in the areas of Malibu, Manhattan, Hermosa and Redondo Beaches (I graduated from Mira Costa in Manhattan Beach) when the ocean and beaches were clean. The local museum sells copies of the book, as well as the bookstores. A copy is also in the local, Kern County Library.

While the book is filled with amusing anecdotes, I devoted this particular chapter to satirizing the entrepreneurial and political structure of America ala Sam Clemens. If you order a copy of the book, you won't fail to see the resemblance between Sam and me. Believe it or not, I'm actually capable of a good deal of humor when there is some joy in my life.

I spent years exposing the corruption so rife in the schools, government and religion. It is rewarding to see my efforts bearing fruit in so many other publications, by seeing people speaking out about these things and carrying the battle to Caesar; as George Washington so well said: "Truth will ultimately prevail where there are pains taken to bring it to light."

And because so many are now doing the job so well that people like myself initiated, I can devote more of my time to bringing truth to light in other ways that are not the purview or area of expertise of these others. My readers of some years will understand and appreciate this new tack in my writing, to my doing the peculiar work of the poet and philosopher rather than the political pundit.

As to my writing as a humorist, there are a number of national publishers interested in some of my other writings but I'm relieved, in a sense, to learn that my peers and colleagues appreciate my sense of humor as well. When you lose that, you've lost it all. God knows how badly we all need a laugh at times. And I dearly love to poke fun at myself. As Walt Kelly so well said: "Don't take life so seriously son, it ain't no wise permanent!"

***

The following material is from, and about, Alice Hill and her organization. Alice and I are attempting to cooperate by the sharing of things that we hope will promote world harmony.

The goal of A. Hill & Associates is:

To have numerous departments such as music, education, law, political, medical and others, all working throughout the world to find ways to better understanding, sharing and caring among people from all races and creeds.

You already know about the hope Alice and I share concerning raising the necessary funds to bring Dr. Philippe Bottero to the U.S. in order for him to lecture in this country. Alice would also like to bring Dr. Boyko Stoyanan, the great pianist, from Japan to this country to do a concert tour across the United States.

Alice has stated that she believes the Drs. Alis from Peoria, Illinois will help with both of these projects and they may be scheduled to coincide with the 1996 International Congress on Communication and the Arts that will be held in San Francisco in July of that year. We ask for the help of all of you to make these things happen.

In a very sober vein, Alice has asked me to share the following story with our readers.

Alice has a friend whose son was recently shot by Oxnard police after he had stolen a pack of cigarettes. According to the police report, the man was shot when he threatened the police with a knife. But the police shot him from the safety of their three, police cars!

To quote Alice:

"A terrible, terrible thing has happened. A dear, close friend, Fredonia Sterling's son, Robert Sterling, age 30, was shot and killed by Oxnard Police on August 29, at about 5:30 in the evening. He died shortly after the shooting occurred."

Alice went on in her letter to share many things about the relationship between this mother and son and herself. Included is information about the history of slavery in this nation. Fredonia had a great-great-grandfather who was a slave and Alice's mother's great-grandfather owned slaves. They researched and shared all of the handed down family stories and compared many of their findings.

Alice makes the following point in her story, a point that I have covered in much of my own writing and research:

"Again, we find ourselves in the same situation as the people living during the civil war period. Our social and economic way of life has not been created by any one person, and there is not any one person who can change it. Our police seem to have been given total freedom to kill at will. They have not been trained in any way about any of the true causes of the mental illnesses (as per Dr. Bottero's research) they have to deal with and because their lives are also on the line, they are filled with both fear and the ignorance caused from improper training and preparation.

"Then, we also have plenty of Mark Fuhrmans both within law enforcement and scattered all through society. My friend's son, Robert, is now just another statistic in this land that all the world looks to as a symbol of Freedom. His mother's heartbreak has been terrible and I feel so helpless when all I can do is appeal to the kinder people in our sick society to help get Dr. Bottero's research findings out to all the law enforcement agencies.

"The policemen are our sons and daughters caught up in our plight too, you know, and they need to know all the facts they can get as well as those who are afflicted by the diseases caused by Rickettsiae. I ask all people to reconsider the plight of the families where mental illness is known. They have both an illness and a stigma to fight. We have to help each other. If government would or could help us we would not be in the dreadful situation we all find ourselves."

CHAPTER SIX

THE OKIE INTELLECTUAL

NOVEMBER 1995

"Nothing can deter a poet, for he is actuated by pure love. Who can predict his comings and goings? His business calls him out at all hours, even when doctors sleep." H.D. Thoreau.

So it is that I, as a poet, intrude myself into so many different areas of life and creation that the result has been a man without common sense, as one woman of my acquaintance some time ago put it. And she was right. In respect to what constitutes common sense in the real world which is filled with so much that is ugly and evil, how explain taking so much time to examine the stars, our only sensible measure of eternity, or a sunrise or sunset and count that as time well spent?

My only defense to the woman is I am compelled, as a poet, to search for truth and beauty in the midst of so much that is ugly and confront those things and people which mar and profane beauty and truth. To be motivated by the love for others, for beauty and truth, is to fall heir to the honest criticism of this woman: A man without common sense!

I was about to put my broom in the refrigerator when I recalled her words once more. I had been building a rock retaining wall in the back of my little cottage in the country. Having swept off the concrete, I walked in the house with the intention of returning the broom to its rightful place; which was next to the refrigerator. I stood there a moment, broom in hand and refrigerator door open, when it occurred to me that my mind was not on replacing the broom to its correct spot. So I just opened the first door I came to. Fortunately, the broom wouldn't fit in the refrigerator and I came to my senses and the broom found its proper harbor.

Now I still do most of the mechanical work on my cars and whatever house repairs prove necessary. I have to do the brakes on my truck before I use it again. Brakes serve a most essential function in vehicles. I now have to worry about focusing my attention properly while replacing the brakes on the truck. Will I wind up, like the absent-minded doctor, leaving a scalpel or forceps in a rotor or drum?

I know I'm not the only one who becomes absent-minded in some circumstances. I'm not the only one who gets up and goes into another room and forgets what he went in there for. But, as a man who has gone to extraordinary lengths to prove the honest criticism of this woman of myself as lacking common sense, I realize that the world has a dim view of those who fail to measure up to the responsibilities of realities. In how many instances did I fail my family in not doing so.

Oh, we may build the tombs of the prophets and poets, we may honor them after a fashion but who, in their right and practical minds, would choose to be one or live with one? But, even tragically, it isn't a choice for the prophet or poet. It is a compulsion. And, as such, results in such people standing before the judgment of the world with no defense but that of Luther: *Ich kann nicht anders*! God help those of us who can utter no other defense of our lives but such a pathetic cry that we can do no different!

As I sit and write this, I am still in my bathrobe. It has a hole in it from a burning cigarette. This happened when an alcoholic I loved and lived with passed out while smoking and wearing the robe. Like many alcoholics, she had learned to pass out in bed with the hand holding a lit cigarette lying in an ashtray. Tragically, this doesn't always work.

Who, with any common sense, would take responsibility for such tragic people and love them? Would I advocate anyone doing so? No. But love compels and flies in the face of common sense. Even at the cost of one's own life and desires for a normal life and life partner.

While the poet and prophet pay the price of such compulsion, it is the responsibility of all to take advantage of what is learned in the process of such a pilgrimage through this vale of tears and before shuffling off this mortal coil. So, to get on with the process of separating the diabolical from the divine, I begin with the following:

Part of the task of the poet is to expose the ugly and selfish that is in conflict with the pure and beautiful. Because of this obligation of the poet, I recently exposed a religious fraud, one Johnny Lee Clary, who was taking advantage of others by his lies and deceit for his own financial benefit.

To this end, I am collaborating with a man, Roy Kendall, in exposing the graft and corruption which led to the Orange County bankruptcy and the theft and malfeasance in public offices involved with the building of the Radisson Hotel and Convention Center in Tulare County in California.

This has involved taking the evidence of such fraud to the district attorney's office, giving the evidence to the F.B.I., to state senators, to the California Attorney General, Dan Lungren, himself. I will be working with Roy in writing a book detailing the chicanery and corruption of conscienceless men and women involved with this scam (and I will be naming them), who don't give a damn about hurting the little people who pay the price of such betrayal of public trust.

The moral breakdown of a society, a culture that leads to such blatant corruption and an attitude of *To hell with everyone else, I'm going to get mine!* whether in the utter selfishness of adultery or the corruption of government has its roots in the relationships between men and women. Allow me to amplify on this statement and see if you don't agree.

The well-known historian, Will Durant, said: "Our knowledge of the past is always incomplete, probably inaccurate, beclouded by ambivalent evidence and biased historians, and perhaps (in fact often is) distorted by our own patriotic or religious partisanship; most history is guessing, the rest is prejudice."

There is no doubt to any objective reader of history that the respective roles of men and women in a society have always predicted the course of nations. And while Durant might be a little strong in his assessment of guessing and prejudice as to history, it is undeniable that historians follow their prejudices in many cases. Hitler, Stalin and our own liberal corrupters of America in the universities provided their own revised histories to suit their pernicious agendas.

The result in our nation has been the total obfuscation of the roles of men and women and a resulting collapse of standards of behavior and the calamity of the loss of hope for the future of our young people. But the actual nature of men and women, their strengths and weaknesses, their distinctive differences are immutable fact and will not be changed no matter attempts to the contrary.

National Geographic of January 1995 had a most interesting piece on New Orleans:

Once renowned as the place of Mardi gras and the birthplace of American Jazz, The Big Easy has taken on a much different persona due to drugs. There have been no race riots in New Orleans since 1900, but the epidemic of drugs has changed that and is the cause of a murder-a-day in this city along with the growing animosity and conflict between it's citizens.

To quote one black man: The neighborhoods are our tribes now! The city of Jazz is dying from drugs! Our kids don't go to high school, they go straight to drugs!

It was Henry Miller who wrote of New Orleans: At last on this bleak continent the sensual pleasures assume the importance that they deserve. (End)

Well, Mr. Miller, your hedonistic view of the source of deliverance from bleakness has a heavy price tag as the sins of the flesh invariably do. The wages of sin remain the same throughout history. When father and mother, when family no longer has the proper significance and honor in a society, the collapse into degradation and perversion of all kinds is assured.

And before I go any further, I make no claims of saintliness in my own life. My own sins, weaknesses and failures go before me in all that I say and do. But if there is any virtue in my life it has its basis in my never having betrayed the love and trust of another.

For example, I was a high school teacher for a number of years. I knew of instances of immorality between teachers and young girls in the schools. One man I knew well divorced his wife and married one of his pupils.

It wasn't unusual for some girl to have a crush on me as a teacher. How easy it would have been to take advantage of such circumstances. That such a thing never happened isn't so much due to any nobility on my part as it was due to the fact that I had a wife and children that I could never betray by such an action. And being very young, I couldn't anticipate the future prominence I would have as a writer or the things I would be writing and speaking about. Looking back, by God's grace, such things did not take place. Such immorality would have precluded my being able to write and speak as I have done these past years and just as surely as the sun shines and the rains fall, *Be sure your sins will find you out* and such a skeleton of the past would most certainly rise to destroy me.

But my years of working with teenagers showed the steady erosion of morality among our young people as they, increasingly, lost any hope of a future, as the epidemic of easy divorce devastated homes and all standards of morality. And, increasingly, government, the churches the so-called entertainment media did their part through corruption and the countenancing, even encouragement, of all kinds of perversion.

The epidemic of drugs in our nation found fertile soil in the loss of hope of a future. And where did this loss of hope begin to evolve? In the disintegration of families.

The basic issue to be enjoined in seeking answers to the problems confronting a society is morality. And morality begins with the relationships between men and women. And it is morality in the home above all else that predicts the future of a society.

The morality of America has been destructing for a very long time. As the homes of America go, so go the nation and other nations as well. And what underlies this moral decline? Divorce.

As a nation, America is reaping the whirlwind of insane laws that make it far too easy for husbands and wives to divorce. The devastation this has caused in the moral breakdown of the nation, its families and, especially its children is now seen on every hand.

The use of drugs, as with alcohol is, in many cases, an attempt to escape the loss of hope of a future, the loss of hope that your life will ever find fulfillment in any meaningful way. For that time that your senses are dulled through drugs and alcohol, you escape the pain of the meaninglessness of it all.

The primary basis of my opposition and confrontation with Caesar and his Big Brotherism form of government is this: I oppose and confront all laws which subvert the family, which work to harm children and destroy hope of a future for them. A recent study has shown that more than half of the adolescents in our nation are involved with promiscuous sex, alcohol and drugs. Yet I warned of this trend more than thirty years ago! As a high school teacher dealing with thousands of teenagers, I watched the steady erosion of morality and hope for a future of our young people as evil men and women worked feverishly to destroy the ideals upon which this nation was founded.

But only recently have the devastation of divorce in its impact on children and the future of a nation begun to be studied, written and talked about openly, candidly and factually. And such studies are putting the Big Lie concerning divorce about better for the children to rest. This has never been anything but an excuse for divorce in too many cases where one or the other partners of the marriage simply wanted out rather than give up any selfishness. Such selfishness always expresses itself in the mind-set that: "There's nothing wrong with me that someone else won't fix! I just have to get rid of the one I have now!"

That children suffer enormously from such utter selfishness never enters the mind of someone who simply has to have it his or her way! And we witness the abomination of the way children are actually used, if thought of at all, in many divorce cases. And these users are going to try to say *Better for the children*! These liars have a place prepared for them, a place called Hell!

I was labeled a moralist many years ago for taking a stand against this plague, which has made family and family values a thing of the past, and, in these times, a tragic joke. But God takes marriage seriously whether men and women do or not. So seriously, in fact, that He says plainly in The Bible: "I hate divorce!" In very few instances does God say that He literally hates something; and this is one of those instances.

In the beginning, we are told, God made a man and a woman to be husband and wife declaring them to be One! Forsaking all others, they were to be true to each other and never to be terminally separated except in the two cases of death or adultery.

God makes a distinction between adultery and prostitution. There are no promises of a life commitment by a prostitute. The prostitute by the very definition of the word cannot betray another. Hence, while the Bible nowhere countenances prostitution, it is the adulterer, not the prostitute, who God says shall never enter His Kingdom!

It is no coincidence that God placed His commandments "You shall do no murder" and "You shall not commit adultery" next to each other in the Decalogue. God equates the two as equally heinous!

Jesus plainly said that the laws of men granting divorce for any other reason but adultery was due to the hardness of their hearts; the reply of men and women then, and now? If that's the case better not to marry at all! How very true this has been in contemporary America.

Now what prompts such an attitude on the part of men and women in response to Jesus' pronouncement? Their hardness of heart. Why not just come out and say you have no intention of settling for just one partner for life? Why not just admit that if you aren't satisfied with that other you have no intention of submitting to meaningless words like commitment and follow a heinous practice of "serial monogamy" rather than fidelity and trust? The sheer hypocrisy practiced by those uttering such words in the typical marriage ceremony makes me want to vomit! The great amount of writing and speaking I have done on this theme has been met in too many instances by criticism, ridicule or silence. Why? Because of the hardness of men's hearts to which Jesus referred.

On the analytical side of the problem, I decided to look at the elements of this tragedy of easy divorce in respect to the relationship between men and women and the distinctive emotional, psychological and physical differences between the two. This in no way mitigates that hardness of heart, that utter selfishness of the adulterer. But such a study of the elements of this aspect of human behavior may help the victims, especially children as they grow older, to deal with the devastation of divorce.

I'm going to introduce new readers to a field of study in which I have been engaged for some years. I will ask that you bear with me as I take a seemingly circuitous path to dealing with the problems I have raised. I assure you it will come clear eventually.

Before I continue, I want to thank so many for their response to last month's essay where I introduced the subject of the importance of the relationships between men and women. I thank those, like Linda, who said I was a progressive man in taking this approach to solving world problems.

And to Lois in New Zealand, thank you for your words of encouragement.

That inner partner, the anima/animus is the Holy Spirit to the Christian.

But there are those who still think of me as a sexual anachronism, a moral dinosaur for having such an attitude toward the relationships between men and women.

I thank those like Mary and Vyvian and so many others who hold out for the ideals of marriage and family, fidelity and commitment and will not give in to a morally corrupt society.

As for the accusation of being a nice man, I was visiting one of my favorite taverns when a girl named Julie, a beautiful brunette, introduced herself to me. This particular place has an excellent soft rock band and I was there to enjoy the music.

As a professional singer and musician, I enjoy an occasional change of pace from Country Western and Ballroom music and I get a chance to visit with the owner, a marvelous woman who has done much to help others in this depressed area.

Since I seldom drink, the barmaid had immediately served me my usual cup of coffee when I arrived. Julie asked if that was all I ever drank? I explained that while I wasn't a teetotaler, as a writer I preferred to keep a clear head at all times. She understood.

While we were getting acquainted, a girlfriend of Julie's came over. She was quite intoxicated. Julie told me quietly that her friend had three, young children at home and needed to get away for a while. That deserves much comment but I must refrain for now.

In no time at all, there were several men trying to hit on the girls. So I became the protector once more, running interference for them. As a result, Julie wound up sitting on my lap giving the impression she was with me. In this way, she could choose who she wanted to dance with and fend off the more objectionable men. And I could enjoy the warmth and softness of a young woman in my arms. I'm still just a mere man.

But one young man was quite insistent. It was at one point of his attempted intrusion that Julie said something quite remarkable. Looking at the fellow she said: "You're a handsome man but this man (indicating me) is a beautiful man!"

Why did this young woman call me this? Because I had not tried to intrude myself on her, I had not tried to fondle her or treat her in any unseemly way; I did not use crude language. I treated her and her friend decently.

The young man came over to me later while the girls were dancing and said to me: "I have to admire you. I just don't understand how an older fellow like you can attract these girls while I can't get anywhere?" He desperately needed, like so many young men, a lesson in poetry and romance.

How many times in such an environment have I had the opportunity to deal with women in such a fashion as to give them some hope that decent men were still available to them, that they didn't have to put up with the crude, even vile behavior of men who treat them as sexual objects. My Birds book is filled with such illustrations from real life. And in spite of those who look down on those that frequent the bars and taverns, these places are filled with people who are good and decent and who seek the company of other decent men and women. Many have tried, without success, to find acceptance in various churches only to be turned away because they couldn't fit in. But these folks are a part of the reality of the poetry of life.

A very lovely lady came up to me the other night and said: "Don, you are the only man I have ever met who truly understands women!" This is probably the ultimate compliment a woman can pay a man. And she knows I attribute any understanding of this kind to my daughters. Everything I know about women, the softer and gentler things women were created for, my daughters taught me. How I wish these things had been learned by my association with the great number of other women I have known. But that would have required a virtuousness and faithfulness I never found in any of these other women.

As a consequence, it was my little girls who taught the necessary lessons a man can only learn by having daughters. And they never knew what they were teaching me as a man. That is the essence of the purity of such love and learning. I have never needed a woman who understood me, only one who would love me.

Like my soul brothers and kindred spirits, Emerson and Thoreau, the preeminent Transcendentalists, I struggle with myself and with God. For this reason, among others, I have not remarried in ten years now and am, consequently, alone. A Truth to live and die by, as per my Dark Dane counterpart Kierkegaard, does not promote a quiet spirit. On the contrary, it promotes a restlessness that women find hard to abide.

But such a Truth does not come by conscious thought processes. Like my brothers, there is the ultimate fact of God, to our minds, being essentially Love. That people live in turmoil and conflict, that the history of man is a history of war, the most unreasonable act of humankind, is a paradox of love.

I keep a private journal filled with my own doubts and struggles, the demons that torment my mind with uncertainties and am able, consequently, to present the poet's music to the world. And to those who would damn me for frequenting the less acceptable environs of society for the spice and reality of life, I pity your own lack of humanity and understanding!

I throw in the anecdotes of real life to point out the fact that men and women think and feel differently in many respects. The needs of each differ in several ways. And we all knew that, didn't we.

In this regard, my readers of some time will recall my project of the Mathematical Model of Human Behavior. It involves quantifying the emotions, among other things.

During the time of my doctoral studies, I began to take notice of a field of physics which was emerging called the study of *Chaos*. The concept being that no matter how chaotic something might appear, a pattern was discernible if enough data were inputted. It was interesting at the time and the present state of computer capabilities makes such a study possible in some most intriguing ways.

There are areas of human behavior that require a virtual astronomical amount of data to explain. So much so that only the most diligent researcher would have the heart to attempt discovery. The additional data coming from the field of genetic research promises to add greatly to our understanding of behavior as well, not to mention things like Dr. Philippe Bottero's work concerning rickettsiae and its impact on mental disease.

Because of so many new readers, I am compelled to provide the basic framework of this approach in helping to quantify and understand human behavior by supplying the following, brief outline. Please, as I asked, bear with me. I assure you it will be worth it in the end.

Having piqued my reader's interest in my work on a mathematical model of human behavior for quite some time, I'll give you some idea of its status and where it is going together with a more thorough understanding of what is involved in an attempt to make predictions of behavior based on scientific criteria. I'll do my utmost to make it, at least, interesting to you.

You don't necessarily have to be particularly adept in the field of mathematics to appreciate what Stephen Hawking has to offer in the subject. His best selling book, "A Brief History in Time", proves this point. I am going to lead the reader into, what I hope will be, like Hawking's book, some understanding of the "Mathematical Principles of Human Behavior", the program I have mentioned to which I am devoting so much of my own time and effort, utilizing some of his findings and speculations. But with a significant difference!

While I have taught high school and undergraduate classes in algebra, geometry and trigonometry, the fundamental theorem of calculus, integral (infinitesimal) and differential, is unique in its contribution to such a data base and is necessary to a degree of understanding the monumental complexities in human behavior.

Another useful tool is advanced statistics (the equivalent of a foreign language) together with an understanding of the mathematics of randomness. Few outside of the field of mathematics know how much effort has been expended by mathematicians in an attempt at pure randomness.

For example, it may not exist at all. A bullet fired straight into the air might be said to fall at random. Not so. If all the data were inputted, you would be able to predict, precisely, the exact impact point of the bullet. But the amount of data needed would be monumental.

It would take very little data to make such a prediction if the need required an impact point somewhere within ten acres. But if the requirement were a prediction within ten centimeters you get the concept. The variables to be factored mount in complexity depending on the precision of predictability required.

It is just because of the daunting number of variables that economists, for example, find agreement difficult. Many a beautiful structure has fallen due to the unyielding stubbornness of an unknown or unconsidered fact. The fatal flaw of the lack of fossil evidence in the theory of evolution concerning mammalian sexuality is a case in point.

Fortunately, my doctoral program included such studies, particularly concerning the variables involved in predictability and trend forecasting. There is a great deal of mathematics and many mathematical principles involved with the study of human behavior. And with the introduction of genetics and the present capabilities of computers, the whole field of psychology is changing dramatically making it ever more essential that the gap between the behavioral and social sciences and the hard sciences be bridged. My mathematical model is an attempt to bridge that gap.

I was talking with a man in one of the local taverns when the subject of semantics came to mind. The true intellectual does not have a larger than ordinary vocabulary because of ego or, like pseudo-intellectualism, to impress others. It is a necessary tool to define and make clear. For example, words like pejorative and adumbration are essential tools of the trade for the intellectual and poet.

Semantic differentials of language are necessary to distinguish and clarify meanings. And clarity of understanding is absolutely essential in order to make the predictability of human behavior sensible. So it requires a mastery of language and mathematics to undertake such a study and make it comprehensible to others.

But I will try my best to keep it simple enough for the math-avoiders to get a grasp of the concept. As I used to tell my students, just keep in mind the fact that you can only do four things with any numbers or variables; you can add, subtract, divide or multiply them. As you will recall from your earliest days of basic arithmetic, these four procedures group into two in which the one provides the check on the other, the inverse operation if you will. No matter the complexity of the mathematical system, the complexity of the problem, this is all you can do in solving mathematical problems from the most elemental to the most esoteric.

In trying to assign a specific value that incorporates the use of both negative and positive factors, the number line is conceptualized with 0 as a point where the one passes through an accepted value of infinity to the other. Whether the vectors of a chart where the rays intersect, the areas, positive and negative, or the assigned values of variables in an equation, the philosophy of something we do not understand or have the capacity or mathematics of even imagining, that point of infinitude, called absolute zero, serves as a practical point of transition, in other words, it is a workable concept.

Workability, however, should never be the sole criteria of considering mathematical possibilities. Theory has a most important place in mathematics, even theory that evolves from imagining possibilities philosophically.

For example it may well be, as Hawking says, that it is impossible to travel at the speed of light based on his supposition that at that speed one would be into the realm of time travel and no one has come back from the future to prove the reality of achieving such speed. But, conversely, one would have to reach such a velocity, by our present mathematical concepts at least, to disprove Hawking; hence, at least for now, philosophical. But the practical limitation of a thing does not cheat us of the ability to imagine its possibilities and the philosophies that arise from such imaginings.

As a result, I take exception to the great mathematician's closed system of the universe, his in-progress theory of reality in which ... the universe would be completely self-contained, neither created nor destroyed - it would just be. As entrancing as I find the theory it not only fails to do justice to a Prime Cause, to the Christian this is God Himself, but it fails to do justice to the philosophical realities of imagination. It might be well to consider Heisenberg's Principle of Uncertainty in this context as well.

But I do understand the necessity of Hawking having to think in his own way of such things because, in his own words, asking what happened before creation is meaningless. Understood from his point of view, he has no other choice. That does not rob those like me of those philosophical realities that, if Hawking were able to intrude himself, would allow of a far larger universe than he pragmatically rejects as a part of his own philosophy.

I think Hawking cheats himself by seeing the stars as cold, still, lifeless, of not having the poetic connection of Creation to draw his mind into other worlds with a more precise science than the one in which he seeks ultimate answers. But I thank God for the genius of Hawking and his ability to seek answers beyond the realm of most common speculations at the same time granting him the sympathy of someone who would intrude such speculations into those other worlds.

I do wonder if, with all his exceeding rare genius, he considers what possibilities exist in even having the capacity to entertain such questions as *Where and how did it all begin* as more than a rhetorical question or trying to enclose the answer in some neat, presumed mathematically precise (more likely imprecise) box?

Such a presumption that excludes a Prime Cause is, in my opinion, likely to fail. If I can succeed in the mathematical model of human behavior it might well cause Hawking and others to take another look at their self-imposed limitations of philosophical data.

In seeking that Holy Grail of all physics, the Grand Unification Theory which would explain The All, it may very well be, to entertain any hope of such, that a much larger part will have to be played by philosophy than is usually the case. By that I mean that some degree of understanding of infinity would have to be at least conceptualized. This of course falls, at present, entirely into the field of the philosophy of physics. This is an area of mathematics that has not received its due attention. Yet who can deny the longing to fill that void of the soul's cry for understanding while looking at the stars, the only sensible measure of infinity which presents itself to us, that longing for a seemingly intuited immortality which the stars seem to betoken?

At present, the philosophical properties of space, matter and time are workable. I assign the term philosophical because of the lack of the ability of our present mathematics to definitively discriminate. The infinitesimal calculus only assigns a point, not an understanding of that point. Such a limitation forces us to assign labels in lieu of real understanding, and still it remains for "Life" to be understood before any complete equation for a Unification Theory.

But Time, for example, by such labeling, is easily understood as consisting of past, present and future. It is not essential for our present requirements of workability to actually understand the calculus of that exact point of transition where the present becomes the past or the future. Nor does the need of workability suffer our not being able to precisely vector length, breadth and height in regards to matter or the space it occupies.

If there were an intense enough need to know, we might well be spending billions on trying to discover the physics of differentiating the mind from the astronomical amount of seemingly, random, chaotic (actually, I believe, symphonic/fractal) patterns of its electro/chemical biology.

But determining a pattern in the firing of the neurons of the brain would not be unlike determining the pattern in a supernova, an exploding star. A thing of such beauty, yet, requiring an astronomical amount of data to discern the sensible order in the seeming chaotic activity involved. Now, rather than exhaust one's inventory of invective, maledicta and just plain, ordinary, everyday cuss words at such seeming esoterica, I'll do my best to speak good old plain American as Phil Harris would say.

All definitions require proscribed parameters, for example; a cup. Now if you go into a store and ask the clerk to sell you a cup he is going to ask you "What kind of cup?" This assumes you are not in the lingerie section in which case it would be a question of size, not kind; little weak humor there.

No, I am not trying to be fiendishly clever; you will have to be somewhat precise in your description of just what kind of cup you are in need of, coffee, tea or milk, ceramic, glass, china, plastic, patterned, plain, large, small, etc. Reminds me of an old Jack Benny skit where he goes in to buy a pair of shoelaces. The most ordinary things can, indeed, become quite complex depending on the variables involved, and if the individual is practiced in making mountains of molehills …

But the use of the calculus methodology is not an exercise in either *reductio ad absurdam* or impossible. Nor will I resort to the Greek analog of the runner who never finishes the race, philosophically. It is a means of precision of definition, and like the concepts of *Weltschmerz* and *Weltanschauung*, must start with a corporate meaning and become ever more and more precise in the mathematical model of human behavior.

The intended use of an item is often sufficient for its definition. You go into a restaurant and order a cup of coffee; you have every reason to expect it to be served in a coffee cup, not on a saucer or plate. Further, while you may get a spoon in concert with the cup of coffee, you don't expect to receive it in attendance with a knife and fork.

Such things are practiced definitions and usually brook little need of elaboration. People know what you mean when you say cup within the context of the use of the word.

We use the words Love and Hate as definitive of certain emotions. But we do so in the knowledge that such words and their corresponding concepts often fail to convey precise meaning, precise definition. Now if we conceptualize a number line with -10 to +10 and assign the most extreme form of Hate the number -10 and the most extreme form of Love the value +10 with absolute 0, the transition point between the two, we could assign a numeric value to all those emotions which fall between the two extremes, 0 being, let's say, the point of ambivalence.

Again, we are forced to labels in lieu of understanding. For example the concept that pure ambivalence exists between love and hate; lacking specifics, we are often forced to generalities. Now while generalities are essential in order to progress from the general to the specific, as in ten acres vs. ten centimeters, there are many potential pitfalls in the transition. Many a beautiful structure has fallen due to the resistance of a stubborn fact that gets in the way of theory.

It is easy to predict human behavior within certain broad parameters. For example, people would prefer to be rich rather than poor, beautiful or handsome instead of ugly, healthy rather than unhealthy, etc. It is easy to predict certain choices when the circumstances are restricted such as those of inmates in a prison.

If all the controlling circumstances are understood, human behavior becomes quite predictable. Historically, human nature remains the same throughout. People still do the same things for the same reasons they always have. People still want the same things they always have.

The complexities arise when choices become ever broader. For example, how account for the unhappiness of those who seem to have it all? Extrapolated to a society that is so advanced beyond the essentials of grubbing in the soil for daily sustenance, the growing sophistication of thought processes that result in a technological society must be confronted.

And such confrontation becomes cruelly ugly when the disparity between the haves and the have nots grows as disproportionate as it has in America. Class struggles, class warfare is assured when such a thing leads to the suffering of the poor while the rich and powerful, when a bloated, corrupt government itself takes the attitude of The Public Be Damned!

I seldom disagree with Marilyn Vos Savant, an extraordinarily intelligent woman I admire greatly. But I take exception to one of her conclusions. When asked what she considered the single, greatest threat to America she replied: The hyphenated American! I would ask her to reconsider and ponder the question of the lack of morality leading to the plague of adultery, divorce and their devastating impact on America and the future of its posterity. And, intelligent as she is, Marilyn might help to sort out the hugely complex equation involved in the following remarks.

"Autobiography of a Face" is the story of an ugly woman, Lucy Grealy. Due to a rare disease, Ewing's sarcoma, Lucy had to have surgery, radiation and chemotherapy. The result was a dreadful disfigurement of her face. Ugly. Bernard-Henri Livy remarks in Men and Women: "A Philosophical Conversation" that we're living in a time that is setting ugliness up as one of its fundamental taboos.

I travel a good deal. I mix with a lot of people from many different areas of life; including the casinos, bars and taverns. As a man, and particularly an unmarried man, I notice women, especially beautiful women. That could be a misleading statement. You have to read my Birds book to get the real meaning of it. I see women as a romantic and a poet, yes. But I'm still a man. And, like a man, I'm attracted to beautiful women. That is the nature of men. It is not a flaw in character, it is human nature. And women are attracted to handsome men. Neither is that a flaw of character.

Fortunately for both men and women, since neither men nor women are usually beautiful or handsome, as we grow in maturity other values come into focus and the emphasis increasingly becomes the genuine character of the individual as important in relationships and often transcends the merely physical attributes. But beautiful remains beautiful and ugly remains ugly—men and women will always wish they were handsome or beautiful; they will always want a partner who is beautiful or handsome.

In regard to Lucy, I quote a syndicated columnist, Patricia McLaughlin, who in writing of her and repeating a point about which I have written so very much said:

"We teach girls that how they look is who they are, and we teach them to worry about it, and we do it very well. Can any other nation (America) boast that, at any given time, two out of three of its teen-aged girls are dieting, along with nearly half of its 9-year-olds? Can any nation match the number of different hairdressings available to us, or the money we spend on makeup and treatment products, or our variety of weight-loss programs, or the number of cosmetic surgical procedures we pay for?

"The carefully cultivated worries of girls and women, from 9-year-olds who're afraid they're fat to grown women who despise their breasts or noses or hips or thighs, support a personal appearance industry that's probably (in fact it is) bigger than the industrial output of some Western nations."

To quote Lucy herself: "When my face gets fixed, then I'll start living." And that folks is the heart-wrenching point! But that is life and that is human nature.

I have written much about the obverse, the curse of beauty in our society that plagues some women. So much so that I have made the statement that there are two classes of people who never know who their real friends are: Wealthy men and beautiful women. Such women become, inordinately, the prey of predatory men. And they are the envy of other women.

As a poet I look at the truth of human behavior and deal with it factually. As a romantic, I seek the beautiful in all women. But, as with Lucy, if an entire society has succeeded in making some definition of ugly a taboo of that society, we all suffer the results.

Therefore, America has become a nation where women grow old and wrinkled, of no value whereas men become mature and seasoned. Hence, the *Jennifer Syndrome*, older men getting younger women, plays into the hands of such a taboo.

At this point, the variables become truly daunting. I have written a book on this subject and reams of essays that only touch the tip of the iceberg.

It would be a life's work, several lives in fact, to delve into the variables involved.

For example, there is a mechanism at work in human behavior that reaches out beyond our world to the stars. But only a very advanced society relieved of the primary needs of life is able to do such reaching as a practical exercise of the mind. And such a society becomes increasingly preoccupied with beauty. And this can become quite a perverse thing.

So, as a true poet, romantic and a man, I not only deal with trying to separate the diabolical from the divine in the beauty of women and God's creation, I deal with mathematics which is rightly called the *Universal Language*. The principles of mathematics cut through all cultural distinctives and provide common ground to all humanity.

I taught many math classes in schools. The schools, as I have said repeatedly, form another part of the equation of the destruction of family and family values. Apart from the home itself, no other institution so directly impacts the lives and values of our children and young people, our whole society.

Coming from the real world of industry and business, areas where the rewards were based on the empirical functions of punching a clock, doing the work and being rewarded with a paycheck, I wasn't prepared for the academic, ivory tower mind-set of those who had no idea of what earning a living by producing was all about.

Consequently, my years in academia were ones of constant frustration, futility and, eventually, confrontation against a system that not only refused reality, but really couldn't distinguish between earning a living and teaching. I didn't make many friends in the educational establishment.

It may seem to be a gross simplification but I must say that the failure in our nation to produce the needed scientists and professionals for industry and business is the inability of the educational establishment to deal with reality. This is evidenced in one most important respect among others: failure to teach the multiplication tables.

Huh?

I know, I'd better explain that outrageous statement. And I will. And I'll get back to ugly vs. beautiful and tie things together.

When the leadership in the universities stupidly decided rote memorization was bad for children, we lost a generation of children who could no longer do arithmetic, spell or write sensibly. Literature suffered from the failure to memorize great works.

While virtually no sensible person would deny that the self-discipline of memorization is an excellent stimulus to brain function and necessary to the learning of many skills, the educational establishment decided it wasn't necessary! So much for sensible when it came to the schools.

I've written so much on this appalling con-job and tragedy of the educational elite foisted on unsuspecting and trusting parents I won't belabor it here. Suffice it to say the situation will never be reversed by, insanely, asking that same educational hierarchy, the people who created the problem, for solutions. And especially by asking those with worthless, basket-weaving Doctorates in Education, a degree that would embarrass any truly educated person!

Freely admitting that the Schools of Education are an embarrassment, a laughing stock and tragic joke on every university campus won't change things either. The point has been made in study after study that the only fix is scrapping them and starting over. Kind of like the solution to a corrupt Congress.

But to return to my outrageous statement about the multiplication tables; no one in the math field would disagree that the times tables are the foundation of all math from the most basic to the most abstract. Failure to know these building blocks dooms one to math failure. And by know, I mean instinctively, you don't have to stop and think about the answer to 8x7. It is there instantly, instinctively. That ability is acquired by rote memorization.

It helped immeasurably to point out the fact to my pupils that there are only four things you can do with numbers: You can multiply, divide, add or subtract them. This is true no matter how simple or esoteric the problem.

I would teach my pupils to think in terms of 3 times 3 = 9 and 9 divided by 3=3. This introduced the inverse operation where the one calculation would be proved by its opposite corollary. The beauty of the balance of thinking of the times tables in this fashion made it much easier for pupils to retain what they learned.

Only the A students I had in math classes knew their times tables instinctively and in this fashion. The B pupils had to stop and think. The C pupils simply didn't know them.

I turned many a C and B pupil into a math literate by insisting they go back to the beginning and memorize those tables. I caught a lot of hell from administrators and others by taking this hard-nosed approach to math literacy but it worked!

I'm about to catch a lot of hell from millions of men and women for insisting they go back to the mathematical corollary of human behavior in respect to the foundation of the relationships between men and women, a foundation as essential to successful relationships, successful families as that of those times tables to mathematics. That foundation is fidelity in marriage, a fidelity that recognizes and honors the compatibility of differences and, forsaking all others, cleaves to each other with that total life trust and commitment necessary to a successful marriage.

And while many won't like the message, stop and think before you kill the messenger. In writing on this theme, I have encountered much interest from readers along with much with which they disagree. But, the disagreements usually arise from the mind-set of a society that has encouraged so-called equality that has done nothing but make a bad situation worse by attempts to eliminate biological and historical standards that will not brook foolish mechanisms of men and women to circumvent.

I have written that when what is best and noble that is peculiar to each sex is recognized and honored, when the compatibility of differences is encouraged, we have the best of worlds. When those differences are used and abused, as in the perversions of pornography, adultery and divorce we have hell on earth!

To emphasize my point, I become anecdotal once more. People will remember a story while they may forget statistical data. The facts may miss the point and people are notorious for excusing the sins of others in an attempt to justify their own.

I have worked within the system in our country called Child Protective Services. I wasn't there two weeks before someone asked if I were a spy or a plant? Why? Because I was different from the others in the system. In what way? I was over qualified.

And it was my qualifications in so many areas of life that enabled me to very quickly determine how dreadful this system of the bureaucracy of government is! Few government agencies with the exception of the American Gestapo, the I.R.S. and a so-called public education system, have such awesome power to destroy families and children with virtually no accountability.

But CPS is a grotesque, mutated reaction to the destruction of morality in our nation. When families cannot have a normal home, when a dysfunctional society rewards unmarried mothers with larger welfare checks for more illegitimate births and penalizes a home with a married, legitimate father and mother working to better themselves and care for their children, the fiendish insanity of such a system must collapse upon its own head!

And then we wonder at the increasing number of bums and riff raff, so-called men who leech off the welfare checks of unwed mothers. And the dope and the booze are natural ingredients of such a deviant lifestyle; a lifestyle that a perverted and deviant government brought about while the universities, churches and so many good citizens raised no voice of dissent!

The very perversity, the travesty of truth, honesty and justice in the face of such insanity of laws is not lost on even the most simple. And just how does a society come to such an insane point? By ignoring the facts of history and human nature, by defying every ordinance of God if you will, by countenancing sexual license in the name of equality and freedom! Who pays the price for such equality and freedom? The children, by the multiplied millions!

So it is that in the name of such equality and freedom divorce is easy to obtain, adultery and fornication are treated as archaic jokes, the purity of womanhood and the best of manhood are buried under the failure of men to maintain the proper head of household status and their failure to accept their responsibility for moral standards and leadership.

The prophets of God have always had a lonely occupation. A society never wants to hear of its needs of repentance; whether a man like Socrates or Jeremiah, when the sins of a nation become such as those that threaten the collapse of that nation, those sins must be confronted.

But it is never the politicians or professional religionists of a nation that come forth with that message of repentance. It is always brought by those men and women with nothing to lose, men and women whose hearts burn with the message out of shame for conditions among their people and love for others, especially the children who have no voice or choice in the sins of their fathers and mothers.

I made many obvious points in last month's essay. For example, we all know that the family is the foundation, the backbone of all viable civilizations. We know that any nation that fails to cherish its children has no future as a nation, nor does it deserve one! Knowing these things how is it that a nation like America comes to such a tragic and sorry pass that it behaves as though it actually hates children?

The great, Russian poets describe America as a nation without a soul. We made the Faustian agreement with the Dark Side and the Glory of Evil in exchange for material wealth and material success, for abandonment to the lust of the flesh in all its most perverse manifestations.

Multiplied millions around the world will be alienated by the message of this prophet because those millions in other nations are as guilty as America of the very same things. It is a global guilt that must be faced wherever these sins, these crimes against humanity, against the children of the world hold sway.

When I said, last month, that no issue is as important to world harmony and world peace as the relationship between men and women, it surprised a number of people. But they had not thought of this in respect to the need for hope of a future for children. Men and women work at their best in harmony when the goal is a better future for their children; when the motives of life are family and all that such an entity means and promises, men, women and children pull together.

A government, the laws of a nation must have its roots and on-going motives and actions oriented to the preservation of its posterity. What is the purpose of a government, a society otherwise? When things threaten the future of a nation, those things must be confronted. It is not enough to discern evil; action is required.

For example, the National Education Association (NEA) at its annual convention in July adopted a resolution to promote the teaching of perversion as acceptable in the nation's schools. The resolution glorifies homosexuals and the NEA has issued a proclamation for the celebration of a Gay and Lesbian History Month honoring perverts in the schools. Nothing surprises me coming out of this morally bankrupt and corrupt organization. As I used to tell parents when I was a teacher and administrator: Things aren't as bad as you think in the schools, they are far worse!

The immutable fact of history that no nation has ever been able to survive such perversion, perversion so destructive to children and families seems to go unnoticed by the so-called educated elite! They have far more in common with the Devil and his demons than civilized people. It is not enough to discern evil; action is required.

A curious statistic: There were over 24,000 homicides in America last year. But there were over 32,000 suicides. People are murdering themselves in this country at a greater rate than they are murdering each other! And far too many of these suicides are teenagers! This evidences a loss of hope.

America is known as a violent nation. But I have to wonder to what extent perversions such as divorce and homosexuality and the perversion of distorted teaching of history promotes such a loss of hope, especially among our young people?

A man who delves too deeply into the dark issues of life, especially when there is no hope of joy or happiness in his life, becomes like Kierkegaard who wrote: "I have just returned from a party of which I was the life and soul; wit poured from my lips, everyone laughed and admired me - but I went away and wanted to shoot myself ... One thought succeeds another; just as one is thought and I want to write it down, comes a new one - hold on, catch it - madness - insanity!"

Next month I will expand on SK's comments. Suffice it to say that if he and Thoreau had married, neither would have died so young nor have been so given over to the Dark Side. That will also require some elaboration to explain.

Like SK, I had a young friend with a genius for music that, after being the life of the party, went home and hung himself. Why? Next month. It isn't the brilliance or genius of men like SK or HDT that makes them quotable or memorable. It is the very way in which they lived their lives and the lessons taught by such lives.

Both SK and HDT would shoot themselves. But they died early enough in life as it was. And they died early because they did not love women and never married. It is in this respect that the comparison between these two worthies and me fails.

My credentials as an academic, a philosopher and romantic, a poet if you will, are well established. But I have outlasted these great thinkers; I have lived, and live, because I love women and children. I had daughters who taught me the lessons these two men never learned, nor could have learned without women in their lives; especially daughters who teach a man things he can learn in no other way. But granted the man must have a father's heart to learn such things, things of the softer and gentler natures of women who yearn to have men respond to such things with the strength of manly gentleness, understanding and compassion.

I love being surrounded by the touches of women in my life, their scents and peculiar, though enchanting to me, ways of doing so many things differently than I do as a man. I love the distinctive, peculiar clothing of women from the most intimate of underthings to the most elaborate of outer adornment. And women were created for adornment as long as it is in good taste.

Those times when a woman is intimate in my life, I thrill to shirts and blouses in a closet with buttons on the wrong side, to the shoes and stockings that are in such contrast to the things I use as a man. It's a blessing in my life when I see her shoes or slippers next to mine, to consider the nearly mystical difference in such things.

This, I tell myself, is the real mystery and romance of the compatibility of differences between myself as a man and the female of the species, that She gender that brings such joy and intrigue into my life as I explore all the differences from the most subtle of clothing and feminine articles of every description to the most intriguing processes of the feminine psyche and thought processes.

I love seeing the cosmetics and array of feminine articles with which these delightful creatures prepare themselves for the attraction of a man's eyes. It's marvelous to see a bathroom crowded with the potions and articles of a woman's presence in the home.

I thoroughly enjoy the elaborate ceremonials that go into the most intimate preparations of women from toenails and fingernails to that crowning glory of their hair. And they do these things for us men! But do men really appreciate such efforts for their benefit? Not usually. In fact, I know too many men for whom such things are, unbelievably, a source of complaint!

A very beautiful, statuesque blonde was recently running her fingers through my hair. She had come over to me and said: "Don, your hair looks windblown." My immediate thought was to tell her it was nothing but a cunning ploy on my part to entice this gorgeous woman to do just what she did, run her fingers through my hair and play with it in an attempt to put it in place.

Was that what she was really trying to do? Not hardly. It was a civil, polite, sexual pretext for her to touch me in a socially acceptable, intimate way and thrill my heart with her closeness and touch. Now that is a romantic moment imbued with all the sexual play undertones, so civilly, romantically understated that the best of men and women appreciate.

This beautiful woman and I didn't have to say anything explicit. The understanding and appreciation of such a gentle encounter between us was simply there. We understood the gentle magic of the moment, as two romantic and sensitive people should. Tragically, I know too many who do not understand such things and the sharing of stories like this is like casting your pearls before swine.

People read my essays because I bring things down to where we actually live. I tell the stories in common language using common examples from every day life to which we can all relate. I have already said that the political battle being fought against the unholy U.N. and its One World Government movement, many good organizations and people are carrying on the battle being fought for the soul of America, for freedom and liberty throughout the world. That I have had a part in starting this confrontation with Caesar and a bloatedly corrupt government is sufficient for me.

My writing now must concentrate on the single most important aspect of the warfare, the relationship between men and women, children and families. That is my calling and mission as a man and a poet.

In respect to the evils of divorce and adultery that must be confronted in our nation and others, I want to tell you a story. This story is a tragedy. It is a tragedy repeated countless times a day across America and throughout the world. It is different in some respects from the ordinary however, different enough to use it to cut to the heart of the matter; and different because I know the people and children so well personally.

It is a story about a close friend of many years and his family; now, his ex-family. He asked that if there were ever a need for my use of his story to help others, to please do so.

Here is one man's story, told in the first person for the benefit of the reader, of the destruction, the murder, if you will, of an American family. When you get through reading it, you will understand my choosing it as an example of this most tragic condition of American society and its contribution to the destruction of a generation of our young people and their hope of a future:

Well, I'm in Lake Tahoe; and under most unusual circumstances. I'm not here to gamble or go skiing. I'll visit all the casinos and watch the people throw money in the slots and drink, toss dice and drink, play various card games and drink.

There are two things parents usually tell their children early on: "Don't drink and don't gamble." Both are excellent advice.

Of course there are a lot of Beautiful People in this posh resort area. As a mere man, I'm usually particularly observant of the beautiful girls and women. I notice how many are with men because of money. How do I know this; because the men are old and ugly, the girls young and beautiful.

Yes, this is a place where money flows as freely as the liquor. I watch as one young woman, in a very short time, goes through a thousand dollars at a $5 slot, shrugs her shoulders and walks away. I see one man lose $15,000 at craps in less than 25 minutes.

But this is Tahoe and, as with Reno, Las Vegas and Atlantic City, people are here to gamble and have fun. A confessed alcoholic confides he is a regular. He dropped about $3,000 before hitting it lucky and won $9,000. He said he was almost ready to go to Gamblers Anonymous but Lady Luck intervened. Then he said: "I know I'll lose it all. I can't keep money."

He was right. I watched as, in less than one hour, he lost over $6,000 of his winnings. There is an old and true saying in the Gambling business: "The house never loses." Of course not! This is a business. The design and elaborate decor of the large gambling (they prefer the word Gaming) establishments is meant to be seductive of quick and easy riches. At this they are eminently successful.

In towns that never sleep and the action is 24 hours a day, non-stop, where neon light pervades the night with it's own seductive allure, you step into virtual cathedrals alive with the sights and sounds of the promise of sudden wealth at the turn of a card, the pull of a handle or one toss of the dice.

But I'm not here to get a story on a town whose wealth is based on people's desire for quick and easy riches via the siren call of gambling. I'm not here to find fault with those who love to gamble or the institutions dedicated to separating them from their money. I'm here to try to help my son. (To be continued next month).

***

The following pertains to last month's international mailing by Alice Hill and me and our efforts to reach the global community.

We received many letters from people in other nations and I wish there were space to acknowledge them all. But one letter from Professor Andrej Paulin of Slovenia pretty well sums up the sentiment of all in which this good man said: Love must be in my viewpoint extended to Love, Respect, and Understanding which is valid both, for relations between women and men, and for relations between men, groups of men, and nations. What believing in God understand as God is for me the GOODNESS in men and women, i.e. love, respect understanding, tolerance, patience, which must be cultivated to overcome the evil.

Alice remarked in reference to Professor Paulin's letter: "Too many religions want to take over God's world and run it by claiming they have a priority on God and His knowledge. This is still God's world and all of the people in it. God is the world's Captain and He loves all of us as long as we carry His love in our hearts for all of His creation. Your letter is much appreciated Professor Paulin and so are your thoughts.

From Alice:

"Hello everyone: If only I could write to all of you personally or be able to mention each of you in this publication. I do appreciate all the efforts, kindness and good wishes so many people sent to Dr. Heath and me.

"A special thank you is sent to Helen Shafenberg from my hometown of Kingfisher, Oklahoma. Helen has always done wonderful, lovely things to help hundreds and hundreds of people through the years. These many people include me and I love you. Helen, I hope every thing is going as well as can be expected for Ernest who had a severe stroke last summer.

"Dr. Mary Myers has been so thoughtful of me. Thank you for your card and for your prayers and love. Ruth Mooley of Tunnel Hills, Georgia, recently sent an appreciated update on things down her way. Thanks Ruth.

"Lois Wells from New Zealand was thoughtful enough to send both Dr. Heath and myself greetings from her part of the world. I had the pleasure of being with Lois in the music program of the International Congress in Sydney and Dr. Heath and I look forward to seeing her in San Francisco this summer.

"Years ago I had a group of children called Los Artistas. These children were very poor and did not have the money to belong to groups requiring fees, dues or other expenses. They paid dues however. Each day they had to do or say something to make someone feel better and each day they had to try to make one little bit of their surroundings cleaner and nicer than it was before.

"I had very dedicated and happy members out doing their good deeds. There will be more news about this next time as we start groups based on this concept.

"Please, Lady Gloria Clayton from Australia and Craig Burgess from New Jersey, U.S.A. Contact either Dr. Heath or myself. We want to start Craig's Adopt a Grandparent program here in this country.

"We have not, as yet, heard from Dr. Bottero in France but hope to soon. His work is so very important and it will help millions of people in years to come. We will share any news of this as soon as it is available.

"I will add that I love all people, as does Dr. Heath, especially those who are fighting for freedom for all people for there can be no lasting freedom anywhere until all people are free.

"For the first time to be available in the summer of 1996, by Arturo Burciaga: the newest member of A. Hill and Associates. A new approach to learning English as a second language in the form of a home study course designed especially for Spanish speaking students who want to learn a second language.

"After 20 years of teaching and helping students to acquire this most difficult skill, Arturo Burciaga, the teacher who was able to learn English with a minimum of a 3rd grade education came to this country in 1962 and, without knowing English was able to develop a system of transcribing every word into a phonetically correctly pronounced word.

"He attended the local schools in Oxnard form 7th grade on. By 1974 he was using the new system he developed to make the task of learning English an easier one for his students.

"During his 20 years of teaching and research, he has decided to market a home study course that will make learning English easier, faster and entertaining."

CHAPTER SEVEN

THE OKIE INTELLECTUAL

DECEMBER 1995

As per Wodehouse, the great Musicals were the last time poets worked in America. Among these great works, I continue to find much of the poetry and music lacking in contemporary America. In some, like "Fiddler On The Roof", I also find a good deal of practical theology and philosophy.

For example, when Topol in his role as Tevye, asks God if it would have spoiled some vast, eternal plan to have been made a rich man, he expresses the genuine sentiment of most of us. And, as Tevye well points out, while it is no disgrace to be poor, it isn't any great honor either. And we cheer.

When his horse pulls up lame, he asks: "Lord, what have you got against my horse? Me, I can understand you taking offense; but my horse? I think when You are too quiet up there; you are considering some mischief against me." Another rather practical question of the Almighty; and we laugh.

We get to the line that "even a poor tailor deserves a little happiness!" And we applaud. But when poor Tevye says, pointing to his wife: "Lord, send us (men) the cure. We already have the sickness!" Ah, gentle reader, it is here that poor Tevye and I part ways. As I do with men like Soren Kierkegaard and Henry David Thoreau.

At 77-years of age, Ann Landers was recently asked what she considered the number one problem in America. Echoing my own findings and writings, she replied: "Family problems. It has always been that way." But I would add, the problems are the result of the problems in the relationships between men and women and that, friends, is a global and historical fact.

One of my favorite people is Sam Clemens. His rare wit and sense of humor are great gifts and continue to sustain me in much of my own writing. He made a point, once, concerning the deplorable lack among the clergy of a knowledge of poker. I have to agree. If only priests and ministers had such interest and skill, they might become more human, more tolerant of the weaknesses and foibles of all us lesser humans.

I take great satisfaction in my ability as a minister, among other things, to engage in an occasional hand or two among friends. Sam would be proud of me, holding out against the tide of criticism of my colleagues in this regard.

But I would add to Sam's comments on this lack among those that wear their collars backwards another skill (along with a deficiency in regards to enjoying a good cigar or pipe) in which they seem woefully unknowledgeable and deficient: Shooting Pool.

Robert Preston's memorable performance in "The Music Man" made the unforgettable point that "Trouble in River City ... starts with a T and that rhymes with P and that stands for Pool!" But Mr. Preston was playing the role of a con man. And, while Billiards might be called a gentleman's game, just like a friendly hand of five card draw, the poor Pool aficionado, especially those addicted to 8-ball, is left with little defense but that he enjoys the game.

Now my ability to give someone a good game of eight ball might be misconstrued as the evidence of a miss-spent youth; far from it. Those who have read my Confessions and Reflections of an Okie Intellectual or Weedpatcher books know I was raised with all the good and civil manners of a Southern Gentleman of the Old School.

But it's funny how easily one is misunderstood when you walk into a bar or pool parlor with your custom stick, take off your coat, roll up your sleeves and go to work at a pool table; especially if your work place is Slugger's Saloon.

Now I love the big table at Arlie's Club. But there have been some tournaments going on at Slugger's where the players are good, friendly folks and most play just for the fun and camaraderie. No one breaks their stick over their knee (or another player's head as in some joints I have been in) over a muffed shot.

Not that there aren't a couple who seem to take the game as a matter of life or death or a challenge to their manhood. And I'm not excluding the ladies. Some of the best shooters I have met have been women and they seem to enjoy it without getting too serious about it and having more fun in the process than the majority of men.

But most of the folks, like me, are playing for the fun of it. I've yet to find any game so significant that it's a do or die thing. Games are for fun, not the serious business of life itself. But much about life and people can be studied and learned by the games people play and just how seriously they take them. I've known people who would draw blood over Monopoly. And where money is at stake, some have been shot for two bucks!

Games and entertainment play an important role in many people's lives, however. All work and no play can be devastating. While such things should never rule your life, we all need an outlet for artistic expression or play of some kind. But when Sports is King and Entertainment is Queen in a society, that society is in deep trouble!

When I am not on the road, the Kern River Valley is the closest thing I have to a place called home. My readers in other countries like France and Germany will forgive me if I become parochial in the anecdotes I relate concerning this small corner of the world. The lessons, political and philosophical, remain quite global and international in respect to all humanity and I know you will agree. Thank you all for bearing with me.

Over the years, I have made many friends here. Due to my writing and some media exposure, I have become well known to the residents of this small area. And I continue to make the lives of some of the folks a little more surreal by my activities and writings.

For example, some of my readers will recall the wedding ceremony I performed for the couple that met in a bar and wished to be married there among their friends. I did say, at the time, it seemed to me to be more like that marriage feast in Cana than most I have solemnized in other surroundings. Well, the opportunity presented itself once more for me to do the honors for a wonderful couple, the brother of a close friend of mine, Dean, and his lady.

The couple had all the necessary paperwork and it only remained for me to meet them at their home and tie the knot. What was unusual about all this? Dean had introduced the couple to me in a bar. And after the ceremony we gathered at the tavern where the newlyweds bought me a drink and I gladly accepted in toasting them. All Baptists will cringe at this but it underscores my problems with those religious people who are too spiritual to meet others on the playing field of the real world.

Recently I wrote a letter of appreciation to a special lady, a close friend who has done so much to brighten the lives of so many people. Little did I know she would take it to the local paper and that they would print it!

PINEY

I have been blessed with a goodly number of friends. Some of these folks like Joyce, Dean, Butch, B.J., Lydia, Greta and so many others I have met at Arlie's Club in Lake Isabella. They brighten my life on many occasions and especially on Friday and Saturday nights when Oscar and Jerry supply some of the best music to be heard anywhere.

Among all these friends, there are a few like Piney, a lovely Hawaiian lady, who always has a ready smile and warm welcome whenever I enter the Club. Piney is one of those rare ladies that make a man feel good just to be around.

Always gracious and kind to me, we will chat and, on occasion, we even dance together. She is a great dancer.

In my travels around the country, I seldom meet many like Piney or my friends at Arlie's. But I tell others about them and, especially those like this gracious little lady, who mean so much in my life.

It is people like Piney that give me hope and inspiration in my writing and my work with others, especially children, hope that there are more like this lovely little lady who make my own efforts in confronting the evil of evil men and women worth the fight.

Thanks Piney, for being such a gracious lady and such a good friend to me. D. H. (End)

Many people came to me or called after this letter appeared in the paper to thank me for writing it. Many expressed the sentiment that it was long overdue for someone to do such a thing. The question that raised in my mind was why hadn't anyone done so?

I raise the issue in my Birds book that the love letters and flowers (if they were there at all in the beginning) usually stop shortly after marriage. Why? But you have to read the book for my answer. Suffice it to say that men desperately need lessons in poetry and romance toward the fair sex.

Why is it that such a small thing, a note of appreciation for the kindness of others, is left undone in so many cases? How many of us should have sent the flowers and notes, should have said the things we wish we had said after a friend or loved one is gone?

For example, the Holiday Season is upon us once more. Friends and families will share Thanksgiving and Christmas. The Prince of Peace will be remembered in spite of all the crass commercialism of a hedonistic society and world at large.

And, for some, the Holidays will be a time of mourning. As with July 4th, the anniversary of the death of my eldest daughter, Diana, and the loss of my family on Thanksgiving ten-years ago due to an adulterous wife, and many will be the remaining, living victims of the drunk driver or some other agent of grief and tragedy.

We have had a rash of tragedies recently in the valley. Two elderly men were killed on the highway. An elderly drunk who had no business even driving drunk or sober killed a young boy! That the drunk was killed as well is no consolation to the family and friends of this boy.

One of the most striking, extraordinarily beautiful, sensitive and intelligent women I know came to me and said tearfully: "Don, we have to do something about alcoholism in the Valley." The boy and his family were close friends of this young woman.

She is one of the few women I look at and wonder if she could be the one who could live with and abide a poet. While we know we love each other, and have even held each other and said the words, this remains the great unknown between us. We are both too aware of the hazards of such a love. And we are both, justifiably afraid. The fear and the love are reflected in our eyes every time we meet, every time we hold each other's hands, in every light embrace. All I could do in this instance was take her in my arms and try to comfort her saying: "I know, Sweetheart." But what is to be done? There is a responsibility factor that needs to be addressed.

In a society such as ours that is so corrupt and morally bankrupt, with a leadership that cares nothing for the little people, who will take responsibility? There is a moral vacuum of leadership among men that, unless corrected, leaves little hope among the masses. And because of this moral vacuum, Americans face those Hitlerian and Stalinist Solutions I so fear.

Why can't life be more like the music- because people don't listen to the music anymore; and it is the music of the poet, more than any other that needs attention. As a poet, I listen to the music and try to bring that music to others. I was fortunate as a child to be surrounded by so much love, great literature and music. And while the music of the poet is often expressed in painting word pictures, no one can deny the importance of the mood-altering aspects of instrumental music and singing as well.

A close friend and perennial bachelor like me whom I have mentioned in other writings is an electronic and computer genius. Like me, he is a musician and loves music (and women). We both find music to be the outlet we need to get away from the ordinary and ugly things we have to deal with in our everyday lives.

My friend played trumpet for years and, along the way, due to love of Latin music, he began playing the Conga drums. So I recently introduced him to a group, Holy Mackerel, in the Valley that was playing a good style of Rock music at Slugger's. While they have a very talented drummer, Paul, I knew that the Congas would be a nice addition to the music this group was doing.

This is going well and I am learning some things I never knew about the Congas. For example, ba ba loo is not the invention of Desi Arnez. Miguelito Valdez used it long before I Love Lucy made it a household phrase. An old Puerto Rican told my buddy the words actually mean Lazarus raised from the dead! The meaning of the beat of the drums was to inspire the spirits in people to life, to resurrect the life force.

Unquestionably the drums really inspire the life force in my buddy. To watch him in action is to be treated to a real show. He really throws himself into the music and people love to watch, listen and dance to the beat of the drums. These tall, beautiful and exotic instruments can be brutal to work, however. My friend learned from an old-timer, Pancho Sanchez, to tape his fingers before playing. This attracts quite a lot of attention as he is preparing to play. The result of all that surgical tape on his fingers makes it look like he has been mixing it up in a barroom brawl or getting ready to step into the ring.

Now both he and I have had our experiences with violence and have the scars to prove it. But neither of us seek it. Yet it cannot be denied that there are always those whose last name should be Hole! We encountered one of these recently at a local cafe.

It was about 2 a.m. and a few of us had gathered for breakfast after the tavern had closed. My friend and I smoke, as do several others. This cafe, at this hour of the morning, cuts us some slack and the waitress is even kind enough to provide us an ashtray as long as there are no complaints from others. My friend and I are civilized and don't want to offend non-smokers.

But this guy came in, a non-local, and as my buddy began to light a cigarette, said loudly: "Hey! Don't you know it's against the law to smoke in a restaurant! I'd sure hate to see this place closed down!" The attitude of this man was most unpleasant.

The Bass player in the band who happened to be in the cafe responded magnificently: "Hey! How did you get here?"

The guy, a little unsettled replied: "I drove."

The Bass player: "Don't you know it's against the law to drink and drive?" We had all seen this idiot hoisting a few earlier at the tavern.

It was at this point that my buddy, all six-feet and two hundred and forty pounds of him arose and said: "Hey! As long as I'm breaking the law why don't I just kill your ass!" At which everyone in the place cracked up at a line that belongs in the annals of history. Things could have become very interesting at this point but the idiot had enough sense to pull in his horns and remain silent. He couldn't get out of there fast enough. I had been quiet, writing the story in my mind as events unfolded; as it turned out, my input would have been superfluous, anti-climactic and a case of over-kill.

Now I would be the last to attempt to defend a habit and addiction that requires you take some noxious weed, roll it in paper, stick it in your face and light fire to it, inhaling the acrid smoke that is guaranteed to produce emphysema and/or lung cancer. Stupid! But my complaint, in this case, is an attitude, especially the hypocritical attitude of this Mr. Hole. Drink and drive? Ok. But smoke in a restaurant? Horrors!

The story has another point. If you were raised in the era when it was the patriotic thing to send cigarettes to the boys overseas, when doctors were used to advertise their favorite brands of tobacco, when illegal aliens were illegal and breaking the law and treated accordingly, when one paycheck took care of a family, you get my meaning.

And, as an aside, who but the enemies of America or any nation would call flagrant criminals Undocumented Immigrants! And who, except the enemies of America, would reward these criminals with medical and other so-called benefits that the vanishing middle class, legitimate citizens, can no longer afford! And no other nation in the world is insane enough to countenance!

And to add insult to injury attempt to justify their own criminal, treasonous actions through the courts under color of law and call such treason Constitutional! These perverted so-called judges and legislators deserve the place reserved to them: HELL! And the sooner the better for the sake of our children and future of America!

You, Caesar, created an entire criminal class of otherwise law-abiding citizens by your perverted laws such as those aimed at drug use and now you have the result that makes welfare and prisons growth industries in America! Did you purposely decide to gut our steel, auto and other industries, eliminating jobs by the millions for greater profits overseas and South of the Border? You bet you did!

As I travel, I meet the good people who cannot find employment, good people who are hurting because of the greed and avarice of money lenders and an elected officialdom which not only has lost touch with American Citizens but who could care less about the suffering of those who have lost jobs, homes and families because of these children of the Devil!

And these conscienceless scoundrels and thieves and mass murderers like Janet Reno seem oblivious to the fact that they are sowing the seeds of rebellion, revolution and anarchy in this nation! They need a lesson from the immutable facts of history and human nature.

You, Caesar, now support your Shadow Government and Brown Shirts through the profits you reap through the drug traffic! And you are so insanely greedy of power and profit, of an *Empire Beyond Reason*, that you think Americans are so simple that they don't know what your pernicious agenda is and what you are doing? Boy, are you wrong! And while the judgment of God may seem to be slow in coming; coming it is! Count on it and tremble in fear as you should! You and your cohorts may have lost touch with the ordinary citizens of America but I haven't!

As to smoking and like things that have suddenly become the purview of a corrupt so-called leadership, just when did Big Brother, Caesar, decide we were children who needed to be forced to Buckle Up, wear helmets, etc.? Well, Caesar, you and your hired thugs and sycophants, your unearned bread masses ala Clinton, Reno, Willy Brown et al. can go to hell as well! And, I repeat, the sooner the better! You traitors can count on my doing my best to hasten the day!

I remain the implacable enemy of the traitors of America, those who would betray us and sell us into world slavery, stealing the heritage of our children, an American heritage of freedom and liberty, that beacon of hope to a hurting world that countless men and women bought and kept with the ultimate sacrifice! And their blood cries out against you! There are millions like myself who can only be silenced by one method! The poet doesn't always spend his time considering the heavens or thinking lofty thoughts, he knows how to fight as well! And the most dangerous and effective weapon against despotic tyranny remains the written word! Since Caesar considers me a dangerous and violent man, why disabuse him of such a notion? But the poet calls them as he sees them. And Truth isn't always a pretty thing.

Roy Kendall, attorney Chuck Lazaro and I met in Fresno on November 29 as a panel on the John Castle TV show concerning the graft and corruption leading to the Orange County bankruptcy and the building of the Radisson Hotel and Convention Center in Visalia. The enemies of America know men like John, Roy, Chuck and I will not let such things happen without giving battle. All that is necessary for evil to prevail is for good men to do nothing remains a truism.

But it took my placing the evidence of the chicanery and betrayal of public offices and public trust of the scoundrels involved directly into the hands of my friend, State Senator Don Rogers, to get the ball rolling. I'll be letting readers know the results of our continuing efforts to bring these conscienceless thieves to account in next month's essay.

The title for the book I am putting together chronicling this betrayal and victimization of the taxpayers might be the infamous line from the old Robber Baron, J.P. Morgan: "The Public be Damned!" At least it summarizes the attitude of these scoundrels and so many others across America in public offices; and now, having said the ugly things that need saying, back to the story.

My friend and I recognized each other as soul brothers the moment we met. It was immediately apparent that we were both men without any common sense and true romantics with a genuine love of women, and both having paid our dues accordingly. But, as I have repeatedly pointed out, men have the divine right to make fools of themselves over women. Better that than so many other things like money or collecting stamps. That my buddy and I have exercised that right on more occasions than most men is another basis of our friendship; this could be (may yet be) a book in itself.

Because of our common love of music (and women) as we make the rounds he and I have become known as the Blues Brothers; could have something to do with our antic, maverick, even, at times, outrageous, outlaw behavior as well as the music. In fact, I had a Bluesmobile ('69 Dodge Wagon) until I gave it to my youngest son. My Maserati, as someone recently pointed out, doesn't quite suit the Belushi image. But it's a case of make-do.

My own taste in music is quite eclectic, my clarinet still fits the improvisational Jazz and Dixieland format and the tenor sax fits a lot of the kind of music I love such as the Big Band variety. And I still love doing guitar work to the better quality C&W music.

Kelly, the beautiful, petite waitress at a local restaurant, R-Haven, said she loved to see my buddy and I come in because we made a great duo. She says my buddy has some of the best one-liners she has ever heard. My task, I told her, is to try to keep him humble, an impossible job since someone recently called him King Conga. But what can a simple Okie like me do?

Now he has a mission and we are discussing a tour in Japan (Cuba and Brazil are distinct possibilities as well) where the people, as those in Latin countries, relate to such music on a mystical, even religious plane. That I may have created a monster by getting him back into the music business crosses my mind. Oh, well, it keeps our lives interesting.

We have a terrific Italian restaurant (That's Italian) in Kernville. Romeo and Anna, the owners, have brought new life to the Valley with some of the finest Italian cuisine you could possibly hope for. When it comes to desserts, Romeo's Napoleon is a true work of art! And his soups? Indescribable! You couldn't find better food in the best of San Francisco's restaurants. And I ought to know, having spent so much time there.

It was an instant bonding with this great couple when they first opened the restaurant and I pulled up in the Maserati. They have one as well! Now there are two such cars in Kern County. But the problem is service. No one in the county does Maseratis.

Serendipity; my buddy has a friend in Bakersfield who owns a garage and specializes in Mercedes but agreed to tackle Romeo and Anna's car. Fortunately I had the service manual for it and my buddy's friend, Dave Mallory, was able to do the required work. I would have offered to do it myself but one Maserati, my own, is all I have time for.

Owning such a car, as I pointed out in my Birds book, is like an affair with a beautiful woman. It isn't impossible to live with one; they just require extraordinary care and maintenance. But the rewards are well worth the extra effort.

The Maserati is one of the best-engineered cars in the world. But the Italians are the true romantics when it comes to building racing cars; a glance at the schematic (which measures about two x three-feet) for the electrical system of the car proves this. It makes little sense to do some of the things the way the Italian engineers do them but with a poetic approach (and enough Vino) to the system, it is made to work. And by applying a dielectric to all the dry contacts, many electrical problems are solved. Some modification to the distributor clamp relieves the necessity of consigning the engineer who designed the thing to the infernal regions. But timing the engine from underneath the car is another matter.

Thanks to my friend, Romeo and Anna, the quality of this poor bachelor's leftovers has taken a unique turn. Now, instead of the usual beans, cheeses of various kinds and non-descript items, I opened the refrigerator the other morning only to be faced with Veal Scaloppini, Chicken Angelo, Calamari, lobster tail and prime rib; tough choices for a simple country boy who usually has peanut butter toast and coffee in the morning.

My friend works as a research engineer in Torrance where my eldest son, Daniel, lives. Now I get to mention topless dancers. Not being into self-abuse, I have never been a habitué of such environments. It isn't a case of being judgmental of such women. I know many women, like some of the prostitutes I mention in my book, which do this kind of work to support their children when deadbeat men have left them without an income or the means of earning a living. And nothing I say or write should ever be taken as an excuse for women pandering to the unholy lust of men. It is an evil system that makes such things, at times, a necessity for some women in a society.

I will maintain to my dying breath that if what is noble and best that is peculiar to both men and women is honored, that compatibility of differences between them that God created would preclude such necessity. If men would accept and maintain their responsibility as the leaders and standard bearers of morality, if marriage and family, children had the priority in our society, if sex were the sacred thing God intended, there would be no unwed mothers having to take up the slack through circumstances that godless men force them into.

My friend's new drum, a Jimba, just came in via New York. It is truly an exotic thing. Since he is staying at my place during the Thanksgiving holiday, he had to go to L.A. to pick it up. The idea was for me to go with him and, at the same time, stay overnight and visit one of his favorite haunts, King Henry's, a topless joint. He would introduce me to the girls and an interesting time was assured. His consideration went so far as an offer to share his favorite, a statuesque Red Head, with me.

Intriguing and appreciated as the genuine offer of friendship was, I had to pass. Not out of any prudishness or nobility of character but the fact that I still have children and others to whom I must give an accounting of the way I live my life. As a result, I have to occasionally pass on some interesting encounters.

Last month I promised to follow up on my peculiar remarks concerning Soren Kierkegaard and Henry David Thoreau in regard to their lack of love for women and children and that accounting for their short lives.

To begin, it is freely admitted that one's mental health, the state of mind has a great deal to do with physical health. This is beyond dispute. We know that joy and laughter, happiness promotes longevity. And there is no other greater source of joy and happiness in a man's life than women and children, than family when it is all it is intended to be.

Lacking these elements to promote mental health, living too long closeted with the Dark Side and delving ever deeper into the human condition without these leavening influences, the man is left too alone and his genius proves his undoing. These great philosophers had little real joy in their lives. As a student of human behavior, and most especially as a romantic and poet, I came to realize that these men, as with many others, lacked a large dimension of life in their writings, somewhat akin to Stephen Hawking's lack of the poetic connection between creation and mankind in his mathematics.

I will state unequivocally, that, as a man, the only real joy and happiness I have experienced in my own life, the motivation to write, sing and make music of the softer and gentler things, the things of real beauty and romance, the things of eternal value has come from women and children. When Thoreau wrote, for example, that as the spider in a garret, he could be happy in a prison as long as he had his thoughts to sustain him, he was wrong. HDT, as SK, placed too much emphasis on the meditative, contemplative aspect of intellectualism. And, lacking that all-important dimension of a complete life experience, wife and children, he was blind to the joy and happiness such things bring to a man.

As a writer and poet, I know, as these men would freely admit, that Truth can only be found through the experiences of life, not through academic disciplines and empirical facts alone. As philosophers both of these men, and so many like them, failed miserably in addressing the real issues of life, the things of such eternal value that they never were able to present the full picture of life and living. These worthy thinkers would never say they knew what it was like to be pregnant or give birth. Only a man-fool would do so. But the world is full of fools.

It is in the philosophies of such men, philosophies that fail so miserably to account for the real basis of strife in humanity, that they too often fall into the camp of those fools that would tell us they know, as men, what it feels like to give birth. Ladies of the world, your fight is against incomplete philosophies of men that fail to consider or cannot understand you as the other half of the human equation!

One of the greatest compliments I have ever received from a Christian man came just the other day. This man owns a Christian radio station and has earned my respect for his integrity as he has battled against the tyranny and corruption of big government and other bullies. He said to me: "Don, I respect you for being faithful in holding the Plumb line against the churches! Keep up the good work." I was humbled at this good man's appraisal of my efforts in this regard.

Can I do less when the great men, thinkers and poets, I have studied and admired are sincerely wrong? But Truth will prevail when pains are taken to bring it to light! G. W. And the best of men will agree with the Truth even to their own hurt. While Faulkner could say to the Nobel Committee that " ... the only thing worth the blood and sweat of the artist is the human heart in conflict with itself," it is a man's relationship with family, with women and children that encounters that psychosis of grief as well as the joy and happiness, that enables him to truly understand the human condition in it's most profound aspects.

As an intellectual in my own right according to the academic community and my peers, I am qualified to bring such an issue before my colleagues and say to them: "These men died young and with incomplete philosophies because they never learned the most important things life had to teach, the things that can only be learned by a loving relationship with women and children."

Without joy and happiness, the realities that become a part of the life force that is only attained in completeness by the relationships with women and children, a man dies before his time. And the most brilliant thinker is blind to such realities and his thoughts, even his genius, suffer accordingly. I am never complete, as a man, without a woman in my life to provide needed encouragement, inspiration, joy and happiness that enable me to do my best as a man.

Extrapolated to the larger view of the history and destiny of nations, it is, as I say repeatedly, the family that dictates the morality and motivation for a civilization, it is family and posterity that is the impetus for the best of humanity and the foundation of a society. And it is the relationships between men and women that dictate the kinds of families within any given society. And men lead, are the responsible parties in the relationships. Where men fail in their duties and responsibilities, where they fail to maintain standards of morality and behavior toward women and children, civilizations crumble and fail.

There is a very real and pragmatic reason that married men live longer than unmarried ones. A man finds complete fulfillment as a man by being a husband and father. Without this, a most important and essential dimension of his thinking processes is vacant, missing.

The foundational aspect of my conclusions in this respect is readily discernible to any objective reader of history and philosophy. But little is written about it. Why? Because men would like to think they don't need a woman or family to be complete as men. And, most importantly, men don't want to accept responsibility (like Adam) as the standard bearers of morality. Wrong! It remains a man's world and men lead and women are forced to follow.

You ladies, you serve the most important function in a man's life by being the motivation and inspiration, the music and poetry in a man's life. It is your beauty as women, as the epitome of the cultivating influence of romance, of the softer and gentler things men were created to live for, protect and nourish and work for.

But if you pander to the lust of men, if you sell out for the short-term of enjoying the wages of sin for a season, the specter of advancing years will most assuredly prove how wrong you are! And the mirror never lies! *Schonheit vergeht; Tugend besteht!* (Beauty fades; Virtue remains).

Concerning virtue, I mentioned something in last month's essay that I knew would stir up a lot of people, the fact that God placed the two Commandments, "You will do no murder" and "You will not commit adultery" next to each other in the Decalogue and I stated the two are equally heinous in God's eyes.

In the Gospel of Luke, the 18th chapter when the Rich Young Ruler asks Jesus what he must do to inherit eternal life, the Lord, curiously, reverses the order and puts adultery ahead of murder. If anything, this proves my point that God equates the two as equal in His eyes.

Adultery is the murder of the innocent; it is the murder of a relationship, the betrayal of love and trust, and destroys something that simply cannot be fixed. So Judas hung himself. Forgiven? Possible. But fixed, made right? No. There is no restitution possible for the taking of a life or such betrayal of love and trust.

When it comes to love and romance, where virtue is absent there are no grounds for such. When women treat sex as of no value, they sell out in the single, most important area of their lives, they destroy the purity of themselves as women. It is only in the ideal of virtue that the best part of men can be realized.

I'll never forget the couple that betrayed their mates and married each other. They spent all their time keeping an eye on each other wondering if they would be betrayed like they had betrayed. Trust? Impossible under such conditions. A marriage? Not hardly.

Make no mistake, men are the romantics and women are the objects of such romanticism. This accounts, as I repeatedly point out, for the fact that the majority of poets, composers, and artists are men. Women are the inspiration for us men. But it takes virtuous women to bring this out in men. It is the due of you women to have a right to expect men to see you and treat you in this light. But only on the basis of virtue do you have the right to demand such regard and respect.

So it is that I bring this issue to light in my Birds book and describe so many ways women betray themselves in this elusive thing called *Romance*. It takes the best in men, however, to encourage virtue in women. Men remain the responsible parties in maintaining the standards of morality and behavior that result in real love and romance, of virtuousness. There are no fallen women unless preceded by fallen men.

As a writer, I live in my head much of the time. Such an occupation, being a very solitary one, I require a great deal of solitude. This, as I frequently point out, has been the bane of my relationships with several women who wound up feeling ignored, a condition that few women can abide.

Almost one might say perversely, I can only enjoy and make use of such solitude when there is a woman in my life. Otherwise, I have to battle loneliness that is the antithesis of solitude. As a result, having loved, and loving many women and children, there is the necessity of getting out and mixing it up in a great variety of life and living.

The history of humankind is a history of warfare. That this has its roots in the relationships between men and women seems to have escaped the notice of the great philosophers and political scientists. Some, like SK and HDT, representatives of the best of philosophers, the best of Existentialism and Transcendentalism, missed the mark in not being able to address this all-important dimension of life. They could not participate in the single, most profound emotion of a man, that dimension of cherishing a woman.

Interesting word *cherish*; simplest definition: To hold dear. But when God said: The two shall be One! Ah, that is another thing than to simply hold dear. For body, soul, heart and spirit to come together with another, to invite and give such absolute trust, love, joy and happiness where each lives for the other's happiness and fulfillment, that is indeed profound and the fountainhead of the best for which men and women were created for the benefit of each other and the world.

Small wonder, then, that the best of human behavior is left languishing when such a thing is most commonly the grounds of use and abuse, a vile spirit of competition and combativeness rather than the compatibility of differences which our Creator intended. The empirical facts of this equation in the realm of the physics of the thing, the Mathematical Model of Human Behavior if you will as per my last essay, includes the following variables:

People, men and women, are inherently selfish. Only love and the resulting cherishing is the antidote to such selfishness. Next, only in the process of parenting is the best of love and cherishing understood and brought out in the family as a whole. In this context, count out all those that do not fit this category of humanity where the understanding is the most crucial element. In this context, the best of thinkers like SK and HDT miss the mark as I said.

When it comes to unselfishness and understanding, only men who have had daughters are able to learn some of the most essential lessons that only the fathers of daughters ever learn. No man with only sons can possibly learn these things no matter how good a man he may be in every other respect!

Then we can discount all those men with daughters who never learned what these little beings were meant to teach. I'll never forget one of the most beautiful women I ever knew, my Lady In Red, telling me that her father never once took her on his lap and told her how much he loved her! As a result, women fail to learn the best about men when a father fails in his love for them. A hugely complex equation begins to emerge which explains the history of humankind being a history of warfare and especially a warfare between the sexes.

Since it is a man's world, since men lead and women are forced to follow, by the time we discount all the men who are unqualified in the area of understanding, compassion and cherishing, there simply aren't that many left who are qualified to provide the leadership the world desperately needs! Leaders emerge in the areas of religion, politics, philosophy, education who are simply not qualified on the most important basis of all, the basis of relationship to family and, most importantly, on the basis of an understanding relationship with women!

There was a world of meaning to the lovely woman I mentioned in last month's essay who came up to me and said: "Don, you are the only man I have ever known who understands women!"

She couldn't have possibly understood the real import of what she was saying. And that wasn't necessary. That she had accorded me the highest compliment any woman can pay a man was humbling enough in and of itself. That she was saying I had the credentials to take a leadership position in helping to promote the healing needed in a hurting world filled with hurting people, hurting children and families, hurting and lonely men and women, Ah, that is really of profound significance! And such understanding comes, in part, by mixing it up with people in every aspect of life and living. This is another part of this hugely complex equation where many, would-be leaders and philosophers are woefully deficient.

Henry James (the writer, not psychologist) could call life "... mostly a splendid waste" because he was not born in want or poverty. With the good things of life, as they are often mistakenly called, comes the ability to squander wealth. But, as with patrons of the arts, sometimes such wealth serves a useful purpose.

Having said this, I hasten to add that Jesus, with complete understanding of the problem, warned that it was easier for a camel to pass through the eye of the Needle (a small gate in the city wall of Jerusalem as per Edersheim et al.) than for a rich man to enter heaven. In the case of James, with time and money to cultivate the finer sensibilities and tastes, there too often remains the missing ingredient of true understanding and compassion. Romantic sentiment without corresponding life experience fails of the mark.

Many worthy men end up knowing that Life is the thing of greatest value but we live as though there were something of greater value. But what is that thing? Ah, gentle reader, what indeed? That is the itch that those, even those of genius, who attempt to attain to the real poetry of life without women and children, without family cannot scratch.

I would not accuse SK, HDT or James of cowardice in not living for wife and family, of not learning the lessons only such can teach a man. But what dimensions of life are missed in the best of men where these things are lacking! And what is missed in the best of the arts and sciences, in religion, politics and philosophy where such lessons are not learned.

As a consequence, my mathematical model of human behavior, in attempting to quantify the emotions among other things, leads to such considerations like love divided by hate equals ... what? Pure ambivalence? Perhaps. But the calculus of such a point of transitional infinitude eludes us at present. We need a more specific mathematics in order to even speculate with any better, specific accuracy.

But such a lack of understanding moves our hearts to look at the stars with wonder and longing. In the never-ending search for truth and beauty, the poet who has learned the lessons only women and children can teach becomes the understanding protagonist in the unfolding drama of life and redemption of all that is ugly and chaotic.

I'll never forget an especially beautiful, young woman who recently said to me: "Don, I didn't know you were such a good pool player." She had never seen me at the table before and I became more human to her because of my ability to tell one end of the stick from the other and know the spots on the table aren't for decoration.

In my years of study of history, theology and philosophy, I became aware of a curious thing among the great thinkers. These men had very little to say in respect to women and children. The married ones seldom, if ever, mentioned their wives; a curious omission.

In retrospect I now realize why. These men were incomplete. They were not poets and romantics, they bogged down in the minutia of the complexities of their thoughts but they didn't seem to have the poetic connection working in them concerning the relationships between men and women.

My studies of the writings and lives of so many great thinkers, philosophers, theologians, artists, composers and poets lead me to the conclusion that women have suffered a tremendous lack of acknowledgment of their rightful place as the other half of humanity. There is an immense missing part in the philosophies of men, no matter how great, concerning this other half of humanity. Was Eve deceived by the Serpent because Adam failed to give her due regard and acknowledgement in her proper role as a woman, as his wife? Possibly.

And while Eve may have been deceived, it was Adam who made the conscious decision to rebel against God and disobey thus incurring God's judgment as the responsible party. And Adam tried to blame both God and his wife for his own miserable performance as a man! No wonder women have a historical resentment against men!

Lest I be misunderstood, I am not into the phony getting in touch with the feminine part of my own psyche; I am not an advocate of the so-called *feminist* movement, Women's Lib travesty or some ephemeral equality nonsense. Men are intended to lead and women are supposed to cooperate in such leadership. But how can any man worthy of the name be respected, supported and obeyed in the leadership role when he treats a woman as a sexual object of his lust, when he fails to accord her due honor as the necessary and other half of humanity?

Nor do I attempt to justify women who sell out to a perverse culture that allows them the opportunity to emasculate men by insane laws that give them a club to use against men who try to lead! My own family suffered such a thing and my children were made to pay the price of such conscienceless selfishness on the part of a woman.

But such a tragedy did not blind me to how men have failed so miserably to give due consideration to women throughout history. The insane laws in America which give women such power to destroy families at will and punish men came about through spineless men who, like Adam, refused to accept responsibility for proper leadership and standards of morality!

It's as though evil men came together and decided to make women equally responsible for their weaknesses and failures by fiat of laws that gave women an equal voice in the very government that is destroying our nation, families and children! And women were deceived, once more, by thinking that, given the franchise, they could make things better! And of course it isn't that simple. There is a historical foundation for the resentment of women, as I have said, where they have suffered tremendously from men, leaders who refused to give them the recognition they deserved as the other half of humanity. It is the failure of men, not women, that is the continuing cause of the conflict. If women long for worthy men who will lead, knowing that men are bigger and stronger and will always win through fear or bullying if nothing else, where are such men worthy of leadership? History doesn't offer much hope of such.

Is it left to our generation to raise the consciousness of men to that level where, finally, women are accorded their due position in the total scheme of things? Not unless men, finally, face up to the fact that they are the responsible parties for leadership in the matter of standards of morality and behavior as God, Himself, intended!

Women and children need, and want and deserve, the protection, consideration and leadership men were intended to provide them. On their part, women and children are to cooperate in the leadership process, not rebel selfishly against men who try to lead honestly.

I don't know if Eve turned out to be a nag. Maybe she resented Adam and maybe Adam tried to bully her. Conjecture and speculation aside, we are left with the resulting calamity that has led to the continued conflict between men and women. It would help tremendously if men and women would face up to the facts of the situation and cooperate in the healing process, giving due honor to what is peculiar to each sex and encouraging the compatibility of differences rather than the no-win competition and combativeness so prevalent in our culture.

Facts like the natural softness and gentleness each would like to show the other in a marriage is not encouraged by the insane laws like those concerning divorce which attempt the phony equality we live and suffer with. If men like myself who would acknowledge the failure of men throughout history to give due consideration to women are to succeed, we must have the cooperation of the distaff side. If I, as a poet, am to continue the fight against the evil which has destroyed the poetic connection between men and women it must be encouraged by women, and men, facing up to the facts and acting accordingly.

A lovely lady came to me recently and said: "Don, I really liked your November essay. It gave me a lot to think about; but the buttons on the wrong side?"

Now she knew I had used that example in a teasing way, and she laughed about it, to illustrate the charming and enchanting way men and women are different. Certainly buttons on the left of a blouse are not on the wrong side, but a different side than men's.

I would be the last to decry the poetic glorification of God's most beautiful, if often inconvenient, Creation. The stars, a sunrise or sunset, the trees and grass washed and scented by a recent rain, the enchantment of a wild, native trout stream, the grandeur of the Tetons and Rockies, so much to excite the artistic exultation of the artist and poet! But even Thoreau admitted:

"What is Nature to me if I have no one with whom to share it?" He spoke better than he knew.

Yet, the greatest intrigue and mystery of a man's life should be that other half of humanity, a woman. In contemplation of that compatibility of differences I mention so often, I find whole worlds to explore. A woman at her best is all the intrigue and excitement the best of pioneers and explorers could wish for. I never tire of talking with these mysterious creatures, of learning the differences in their thought processes from my own as a man. And what can possibly compare with holding such warm, soft beings in your arms, of the profound act of making love to them and, most importantly of all, having that love returned in kind?

But as I have already pointed out, when so many things such as the cherishing of a woman are missing in a man's life, how is he to understand the most profound aspects of human behavior? He simply can't!

Perhaps it is because I have never lost that best part of the man, the child within, that child who still finds wonder, enchantment and magic in Creation and has never lost hope that the story ends with all living happily thereafter that I remain, in spite of all the evil I encounter and do battle with, the poet.

I learned long ago that it does no good, as a man, to be able to bench press 300 pounds if you fail in the most important aspect of manhood, if you fail in the gentle strength of showing love, consideration, compassion and understanding toward this other half of humanity. These are the characteristics of a real man who is absolutely confident in his manhood. And women know and respond to this.

But, as I frequently point out human behavior is complex in the extreme. To cite just one example and bring it down to a very common level, I am often told by men and women that they don't want someone who wants to change them.

Now it has to be admitted that some forms of behavior do need to be changed. For example, a man might be an addict to pornography. I know men in this category and I can think of few things so destructive to mental health and so harmful to women and children than this filthy material the only purpose of which is to inflame the lust of men and make money for its publishers and promoters.

But on a lesser scale it is true that if a man has an annoying habit of some kind like chewing tobacco he may well have to change in order to attract a woman and vice versa. Few would recommend smoking or any drug addiction as a desirable or attractive trait. As a smoker, I ought to know.

This, of course, is not what people mean when they say they don't want someone who will try to change them. There have been things I would like to have changed in some of the women I have known. There were a multiplicity of things, I'm sure, they would have liked to have changed about me.

But changes in the persona of the individual are difficult at best, even when warranted. And none of us usually ask someone: "Please change me!" Just doesn't happen that way.

Reacting to a guy who was coming on to her rather heavily, a lady recently told me she had lived with someone with an attitude for a long while and wasn't looking for another one. What was she really saying? Though the term has become quite common, I'm not sure what specific kind of *Attitude* she was talking about but it was obviously one to which she didn't wish to accommodate herself.

I've encountered a number of Attitudes that I wouldn't want to try to accommodate myself. One of the most common, and I would guess it was the one this lady was referring to, is an attitude of selfishness which denies the other person his or her value as a human being, a person in their own right.

Another of my mentors of great wit and insight, Walt Kelly, died early in life; partly because he often looked at the world through the bottom of a glass or bottle. But he, as SK and HDT, missed the most important dimension of life and living by not paying heed to that omission of women and children in the total scheme of things.

I mentioned a young man of musical genius, a close friend of mine, in last month's essay. Like me, he was trained as a classical clarinetist. But after being the life of the party one night, he went home and hung himself. Looking back, I realize he had never had a girlfriend.

It has been the joy and happiness that women and my children have brought to me that has enabled me to escape suffering a similar fate. Yes, there has been the tragedy and grief as well, the psychosis of grief from death and the betrayal of love and trust to struggle through and choose to live rather than die.

But a man without women and children in his life, without family, can never understand what the real dimensions of joy and happiness are. And, lacking such inspiration, generally fails to understand the real dimensions of life itself regardless his peculiar genius in other areas.

So I present this challenge to the academic community world-wide which has failed so abysmally to present a truthful picture of Intellectualism and Poetry, which has refused to deal honestly with the failure of men throughout history to acknowledge the contribution and necessity of the softer half of humanity and look to itself and examine the basis of such historical failure.

Since the problem is of immense complexity, it will take the efforts and cooperation of a great many to bring light to this omission. For example, the issues of pornography, homosexuality, divorce, violence against women and children and the devastating impact these things have on women and children, families must be honestly and factually addressed.

Finally, there can be no hope of world peace, of world harmony unless the questions are dealt with, unless men and women can live together in compatible peace and harmony. And this will not take place, (and has never taken place) unless the questions are honestly faced and men and women cooperate in the answers. Issues I raise in my book like women as prey and men as predators must be honestly faced as well. No man, as I point out in the book, could survive a day having to think as a woman who must learn from childhood that she is the prey of men and how to deal with this. That this necessitates the protection of good men and good laws governing a civilization is beyond dispute. But it will take men who are qualified and enlightened to the distinctive needs of women and children, families to lead and make the essential and necessary changes.

I have written much on these issues and next month I will expand on some of these things I have just mentioned. I leave the reader with this final anecdote: I recently posed a question to a friend who considers himself a good thinker and believes he understands a lot about women. I asked him: "When an attractive woman walks into a room or a bar or any environment with a number of men, what is the single most important thing she must control about herself?"

He thought about this for some time and suggested several things, none of them correct. I could have asked the question of millions of men and few would answer correctly. But most women would know, especially the attractive ones.

I invite the reader to let me know what you think the answer is. I'll tell you in next month's essay. But it is something none of the great philosophers and thinkers takes into account. And it's an omission indicative of the failure of such men to deal with the most important realities of life, their failure to consider, understand and take into account the whole other half of humanity in their, consequently, incomplete and erroneous philosophies.

Next month, I hope to go into some depth of exploration concerning the reasons for a lack of romance in our nation leading to the conclusion that America is a nation without a soul. One point: Few men or women are able to overcome the circumstances of a lack of real romance in their lives so they sublimate the normal desire for such in many ways, not all of them socially acceptable.

An escape into the mysteries of religion ala the monkery or nunnery or the shameful antics of so much TV so-called *evangelism* is one way out for some. But an inability to deal with reality as in the case of most professional religionists that results in escaping into the mysteries of religion is, at least, socially acceptable though such acceptability doesn't speak well for a society. Such things contribute their part to the suffering of the ideals of beauty and truth, to that omission of women. The historicity of this part of the equation needs much attention by qualified scholars.

I spend a good deal of time with the Dark Side of human nature in its multiplied manifestations. The tyranny of despotic governments is one of these areas that consume much of my time and effort. Take the subject of Special Education in the schools for example. Few outside the system of the schools know how this Empire has been built or the part it plays in the destruction of children, families and real education, of how it cooperates with CPS and the prominence it has in Outcome Based Education (OBE) and Goals 2000.

If a family is trying to enforce discipline, values and proper authority in the home, the children of such a family are going to find themselves tracked to Special Education. In the process, the family is going to be subjected to close scrutiny of mental health professionals.

The Resource Specialist will involve the panoply of school personnel from the school nurse, the teacher, the school psychologist, the principal, the speech pathologist, etc. and recommend a course of study to correct the child's learning disabilities and promote the child's mental health. That all this is in conflict with the desires of the family is of no consequence. The school rules, not the family. And if the family becomes too difficult, there are always the offices of CPS to bring to bear on the problem.

My own brief tenure with CPS was more than sufficient to analyze the problems with this infamous agency of Caesar. As a Resource Specialist with the Stanislaus County Department of Education, I had to deal with CPS on a daily basis. Later, employed by CPS directly in Tulare County, I learned first hand the dimensions of the power of the agency to destroy families with no accountability for its actions, and like the schools hiding their sins under the "Cloak of Confidentiality."

I learned of the collaboration of the courts in such trampling of the rights of mothers and fathers to rear their children in contradiction to the mandate of the schools and other government agencies. Documents, court records, proceedings and testimonies are altered at will.

Social Workers are made to support these evils by the coercion of supervisors who are intent only on building the empire of Social Services and protecting their own power and paychecks. Very much the same way the schools operate.

A father recently told me his little girl asked him if Polly Klass didn't scream when that animal tortured, raped and murdered her? How many fathers like this man or me doesn't find such a thing the cause of nightmares?

It is when men's laws are in contradiction to God's laws that such monsters of Satan roam our streets freely. God's law would have immediately killed such a monster before he could rape and murder a child. And like Polly's father, I would have gladly killed the monster by my own hand. And I wouldn't have made it a quick death or a merciful one! I would make him scream just as he made that child scream! That is Justice, not revenge! And no bleeding heart better dare try to tell the mother or father of such a tortured or murdered child any different! You can share the same pit of fire reserved for the vicious, conscienceless satanic monsters you take up for!

I've seen too many such perverts in control of our schools, of Social Services, in the Judiciary, in legislatures and Congress, in the hire of the IRS, the FBI, BATF, in local police agencies, in local governments, in the fields of mental health and medicine, in the legal profession, in the offices of District Attorneys.

And don't you find yourself asking why? Like old Asaph, I ask why the wicked prosper, why the judgment of God seems to slumber? And then I confront the logical answer. When perversion pays, be a pervert!

Further, when the laws of men come into conflict with the laws of God and the laws of men prevail, where does that leave us? It leaves us with the unheard screams of the Polly Klaas's and those millions of babies who die before they can even make their screams heard!

This month I have done radio and TV shows, given speeches to various groups and tried to keep up with telephone calls and correspondence. This involves addressing the areas of abuses in Education, mental health, government agencies and so much more. And I try to keep up with the writing as well, a gargantuan task overall. And the travel involved with all of this? Where is there time to do it all?

The fact that I have become a most unwilling expert in the areas of so much abuse of authority such as that of the schools, CPS, law-enforcement, etc. makes the demands on my time extraordinary. I get very tired folks. And adding to the tiredness is the haunting fact of Thoreau's comments from his tract: On the Duty of Civil Disobedience. In regard to bureaucrats:

They seldom make any moral distinctions and are as likely to serve the Devil, without intending it, as God!

How does it become a man to behave toward this American government today? I answer that he cannot without disgrace be associated with it. I cannot for an instance recognize that political organization as my government which is the slave's government also (While Thoreau refers directly to Negro slaves, we may safely extrapolate his intent to all of Caesar's slaves in America today).

All men recognize the right of revolution; that is the right to refuse allegiance to and resist the government when its tyranny or its inefficiency are great and unendurable.

When oppression and robbery are organized (as with our present government), I say, let us not have such a machine (such a government) any longer.

Can there not be a government in which majorities do not virtually decide the right and wrong, but conscience? Law never made men (or women) a whit more just.

Thoreau's comments, as those of Jefferson and so many others, are the focus of much of my writing concerning the tyranny of Caesar and his agencies like those of the schools, CPS, etc.

CHAPTER EIGHT

Being a simple country boy, modest, unassuming and self-effacing (to a fault some have said), and of no particular ambition but going fishing and making love to every beautiful woman I meet, it seems patently ridiculous for me to be writing books.

But I have written a book. Actually, I've written several and they are good books. But with "HEY, GOD! What went wrong and when are You going to fix it? I have written a book."

There were difficulties. During the research and writing I had to put off many tasks that had a cumulative detrimental effect. For example, I had to forego the annual (more or less) washing of my windows and chores such as dusting and removing cobwebs from implements of infrequent use like the TV, stove and vacuum cleaner.

Some correspondence suffered as well. I lost $10,000,000 by failing to mail my guaranteed winning number to Publisher's Clearing House and a free Caribbean cruise, a free trip to Vegas and my free gift of Ex-in-laws, Episcopalians, and gopher repellent; satisfaction guaranteed.

But there was one benefit from the total absorption of the book; I forgot to shave. As a result, my beard, requiring little effort on my part to grow, will be suitable for playing Santa Claus for the grandchildren this Christmas.

With HEY, GOD! I know I have written a book; a book some have told me would change the world if enough people read it. That's nice. The world needs changing. Of course if that should happen, reserving the caveat that the book results in changes for the better, I deserve the Nobel and Pulitzer.

But I'd settle for Audrey Hepburn. I would settle for Julie Andrews as Maria in The Sound of Music. The reason I place Audrey in such a prominent role in my life is because she deserves it. She is an inspiration. Not because of Breakfast at Tiffany's or My Fair Lady. But because she was a beautiful woman, a beautiful person, because she loved children; and, because Audrey personifies, like Julie Andrews in her role of Maria, what a man like me has always sought in a woman; real romance.

Because I'm a poet, musician and romantic, I lose myself in the great Broadway and film musicals. I have sung to women and had some sing to me. It hasn't been a fantasy, it has actually happened. I've loved several women and they have said they loved me. But the music ended quickly in most cases. Maybe because I needed Audrey or Maria but never found her. The idealization of the poet's love is holding that woman, looking in her eyes, singing to her and having that look and that song returned in kind.

Failing this, the best I could do was to offer my faithful love, the kind of love that keeps its nose to the grindstone, caring for wife and family and, in short, working out your love in the traditional ways. Tragically, the poet may slumber, but he never dies. He lies there, growing restless and, at last aroused, becomes something the great majority of women do not know how to accept. But the majority of women don't know how to have a man look into their eyes while he sings to them.

The majority of men and women know nothing of writing love letters. The poet is compelled to write them. The majority of men and women know nothing of opening their very heart and soul. Again, this is a compulsion of the poet. A poet knows little of secret compartments of the heart and mind, he tells all, even when that all is hard and ugly. He does not know how to practice the hypocrisy of presenting a carefully barbered and perfumed, well-tailored facade in the place of the truth.

But it doesn't take a poet to dream or want those dreams to come true. All those possessed of a conscience, a soul want to love and be loved. We want an ending where the lovers live happily ever after. And we want that happy ending for ourselves.

What does it take to play a part convincingly? How did Shirley Jones and Julie Andrews learn to sing to a man and look so convincingly in love with Gordon MacRea and Christopher Plummer? Shirley and Julie knew how to love. They were in love as they played their parts. For the men and women who give us our enduring fantasies of such love and romance, the best know how to love and, while the play goes on they live that love.

But you must be practical! Yes, there is no getting around that one. Love and romance don't go well with an empty stomach and no roof over your head. However, even provided the necessities, few women ever find their Knight and few men their Audrey, Shirley or Julie. Now, in the September of my life, I have come to some conclusions as to why this seldom is the case, why the right man and woman have such difficulty meeting each other.

If I have to settle for Audrey in my reverie, if we are only able to have each other in our dreams that will have to do; at that, it is more than most ever have. Why? Because I know my Audrey, wherever she is, is faithful to our love in spite of the fact that we never found each other in this life. Granted that sounds a poor substitute for the reality. However, I maintain this is more than most will ever have. Why? Because Audrey and I know real love and romance; we know there is no substitute for this regardless the realities.

Somewhere out there is Audrey, a woman who knows the love I have just as I know the love she has, a love that regardless of never finding its fulfillment in each other keeps the dream alive, keeps us alive. It is the kind of love that inspires to the best art, music, literature of humanity, and the kind of love that moves hearts and minds in these things, that has true immortality, deathless because it is the very heart of God himself!

There is a faith in love to be considered. Those who have such a faith are saved by it. They are the true believers that know, in their hearts, that no matter what, love conquers all!

I live, and move and have my being in love. I live in the music, the poetry, literature and art of love. I always have, though the poet gave place at times in order to meet the necessities of practicalities. I nourished the poet at times with a wilderness trout stream where the joyous, chuckling, sparkling water cascading over rocks, spraying and flashing into countless diamonds shooting off refracted, iridescent rays of dappled sunshine, plunging through short rapids became gleaming waterfalls descending into crystal clear pools. I would take him to the oceans where the scent and sound of the sea and the crashing of the waves against dazzling sands or rocky shore left marvels in their retreat. And watch a bloodburst sunset in wonder at that magnificent vista of water across which lay the islands of imagination, of the *Bali Hais* of the mind and soul.

Then we would go to the desert, so clean without the corruption of fences, asphalt, concrete and man-made structures and marvel at the sere vastness with nights so clear we could count every grain of sand in the moonlight. When I made music with clarinet, saxophone, guitar or my voice, the inspiration in the music was Audrey. Her name at the time might have been Susan or Ann, but it was Audrey that remained, Susan and Ann never did.

In the yard of my little house in the country, I sit outside of a summer evening and watch the sunset gradually give place to a platinum colored twilight. The trees and the hills in the distance become dark silhouettes and stars begin to appear in the canopy of heaven and I listen to my private, heavenly choir of the rustling of the leaves and branches by a warm, scented breeze and the last music of the birds now beginning to be replaced by the peeping of tiny frogs and the chirrup of crickets.

Evening deepens into the quiet, smooth velvet of darkness and I gaze at the stars, Ursa Major and the immense Milky Way and Audrey is with me though I sit alone. And at that, I'm not nearly as alone as countless who don't even see the stars or even consider sharing them with another.

I don't blame Susan or Ann for not being able to abide the poet; they felt ignored by him. His thoughts were on Audrey and they simply couldn't be them; it wasn't their nature. At first, they thought they were Audrey. There were the times when they thought they shared the enchantment of God's marvelous creation, that they even thanked the poet for pointing such things out to them.

The poet would place a rose on their nightstand. He would try to tell them the thoughts of his heart. He believed the closeness of their warmth and softness as women a sacred thing. But invariably, Susan and Ann would prove they didn't really value the things of the poet. They couldn't be Audrey. The poet, because he couldn't betray, would simply retreat and go to sleep. Eventually, Susan and Ann would find someone else, someone more practical with common sense and not given to dreams.

I don't know that Audrey would have agreed with some of the things I wrote in my book, HEY, GOD! But I know she would have agreed on one of the direct results of the book for the protection of children. Looking at my criticism in the book of the churches failing to take the leadership in being agents for positive change, it occurred to me that I should put my money where my mouth is.

As a result, I have proposed a Constitutional Amendment for the protection of children. I wish Audrey were here to help me with it. I know she would. The proposed amendment reads as follows:

AMERICANS FOR CONSTITUTIONAL PROTECTION OF CHILDREN

Proposed amendment to the U.S. Constitution

An adult convicted of the molestation of a child will be sentenced to prison for a term of not less than ten years.

If the child dies as a result of the molestation the person(s) convicted of the crime will be sentenced to life in prison without the possibility of parole.

A child as defined by this article shall be one who has not attained their sixteenth birthday.

The Congress shall have power to enforce this article by appropriate legislation.

There is not a single Constitutional Amendment that specifically addresses children. Yet we pay lip service to the dictum that: No nation that fails to cherish its young has a future as a nation. I always add: Nor does it deserve one!

I have initiated a proposal for an amendment to the U.S. Constitution that would protect children at the most fundamental level, protection from molestation.

It is essential that such protection be universal. An amendment would serve this purpose. If child molesters knew they faced federal prosecution and life in prison without parole, it would be the strongest kind of deterrent and save many of the Polly Klaas's.

People have lost faith in our system of government. And how can the people have faith in a system that cannot even protect their children? An amendment would empower the people by giving them a chance to stand up and take action in a cause that declares our love for our children.

It simply cannot be left to the several states to do this on an individual basis. The laws protecting children from molesters are too ambiguous, voluminous and far from being in accord from state-to-state.

For the first time parents, family, a nation can directly address a specific, positive step by which *We the People* can show we care about children and family values. It is my earnest conviction that this would be a mechanism that could draw our nation together in common cause.

When you consider the fact that fully one-third of little girls suffer some form of molestation, this goes a long way in explaining some of the major problems in America. This amendment would serve notice that the people of America intend to protect the rights of children to be children in all innocence, that Americans cherish their young, our posterity, that we are, in fact, a moral nation.

Just the fight for such an amendment will pay vast dividends in making the enemies and predators of children, of family, the enemies of our posterity, declare themselves. I can think of no better way of bringing good people together in common cause. Our children have no voice or choice. It is our duty to speak and act for them.

Such an amendment will reduce prison and welfare populations. In the shorter term, it is well-substantiated fact that babies having babies are to blame for an enormous burden on taxpayers.

These babies of girls as young as eleven-years-old are invariably doomed to substandard care which increases medical costs. As such children grow, they are far more likely to be anti-social, illiterate and begin early, criminal activities loading our juvenile justice systems, and, eventually, our courts, jails and prisons.

If adult molesters of such girls faced life in prison, I guarantee there would be an immediate impact on this problem that is contributing to so much heartache and fiscal difficulty in our nation. In the longer term, there will be fewer such children growing up to a life of crime, thereby reducing prison populations. Fewer such children being born will have a dramatic effect on our economy by reducing the problems they create for the schools, medical care and other financial burdens to the taxpayer.

A somewhat more subjective, but to me, major factor is what this amendment will do for a lower divorce rate and the strengthening of family in this nation. By reducing the number of stepfathers and other predators who prey on the child victims in homes, people will be much more inclined to consider this in marriage or live-in arrangements.

Unquestionably, when we are dealing with the fact that over one-third of our little girls are molested in one way or another, the trauma carries into their adult relationships, especially marriage. By radically reducing such molestations, we have taken a huge step toward establishing healthy marriages, and, by extension, a healthier society. Consider the boys that are molested and the enormous cost, mentally, socially and fiscally to America. Such boys are far more likely than others to be involved in crime and sociopathic, anti-social behavior.

This amendment will virtually eliminate the inhumanity and national disgrace of child prostitution. By force of law, it will encourage sexual restraint, self-discipline and responsibility and greatly reduce the number of abortions. It will also dramatically impact Child Protective Services, forcing that agency to act in a far more humane, responsible and professional manner. There is no doubt in my mind, having worked in this agency myself, that with the power of such law as this amendment, CPS will have to do a better job of identifying, establishing factual case evidence and removing the predators of children. Even if this were not a question of morality, the fiscal impact alone makes it deserving of our best efforts.

My hope for passage of such an amendment is based on several facts. One being that it hits at the heart of all Americans regardless of race, creed or political views. Also, if the fiscal impact can be made clear to Americans, this alone would insure passage.

For my part, I will try to make the message one of empowering the people to take action against an evil on which we all agree, action that *We the People* can take in spite of Caesar! If we can succeed in just this one thing, you know the hope it will give Americans that we really can do something positive for the future of our children, for the future of America!

With success in just this one thing to start, imagine where Americans, inspired with such hope that they can take control and make positive changes for the better, might be able to go from here in correcting some of the other evils that are destroying America!

Few people know the actual laws concerning molestation. Having worked in the schools and CPS, I had to know them. In dealing with the arguments against this amendment, I have to confront much ignorance on the part of those who do not know such laws but have much assumed knowledge about the subject.

One example of such ignorance is the person who said to me: "You can be arrested if a child accuses you of molesting him! Incredible as it seems, this man actually believed this. Why? Because he had heard something somewhere! You would think such ignorance impossible. But it's out there and has to be confronted.

No one can be arrested on the basis of a child's accusation. Yes, a report might be taken by the police and/or CPS. But an arrest is predicated on evidence and investigation, not simply an accusation whether by child or adult. In this respect, the laws concerning suspected or alleged molestation are no different than the multitude of other laws governing the actions of police leading to arrest and prosecution for a crime.

Yes, the reputation of a person can suffer simply on the basis of such an accusation. But that is true of any number of other things that can destroy a person's reputation regardless of guilt or innocence. As with any crime of which a person is accused, guilt must be established beyond doubt. The amendment must automatically follow due process, a right already established and guaranteed by the Constitution. What the amendment will accomplish by federal guarantee is prosecution of those who have enough evidence against them to be arrested and charged for the crime, not suspicion of the crime.

The most pervasive argument against the amendment comes from those who believe the amendment is too draconian, from those that believe that the child molester is sick, not a criminal. The crux of this argument is the perception that child molestation is not the result of criminal intent, that it is not serious enough to incarcerate a person for life. I will answer this by saying that first and foremost; a child has a right to be a child, to be raised in a loving environment in all the innocence of childhood. No one would disagree that molestation emotionally scars a child for the rest of his or her life. Try living with that! The molester has done something to the child that literally imposes a life sentence on the child!

The molested child is likely to engage in aberrant, sexual behavior. This perpetuates a vicious chain of victims. I know personally of one case where there were 32 counts of molestation involving eighteen children molested by one person! Out of those eighteen children, some will go on to molest others. Only keeping the molester in prison will break this chain.

As to being sick, this is a sickness that admits of no cure in spite of claims to the contrary. You're a psychologist or psychiatrist who subscribes to the sick theory. Very well, treat the molester in prison where he belongs! I suggest, however, that the molester be separated from the general, prison population or separate facilities be provided.

The molester is a predator. If a mountain lion leaves its natural habitat and starts preying on pets, even children in another environment, we don't say: "The poor lion must be understood and treated for its aberrant behavior." No, we hunt down and shoot the lion if it has attacked a person. Why? Because we know an animal like a lion that behaves in such a manner is not susceptible to treatment to correct such behavior. It will never learn not to attack people.

Few of us would have any compunction about shooting a lion or mad dog that threatened a child. That thing is trying to kill the child! you say. Since the molester, in most cases, is not trying to kill the child, we don't consider him a mad dog. But he is. But in the instance of a molester who makes a child of thirteen pregnant, what happens? Abortion. But if not abortion and she has the baby, what happens? Typically she goes on welfare. And, as happens many times, the baby is born with defects and the hospital and medical costs ($5,000 a week to keep a crack baby breathing!) to the taxpayers are enormous!

If the molester is arrested and imprisoned he gets out continuing his depredations. Will the molester be responsible for the babies he has fathered? You know the answer to that one. The baby, and typically, the child-mother become a lifetime cost to the taxpayers. The victims of molesters go far beyond the child molested.

Because the victim of molest is not murdered the death penalty is not appropriate for the child molester. There is a victim but the victim's life has not been taken. As to the murder of the innocence of the one raped or molested? They will have to cope as best they can.

But it will help immeasurably for the victim to know that the mad dog, the predator will never have opportunity to do such a thing to someone else! And it will help immeasurably for the victim and witnesses to know they need never fear this animal coming for them when released from prison, that there will never be another victim of his depredation! And I maintain the victim has this right to that much peace of mind!

Ask yourself why molestation is not taken as such a serious matter in society? You may surprise yourself at some of your answers. The bottom line to this is that we, as a society, have been trained not to think about it so seriously.

Since girls, far more than boys, are the victims of molest, this points out a problem of tremendous magnitude concerning a society's attitude toward molestation. Girls and women are there to be used by men! Girls and women do not have the value of men!

My books: Hey, God!, Birds With Broken Wings, and The Missing Half of Humankind: Women! address the truth, the facts of this problem. But you would have to read these books to gain an appreciation of the monstrous magnitude of the problem, its history and dimensions, its impact on the whole history of the human race and how it affects virtually everyone today!

Suffice it here to say that the problem of the relationship between men and women is the most difficult, intractable problem with which the human race has to deal, a problem of such complexity and intractability that it has never admitted of a solution! Yet look at its importance. As goes the relationship between the sexes, so goes a nation. But, I ask in the book: Why are women totally excluded from philosophy and theology? I answer: Because they have no value! The natural, historical resentment of women is thus easily understood. Molesters act on this premise. They know girls, women, have no value and as a result society, led typically of men, will not act against the molester effectively.

We keep boys and girls in school until they are 17 or 18 years old. But do we consider such teenagers children? No. That is the reason for the amendment dealing with children under 16. It isn't because 17 and 18 year olds are adults. But our society treats them as such sexually. These children are marrying in our society. Our entertainment media encourages, extols their sexuality. We have taught such children that they should be sexually active or there is something wrong with them!

It would be naive indeed to think that children as young as six and seven aren't getting this message as well and responding to it. And just as children are now raping and killing children thanks to the messages received primarily through the sex and violence of TV, videos and movies, the so-called music they are exposed to, the pornographers, pedophiles and molesters have taken advantage of an amoral climate to increase their activities to the most dreadful detriment of our future as a nation!

I can think of nothing as effective to changing our direction as a nation, to tell our children that we do love them and care about their future as this amendment. Draconian? Only in respect to what we, as a society, have been taught to accept and live with.

But who have been our teachers? The psychologists and university professors who have multitudes of theories but do not contribute anything in the way of substantive solutions, the entertainment media that is selling the sex and violence as normal? Or are they those homosexuals and molesters in the Congress and judiciary who like little boys and teenage girls? Nothing you can name will so expose and call down the wrath of the enemies and predators of children, and our nation, as this amendment!

But parents, people who love children and America, who know the future of our nation rests on our children will be in favor of the amendment. This is not to say that some honest people won't have difficulty with it. And that is their right as Americans. I ask these, however, to examine the amendment and its ramifications as objectively as possible. This, I fully realize, is asking a lot, especially in view of how we, as a society, have been so successfully propagandized and brain washed in viewing molesters as poor people who need treatment for their sickness. But unless the chain is broken, it will continue to grow worse and worse with no end in sight.

I have a perfect example of how difficult it is to face our prejudices. A friend of some years recently dissociated himself from me because of a letter to the editor I wrote. This friend was ordained as an Episcopal Priest but went into selling real estate.

I quoted Sam Clemens' remarks concerning an Episcopal minister, one reverend Sabine, which were not complementary of this man of the cloth. I certainly did not, nor did Clemens, denounce all Episcopalians. And in Sam's defense, he had the highest regard for the Gospel and Jesus Christ and had some close friends who were ministers though he loved poking fun at the hypocrisy of religiosity.

To make matters worse, I mentioned something in the letter about the distrust people have of used car and real estate salesmen. This friend, this outstanding example of Christian living, a man with a good heart astounded me by calling and abusing me terribly for the letter.

I was dumbfounded by his hypocrisy! I never thought him capable of such a thing. I pointed out to him, when I could get a word in, that if Clemens had made his remarks about a Baptist minister, my friend would have laughed. I pointed out that next to congressmen and lawyers (samo, samo) used car and real estate salesmen come next in public distrust.

Now I have a good friend, a state senator, who never takes exception to my generic remarks concerning politicians. I know this man, an honorable man, is the exception to the rule and he never takes my remarks personally knowing full well that politicians, by and large, are scoundrels.

But my friend, a good Episcopalian and real estate salesman, could not see the hypocrisy of his stand. He could not accept that while he might be the exception to the rule, the public opinion of used car and real estate salesmen is one of proverbial distrust. Worse, he took my letter as a denunciation of him personally. He had no basis whatsoever for doing so.

The point being that when blind orthodoxy and prejudice hold sway, it is extremely difficult for the person to recognize it in their own life. Like the religious person who reads the Scriptures and never sees the obvious contradictions and corruptions in the texts, who knows nothing of good textual criticism and scholarship and worships a book rather than the truth of God; there are those, like those Pharisees of old, who are willingly blind!

Go ahead and knock the Baptists and Catholics, lawyers and used car salesmen but Episcopalians and real estate salesmen are sacrosanct and above reproach! Right. But my friend needs to take a look at the vast number of complaints to the state real estate board and lawsuits against realtors. They run a close second to auto mechanics that still hold the top spot.

Does it occur to people like this good Episcopalian, since he is so righteous, to fight for cleaning up the mess in his own backyard so he has an organization that is, in fact, above such reproach as that of Sam Clemens? Not likely. Whose ox is gored? In the case of people who are merely religious, people who have no interest in the real truth, I expect no help with this amendment. While there are good people in the churches who will help in its passage, it is not a church issue; it is a We the People issue.

Further, I think it reasonable to accept as a fact that a Hindu, Buddhist, Moslem, Jew, Republican or Democrat loves their child as much as any calling themselves Christian. But there is a most disturbing factor that has to be considered in this. I deal with it in my book. The fact is that we may be talking about a genetic factor, at least in part.

There is such a thing as learned behavior. In other words, there are behaviors that can be learned or changed and have nothing to do with genetics. I suggest in my book that in some cases we are dealing with people that have no conscience, people like the serial killer that may, in fact, be of another species.

Before you write this off, let me offer one point for your consideration. Recent studies with mice have located a mother gene. Mice without this gene do not nurture their young and let them starve to death. In my book I write of studies in subatomic particle physics and how such things may impact on behavior, especially in the paranormal having to do with things like precognition, prescience and telepathy.

No one questions that such things are factual; we just don't understand the mechanism at work in such cases. And, to date, they are not understood well enough to submit to strict, scientific examination in a controlled environment making replication nearly impossible.

I also suggest in the book that when the Bible refers to the seed of the woman and the seed of the serpent, we are talking about two, different species of creation. The cold-blooded murderer and sadist may be a child of the Devil quite literally. The compassionate children of God may be another species quite apart. Now if studies in genetics, together with studies of subatomic particle physics and Psi (paranormal research) should determine that there is, in fact, two species of creatures called Man?

Ion therapy works. Anions, negatively charged atoms, are beneficial in cases of depression. We don't know why.

The discovery of the antiproton in 1955 and the antineutron in 1956 proved the existence of antimatter. A mirror, opposite image or doppelganger, of the proton, neutron and electron means, theoretically, that there may be planets and stars out there somewhere made of antimatter.

But such material could not exist with what we call normal matter. The two different charges, brought together, would result in their mutual destruction with the resulting release of tremendous amounts of radiant energy. I mention these things only to point out the fact that with the existence of things beyond our imagination, beyond our field of reality, there exist realities we know little or nothing about. As with my story of Karrie and the bear in the HEY, GOD! book, there is a bear coming that, like the Scopes trial, the churches and religion in general are not prepared to deal with.

The recent announcement of a computer to be completed in 1999 that will have such huge capacity as to be able to emulate an atomic explosion may be the leading edge to astounding discoveries in particle research. What we have been lacking in studies of Psi is the ability to discover patterns of brain function and how atomic and subatomic particles impact on our emotions, even physical health and how gene patterns predict certain behaviors. A computer that can emulate a pattern in an exploding star could conceivably discern patterns in brain function, those fractal/symphonic billions of firings of neurons, and account for anomalies of behavior, even Psi abilities.

I have one of the most devious and cunning minds you could possibly imagine. I have lived the life of the most successful con man; that is the one who believes in his own virtue! I know how to manipulate with the best. And I know full well those thoughts that most of us have, those monstrous things that come unbidden to our minds that if any suspected us of such thoughts we would die of mortification!

I was one of God's hard-cases. I could excuse anything on the basis of rationalizing it away. If I was convinced I was right, by the deceitfulness of my own vile heart, I could make it a holy cause with the best of them and bless it with a text!

There is a man I know who has made his family pay a high price for doing what he is convinced is right. He has driven the family into penury for what he believes is a work for the honor of God and the saving of our nation. He is wrong! I was such a man myself. It took the loss of my family together with some other extraordinary circumstances to bring me to God's view of the matter. As Christ is the head of the Church, so is a man the head over his family. Well and good. That's Scriptural and men applaud. However! That man is the head over his family for the good of that family just as Christ is the head over the Church for the good of the Church!

Men, your first responsibility and obligation before God is that family! And in the words of Scripture: If any not provide for his own he is worse than an infidel and has denied the faith! I Timothy 5:8. What could be plainer? Looking at this objectively, it makes perfect sense: As goes the family so goes a nation! And so goes the Church!

Because of my own sin and failure, my own mistakes in so many different areas of life, I have become a most unwilling expert on the wrong things to do, of the dark side of our fallen nature, the Old Corrupt Adam! So when I speak of such things, I know whereof I speak. And the things I have tried to call attention to have been bought with a price. And sometimes the innocent victims of my own self-righteousness paid the price.

With that thought in mind, I close with the admonition that the churches will never be agents of change for morality, for substantive change for the Good until they examine their wholly untenable dualistic, failed theology. I adamantly oppose the position that evil is essential for good!

No form of Calvinistic lapsarianism, supra, infra, etc. to which all philosophies, non-religious as well as Christian, Jewish, Moslem, Buddhist, etc. subscribe in one way or the other will do. All dualistic philosophies of men that would try to make God responsible for preordaining evil fail upon honest examination. If we were on the right track in any of these, war, being the most unreasonable act of man, would cease and peace would reign supreme!

Such an honest examination of the present orthodox abandonment theology teaching that God alone will overcome the evil and that we, as gods are not responsible for subduing evil would, I believe, be the catalyst for the churches finally finding common ground of agreement. But I don't minimize the extreme difficulty facing the churches in trying to deal with orthodox prejudices centuries in the making.

Tom Paine, most would agree, was not a nice guy. But without him there would never have been a War for Independence birthing the freest nation in history, a beacon of hope for the rest of the world. It was essential that Paine faced the truth and dealt with facts to pull the colonies together in common cause. But it was equally essential that he move the hearts of the people.

Oddly, it was "infidels" like Paine and Franklin, men who questioned orthodox religion that gave us a nation conceived in justice, liberty and concomitant personal responsibility. It was not the churches, but not so odd once you have examined the orthodoxy of the churches.

A theology that deals with the facts and moves hearts is essential for these times. The present theology of the churches has failed to do this and the price is the potential for our nation to become enslaved to a world dictator, a French Revolution and anarchy.

You cannot sugarcoat such possibilities by saying only those things pleasing to the ear and expect action by the people. By trying to pass off a theology that is unable to take decisive action against an evil system, against evil people, you join yourself to accommodating the evil.

I love children. In our present welfare and prisons society, our growth industries, I confront an ugly fact of present life. I was a classroom teacher during the change when it became risky to put a friendly hand on your students or give them a hug of encouragement, when the vulgarity and profanity of teachers exceeded that of the students.

A couple of little neighbor girls like to visit me. I'm a grandpa and, at first, I was delighted to see them. There was no father in the home and one could only guess at the circumstances that made these children need a loving grandpa.

But I'm unmarried, living alone. I realized that all one of these precious little girls would have to do is make any kind of statement, or be led to make some statement, that could be construed as improper behavior on my part toward them to, at the very least, make me a candidate for prison. I'm forced under the circumstances to try to make it clear to these little ones that I cannot have them visiting me. That is hard, that is cruel. Especially toward little ones that need all the love they can get.

Now if the molesters of children were killed like the rattlesnakes they are, not many dirty old men would have to be exterminated before they got the message and little girls and boys would be safe from such predators. But can you imagine the churches of today taking the lead in such action? Not hardly.

There is always a high price to be paid for excellence whether academic, artistic or industrial. Excellence in pursuing the Truth in the cause of freedom and justice requires the very best effort of time and resources. And it cannot be done by allowing the rattlesnakes to have it their way by perversions of laws that pervert the cause of justice and some fuzzy-minded distortion of civilized behavior. Reptiles like rattlesnakes know nothing of civilized behavior, of law and most certainly have no conception of justice.

By the compulsion generated through long years of experience and study, I am far removed from accepting a status quo that is the enemy of all that is pure and beautiful. Like most of you I want happy endings to love stories, I want Tony and Maria to be the winners in West Side Story. And they could have been if it had not been for the ugliness of orthodox prejudices.

But there are evil, ugly monsters in the guise of humans who not knowing of the love and poetry of romance and having no chance of such in their own lives, try to profane and destroy all that is beautiful. These children of the Devil, as the serpent in the Garden, know how to deceive by bringing God's righteous love into question, by getting others to believe that there is no reward for virtue.

I want to work for a world where the Tonys and Marias have a chance, where my children have a chance for the poetry and music of life. I will never accept that it cannot be done, that good people are going to continue to cave in to the Cainites by default.

But I know this can never happen without just standards of morality, without doing battle against the enemies of righteousness. And this will never happen as long as the enemy continues to be so successful in subverting the truth by calling people like myself bigoted, homophobic, etc. for standing up for the Truth! These perverted liars have their appointed place set for them in the Lake of Fire. But I will continue my best efforts to make that an expeditious appointment for them. A race that can produce the music and poetry that we have, that can love as we can, cannot help but have within it the capacity to fight for these things.

I never tire of the great Broadway musicals. I have said to repeat Wodehouse that they represent the last time poets worked in America. Why is this? What happened to the inspiration of the genius of romance that produced such masterpieces of the art of love as The Sound of Music? There is a greater and more powerful sermon in this great musical than any I have ever preached or heard! Why have such beautiful works of art given way to the loss of the hope of such things and fallen into the hopelessness of the ugly, vulgar and profane?

An evil system has been allowed to rob our children of love and romance, of hope of a future. And unless we take a stand, no, more than a stand, unless we decide to do battle, what can we offer our children?

Children have a right to be able to dream. That young girl and boy have a right to hope for love and romance. But only if they are taught to honor virtue. And where is the reward for virtue to be found if our children are constantly confronted by the successes of evil and the wicked continue to prosper? Virtually no one would realize or admit that they are blaming God by their prayers. Yet that is exactly what most people do when they ask things of God which is their responsibility!

I know, personally, that many people subscribe to agnosticism or atheism because they cannot, in all intellectual honesty, subscribe to the superstitions and myths of organized religions. I wish the churches would pay heed to this. But I think it would be helpful to such people to consider that God is not guilty of the image many religions impose on him, that he is, in fact, preeminently a God of Reason as well as Love. I ask such people to give God a chance devoid of religious interpretations of him.

For example, my children had a right to expect me to act for them in many ways as their father. They had a right to expect me to love, feed and clothe them, to provide for them all the necessities of life. Of course, in love, I tried to give them all I could, and, most importantly, I tried to prepare them to face an adult world. But when my children were grown, it became their responsibility to provide for themselves; to act and think for themselves. One thing remained unchanged; my love for them. I continued to work for them as I could, to advise them when possible, but the work of adults was now their responsibility.

If any of my children make a mistake that puts them in a position where, in spite of my love, there is nothing I can do for them, they have to bear the consequences. For example, a grown son commits a crime and goes to prison. Not all the love of the parent can free the child. If he commits murder, not all the love of the parent can redeem that lost life and make restitution. The child no longer has a right to ask the parent to undertake for him in such cases. Nor does the child have a right to continue to ask the parent to feed and clothe him, to ask the parent for those things that are adult responsibilities the child should reasonably provide for himself.

As parents, we always want to do all we can for our children. But we realize that once grown, they must bear the consequences of their own decisions. The one thing that never changes is the love of the parent for the child. It is that constant, never failing love that the grown child should always be able to depend on. And that continuing love is the thing from which the child will always draw strength.

But how much of prayer is actually the adult son or daughter of God blaming him for not providing things that are the responsibility of the adult child? If we are grown adult children of God, why ask him to do things or provide things that are our adult responsibility? God's love, as with any parent, should be the strength of our actions. We have a right to depend on his never failing love and guidance in making decisions that lead to action. But the actions are now our adult responsibility!

Yet we will come to God asking him to do things that are our responsibility! We ask him to do something about the suffering in the world, about continuing wars and conflict between people! Are we not, in fact, blaming God for those things that are our responsibility? Of course we are! We ask God to deliver us, to bring judgment against the wicked when it is our responsibility to take the necessary action to confront evil and overcome it! And then we will blame God for not doing that which is our responsibility!

There are things I cannot do for my grown children. There are things our Heavenly Father cannot do for his grown children. But unless we stop moaning, bitching and complaining, unless we stop blaming Dad and do the things that only we can do, not him, nothing will change for the better.

Don't try that God can do anything! line on me. It won't wash and it never has. That is a cop-out, pure and simple, that is the party line of man-made religions from time immemorial! Only when we learn and accept the fact that God is limited in what he can do for us will we be able to take our lives in hand as responsible adults and fight to win against the evil! As long as we continue to blame God, making him the scapegoat for our miserable failures, we cannot hope to do battle against the wicked successfully! While the great majority of people will reject what I have said, I suggest that if they think of this sensibly and objectively apart from their prejudiced, blind orthodoxies, they will see the logic of it. I have many friends who, out of consideration for my welfare, out of genuine concern for my soul, have tried to dissuade me from some of my heretical views, who have cautioned me not to put such things in print.

My question to you, the reader, and my friends is this: Prove I'm wrong and tell me how your orthodox positions are changing things for the better, how you are fighting the battle against evil to win? Show me how your interpretation of Scripture, how your ideas of the nature of God and man are giving you victory against wickedness and wicked people? How are you making a difference in the care, protection and feeding of the millions of children who are suffering? How does your theology actually work in a practical sense?

Bottom line: My friends have no answers to these questions. They continue to hold on to an abandonment theology, dualistic doctrines that make God responsible for evil, not them. Like the child caught in a lie or petty theft, they will try to deny this. All they know is that I'm wrong and they have the truth. They just aren't able to prove it.

And, after all, since God is in control of everything, since Jesus is bound to show up eventually, it isn't even our responsibility to fight! But to continue to hold the view that God can do it on his own, that he does not need our help and cooperation, that we are not, in fact, gods ourselves with that family responsibility, is to face the continued successes of the wicked.

Now you know the title of the book is a legitimate question, but it is not up to God to fix that which is our responsibility. To ask, *Hey, God! What went wrong and when are You going to fix it?* is not to blame Him for our failure. I believe God made errors out of love just as we do. But we learn through the errors of love, we learn to discriminate as we grow up. Yet the ideals of love never change. Love cannot live in suspicion and distrust; it never becomes cynical. It never fails in hoping that this time, it will work, that the one loved and trusted will never betray.

I will probably die a poet. Why? Because in spite of the many errors and failures of love, in spite of the continual betrayal of love and trust, I cannot let go of the dream and I cannot stop loving. It's a gift. And I have just described the heart of God himself, and by His Spirit this gift of love lives in his children.

It takes two artists working together to make the dream come true as God intended between a man and a woman. But when the dream comes true, you have the foundation for virtue and goodness in a family. And from the family comes the virtue and goodness of a nation.

When those things are being done that make the family the most important priority in our nation, and then we will be able to have hope. And only then can we offer such hope to our children! We have a long way to go but I maintain hope. Perhaps, as with Napoleon's dream of wars fought and won without cannon and bayonet, we can let go our prejudices, the solution of the paradox of good and evil may yet be understood.

But it will take Renaissance Men, men and women, studied in a multitude of different disciplines rather than specialists, to discern the patterns in so much seeming chaos enabling us to make sense of it all and suggest courses of action. Some of these people will have to be expert in the philosophy of physics as well as human behavior. They will have to have the genius to be able to bridge the gap between the hard and the social/behavioral sciences. To bring the arts and the sciences together on a common ground of understanding has been the Holy Grail of the true poet, his personal Grand Unification Theory.

While people tremble in fear of a bloody French Revolution in this country, if enough of us help God, as is our responsibility as gods, according to Jesus Christ, as adult children of God, we can move mountains!

CHAPTER NINE

September 1996

PROPOSED AMENDMENT TO THE U.S. CONSTITUTION

An adult convicted of the molestation of a child will be sentenced to prison for a term of not less than ten years.

If the child dies as a result of the molestation the person(s) convicted of the crime will be sentenced to life in prison without the possibility of parole.

A child as defined by this article shall be one who has not attained their sixteenth birthday.

The Congress shall have power to enforce this article by appropriate legislation.

NO NATION THAT FAILS TO CHERISH ITS YOUNG HAS ANY FUTURE AS A NATION.

NOR DOES IT DESERVE ONE!

Not unexpectedly the proposed amendment has really sparked a feeding frenzy among homosexuals. They really want my hide. Well, as long as that's all they want, they're welcome to it. An interesting note: Some people have responded with dismay that I have encountered any opposition to the amendment. One very intelligent woman replied: "Why should anyone oppose it?" She was truly dumbfounded. Apparently this lady has not seen "Philadelphia" starring Tom Hanks of "Forrest Gump" fame.

Being a student of propaganda, among other things, no one can possibly fail to objectively see Philadelphia as a stroke of propaganda genius. The point Hanks and the film make: Homosexuals are sensitive, artistic, loving, misunderstood, are no threat to anyone and are unjustly discriminated against.

As a piece of propaganda, the film is unsurpassed. But it is propaganda. And as such, is supposed to make all us straights feel guilty and deep sympathy for the poor, misunderstood homosexual. We are supposed to feel guilty that the perversion of homosexuals is repulsive and repugnant to normal people. But it is! And rightly so! And are you afraid of AIDS? You ought to be! The film is supposed to preach a message of tolerance. But look beyond the heart-tugging, artistic and sensitive portrayal of that poor tortured soul being so ill-treated and look at the real message of hatred and bigotry it teaches. And what is that message? That we are supposed to hate, despise and punish those that rightfully find perversion repulsive and repugnant, those that know these people and their abominable practices have brought into our society untold heartache and AIDS!

In other words, hate the sexually normal, straight people and call them bigoted, prejudiced, ignorant, homophobic, and glorify the poor, downtrodden and misunderstood homosexual! Philadelphia is a slick message of hatred of normal people with normal reactions to perverts and a deadly disease! But where is the Hollywood masterpiece depicting the tragedy of infants and children, innocent men and women infected with perversion-caused AIDS? Would Mr. Hanks be asked to play the starring role in such a film? Would anyone of his star caliber even risk such a role if one were made possible?

Homosexuality in Hollywood has a long and ignoble history. Remember Rock Hudson? But why, I ask myself, would the entertainment industry try to glorify such perversion? It isn't just because of the money, of that I can assure you. Media like the L.A. Times has glorified the homosexual attorney, Evan Wolfson, for his taking the case of legalizing homosexual so-called marriages before the Hawaii Supreme Court. Wolfson portrayed as another typical sensitive homosexual artistic genius is a media darling.

A recent letter to the editor of our local paper, The Kern Valley Sun, by a John Nicholson is typical of the propaganda campaign of homosexuals. Mr. Nicholson actually wrote the following remarks: "Take homosexuals out of the church, state, medical and artistic professions and those professions would collapse!"

Making outrageous claims like this and equally outrageous claims of proof of genetic causes of homosexuality is a common propaganda ploy of the homosexual lobby. Not content with such outrageous, outright lies, Mr. Nicholson, like most homosexuals, does the usual pointing to Jesus Christ for approval of perversion. I don't think Jesus is amused. But then, a sense of shame is not the strong suit of the defenders of perverts like Nicholson.

We need some straight talk (no pun intended) about this issue. Why is it that normal people cannot make their voices heard over the clamor of San Francisco's gay pride parades and propaganda like Philadelphia? Why have the homosexual lobby and its activists been so enormously successful in tarring straight, normal men and women with labels like homophobic, an oxymoron because a phobia is an irrational fear and what sexually normal person is actually afraid of perverts? Tell the lie often enough as per Hitler and ...

If you knew of the perversion in the halls of power in this country you would understand. When leaders live without moral restraint, they can hardly stand up for virtue! We are sensitive to name-calling. If we try to close our borders to illegal aliens, if we point out the fact that prison populations are largely black and brown, if we reasonably ask that English be the official language of America, if we mention the fact that AIDS is the problem it is because of homosexuality, if we want to remove molesters from society, we are called racist and homophobic.

But facts have a way of catching up with a society. Not all the quasi-noble rhetoric of propagandizing liberals will change those immutable facts. A nation that cannot control its borders, that fails to adhere to standards of common decency and virtue that cannot offer its children hope of a productive future is courting disaster.

The first international conference on the subject of child molestation has just taken place in Stockholm, Sweden. 130 countries were represented. The recent excavation of the bodies of girls who were murdered by a pornography ring in Belgium gave impetus to the conference. UNICEF estimates, conservatively, that 1 million children are forced or sold into child prostitution and pornography every year.

I found it fascinating that Roger Moore of James Bond fame was willing at the conference to admit to nearly being molested as a young boy. And there are multiplied millions of people out there who could tell the same story! I meet them all the time. The fight for this amendment will give these millions of people like Roger Moore the courage to tell their stories. And the homosexuals know, and fear, this happening.

The perverts cry that just because they are homosexuals does not make them child molesters. Why, then, are they so opposed to an amendment that specifically names only child molesters? I think reasonable people can figure that one out so I won't insult your intelligence by attempting to give an answer.

I don't believe it any coincidence that President Clinton's recent announcement about legislation requiring the national registration of sex offenders came immediately after his receiving a copy of my proposed amendment. It has been proposed in the California State Legislature that child molesters be given injections to lessen their sex drives. Governor Pete Wilson says he approves.

Now when you all stop laughing for a moment I would like to reply to this. Big talk about such things like injections, castrations, and registration of sex offenders always makes good political rhetoric. But here comes the A.C.L.U., the homosexual lobby and the U.S. Supreme Court! And there go the politicians. I recently made this very point to President Clinton.

Nor do I believe it the same kind of coincidence that California Governor, Pete Wilson, comes out in favor of so-called chemical castration immediately after his receiving notice of the amendment. But what is going to happen to such legislation when the A.C.L.U., the homosexual lobby and the Supreme Court get into the act? You already know the answer to that one.

The High Court will, inevitably, give the perverted minority the right to continue to flaunt perversion and to hell with We the People and our children! Only a Constitutional Amendment will get around this arrogant court for the sake of our children! When it comes to a vote for minority rights, regardless the perversion of that minority, this morally corrupt court invariably votes perversion versus virtue! But virtue is not the strong suit of this court.

A curious fact: State Governors are not stupid or naive people. Why, then, are they responding to the amendment negatively and trying to insist that it should be handled by the individual states when they have already failed so miserably to protect children from molesters? Political posturing is the only answer. These governors know, full well, that any attempt by the states to address the problem in the terms of my proposed amendment will be shot down by the Supreme Court. I have had to tell people that even though the amendment process will take several years to accomplish, trying to accomplish this needed legislation at state level only to have the Supreme Court call it unconstitutional as it consistently does with any legislation encouraging virtue and morality would waste years!

If the states cannot get such a court to cooperate with denying illegal aliens welfare, to cooperate in controlling our borders, when such a court seems determined to deprive Americans of any cultural distinction as Americans and is obviously sold out to the proposition that our nation is not to be distinct in encouraging self-reliance and responsibility, when this court is determined to undermine any attempt to encourage small business and the rights of property owners to do with their property as they will, etc., don't try to tell me that state governors who say this amendment should be handled at the state level are engaging in anything but political rhetoric!

And why should the governors be opposed to something that is not a state but a national problem, one that all Americans everywhere should give a single voice to? Political posturing. I think the governors of our states need a message from We the People that molestation is a national concern, not a local one. And it isn't something they should be using, like governor Wilson's bound-to-lose-and-he-knows-it injections, to suit their personal, political ambitions! If Mr. Wilson wants to get real, let him support this U.S. Amendment!

I suppose I have to make some kind of comment about Ross Perot. He bought a third party to satisfy his ego. That same ego would not stand aside to allow better qualified men a chance to advance this third party. Consequently, the Reform Party will be nothing but a hollow gesture, much like the Libertarian Party.

My political nature forces me, at times, to call a spade a spade. For example the recent, much ballyhooed meeting of militia in Washington D.C. Touted as expecting at least 15,000 in attendance, only about 300 showed up. And at least one-third of these were reporters! I could have projected the small turnout. Why? Simple. There are too many petty egos and private agendas among the patriot groups. There is no single, coalescing factor or charismatic individual to pull the various groups together in common cause. I would suggest to these people that they take a hard look at my proposed amendment if they want to take up a serious attempt to help the America they claim to love so much rather than spend all their energies in dressing like Cuban expeditionary forces and shooting around trees with pellet guns.

Another typical example of misplaced priorities and a lot of money and effort expended for personal empire is Dr. James Dobson's Focus on the Family. I remember Dobson well from his salad days of itinerate preaching from place to place for small fees and love gifts. As a courtesy, I sent his organization a copy of the proposed amendment. After all, Dobson talks a great deal about how much he loves children, of the great work he is doing for family values. What did I get as a response; a letter requesting a donation to his organization but not a word about the amendment; that's what I call real chutzpah.

Was I surprised? Not at all; I've had too much experience with Christian organizations to be surprised. Long on shameful begging, short on action. Now I do admire the work of Focus on the Family and the information they provide is valuable. But is it making any real difference in turning America around, in offering any real hope of a future for our children? No. No more than the patriot groups that talk a lot and do little. A great many churchgoers are in for a surprise when they ask their pastors, priests or rabbis to support the amendment.

When it comes to the question of discrimination, let's face another unpalatable fact, one of thousands of year's duration and one few have the courage to address honestly and sensibly. I have written extensively on the peculiar fact that women, throughout history, have been excluded from philosophy and theology, of how this has impacted on the history of humankind and helps explain why the history of the human race has been that of conflict and warfare, a fact that contributes not a little to the problem of homosexuality. Of that great library of books, The Great Books of the Western World, not a single woman is a contributor. The Bible: No women allowed! Theology: No women allowed. Philosophy: No women allowed.

There are a host of reasons for this "Missing Half of Humankind: Women!" as I titled my book on the subject. Many of these reasons, like the difference in brain functions between men and women, the biological physical differences, the different emotional needs and dependencies, are quite legitimate.

But there are other reasons, less legitimate reasons that have led to the exclusion of women. A major one being that most intractable of human problems defying solution for lo these thousands of years: Why men and women fail to communicate at the level of the compatibility of differences, why the relationship too often devolves into competition and combativeness, use and abuse, resentment, even betrayal and hatred.

That Five-foot Shelf of Books: "The Harvard Classics." Billed as the work of the Immortals, a set of books intended to be all things to all men! How many women writers included? Take a look for yourself.

There's no getting around it ladies, it's a man's world, men lead and you are forced to follow. Homosexuals and molesters generally disdain women and speak derisively of them. Some of the vilest, most vulgar language and stories imaginable against women have homosexual and molester origins.

I often mention Sam Clemens (Mark Twain) for several reasons. One of them is that he was so very human and humane. Another reason is his insights concerning human nature. But a very major reason is that Sam never lost the best part of the man, the child within, who dreams and holds on to the ideals of childhood. One of these ideals had to do with the virtue and purity of women.

Sam had a pure and loving wife, Olivia (Livy) Langdon, and daughters. His wife and daughters were his very essence of life, his reason for being. And no matter what his weaknesses and vanities he lived the life God approves in the most important aspects of all; that of a faithful, loving, and devoted husband and father and a true humanitarian. What led Clemens to his depressed and cynical view of humanity: Death; and a corrupt view of God because of death.

With so much death in his family, his brother, his infant son (and his blaming himself for their deaths and that of a man to whom he gave some matches who died of a resulting fire), his beloved daughters, with so much hypocrisy in government, business and the churches, Sam had a full plate of causes for depression and cynicism. So great was Sam's depression and cynicism at the end of his life that in his Autobiography he called "death the only unpoisoned gift the earth ever had for men."

These things and so much more in Sam's life made him despair of the human race. His genius certainly contributed to his depression. He knew he was wrong, and wrong about a lot of things, he just couldn't get a handle on the problem and died without ever really understanding. He was acknowledged a master of humor in the category of Rabelais, Swift, and Voltaire but with his generally fair but rough genius in writing. The irony of that has never been lost on me, nor would it have been on Sam.

Neither Sam nor I are given to an art of bon mots or purposely contrived, mechanical stratagems evocative of a George Will or William Buckley in attempts at self-aggrandizement and erudition. The South and the West have given Sam and I a heritage where play-toy, picture show, fine as frog hair are a natural part of our expressions of humanity, not contrivances aimed at psuedo-sophistication.

Sam was often vain, often naive, he tried to profit as others caught up in the Gilded Age but never lost his humanity and his concern for the suffering of others throughout the world. Sam had a heart. Literary critics, being critics, have divided opinions on Sam Clemens. I would like to correct at least one error. Sam Clemens was never an agnostic or atheist.

He chastised religious hypocrisy unmercifully. But he had the greatest reverence for God and Jesus Christ Accused of irreverence myself by orthodoxy, like Sam I would point out the fact that if that Baptist or Roman Catholic was a Christian first and a Baptist or Roman Catholic second, we could probably agree to disagree on many other peripheral issues. And, like Sam would, I point out the obvious that in order to be irreverent, there has to be an object of reverence. I do not revere any man or institution. My reverence is strictly reserved for God and Jesus Christ, not you or your institution!

Nor do I reverence a book, the Bible. I honor it as the best source of fact concerning God and Jesus Christ, of much of the history of the human race. But I'm a scholar of the book, I know of the holy tampering and corruptions of the text itself. Yet I encourage everyone to read the Bible as the best book ever written, as the finest source of God's teachings and the best influence on morality, on virtue He has given us.

But I will never revere those institutions and their representatives that have done, and are still doing, so much damage to humanity, those institutions and people which have so thoroughly obscured and obfuscated the very nature of God and His Word, who have shamed Him by their peculiar doctrines and even disgraceful, hysterical antics as per the charismatics to further their own nefarious empires and agendas!

Most of us who have buried a child or spouse, who have suffered the sundering of our families through divorce, who have suffered some cataclysmic health or financial disaster have felt anger with God. Sam and I are no different in that respect. I worked through my anger to understanding in my book HEY, GOD! But Sam didn't have the academic training or background that would have enabled him to deal with the issue as I did.

But Sam was intelligent and he could read. He saw the obvious contradictions in Scripture, the contradictions of the books of Samuel, Kings and Chronicles, the varied account of creation in Genesis, the contradictions like the purchase of the property where Judas hung himself, the contradiction of Moses being a coward in the Old Testament and a hero in the New, the contradiction of the withering of the fig tree in Matthew, Mark and Luke and a host of others.

And I know Sam, as an avid Bible reader, had to wonder, among many other things, about the three, different accounts of how Jesus stopped the mouths of the Scribes and Pharisees in Matthew 22:46, Mark 12:34 and Luke 20:40. Sam and I wear the garment of heretic because we question God. We ask the questions that organized religions never ask. And Sam would agree with me that God has made errors of love. To even infer that God has, like any parent, made mistakes, that He is still learning, that Jesus learned things, is enough to consign us to the infernal regions!

Holding the position I share with Sam and Thoreau, that most religions profane God with their hymns, prayers and sermons; that they ignorantly, prejudicially hold doctrines that fly in the face of actual knowledge and fact does not promote harmony with me and most church-goers. If Sam had been able to take the view that God is not omnipotent, omnipresent and omniscient, the teachings and superstitions of the religions of which he was familiar, particularly Calvinism, he would not have blamed God for those things that are the fault of human beings.

Virtually all religions are dualistic, blaming God for evil. There is another view but that requires far more explanation than can be contained in this essay. My book, HEY, GOD! goes into great detail about the subject. But it took a book of some size to do it justice.

Suffice it to say that humankind is responsible for evil and good people better get their act together to do battle against it effectively. And they better quit asking God to do things he cannot, things that are our responsibility! By good people I am talking about those that live the Gospel, that live the message of love for one another and accepting responsibility to act out that love in their lives!

Instead of listening to the righteous and legitimate complaints of Sam Clemens and Henry Thoreau, as they should have, the churches closed ranks and declared them deists, heretics, agnostics, atheists or infidels! But Sam's best, life-long friend, a Methodist minister, Joseph Twichell, together with Olivia sustained his battered faith in God and Jesus Christ. The love of these two people together with the love of his children undoubtedly led Sam to his scathing parodies of the paleontologists and evolutionists of his time. He saw the obvious fallacies, even hoaxes, being perpetrated against the gullible in the name of science as well as religion.

Even today, Sam's clear thinking in regard to these is found in the failure of the Spenserian and Carnegian Social Darwinism. And though Sam was saved financially by the robber baron and, in Sam's words, Standard Oil Fiend, Henry H. Rogers, he remained the enemy of those who would lie, cheat and steal in the course of acquiring riches.

Clemens drank the curse of love to the fullest. But he couldn't understand it. He felt betrayed by his love and died a cynic of absolute goodness without hope for humanity. Yet, he had experienced that very goodness in his wife and children. Sam was a victim of religiosity, pretended understanding of God by the professionals of his time. In spite of this he, along with William Howells and Henry James, was the spokesman for his age and his gifts compelled him to exercise those gifts for the good of the very humanity he lost hope in.

So very fallible in not always using his gifts to the best purpose, in his raiding tours as he called them to cover financial loses, he remained, for the most part, an honorable man to the end. I credit Sam's failings not to acquit my own but to give him his due as a fallible humanitarian. He was living proof of the words of Jesus that the righteous enter into life through much tribulation.

Even Sam's severest critics have to acknowledge we would be the poorer without his having lived and wrote. Even these critics have to acknowledge that his genius would not have been able to work itself out without his having suffered as he did. To continue to work when life has lost its savor, that is the compulsion of the true artist and poet for which he can take no credit. But as with Jesus Christ, the world owes a debt to him and those like him of which it remains largely unaware.

Sam, I believe, now knows the truth and knows he was mistaken about God. Our Father in heaven did not make the children of the Devil. And the world would be a kinder and gentler place if those who call themselves children of God would grow up and accept their adult responsibility for the world we live in! Quite frankly, if Sam were alive today, I know I could count on his help with this amendment. The churches?

Thanks to my comments concerning the Supreme Court, there have been a few people who have been so busy trying to abuse me they don't have time to examine their own ignorance. I was a teacher for many years so I'm used to dealing with ignorance. It's a teacher's job to dispel ignorance. I suggest these people look at the decisions of the court since the Civil War, the time that the congress together with the court acted in such a blatantly scandalous way that even some Northern lawmakers were aghast and tried to interpose.

The wholesale abrogation of Constitutional rights in a Northern frenzy to punish and plunder the South is something from which the court and America never recovered. Southerners never hated Negroes until the actions of the North and the Supreme Court made them hateful resulting in retaliation and laws designed to preserve what civilization remained to the South.

No one with any claim to legitimate criticism of my remarks concerning the high court dares try to do so in the light of a scholarly study of the court since the time of the Civil War. And I suggest they start with Professor Claude Bower's definitive work of that period entitled: "The Tragic Era."

From there they can go on through the Gilded Age and the cooperation of this court in selling out the common man for the interests of Big Business, through the F.D.R. years of entrenching a Socialist doctrine of the Welfare State! Then start looking at the giving away of the American Store, the American Dream in favor of the perverts! And I'm not talking just about homosexuals!

Those who would argue the point only emphasize their own ignorance, sometimes quite loudly as ignorance is childishly prone to do! But I'm used to people without formal education telling me a Ph. D. doesn't mean anything. Yet that is the arrogance of presumed knowledge, i.e. ignorant, prejudicial bigotry. Kind of like when the kids start thinking dad and mom just don't understand.

But it was just such kids who wound up buying into Lucy In The Sky With Diamonds and Strawberry Fields Forever! The so-called adults in the homes, schools, government and churches let it happen! Now all the political rhetoric about a *War on Drugs*! Who's kidding whom? Not until we have something better to offer.

Fortunately, as a teacher, I knew I was dealing with ignorance. It was my job to teach and I never had any trouble distinguishing between teacher and pupil, between who was there to teach and who was there to learn. And I was a good teacher for those willing to learn. But over the years, I had to accept the sad fact that there were always going to be those who know better than the teacher, those children who, to the shame of their parents, hold forth in attempts to correct the parent.

Well, kid, you may know better about some things but you better do some living; you better raise your own family before trying to correct dad and mom! Now it's your turn to deal with the corrosive facts of drug abuse and immorality!

Insurance companies know the facts about driving. But what sixteen-year-old isn't a better driver than his dad! Just ask the kid. But when the kid starts paying for his own insurance, he comes up against a hard fact; he's a far greater risk than dad and mom behind that wheel.

Does that mean anything to a child? No. He's still the better driver. Just ask him and he'll tell you how unfair insurance companies are, how they discriminate against his obvious superiority! It isn't just the parents that don't know how good a driver he is, insurance companies don't know anything either.

I have met many of these kids in their forties and fifties. I'm meeting many of them thanks to this amendment. They obviously know better than the parents of Polly Klaas, they know better than the facts of history, they know better than any of the factual statistics that could be brought to bear concerning the multiplied millions of victims of molesters and the astronomical cost to our nation morally, emotionally and fiscally!

Since the great bulk of these experts are not doing, and have never done, anything productive to making America better for children, they deserve to be ignored. Their inaction speaks volumes of their genuine lack of concern. They content themselves with bitching and complaining about those who take action.

And we can well afford to ignore these *patrons of virtue*; there are more than enough really virtuous Americans to carry the battle. The others aren't going to do anything anyhow so why waste time on them. I only spend this much space on them to show what asses they are.

Many agree with Jefferson and Thoreau that revolution is an inherent right and duty of a citizenry. Certainly America has the precedent. My proposed amendment is revolutionary. No question about it. But it shouldn't be, and that is a tragic commentary on our nation in its present circumstances. But it would never have occurred to the founding fathers that there would ever be a need to confront such blatant immorality in this nation as to require it being addressed in the Constitution or Bill of Rights. An amendment protecting children from perversion would have been unthinkable even forty years ago.

Yet, if perverts are going to continue to flaunt their perversion and continue to agitate for legal sanction of such perversion, it must be confronted in unmistakable terms. We, as Americans, are either going to take a stand against it or not. The proposed amendment gives We the People a chance to take such a stand.

With over 20 years of experience as a teacher, having worked in so many different capacities with thousands of children, I believe I have some relevant suggestions to parents. Give all diligence to exposing your children to things like chemistry, biology, computers, good music, art and literature. Buy that chemistry set and make sure it is accompanied with a decent microscope. Get an erector set and help your child put things together. Let the child have a chance to try various musical instruments and encourage his or her becoming proficient with at least one of them.

Sing to and with your children. Sit with them and watch the old Broadway musicals as early in life as possible. Show them there is more to life than the violence and inane sitcoms of TV; show them life does not have to be brutal. Read to and with them. Encourage the memorization of children's songs and mottoes of life. And make sure they memorize their multiplication tables at the earliest. Help them to start writing by encouraging them to write what they see, feel and think as soon as they can.

Take them to the ocean, forest and desert. Provide a hammer and saw and let them try to build a doghouse or a birdhouse. Get the watercolors and clay and see how they respond to such things. Don't make the tragic mistake of expecting the school to do the things that you, as a parent, should be responsible for!

A garden is a good experience for children. So is anything you can practically do to get them to relate to birds and animals. Aquariums are always a good idea even if dad and mom do wind up taking care of them.

I have a prejudice that it is good to teach children to fish and shoot, that children should learn to build model ships and planes. But not the plastic junk; I mean the real things that require wood and real blueprints, not insert tab A in slot B.

In short, try to expose your children to as many experiences of life as possible and observe, find out what your child's interests and gifts are; what things to encourage in the child's life. Then take the time to encourage these things.

Did I do all these things for my children? No. But I tried and in many ways I gave them many experiences denied most children. They traveled wilderness places, learned to fish and shoot, build with hammer and saw; they were surrounded with good books and music.

But grandparenting is definitely better. We don't get our children with a how-to manual. Raising children is definitely on the job training. This is why grandparents can be so important in children's lives.

We grandparents have already made all the mistakes we would like to warn our children of when they have children of their own. What a list I could make of the things I would have done differently with my children that I can now apply to the grandchildren!

In our defense as parents, if we had known better we would have done better. And it is only reasonable to expect age to bring a degree of wisdom we did not have when we were young and muddling through so many things.

My Ph. D. is in Human Behavior, my academic specialty. This, together with my many years of working in various school districts including the ghetto of Watts and the barrio of East San Jose, my close association with Child Protective Services and later employed directly by the agency gives me a wealth of background to address the subject of child molestation. This helps enormously in leveling the playing field when I have to confront homosexuals and others who claim molestation isn't the problem I contend it is.

My greatest task is educating people to the problem. The great majority of people don't realize how prevalent molestation is and how devastating it is to the children and in later adulthood. People certainly are not aware of how greatly this has impacted on American society as a whole.

One of the reasons the magnitude of the problem is so little known is the fact that it isn't taken nearly as seriously as it should be. By making sex common, by the way the subject has been degraded through media, the children have been made the victims of a lack of concern.

The dirty secret of America is molestation. It is tragically, shamefully common. Multiplied millions of adults were molested as children and have never made it known. They are ashamed to tell about it. If I had been molested as a child, I don't think I would want it known.

But I had two, close calls; once by another boy a little older than me and the other by an adult in his forties.

I describe the incident by the boy in my book: The Lord and the Weedpatcher. The other I have never before talked about. But it is time.

This man was married but homosexual. He also had a stepdaughter he was molesting and this with the knowledge of the mother; a not uncommon thing. He worked as a surveyor and the incident occurred when another boy and I were pulling chain for him as he surveyed a local tract of land nearby our mining claim.

I was too young and unknowledgeable to really understand what was going on with this man, I only knew his advances were wrong and repugnant, repulsive to me and I wanted nothing to do with him. But even though I didn't really understand, I didn't tell anyone about the incident. The major reason was the fact that I was living with my grandparents.

My grandfather was a large, thoroughly masculine man and had a violent temper when aroused. Somehow I intuited that had I made this man's actions known to my grandfather, my grandfather would have killed him. And I didn't want my grandad to get into that kind of trouble over me.

And there was something else; I was ashamed. Though I had managed to rebuff this man successfully, I was ashamed. There was no reason for this yet there it was. I had done nothing to encourage this pervert. Why should I be ashamed? As a mature adult, having full knowledge professionally, academically of the mechanisms of the mind as they relate to such things, I understand.

The victims of rape commonly blame themselves, at least in part, for the rape. Though the victim has done nothing wrong, there is a sense of shame often attaching to being violated. A part of our human psyche reacts in this way to our being violated sexually. This in spite of the fact that we are the victims!

Children often feel this sense of shame in spite of the fact that they are totally incapable of understanding it or even the act itself. They just know it is horribly wrong. The molested child seldom tells of the molest; They don't know how. The older child is often restricted by this sense of shame.

As a result, there are multiplied millions of adults out there who were molested as children but have never made it known. But their adulthood has been tragically impacted by it, usually manifesting itself by failure in employment, education and failed relationships with others in one way or another. And, too commonly, by the molested becoming molesters themselves!

I had to make a call on a home once where there was suspicion of molestation. Due to some unusual circumstances, the people had been notified of my impending visit; a case of the failure of CPS to do its work properly. When I arrived, the front door of the house was open but there was no evidence of anyone at home.

Entering cautiously and determining that there was no one there, I looked through the house. It was evident from the disorder throughout together with still-warm foodstuffs and coffee on the kitchen table that the residents had made a hasty departure before I arrived. I learned later that someone within CPS had alerted these people, stupidly or purposely, of my coming.

In one bedroom I found a number of used condoms and their wrappers strewn about together with a large, open jar of Vaseline. A sheriff's deputy assigned to meet me finally arrived and I showed him the evidence of what I suspected was going on. He was horrified! The result of this a man and a teenage boy were eventually prosecuted for the molestation of some thirteen children ranging in age from two to fourteen years of age.

Another time I entered a child's bedroom in an apartment and saw the bed broken down at one corner. Curious about this, I lifted the bed and saw a number of wine cooler bottles; several used condoms and a large, open jar of Vaseline. I later learned that the child, a boy, had been visited by another boy, who was known as being a molested child. The mother of the boy, with full knowledge of this, had allowed this molested child to stay with her own child.

The mother, though married to another man at the time, was having an adulterous affair with her boyfriend in the adjacent bedroom. I had to wonder how she could knowingly expose her own child to such obvious immorality and danger, how she could be unaware of what was going on with her own child in the room right next to hers!

The mother, of course, denied any wrongdoing, denied any responsibility of putting her child at risk. This in spite of the obvious evidence to the contrary. But the family court in the county found otherwise.

As an aside, why the Vaseline? To those blissfully ignorant in the area of molestation and homosexuality among children, Vaseline is the product of choice for two reasons: One, its common availability. Two, children are usually unaware of substances like K-Y Jelly or it is not as readily available to them.

The two incidents I have just described did not take place in a welfare ghetto or barrio but in middle class white environments. But let's talk about the problem in areas like Watts and East San Jose, environments where the problem is pandemic.

I'm reminded of the scene in the Godfather where the Mafia Dons, with a great show of self-righteous concern for children, make the decision to deal in drugs "but will confine the business to the coloreds since they are only animals anyway!" You have to have traveled, worked and lived in places like Watts to understand the thinking of those men. To them, the inhabitants of places like Harlem and Watts were animals. You have to have seen the colored boys and men urinating against a door, a wall or fence in public on a main street in full view of all. You have to have seen the urine-rusted metal of doors of public places in downtown Atlanta, to step around human feces in public places to understand. And when you have traveled, worked and visited in such communities, when you have been in the homes in such communities, you begin to understand the magnitude of the problem.

Where welfare, drugs, alcohol, crime and violence, prostitution are a way of life molestation is pandemic, it is an inherent part of the culture. Through welfare, the polite, civilized middle class has paid the inhabitants (the animals) of Watts and Harlem, of East San Jose to stay in their place. In this way, the problem could be ignored. But with this reverse blackmail coming to an end through recent legislation, what is going to happen when the payoffs stop and these Mafia described animals stop getting their taxpayer financed checks in the mail?

My proposed amendment is revolutionary. For more reasons than many could possibly know. But I know. I have been educated to know in the academic environment of the university, in Watts, East San Jose and Atlanta, in lily-white middle class communities and my work with thousands of children. I know.

My question is whether the coming revolution will be one of a revolution directed at the saving of our children, our posterity and future as a nation or will it be a revolution of anarchy and the breaking down of our civilization and lost hope of civilized answers to our problems? Will we be forced, more and more, to those Hitlerian Solutions I have warned of for so long? Will we face, finally, the situation that forced that old Roman Senator to say: "We have come to the place where we can no longer endure the problems or survive their solutions?"

Part of the educative process I have to be involved with is confronting the prevailing ignorance of Americans concerning our U.S. Constitution. I have had a few people ignorantly try to tell me the Constitution doesn't make laws! Some may laugh at this kind of ignorance but it's out there.

Notwithstanding the fact that the Constitution itself is an instrument of law throughout, look at articles XIII, XV, XVIII, XIX, and XXI together with the common addendum: The Congress shall have power to enforce this article by appropriate legislation, i.e. law.

Some people have expressed fear of arrest due to false allegations of molestation. Look at articles V and VI in the Bill of Rights guaranteeing due process! Amendments cannot infringe on this guarantee. Some have expressed the concern that we will need more prisons to handle molesters. The long-term result of the amendment will be a reduction of prisons by reducing the criminal behavior of adults that often results from molestation!

A great many people are going to be forced to clean up their act in regard to drug and alcohol abuse and so-called casual parenting out of fear of life in prison for the molestations that these things frequently lead to! People are going to have to take far more interest in children, in family, especially when it comes to divorce. Women with children, particularly girls, will have to face the fact that a stepfather or boyfriend is far more likely to molest than the natural father.

New Jersey is considering new smog legislation that will virtually guarantee no car more than ten-years-old can possibly pass. New carmakers are smacking their lips. And more of the poor will be walking. Carnegie may be dead but his preaching of the survival of the fittest, that millionaires are God-ordained to rule and care for the great unwashed, the sheep, lives on. With Caesar's help and the continued erosion of our freedom as Americans, the clanking chains of Carnegie's ghost grows ever louder.

At the beginning of this essay, I mentioned the paucity of real friends most people ever have. I have been fortunate, in a sense, of having a great many more friends than most. But most of my friends are dead. In another sense, that is not true for I count among my friends men like Emerson and Henry Thoreau. They, being dead, yet speak and I often find my thoughts engaged with their own. In this way, we have many an entertaining and instructive conversation.

Recently re-reading E.B. White's essay on Thoreau I was struck with the fact that it was fortuitous that I made the acquaintance of the inhabitant of

Walden while I was quite young. Last month I wrote that unlike most men, I have really lived. Henry would agree with me. But unlike Henry, I do not find fault with those who have not lived.

That I have never been able to settle for the routine, the desperately quiet lives that most men live, those heroes at their lasts and anvils, is not necessarily to my credit or to their shame. But Henry died young and I have lived long. Given the opportunity of long life, I'm sure he would have ameliorated some of his criticism of those who live their lives of quiet desperation.

I will, undoubtedly, die an advocate of living simply. Not because I consider myself better than others who seem to thrive on the business of business, but because I think those who live for the acquisition of material wealth not only cheapen life in the process, I think they harm a better priority. That is, like Carnegie, if a man is successful in acquisition, he invariably begins to think himself better than those who choose simplicity. And this is wrong.

But neither Henry nor I would advocate or countenance sloth or indolence as desirable traits. Begging does not suit us; especially the kind of begging that is the result of sloth and indolence.

There is a necessary compliance of familiar manners, speech and dress that is appropriate to civilized living. But my shirt and shoes, if clean and in good repair, should not be the measure of myself as a man. And while, for the sake of a culture and civilized manners, there is a need to acknowledge conventions, the need is to not be brought into captivity to them.

A plant must grow according to its nature, and so a human being. But the plant is not nearly as resilient as the human and will quickly die out of its necessary element. The fact that a child, a man or woman is dying out of their element does not show as quickly. Like the dry rot, though, it is there nonetheless.

But I am not going to criticize those who, able to make the choice in all sensibility, find they need a great deal more than I do to carry on their affairs of daily living. Nor do I have to eat a Woodchuck to prove I can eat a Woodchuck. I will eat him if in doing so; it is a benefit to my own choice of living.

The world is far more wonderful than convenient and to provide for wife and family is the sum of the greatest quality of a man. It is here that Henry and I part company. I have lived better, more fully than he because I am not a coward. And make no mistake, men as admirable in so many ways like Henry and Soren Kierkegaard are cowards when it comes to accepting the ultimate responsibility, that of family.

Yet, as with children who can hardly be expected to bear heavy responsibilities, I enjoy my time with my friend Henry because we do share much in common. This because I have never lost the best part of the man, the child within, who still finds the seemingly erratic flight of a butterfly purposefully beautiful and enchanting.

I thoroughly enjoy watching the quail and birds in my backyard. I enjoy having the squirrels come to my back door for a cracker or bread crusts. Simplicity in this kind of living in association with my feathered and furry companions suits my habits as a writer. But by accepting the proper role of a man, by accepting the responsibility of wife and family, I learned things that are unlearnable in a softer fashion.

I wouldn't trade for the lessons I have learned in wilderness living and travel. But they don't compare with the lessons learned as a husband and father. Nor do I, as a poet, ever see the stars as more meaningful than loving a wife and children. And not being a St. Francis, I don't confuse the quality of my relationships with people as less desirable than that of the critters.

We do need, however, to be reminded by people like Thoreau that there is always the risk of filling our lives with the impedimenta of living to the extent that we ignore the stars and, consequently, lose the capacity to dream. And there should always be a time for feeding the squirrels, for watching a sunrise and sunset.

Another man I much admire is Charles Dickens. I frequently recall his "Night Walks," an essay he wrote when he, like me, was tormented with the demons of what he saw and knew of the suffering of children and others. So insomnia is the natural result of knowing and experiencing too much of the dark side of the race called human.

Dickens, speaking of the Victorian Age as much as Sam of the Gilded Age was the instrument of genius and sensitivity that brought about much of the legislation in England and America designed to correct some of the worst abuses of children. In his night walks, Dickens pondered the extreme cruelty and injustice represented by Old Bailey, contrasted, perhaps more properly mocked, by the spires of Westminster. Acknowledged more humanitarian than Christian, Dickens, like Clemens and Thoreau, was far more sensitive to the humanity and justice of God and Jesus Christ than orthodoxy ever has been.

The story of Scrooge and his transformation is rooted in the hope of men like Dickens that people will do better if they know better, that there is an inherent ideal of absolute goodness that can be prevailed upon in calling good men and women to action against evil. It isn't essential that good men and women be perfect, that they always be correct in their assessment of the need of action. Most certainly Clemens, Thoreau and Dickens would make no claim to such perfection.

What is essential is good leadership, the kind that a man like Dickens offered to his generation, and agreement on a common course of action. The failure of so many well-intentioned people and organizations today in America is that lack of leadership and agreement on a common course of action. It brooks no contradiction to say that any course of action that does not have as its goal the saving of our children and the offering of hope of a future for them where life is wide and full of promise is a wrong direction, a wrong emphasis. Unless petty egos and private agendas submit to common cause for the sake of our children, other courses will do nothing but result in a diaspora of all other attempts to reclaim America for our posterity.

I hadn't seen Sam in quite some time so I was surprised by his visit. And I could tell he was deeply disturbed. A sensitive man of deep feelings, he figured prominently in some of the stories in my book, Birds With Broken Wings. Sam and I have known each other for many years and have shared many things of the heart.

"Don," he began immediately, "I had to come over and ask you about a very great problem I'm having. I don't know that you have an answer for me but I know of your genuine love and concern for children. Your work for this amendment is honorable and I'm helping as much as I can to let others know of it. I know you are qualified to advise me on this problem even if you don't have an answer that will satisfy me.

"As you know, I live alone. But I have grandchildren and love being around little ones. I have a new neighbor, a single woman with three, little girls. I've seen a number of men in and out of the place at different times of the day and night.

"The little girls came to visit me shortly after they moved in. The smallest is no more than two-years-old, the next about three and the oldest, eight. They are beautiful little girls but the middle one is an absolute angel. She has long, ash blonde hair and the most beautiful gray eyes, so wide and filled with innocent trust and wonder that just melt your heart.

"It was the eldest girl that really disturbed me. Like you, I've had a lot of experience working with abused children. I have a finely tuned instinct about molestation and I knew, at a glance into her eyes, that this girl was a victim. Against my better judgment, I gave them all some candy but didn't allow them in the house. You know how hard it was for me to deny asking them in.

"They have been over several times and don't understand why I don't ask them to come in. What can I tell them, Don, and what can I do about my suspicions of molestation of the older girl? And it is only a matter of time until the other little ones become victims as well, you know that!

"You know, Don, I throw food scraps out for the squirrels and birds just as you do. But I can't keep encouraging these little girls to come over by giving them candy. I can safely feed the birds and squirrels and give them treats, I could safely invite a squirrel or bird into my house but I can't let these children come in or give them anything! In other words, I can show more kindness to birds and animals than I can to these children! That's just plain wrong!

"I know how easy it would be to ask leading questions of the oldest girl and get answers that would confirm my suspicions. But I would have to invite her into the house and lay the groundwork of trust to elicit the answers. And that is just too dangerous."

"Sam," I finally broke in, "you're working yourself into a state of mind that isn't healthy or helpful. First, you can make an anonymous report to Child Protective Services. They may already be involved. And they can check to see if any of the mother's visitors have criminal records, particularly if the mother is receiving funds or food stamps from Social Services. But be aware that if you make such a call, you risk your phone number, hence your name and address, becoming known to CPS. But you specify anonymity in case something happens to bring the situation to court. Some of the people in such cases can be very dangerous and CPS isn't exactly the most circumspect or professional organization. Beyond that, there is nothing you can do but protect yourself as you have been doing, hard and cruel as that is, and keep your ears and eyes open to anything going on at your neighbor's place that might be helpful to CPS or the police."

Sam and I shared our mutual hurt and frustration at the fact that there was little anyone can do in such a situation except what I described to him. The little ones did, however, have one thing going for them: A neighbor, Sam, that cared. It could make all the difference, even save a child's life. The tragedy for Sam is that he can't show how much he cares to those little girls.

But the Amendment can change that. If my own night walks become more frequent it will be because I know children are dying every day for lack of this amendment. And many will die needlessly every day that it takes to get the amendment passed.

In my capacity of minister, I still officiate at an occasional wedding; and funeral. I have buried the infant, the child and the adult. It is a hard thing to do, but especially hard in the case of the babies and children. And I seldom volunteer my services.

It is too easy to lie down at night and see myself standing over that graveyard in Belgium, filled with Polly Klaas's, tortured, mutilated bodies of those little girls. What can I say to these little victims of conscienceless beasts that used them, tortured and murdered them? There are no adequate words, they will not come to me, and words could only further profane what happened to these children. Only action will suffice. I know this, and it is the source of the nightmares that civilized men and women must have knowing the same thing.

Then there crowds in on my mind the countless, unmarked graves covering America, the graves of these little victims that fill the roles of Missing Children! And I further know the roles are not complete. Some of these graves contain the babies and children never reported as missing!

For the families of Polly Klaas, Melissa Russo, Julie Lejeune and so many others, the nightmares will never end to the day they die. A pornography and pedophile ring, some members of which were highly placed authorities in Belgium, used Melissa and Julie. Child molestation reaches into the highest levels of the judiciary and government. And these unholy, perverted monsters protect their own whether in Bakersfield, Washington D.C. or Belgium.

Little Melissa and Julie were only eight-years-old. They died in a dungeon without food or water after being brutally raped many times. Videos were made of these rapes to satisfy the unholy lust of beasts in the form of men. You try living with the nightmare of your little girl being murdered in such a fashion! Just try closing your eyes at night with such a constant nightmare ever before you!

To further add to the nightmare, the murderer of these little girls, Marc Dutroux, had served only three years for the rape of five, little girls, the youngest only 11-years-old! But this beast was released for good behavior! As in this country, the psychologists, psychiatrists and judiciary seem to be on the side of the molester.

Only a U.S. Amendment will keep these beasts away from our children. Only this amendment will save our children from the judges, psychologists and psychiatrists, in cooperation with the pedophile and pornography Mafia, who keep releasing monsters like Marc Dutroux and Richard Allen Davis to prey on their little victims!

I lost my eldest daughter to a motorcycle accident. The psychosis of grief took a long time to heal to the point where I could behave in a rational way. But in some ways, the psychosis of such a loss never departs. It is always there when you bury a child.

But Diana's death still left me with me some soft memories, ways of recalling her that do not have the torment that these other grieving parents will live with till they die! I do not wonder that the parents of these children will never be able to live a normal life again. And where is there any justice for these children and their parents, their sisters and brothers? Where is the justice for the little victims of such beasts?

Please don't wonder, as I sit alone writing about these things, that my own mind is not always at its rational best. Dispassionate objectivity is not easy to achieve when you are compelled to write about such things. But if I allowed myself to drift into the kind of grief that accompanies the knowledge and experience of such things, I realize I could not do the work required, I could not be a voice for these little victims.

As a result, I force myself out into the world, I sometimes force myself to read and listen to the music, feed the squirrels and birds and seek the things, and the people that promote softer and gentler memories and give me hope that goodness and virtue will yet prevail. But in the best of circumstances, the nightmares will always be there, I have learned to accept this.

I used to get angry with God about so much suffering of children throughout the world. That was until I understood it not only was not His fault, there was little He could do about it! That jars terribly with the usual concept people have of God. After all, God can do anything is the party line of all religions.

But I came to a point in my life where I had learned and experienced enough to question this religious dictum. And I found it terribly wanting in the face of facts. I was an avid student of theology but I finally had to confront the fact that there really is no such thing as a truly systematic theology in any religious system. They are all filled with errors and contradictions. Only in understanding this was I able to come to terms with the fact that it is our responsibility, not God's, to confront evil and do battle against it.

We are supposed to be the adult children of God, taking on the role of adults with that same responsibility we normally expect of all adults. But we act like children religiously, demanding of God that which is our responsibility.

Supposing that God *is but can't* would go a long way in getting people to accept their responsibility to act. Accepting this, my anger became properly directed at those good people, those patrons of virtue that talk so much and do so little. Further, while I became increasingly angry about the apathy and complacency of those that think themselves good, a perfect hatred began to take form against those evil, wicked monsters that use, torture and murder the children.

Are you one of the good people, especially one of those religious, good people? Have you a more substantial philosophy or theology than mine? Not if it is one that allows you to blame God for that which is your responsibility, not if it is one that allows you an easy conscience in the face of such suffering and brutalizing of children while you wait for God to fix things as you do your duty of going to church, singing, praying and sermonizing while doing nothing substantive to confront such evil!

You must forgive me, knowing what I do, if I seem impatient at times to get this amendment the attention and support it deserves. Children are being tortured and murdered every day without it. If you think yourself good, then do good and quit profaning God in your prayers, start doing the things that only you, not God, can do, the things that are your responsibility, not His! Jesus Loves the Little Children of the World. But Jesus isn't here. You are!

I am only now getting responses to my mailing to the governors. The mailing to the 100 state senators will go out this week. I know you will be most interested in their replies; which I will publish.

Many readers are still writing or calling asking what they can do to support the proposed amendment. I will repeat what I wrote in last month's issue of AP: One thing everyone can do immediately of great importance is to write or call your elected representatives in government, local, state and federal to tell them of the amendment and your support of it. You can also inform your local radio, TV and newspapers.

I will send you a copy of the amendment together with the six-page pamphlet explaining and justifying it. When funds permit, I will be putting together a booklet you may hand out to others to educate them to the purpose of the amendment.

We will need signatures of registered voters supporting the Amendment. I will send you a master signature sheet from which you can make copies in order to gather signatures. This is extremely important. There is a need for people to represent the organization in their respective communities. Please let me know of your willingness to accept this obligation.

CHAPTER TEN

Having received several comments about the August essay, I feel I need to address a few before getting into the issues surrounding the U.S. Constitutional amendment I have proposed.

First and foremost, for those ladies who wrote or called expressing the generous and kind wish that they could be Audrey, I sincerely thank you; this in spite of my picture being on these essays. That is truly inspiring to a poet and to me as a mere man.

While most people responded in a gratifyingly positive manner, I did have a couple of minor criticisms. These objections were from people trying to defend Episcopalians, real estate and used car salesmen.

Now folks, I do not, any more than Sam Clemens, have it in for Episcopalians. One of my best friends is an Episcopalian priest (at least until he reads this essay, possibly). Real estate and used car salesmen, like politicians and lawyers, are another matter.

My comment had nothing to do with the Episcopalian minister caught in an unnatural act with a neighbor's rooster. I am quite certain the story is apocryphal. Just as, I'm equally sure, was Peter Falk's comment on the Albanian gardener and a neighbor's German shepherd. Neither Mr. Falk nor I hate Albanians. Why some of our best friends ... etc!

And far be it from me, noble soul that I am, to cast aspersions on Episcopalians (or Albanians) by repeating scurrilous stories about the priests of that pure institution, of dallyings with choir boys and nuns, of what goes on behind the cloistered doors of their peculiar institutions.

Personally, I'm somewhat opposed to the beating and raping of nuns, Roman Catholic or Episcopalian. But, then, beating nuns has never has been encouraged by most civilized folks, Episcopalian, Albanian, Baptist or otherwise. And to my own credit as a genuinely nice guy, I probably don't know more than two hundred jokes about nuns, Episcopalians and Albanians and hardly ever tell the three worst ones.

I was born in Weedpatch. Raised as a card-carrying redneck, I have a host of jokes about Okies. Known in some circles as The Okie Intellectual, I take pride in my ability to tell Okie jokes.

The fact is that I use my humble origins to poke fun and prick the balloons of pompous asses that think themselves above the common man and woman. I take great pride in my ability to *aw shucks* it with the best of these pretenders to intellectual superiority. And it should go without saying that when we lose our sense of humor, we have lost it all! When we cannot laugh at ourselves, how dare we presume to laugh at others!

During a brief stint in Vegas as a child (our mother had married a disk jockey employed there) I got to see a woman I was in love with, Marie Wilson. Some of you will recall the show "My Friend Irma" in which she starred.

She, Dean Martin and Jerry Lewis were hyping the movie "My Friend Irma Goes West" in front of the Golden Nugget. I remember the sight of Jerry Lewis being towed on roller skates behind a Cadillac convertible down the Vegas strip as though it were only yesterday.

My childhood dream girl, just a few feet away from me up on that stage in front of the casino in person! What a thrill! If some have wondered at my love of poetry (in the ancient sense of the word, not the rhyming pulp or attempts to be clever that try to pass) Marie explains it. I never tire of her recitation of an especially heart-tugging sentiment that stirred my innocent soul.

There she was dressed in a flowing, white gown; her long angel-golden hair shimmering in the neon light of this magnificent casino. Dean Martin passed her the mike and this beautiful girl recited this moving and marvelous example of great poetry:

Of all the fishies in the sea,
My favorite is the bass.
He climbs up in the seaweed trees,
And slides down on his hands and knees.

Thus, you never know what will strike a responsive chord on the innocent heartstrings of a child. Admittedly, some will have difficulty seeing how the noble purity of poetry and romance could blossom in the heart of a child through such a sentiment. But I guess you had to be there.

A few of my detractors would say it goes a long way in explaining my perverse sense of humor. Let the carping critics of my humor try to outdo Irma. But then how many children today have the opportunity to go out in the morning and shoot a dozen quail, bring them home and dress them, arrange them on a bed of sage dressing in an iron pot and, baked in a wood stove, served for Thanksgiving dinner that afternoon? Mine was not the ordinary childhood in many ways.

The reader should know in regard to Irma's poetry that as a child I was also learning the lyrics of songs like I'm a Lonely Little Petunia in an Onion Patch, Mairzy Doats and the classics of Spike Jones and Phil Harris. What child today knows how much real fun music can be?

But because mom and the grandparents loved music, I was raised with the greatest of the Big Bands as well, Orrin Tucker, Glen Gray, Paul Whiteman, Jan Garber, Jimmy and Tommy Dorsey, Glenn Miller and Benny Goodman. Speaking of Tucker, I was too young to realize how provocative Wee Bonnie Baker and her lyrics were. I just enjoyed the music.

Unhappily, mom's career in the chorus line was cut short due to a broken leg from falling off a stage and my grandfather's movie career playing a gambler in silent movies ended when he got religion and never looked back. As I said, mine wasn't the usual childhood.

With that kind of background, plus picking up clarinet and saxophone early in life, I never want for music to set the mood. And I often write with the appropriate music playing. I'm grateful for a good collection of vinyl and tapes.

As hard as it is to believe, in 1953 the number one song on the charts was the Ames Brothers rendition of "You, You, You." As beautiful and romantic a song as you could ask for. But that was a time of great Broadway Musicals as well.

But trouble was ahead, the morally bankrupt Darwinian Socialists of the Supreme Court and the universities were going to remake America into their version of a Utopian Welfare State with justice for none and usher in a period of breaking the back of taxpayers, dumbing down the schools and selling out America and the birthright of our children!

They succeeded admirably. In so little time, if it feels good, do it became the theme and the standards of morality and justice took a dreadful beating. Clark Gable's "Damn" went on to "Catcher in the Rye" in our schools and then arguments over whether Playboy should be in school libraries and homosexuals should be able to get married and teach our children that theirs is an acceptable lifestyle. Well, there's always a price to be paid when real art, love and romance are traded for depravity and vulgarism. Hold up a mirror to 1953, to the music and art of that period and see what 1996 reflects. We have indeed come a long way; the wrong way.

I didn't choose to be a poet. It just happened. On reflection, I had so much of such great value in my life of real adventure, art, music, love and romance (and, of course, the grief and tragedies too common to life) that I just kind of slipped into it.

I have wondered how any reasonable person can refuse to see facts. But such is the case. We call it blind prejudice, an exercise of the will choosing not to see! Few can afford to be poets. As Melville said: "The truth, it don't pay!" I didn't intentionally take a vow of poverty when I decided to write the things I believed people needed to read, it just worked out that way.

But I don't find it any sacrifice on my part to live simply, without the toys I used to think I needed. It took a while but I finally realized it isn't the one with the most toys when he dies that wins, it's those of us who have really lived!

It takes a few of us to be the reminders of what is of real value, who have earned the right to tell the truth about what is dirty and vulgar and what is real beauty. That right is earned on the actual battlefield of reality, of actual life in all its varied facets, in the classrooms of the university and family, in studied contemplation of Creation.

A lovely lady sent me a picture of Hemingway with Martha Gelhorn taken in 1940. She had pasted a heart on Hemingway's breast. I keep that picture where I can see it as I write for several reasons. Hemingway, his father, a sister, a brother and now, a granddaughter, Margaux, committed suicide. As long as I have a heart for others, the depression that demonized Hemingway and the others will not do me in.

But no real artist of any stature, any real poet or gifted writer will escape the psychosis of grief. Jesus well said the righteous enter into life through much tribulation. No one who truly lives will escape it.

If people cannot, or will not see what was traded for the art and music of 1953 compared to what we have today, they are simply refusing to see the facts. But I'm going to keep reminding them.

Say, how about that Martian Meteorite! Wasn't it comforting to all of us to have Jerry Falwell say it didn't mean anything to his Old Time Religion! But of course the flogging of William Jennings Bryan by Clarence Darrow didn't change Bryan's mind either. Any fool knows God put those old bones in the rocks just to test the faith of real believers! And anyone that doubts can go to hell! In love, of course.

But it does good science no credit to believe in a thoroughly discredited Darwinian evolution that has been as destructive to reason as the Darwinian Socialists to civilization. Reason and planning are still the hallmarks of intelligence, even among scientists. Unhappily, there seem as many dishonest scientists in this regard and as bigoted and prejudiced as the religious charlatans.

According God more good sense, intelligence and reason than some scientists as well as Falwell, Robertson and their fellow gospel-peddlers, I found the discovery exciting and the thought that Mars might once have supported life of some kind, that Europa may, in fact, have water under all that ice should give us all a wider view of God's creations.

The ancient rock also gives men hope that the planet Playtex is actually out there somewhere after all. Just foolin' ladies; I love you even if you don't have pointy ears. I don't really think the model can be improved by a green tint and purple hair. But I'm still of the opinion that if there is proof of intelligent life elsewhere in the universe it has to that they leave us alone.

While I live a bachelor life, I'm as tidy as a writer can be. But living in the country has a couple of drawbacks. Alas, there seems no Utopia.

There are bugs to contend with. This summer has brought a plague of ants. I drank a considerable quantity this morning. No, it wasn't on purpose. I'm often up at odd hours and usually have coffee as I write. Sometimes I leave a half a cup or so and take a drink while I'm waiting for Mr. Coffee to do his thing in the morning.

Well, this morning it was still dark when I got up. I drink my coffee Southern style, cream and sugar.

I had left a partial cup on the table in the living room. I had turned on the coffee maker and going into the living room in the dark (home is where you don't bump into things in the dark); I got my cup and took a healthy draught.

My taste buds quickly detecting the strong flavor of ants immediately activated neural transmitters instantly communicating to my agile mind that something was amiss. Coffee should not taste like ants.

The nociceptors at approximately 1,300 per square inch of skin, instantly conveyed via spinal cord to the switching station of the thalamus to the cerebral cortex and limbic center the sensation of little critters crawling all over my face and hands. Ants! that computer-like genius of the cerebrum strongly suggested.

Rather hurriedly, I went to the kitchen, turned on the light and behold! My quick brain proved correct in its assessment of the situation: Ants! Lots and lots of ants swarming all over the coffee cup and, incidentally, me.

Of course I'm not altogether sure how many of the little fellows I ingested, but it looked like a couple of hundred were sent down the drain of the kitchen sink. A quick shower took care of the ones in my hair and elsewhere on my body. More ants sent off to a watery Ant Valhalla.

Not generally given to exotica in food and drink never having cultivated an especially epicurean palate, I have never had a hankering for chocolate covered ants, or ants in any form, not even ant-flavored coffee though I do admit to having had some coffee that might have been improved by a dash of formic acid.

I managed during the day to trace the source to a large anthill outside my back door and applied a liberal dose of Diazinon. As an aside, it's always a good idea to check out shoes and clothing in the country. Before putting on my pants to go outside (being a civilized man) I shook out a rather large spider. They also seek a harbor in my slippers on occasion. The crickets I don't mind as much as an uppity spider. And since I only have the one resident lizard in the house, he can't be expected to handle all these invaders.

Ants and spiders are a fact of life we must deal with. Cockroaches are another matter. Keeping a clean kitchen and not given to leaving food crumbs about, only coffee, I have never had a problem with roaches. You are probably wondering what the point of all this is? Here goes.

I offer the following as a token of my lack of malice toward Episcopalians, that I exercise my acerbic wit indiscriminately: Let's now speak a good word about politicians, lawyers, used car and real estate salesmen, let's hear it for the cockroaches!

Let's face it folks, little difficult to find a good word for cockroaches. Obviously there are many good people making an honest living through used car and real estate sales. But, like congressmen and lawyers, the professions themselves are so riddled with scoundrels they have an earned reputation of distrust and, as a consequence, become subjects of derision and unflattering humor. And if you can't take the heat, clean up the mess or get out of the kitchen!

As I muse on that thought, I light a good cigar, lean back in my chair and with the omnipresent cup of coffee (*sans* ants) and the soothing, sylvan, cacophonous strains of Spike Jones' "None But The Lonely Heart" and "Charleston" in the background, I reflect on the absurd and perverse incongruity of how people will applaud Commit a Senseless Act of Kindness and argue against a Sensible Act of Kindness as per the following:

AMERICANS FOR CONSTITUTIONAL PROTECTION OF CHILDREN

PROPOSED AMENDMENT TO THE U.S. CONSTITUTION

An adult convicted of the molestation of a child will be sentenced to prison for a term of not less than ten years.

If the child dies as a result of the molestation the person(s) convicted of the crime will be sentenced to life in prison without the possibility of parole.

A child as defined by this article shall be one who has not attained their sixteenth birthday.

The Congress shall have power to enforce this article by appropriate legislation.

NO NATION THAT FAILS TO CHERISH ITS YOUNG HAS A FUTURE AS A NATION.

NOR DOES IT DESERVE ONE!

Senator Rogers is among those honorable men in government I am privileged to know and call friend. And knowing of his love for children, family and America, I knew I could count on his efforts on behalf of the amendment. It will take the efforts of good men and women like Don for We the People to carry the battle ahead.

My proposed Amendment for the protection of children from molesters, a breed of cockroaches apart from all others and beneath the contempt of all those thinking themselves civilized, is meeting with some interesting responses. I envision myself addressing a stadium full of people, a hundred-thousand strong, and I ask the audience this question: Will all those who believe molesting children is good please raise your hands!

In all this throng, no one raises their hand. Why? Because like beating nuns, civilized people know molesting children is not good.

There are those who believe we should follow the Old Testament injunction to stone the molester to death- Immediately. There are those who believe he should be treated as mentally ill. There are those who believe he should be incarcerated for life.

For the sake of a civilized humanity, I urge that the molester be incarcerated for life without possibility of parole. This breaks the chain of molestation, an essential and absolute necessity for the sake of a civilized humanity. A man in Texas recently confessed to the molestation of hundreds of children! How many more will be saved by his being imprisoned?

Life without possibility of parole encourages the victim and witnesses that the molester will never again be loose to molest or seek revenge. The victim and witnesses deserve this peace of mind. Society owes them this much.

I further suggest that the molester be kept apart from the general, prison population or separate facilities be provided. It is only fitting that the molester be restricted to his own kind; let psychologists and psychiatrists treat the poor sick mind of such cockroaches in the slime of their own, private environment.

Society must serve notice by this amendment that such bestiality will not be tolerated among a civilized people! But the molesters are not the only cockroaches this proposed amendment is flushing out from under their respective rocks. I have already had offers to help with the amendment from other species of insects and reptiles.

One such offer was to put the amendment on the Internet; for almost $7,000. Now I'm not naive enough to think publicity for the Amendment can be had at no cost. But damned if I'm going to have people on the side of this for their personal gain!

I have just one question of such cockroaches like those who want to support the amendment if they can use their names and organizations for profit: Where were they when the children needed them? Bottom line: I'm only interested in the help of people who are willing to sacrifice for it and keep their selfish interests and petty egos out of it! Others need not apply! This amendment is for the children, for America, not you!

Thoreau well said he could find 999 patrons of virtue to every virtuous man! There should be one inviolable right for every child in the world, the right to be free of molestation! These patrons of virtue are those who pay lip service to it but fail to support it by their actions. It is the inaction of good men and women through which evil prevails and gains the ascendancy in a society. Who in their right minds could ever believe in disinterested virtue? That won't fly!

It is not enough to discern evil; action is required! Why, I have to ask myself, is it that so many think themselves good when they take no action against evil? I know good people; at least they consider themselves good, who cannot give an answer when asked about absolute goodness. Many of these are religious people who point to God or Jesus as their definition of absolute goodness. Of course this is a copout that might relieve their religious consciences, it makes no demands on them personally to be good or do good as mere human beings, and it relieves them (they rationalize) of the responsibility to take action against evil. That's God's job, not theirs, they say.

But I long ago cast my lot with the founding fathers who accepted their responsibility to take action. Yet many good people find fault with these men for not doing a perfect job. I would ask such patrons of virtue what they have done to improve on it? Virtually no one disagrees that absolute goodness must exist in some form somewhere. It must exist in order to have any hope that good can do battle against evil and prevail.

I propose that if the people of a nation cannot recognize their responsibility to guarantee, to the very best of their ability, to cherish and protect their young, such a people are incapable of recognizing absolute goodness and fully deserve the tyranny of the wicked! If such a people are incapable of recognizing this absolute goodness, this absolute, empirical necessity for their continuance as a civilization, they face dissolution as a culture, as a viable society and nation.

Molestation, homosexuality, pedophilia, and pornography: Where in history have such things ever been the proud monuments of a culture or any nation? Rather have they not invariably been the hallmarks of a nation in decline, reflecting a society degenerating to depravity and inevitable destruction of a civilization?

Far too many patrons of virtue, faced with the enormity of the task, will put their hands in their pockets and sit down saying they can do nothing! It is hopeless! they exclaim. I say a pox on all such, particularly when these same patrons of virtue have the temerity to claim rights that noble, better men and women paid for with the fullest measure of devotion, rights that such patrons have taken for granted as though liberty can be had at no cost to them!

I say to such: Confront the evil, do battle against it or stop claiming a heritage that you insult! Stop thinking yourself good, for heaven's sake, when you profane such a heritage by your talk without action! You dare think yourself better than those evil and wicked men and women who achieve success on the back of your apathy and complacency!

Does this amendment guarantee protection of children? Show me a law that makes any such guarantee of protection; that is flawless in its application! Law is for the lawless, not for the law-abiding. Law is designed to punish and protect by the threat of punishment. No law guarantees freedom from lawbreakers. But the amendment does guarantee punishment. It is the deterrent value of law in a civilized society that serves the purpose. And a nation is known by its laws.

There are those who say that America is so far gone down the path of moral depravity that We the People can no longer change its course! I refuse to accept this. I know too many good people, people of the moral fiber of those who died for this nation, to accept any such defeatist pronouncement!

I think a lot of these people are like the guy who went to see a doctor about a pain in his stomach. The doctor asked him if he knew what was wrong and the guy said "Of course! There's a frog in my stomach."

The good doctor, knowing he was dealing with some kind of nut, gave the man an enema and while doing so, slipped a dead frog from the laboratory into the excreted material. Seeing the frog, the man went happily on his way, his stomach in good shape. The story is attributed to Doctor Bethune who is supposed to have said "The man really needed the enema for his body, but he needed the frog for his mind."

The people who think America is too far gone to reclaim, who believe without even thinking or trying, that this amendment isn't needed or can't pass, are like the guy who really needs an enema but also needs to see the frog. The amendment is designed to cure the real ailment, but their prejudice is that a frog is to blame for their sickness. As long as these people keep blaming the frog, they can do nothing. They will keep the frog, and the pain, and refuse the enema. Yet I can think of nothing as appropriate as the purgative enema of this amendment to begin to expunge the painful filth that has been allowed to accumulate in the American Body. Not a pleasant remedy but an essential one.

It takes a devious and cunning mind to come up with a story about a young boy who cons other boys into doing his work for him. And to get the other boys to pay him for doing so! Now you gotta admire a con of that magnitude. That Sam Clemens had such a conniving and devious mind is reflected in this story about Tom Sawyer. Why anyone with a lick of sense knows Sam was the brains behind the con!

There is nothing as common as the failure of genius. It's not what you've got, it's what you do with what you've got that counts. Now we all have a gift or gifts. Some are great artists, composers, architects, musicians, and writers. Sam and I were gifted as con men.

Much as I admire Sam as the most gifted, natural born liar this earth has ever seen, I don't think I need take a back seat in this department. No, sir! Being number two, I try harder. When I get together with other fishermen, I'm the first to say I've caught more and bigger fish than they have lied about! Given enough time to consider, I can contrive a devious answer to the most innocent or innocuous question.

I think my genius in this department has been neglected by not applying it exclusively to politics (or TV evangelism or real estate sales). I'm a natural. You know the old cliché: If you've got it, flaunt it! And when it comes to the well-contrived, well constructed and executed lie and con, boy have I got it!

Now there are a few misguided folks out there that think this is nothing to boast of. Why I know good men, even ministers, who think I should be ashamed to tell others of my extraordinary abilities and talents in these things, that I should never expose my proficiency with a cue stick or my familiarity with an honest, friendly and gentlemanly game of five-card draw poker. They are wrong!

I offer the following example for the consideration of good people, of God-fearing, church-going people:

Suppose I ask Bill Clinton to support my proposed amendment to the Constitution?

Now I write our president and tell him I believe it my duty as a citizen to let him know, as my president, the elected leader of the United States of America, of the amendment.

Here is a man described as a draft-dodging, womanizing crook! And I offer him the opportunity to go down in history (depending on the forthcoming election) as the president of the U.S. at the time of this amendment, an amendment beyond the magnitude of the Emancipation Proclamation, an Emancipation Proclamation for children, the slaves of molesters, putting Clinton in the category of Abraham Lincoln! Yet this is precisely what I have done! And if President William Clinton has the political savvy of a warthog and is as shrewd and intelligent as I credit him, he will know he doesn't dare turn down such an opportunity for greatness.

Now if this is not the act of a genius for deviousness and cunning you tell me what is! In one fell stroke, I have achieved a con even Clemens would bow to, a con so successful I can declare it openly and even the victim, the President of the U.S. will thank me for it!

But I'll kiss the hand of every voter who stands up for this amendment. I believe even the President loves his child. I can forgive and overlook a lot in people who genuinely love children irrespective of their personal creed or politics. Republican, Democrat, Libertarian, Christian, Jew, Moslem, agnostic or atheist, there are no boundaries of separation in loving our children, protecting and providing for them the hope of a future devoid of being the prey of the predator/molester.

In talking with my very good friend, Linda, the last lines of I Corinthians 13 came to mind: "And now abides faith, hope and love. But the greatest of these is love." The question we were discussing was whether faith and love might be synonymous? Linda had showed me her mustard seed. Many of you have seen these small glass balls containing a mustard seed.

The parable in Matthew and Luke is a familiar one to most: "If you have faith as a grain of mustard seed, you can say to this mountain, be cast into the sea and it will be done" hence the expression, "Faith that can move mountains."

My book, HEY, GOD! has prompted several people to write or call thanking me for removing the tyranny of religion from their lives. For this I am most grateful.

The New American, The Freeman, Frederic Bastiat, Ludwig von Mises, James Dobson and Focus on the Family, etc. all fail to get at the root of evil. Not all the problem-solving ethics of good men and women will ever be successful until Americans are united in common cause against evil.

All the above have their particular agendas in correcting errors and educating the American public. And, for the most part, the information they provide is good and necessary to have an informed mind and pursue courses of corrective action.

I never tire of Thoreau. While most certainly not in agreement with some of his points, like friends, we agree to disagree at times. I don't always agree with Ben Franklin, Tom Paine, Thomas Jefferson, Sam Clemens, H.L. Mencken, Walt Kelly or Tom Lehrer.

Yet, Thoreau makes points to which we should all pay heed. I still urge everyone to read his tract on The Duty of Civil Disobedience: "Let every man (and woman) make known what kind of government would command his respect, and that will be one step toward obtaining it."

My one step after writing and speaking of the abuses and tyranny of Caesar for so many years is this Amendment. Yes, good men and women see the Amendment as simplistic, as asking "Who is in favor of nun-beating?" But these good people fail to realize that beating nuns is not a problem.

Molestation is. If nun-beating was the problem, I can see all these good people fighting to get in line for an amendment opposing it.

Why should they oppose an amendment that addresses a real problem rather than a hypothetical, nonsensical one? Ah, that speaks volumes about the mind-set of Americans who have been trained not to see the problem in all its monstrous ramifications, who fail to take action rather than just talk! And it speaks directly to all those so-called *men* who think girls and women are there to be used for their pleasure and abuse! Especially those *fathers* of the babies of young girls who take no responsibility for their rutting like animals.

If good people will take the time to think through the arguments for the amendment, I'm confident they will see the wisdom of it. They will have to face the question of why those who make their millions through the sexual exploitation of children and women oppose it, why some seemingly patriotic and religious organizations oppose it, why some judges and lawyers oppose it, why high-ranking officials of government oppose it.

While I have the greatest respect for those good people who disagree with me, and I fully understand the grounds for their disagreement, I do ask that they be willing to acknowledge their personal prejudices and confront them, that they be willing, personally, to make Thoreau's first step before rejecting the amendment out of hand.

In other words, stop being a patron of virtue and choose to be virtuous! If you fancy yourself having so-called *intellectual problems* with the amendment, try putting yourself in the place of Polly Klaas as she was tortured, raped and murdered! Or put yourself in the place of her family, a father, mother and grandparents who will suffer this nightmare the rest of their lives! And try to imagine, as a part of the nightmare, them living with this animal bragging about how he masturbates to the image of his murder of their little girl! At this point you will understand my saying: To hell with your intellectual rape of the absolute good in favor of your groundless and virtue-less arguments in opposition!

If this amendment had been in place, the animal that tortured and murdered Polly would have been kept in prison when he first molested a child and this little girl would still be alive! People who express the fear that the amendment will cause people to be subjected to greater risk of false allegations of molestation need to get their brains in gear. I can name hundreds of allegations you are presently subject to from doing drugs to beating your wife. Are you objecting to the risk of the laws governing these allegations? Moreover, do you for a moment, think that just because I accuse you of beating your wife that you are going to be arrested and hauled immediately before a judge on the basis of an allegation? Come on now!

I repeat what I have said earlier, we still have a Constitutional guarantee of due process. If due process fails, it usually fails on the side of the criminal and against the victim. The amendment, on the contrary, will force agencies like Child Protective Services to do a much better job of investigating cases of child abuse. Having worked for the agency, I know how it presently operates. There are few, truly qualified personnel in CPS. With the amendment, the agency will be forced to hire people properly trained, not just those with the Mickey Mouse degrees in Social Service basket-weaving courses. I'll give you just one example of many I could give of the lack of qualified personnel in CPS.

When I was interviewed for the position, one part of the process was roll playing. I was asked to determine if a young girl's allegation of molestation by a stepfather was true or not. Now there were two women and one man on the interview committee. You'll never believe who played the part of the young girl. The Man! Was it because he was a homosexual? That's the definite impression I got from him, Social Services does use homosexuals in the organization on purpose! But this opens a Pandora's Box to a host of problems within the agency.

Like the schools, Social Services attract molester candidates for positions for the obvious reason that they will have ready access to children. Homophobic? No, just the facts. But then who would have guessed we would ever witness the travesty of homosexuals trying to get legal sanction for their marriages? Insanity! There seems no end to such depravity in a society that acts, more and more, like it hates children and families! And I too well remember how Anita Bryant was vilified and crucified for her stand against homosexuals as teachers in the schools. But she was right!

We need people trained in the law, people with proper training in psychology, people who have had actual experience in working with abused children. And it should go without saying that homosexuals are the last people who should be working with such children and families! And it would be the height of inexcusable, ignorant prejudice to be blind to the activities of homosexuals in their attempts to legalize their perversion and the attempts to stifle this amendment! The amendment will force universities to design the kind of curriculum and standards that will assure properly trained graduates. But as a society, we better get rid of the fox and start watching the hen house ourselves.

Because of the huge responsibility that attaches to the amendment with the concomitant risk of monumental lawsuits against it for not performing responsibly with facts in hand rather than mere allegations, CPS will have pressure brought to bear on this agency and the schools and universities to perform responsibly which is greatly needed and long overdue.

While I was waiting outside the courthouse one morning to give testimony in one case, a man approached me with tears in his eyes. He said to me: "What gives you people the power to just come into a man's home and take his children away from him!"

My answer to him: "Do you know who your elected representatives are, are you a registered voter, did you even vote in the last election?" He admitted *no* to all these questions.

I then said to him: "You're asking the wrong question of the wrong man! It is your elected representatives who are responsible for this, not the people in a system designed by those representatives." And maybe men like this father will register and vote; will become educated to what is needed to really protect children from real abuse! And the only way to address the wrongs in the system is to make it accountable by taking it out of the hands of these elected representatives through the action of We the People!

Once removed from the bureaucratic, non-accountable (like the public schools and I.R.S.) autocratic present structure, CPS, with the demand of this amendment, will be forced to accountability! If the proposed amendment generates the kind of discussion it needs and deserves, good people are going to have to face their own responsibility for the kind of morality they preach we need in this nation, a morality that they have not taken any positive action to encourage! And this brings me back to my discussion with Linda.

James in his epistle points out the fact that faith without works is dead, meaningless rhetoric. Jesus said that we will know people by their works. He is also quoted in all three synoptic Gospels as saying: "It would be better for a man to have a millstone tied around his neck and be drowned in the depths of the sea than to hurt a child!" And you know Jesus wasn't talking about the disciplining of a child in love. No matter the race or creed, all people acknowledge the truth of this, as all people give lip service to loving children. But look at a nation's laws; look at the living conditions, and the hope of a future for its children to find the truth.

In the case of America, we have passed a plethora of laws demanding child-proof caps on bottles, child-proof cigarette lighters, child seats in cars, we have multiplied organizations directed to the needs of children and yet, as a nation, we have failed to address one of the most fundamental rights of a child, the right to innocence. Without that innocence, a child loses the best of childhood, and with that loss a nation loses the best of the adult's ability to contribute to the softness and gentleness of virtue without which a hard and callous society results.

It is a commonplace of history for a people to become inured to evil and callous to virtue. We seem to have reached that point in our own history as a nation. We need to fight for this amendment in order to know, as Americans, whether we do, in fact, cherish our children, whether a child has a right to innocence and should be raised virtuously.

There can be no doubt that the proposed amendment will be an accurate barometer against which Americans will be able to measure their genuine love and concern for children. And as a nation, we need to know this. We need to know whether there is enough morality, enough virtue to do battle against evil and win! And if Americans cannot take a stand on such an obvious moral absolute of goodness, we need to know this also. It is my fervent hope that this amendment will be the turning point of this nation back to the virtues that made us the most powerful force for good in history and a beacon of hope to the rest of the world.

June 30th of this year, San Francisco hosted the 26th annual gay pride parade. It is estimated that 317,000 participated including Roberta Achtenberg, senior advisor to the department of Housing and Urban Development, the highest-ranking lesbian in the federal hierarchy. Not to be outdone by the feds, there was Willie Brown, the city fire chief, Bob Demmons and police chief, Fred Lau.

Two regional Methodist groups recently voted to welcome homosexuals and Presbyterians voted to allow the ordination of homosexuals as long as they promised to keep it in their pants (technically called a vow of celibacy). I suppose naiveté in the name of religion isn't confined to the snake handlers of Appalachia.

It is no wonder that Supreme Court Justice, Clarence Thomas, went back to Roman Catholicism. Say what you will of the Roman Church, in spite of its ignoble history and many failings, of its being steeped in ignorant superstitions and mythologies, its stand against perversion is clear and unwavering as opposed to many Protestant denominations. But for centuries the RC church has shielded the perverts preying on children in its own ranks.

To point up a fact of hypocrisy in government at the highest level, when Thomas was asked about his re-conversion, he refused to give an answer. And how could he, a Supreme Court Justice, admit it was to personally escape the homosexuals while being a member of that High Court promoting perversion!

By the arrogance of a Supreme Court dedicated to re-inventing the Constitution, with total disregard of virtue and the wishes of the majority of good Americans, a minority consisting of perverts are free to flaunt depravity and perversion, even insist that it be taught as acceptable in the schools and insist it be given special privilege of law! Yet children are denied protection from predator/molesters at the very federal level that has been grotesquely distorted to protect the perverts! Is this what We the People really want America to stand for? I think not!

The moral and ethical dilemmas that we must face honestly as a nation are not going to get better for our children unless we take a stand. How many real Americans think we should have open borders for people to cross at will? How many think we should simply allow foreigners to have babies here at taxpayer expense to become instant citizens and go on the dole? Insane! And because literally insane, national suicide if you will, unheard of in any other nation in history!

In talking about the amendment to so many people I have had to point out the absolute necessity of bypassing the Supreme Court by the amendment process. This court that has arrogantly trampled the will of We the People so many times by re-inventing and grotesquely distorting the Constitution to their Socialist agenda and despising virtue, would immediately cry that the amendment is unconstitutional if the people of any state tried to put it in their state constitution. This court must be put in its proper place of serving the will of We the People, good and virtuous Americans, it must be by-passed and only a U.S. Constitutional amendment can do this! Let us resolve to give our children their needed Emancipation Proclamation, freeing them to be children, granting them their right to the innocence of childhood without fear and turning America back to virtue and goodness through this amendment!

It is sad that there are so many men out there without daughters. My eldest son never married. He hasn't the foggiest notion of some of my feelings as a father toward his sisters. Now Daniel is an exceptionally intelligent young man. But he makes the all-too usual mistake of assumed knowledge to which we are all heirs in one way or another. Being intelligent, he thinks he knows and confuses feelings with knowledge and experience. But he's certainly not the only man who would ignorantly and arrogantly tell a woman he knows what's it's like to be pregnant!

So my boys, Daniel and Michael, would accuse their dad of being chivalric toward the girls. Just like all brothers of sisters. Understandable since the boys got the brunt of physical discipline, among other things, rather than the girls. A father hopes his sons will grow up to be men and his girls to be ladies and is inclined to corresponding discipline. The boys, of course, know this is imminently unfair.

Too much of manly love toward the boys? Perhaps so; it's a tough world they face and men commonly try to raise their sons with the toughness to deal with it. As a result, the boys often don't get enough softness and gentleness in childhood.

Most destructive of all is the infamous double standard that many men pass on to their sons, that girls are there for their use and abuse, that boys are to be experienced and girls are to be chaste, a lie straight out of the pit of hell itself!

But until I had my little girls, there were most certainly some things I would never have learned about women. And no one would have been able to convince me that I didn't know what it was like to be pregnant. My own pompous foolishness in this regard probably surpassed that of my sons'.

When it comes to pompous arrogance concerning things never experienced, few rise above Soren Kierkegaard who wrote so much about women, family, love and romance yet never married! Now that takes an arrogance above and beyond even that of which I'm capable!

At least I have learned there is no getting around this; as Clemens so well pointed out: "Some things are just unlearnable." Men like Kierkegaard will assume they know regardless of the facts against them. The prejudice stands and will not be moved, at least until they have little girls of their own.

I think the boys, like most men without daughters, chaff mightily under the truth of my statement: "There are things about women that simply cannot be learned unless a man has daughters!" Among these is the all-important softness and gentleness a man can only learn from these little girls, things women seem to lose as they grow up and boys seldom learn from sisters.

So it is in our corrupt society that women lose the capacity to teach these things to men. And being unable to teach such things, no longer being in a position to demand respect and an appreciation of themselves as women encouraging the compatibility of differences to prevail rather than the present norm of competition and combativeness, men do not learn from women. The men, growing up callous to the softness and gentleness of women, take full advantage as predators and seducers.

It takes a mighty good man to confess to such ignorance. I was not such a mighty good man. God knew I had to have daughters in order to correct my pompous, bigoted, prejudiced and arrogant ignorance. No one was going to tell me I didn't know what it was like to be pregnant!

But, alas, my winter victory over the tragic loss of my springtime is summed up in "Old too soon and smart too late." So many things that make sense now could have saved a lot of heartache back in the spring. A paean in praise of finally gaining a degree of wisdom? No. What is a poet if he is afraid, if he does not feel free to express his thoughts and feelings?

I have my songs at twilight, I can still hear Love's Old Sweet Song and even though I have never had a kiss from a woman that was not betrayed I still thrill to Jeanette MacDonald's high C's, of the love I have known no matter how temporarily given.

While winter stares back at me in the mirror, spring lives in my heart and mind. The strength of my youth was not entirely wasted on the young;

the years inside the prisons of factory walls were devoted to wife and family. And while the spirit of the poet had to give place to the necessities of life, there was never any thought of selfish sacrifice. A man is a man for that. And while the flickering shadows of memory do not bring to mind a faithful kiss, there are memories of the softness and gentleness of love, more love than most men will ever know.

What dark force insists that we say farewell to dreams? Only if we forget to listen to the music, one of God's great gifts he intended to sustain us. The vain philosophies and pathetic, pretended poetries of men without wife and children, men like Thoreau and Kierkegaard who missed so much, whose genius could have been so much more, miss the best part of the music of life.

The poet is called on to be the guardian of what would otherwise be lost. If you are trying to live without the music, you are defeated before you enjoin the battle! Because the battle is for family and children, for the actual music and poetry of life! For genuine love and romance!

There is an enormous amount of lost, unknown treasure of which our children have no knowledge. I still need a candle or oil lamp to reclaim some of that treasure as I sit in such soft light and consider the fact that I have really lived, never settling for a quietly desperate existence! And while I have lost many a battle, the enemy always knew he had been in a fight!

No poet has any right to the name unless he does battle against the enemies of what is pure, the enemies of beauty, virtue and romance. He is compelled to confront the ugly depravity, greed and corruption that would profane those ideals of the Absolute Good!

And having really lived, there is an excitement about what I hope to carry with me into my greater life among the stars! I have been enormously blessed with having fought the fight for wife and children, for being able to make music and sing, for being able to express my feelings in writing and have others tell me I have blessed them as well in doing so. I have been blessed with a life that makes the candle and oil lamp significant in my life, where the quiet is not always lonely. I have been blessed with the trust of so many children, of the sharing of their hopes and dreams.

No matter the meanness of our circumstances, if we have the music we can make it. I tried to make music important to my children. How many would never be involved with gangs and crime if they had been given a clarinet or guitar? Few things are as rewarding as being able to make music. The joy and self-esteem of such a thing can make all the difference in a child's life.

But it should go without saying that it must be the kind of music that inspires joy and fun, love and romance, not the trash our young people have been sold as *music*. You simply cannot compare Blue Champagne and noise glorifying drugs, perversion, violence and irresponsibility!

And in the lengthening shadows of life, if in the soft light of an evening by candlelight you can call up the following from the recesses of memory, you will know it has all been worthwhile: "When my life is through, and the angels ask me to recall, the thrill of them all, then I shall tell them I remember you."

And that folks is the stuff of the stars, what we were created for, what we must restore to our children!

CHAPTER ELEVEN

I wonder how many of you remember the movie "Gidget?" It came out in 1959 starring Sandra Dee, James Darren and Cliff Robertson with the Four Preps, Darren and Morris Stoloff doing the music. Having lived the life of the Lotus Eaters with the music of Camelot and clean, uncrowded beaches with no graffiti in sight where the movie was made, it was my era and my life during the late fifties and early sixties.

Leaving the wilderness of the Sequoia National Forest and my life among the critters on the mining claim, I found myself in Redondo Beach and soon made myself familiar with Hermosa, Manhattan Beach, Santa Monica, Venice and Malibu. The transition was eased by the music that I continued to play and sing, music as common to me in the wilderness as it was in Camelot. The kids at Mira Costa High School in Manhattan Beach where I graduated knew and loved the same music so, by continuing to play in the school band and at dances together with my job at Floyd and Gil's Auto Body Shop on PCH (Pacific Coast Highway to the non-cognizanti) in Redondo, I gained acceptance to this new environment.

To watch Gidget now is to realize how much our children have lost. Toward the end of the movie, Gidget and her mother look at a motto on Gidget's bedroom wall. It reads: "To be a real woman is to bring out the best in a man."

After all these years, I am surprised to find myself much more in love with Gidget now than I was then. Perhaps it's because in our maturity, having learned and understanding what is of real value in life, neither Gidget nor I will ever really get old. In our minds the ideals of love and romance remain unshakable and hope of the future will never die.

Gidget, as with Audrey Hepburn and me, did grow up. We learned to love others, to love children. And in learning to love, we never got old. So I watch what is now an old movie and Gidget and I are young once more in the true environment of a Camelot that promoted the best of innocent love and romance, the best of a hope for the future and the Four Preps together with Morris Stoloff always provide the music in the background, the sea and shore remain clean and uncrowded, filled with the scent and sound of the kind of magic only the Pacific Ocean and the old South Bay could provide.

As I write this, I am sadly aware of how few people can truly understand what I am trying to say. It is a tragic loss to our children that they don't even know what it is that they have lost. So I suppose someone has to recall it for them, someone like myself who was there when it was all real, when it was actually happening and Gidget and I were in love and knew it because she, as a real woman, brought out the best in me as a man; she was the poetry, the music and the inspiration that a real woman should be for a real man.

It's the responsibility of the poet, the maker and recounter of his age, to never let the magic die but to pass it on to the next generation. It remains the definition of true poetry to be a recounting of the actual but in a way as to be memorable. And nothing but a real woman like Gidget can inspire the poet to his best.

My own poetry is much of that of the essayist. As such, it is intensely personal as both poetry and the essay, by definition, are supposed to be. The poet and essayist is an intense examiner of his own life. It is through self-examination, meditative, reflective, studied that the experience of his own life lived in conjunction with others becomes remarkable and so he is compelled, finally, to remark.

Michel Eyquem de Montaigne (1533-92) is the father of the *Essai*. As he pointed out, he did not set out to make himself a study for books. It just happened. Before Montaigne, it was thought unacceptable to set one's life out in such personal terms as he did. This was held strictly as the purview of the poet only. Montaigne freed the poet to incorporate the essay, this method being far more liberating to comprehensible expression to the masses of people. In later times, this degenerated to a form that became what is called prose. But a good, poetic essay is read pen in hand and, just as a good piece of music sets the mood of tapping your feet and clapping your hands or instills a mood of love and romance, the heart and mind are moved to respond.

Along with Gidget, we had "Rebel Without a Cause, Picnic" and some of the best Broadway Musicals ever made. Things were beginning to get confused. The Theme From Picnic or Moonglow, Morris Stoloff providing the music for the movie, is one of the most beautiful compositions. I still thrill to it, especially the Mcguire Sister's version, and always will. But you lose something if you don't visualize Kim Novak and William Holden dancing to the music.

Literature just before and after the turn of the century was already tending to a realism that exposed many of the evils of the time. Life was not all sweetness and light, it never had been. Much as I admire the genius of Faulkner, Tennessee Williams and some of Arthur Miller, I still hold to the fact that a humanity that can produce such masterpieces of beauty, love and romance like the Musicals and Gidget must have within itself the potential of overcoming evil. A humanity that can portray Gidget cannot give itself over entirely to cynicism or brutality. Gidget gives me ever-renewed hope that she and I, together, can still speak for the children. Gidget and I are not naive. We are believers in love, truth and justice. And knowing the best of these, we are able and willing to fight for them.

I would have counseled Kim Novak not to run off to William Holden until he had something to offer a wife. I would have told James Dean that he better get his act together and behave responsibly before his little friend or Natalie Wood got hurt. But Holden told the truth when he said to Kim Novak: "I can amount to something with you!" A real woman brings out the best in a man. A real man and woman know that love has responsibility. And it is a responsibility that is gladly embraced.

I am not naive. But I know the most powerful force in the world is love. And I have learned that love is not naive. If the love is real, William Holden and James Dean will get their act together. Gidget will bring out the best in a man.

Lacking naiveté, I know how this generation would respond to a movie like Gidget. They would laugh at it- that is if they could sit through it. Tragically, they would not understand their laughter. But they have never known a life untouched by the brutality of drugs, immorality and violence, a brutality of life that has made virtue, love and romance quaint anachronisms.

Certainly I'm transported when I watch the movie to the magic of that time I lived and experienced with Gidget. I don't have to overlook what is now thought to be the ultra-simplicity of it and the lack of technical sophistication and Spielberg special effects. But, unlike the children of today, I also know it wasn't a sham. It was real in its most important parts, real in a way that makes such a tragedy of the lives of our young people today, real in making self-discipline and the accepting of responsibility and making a life commitment to another a part of genuine love and romance.

When Cliff Robertson looks at Sandra Dee and says: "She may be pint-sized but she's quite a woman," he knew what it was all about. When James Darren looks at Gidget and tells her she "represents real responsibility for a man," he knew what it was all about. And Gidget knew what being a real woman was all about when she brought out the best in these two men.

Neither Gidget nor I would understand it back then. We understand now. But that motto on her bedroom wall had been passed down from her grandmother to her mother and then to Gidget. Grandmother and mother knew and in time Gidget would come to know and, hopefully, pass it on to her little girl.

When Moondoggie and Gidget finally face each other as Francis and Jeffrey, the pledge of their love is enough, all of the commitment to each other in that college pin, the anticipation of what lies ahead for them is the thrill of a lifetime never to be repeated; and never needed to be repeated. To know real love and romance is a lesson once learned never to be forgotten.

The world desperately needs Gidget, the girl for whom the pledge of love is enough, the girl who lives in such a way that commands the respect of boys, who, as men, come to understand the supreme value of what Gidget represents and encourages it. A large part of my Birds book is given to a description of the tragic loss, especially to girls and young women who have had little but brutality and smashed dreams in their lives, who never had the grandmother and mother Gidget had.

The proposed Amendment might turn our young people's lives around, it might provide a moral and virtuous environment when girls can, once more; dream of Knights in shining armor and boys will be encouraged to respect and prize virtue and purity in girls and themselves. Too few of our children are being raised with any awareness of how vital to self-esteem and self-worth morality is, of how important it is to value yourself before you have something of value to offer and have the right to expect that value appreciated by another.

Parents who try to raise their children with the right values and morality face seemingly insurmountable obstacles everywhere they turn. A whole society seems to be the enemy of such things. Yet we know, as a society, that such values are needed for any hope for our children, the future of our nation.

Only the innocence of childhood can accomplish this. I have had to live this long to appreciate this fact. I have had to live this long and experience what I have of real love and romance together with its betrayal to understand. Therefore I do not criticize our young people for not understanding. It is not their fault, but mine and those of my generation for not holding on to the ideals of Gidget.

She and I did not know what we had when we were young. How could we? We were young. We know now. But we knew we had something beautiful, something that made life wide and full of promise. It takes the years to teach us and give us understanding of that something.

This is why it takes a poet to preach the message, someone who can be a fool to so many who will never understand and risks it all for those who can. To make the need of innocence known is a difficult message in the face of the loss of so much innocence. Few of my generation ever learned the lesson; few ever experienced real love and romance. I know this when it is impossible to see a movie or hear the music of love and romance in our lives, when we are bombarded with noise and violence all around.

The need for this amendment grew unconsciously in me. It formed itself from the loss of so much of the softness and gentleness I wanted for my children, for all children. It formed from the writing I began to do in an effort to help change the direction I saw America heading. The background and experiences of life were all there to bring such a need to my attention. Gidget came to represent what I knew I had to fight for and how to do it.

At the time the movie came out I was dating a girl, I'll call her Susan, who confessed in tears that she had been molested by her stepfather. Her mother knew about it but did nothing. The best the girl could do was to get a lock on her bedroom door. What could I possibly say to this beautiful, young girl as I held her in my arms and tried so clumsily to assure her that in spite of what this wicked man had done, she still had a life ahead of her, that not all men were like him?

But Susan still had a senior year of high school to finish, she still lived in a house where this man might force himself upon her again and she could not depend on her mother to protect her. In those days, you didn't just pick up the phone and call CPS. And even if she could, the blasting of the home would have left her ... where? Her mother needed the provision of the stepfather and if he was arrested and they lost his income they could be out in the street.

Over the years I came to realize how prevalent this tragedy actually was. And Susan and Gidget became a contrast by which I was able, finally, to grasp the magnitude of the problem. Like Gidget, Susan was a very beautiful and talented, petite girl. She played the lead in the Senior Play, she was a contender for Prom Queen and, to all outward appearances, had it made.

But her private life was hell and I was far too young to understand and help her. She began to drink and the mother and stepfather didn't dare try to stop her out of their own fear that the ugly secret would become known. Susan partied every chance she got. Being so beautiful, she didn't want for attention from boys and that, with the increasingly heavy drinking, finally sundered our relationship.

Since I couldn't know at the time what Susan needed, how her self-esteem had been so thoroughly shattered by the molestation and conditions in her home, how the shame she carried made her act as she did, we parted. By the time I wrote the Birds book I understood the problem and was able to draw the necessary conclusions. And one of these conclusions was the scourge of easy divorce in this country. Parents divorce with utterly selfish disregard for children, with little or no concern for the little victims of such selfishness. As one woman told me: All I want is my freedom!

If Gidget's parents had been divorced, if she, like Susan, had been attacked by a stepfather there would have been no innocence and purity, no virtue that would lead to that pledge of love between her and Jeffrey, no promise of that wide life ahead so full of promise and so worth working and waiting, faithfully, for. Now we live with the cynical, betraying laughter of our young people who can't possibly believe in the message of Gidget, who laugh at that motto on her bedroom wall, who laugh at waiting for sex, who laugh at the patience of responsibility and self-discipline for the sake of the future.

My generation is to blame for allowing the message of Gidget to fall prey to such laughter. As the generation before Susan betrayed her, my generation betrayed Gidget. If this nation had dealt with the problem of molestation as it should have, if our previous generations had taken it as seriously as they should have, maybe Susan could have lived the life of Gidget and have become a woman who would have brought out the best in a man. But Susan was destroyed by a society that refused to take the problem seriously, that has steadfastly refused to acknowledge America's dirty, shameful secret.

As the recent meeting in Stockholm has evidenced, it isn't only America's dirty, shameful secret. The selling and stealing of children to satisfy the unholy lust of beasts in the form of men is worldwide. And as was discovered in Belgium and is just as true in America, these beasts often hold high positions of power and authority in the judiciary and government.

Only the proposed U.S. Amendment dealing with molestation will solve this problem, will take these beasts from their thrones of power and remove them from preying on the innocent. It will break the back of the pedophile and pornography Mafia!

Do not be surprised at the seeming apathy of government leaders, even their open hostility to this amendment. The power that perversion holds in the highest levels of our society and government is a monster that will fight against any attack on it.

To the tragic dismay of the parents of Polly Klaas, Melissa Russo and Julie Lejeune, they found that the monsters, Richard Allen Davis and Marc Dutroux, were protected by judges, politicians, psychologists and psychiatrists. Dutroux had only served 3 years for the rape of five, little girls. The youngest was only 11-years-old. Yet, the judges, politicians, psychologists and psychiatrists, as in the case of Davis, had released him for good behavior!

Only as Americans, as We the People, can we hope to do battle against this molesting monster. Far too many such monsters fill the ranks of Hollywood, of church, school and media leaders, politicians, judges, psychologists and psychiatrists. This is why I have brought this issue to We the People, bypassing, out-flanking the monster. We The People have the God-given right, duty and responsibility to revolutionize against the tyranny of the monster.

Susan and I were betrayed by generations before that failed to take action. Every girl should have the right at a chance to become Gidget. Every boy should have the right at a chance to expect Gidget in his life.

The word corny is always used with derision. But it is usually a mask for the deeper feelings of loss, a false bravado in the face of the knowledge of that loss. There are multiplied millions of older women who recall Gidget, who would give anything to go back in time and have been able to make that choice for responsible love and romance, to be worthy of her Jeffrey. And there are the multiplied millions of older men who would give anything to be able to go back in time and live worthy of finding and winning Gidget.

That sense and knowledge of such monumental loss in so many millions of lives haunts our whole society, it is a dark Specter that confronts us everywhere we turn. Our young people can be excused for their ignorance, we, who should have been their teachers, cannot.

But the loss of such holy, sacred innocence is manifested in drug and alcohol abuse, in the mounting crime and violence of our society, in the disintegration of families and the increasing loss of hope of a future for our children. And that word, *Corny*, becomes increasingly a fitting epitaph for a nation dying for the lack of hope for Gidget, dying for a lack of genuine love. Yet Gidget is reflected in the eyes of millions of little girls. The Jeffrey's are possible in the boys who are taught that purity and virtue are manly things. And, believe it or not, there are millions of young boys and girls out there who want to believe in Gidget and Jeffrey even now. Even though the peer pressure is enormous, even though an entire society seems their enemy, these young people fervently wish their lives could be so *Corny!*

But as a society we have failed them, failed to protect them and provide them an environment where they can reasonably expect the best that true love has to offer them. And we have failed to teach such love, failed to show them how to find that love for themselves. In short, we have failed to cherish our children. Tragically, that word *cherish* has fallen to the low estate of the word corny. But Gidget and Jeffrey found it in each other and they would grow to understand it. Cherish, to them, became the meaning and essence of their lives, the sum of their own fulfillment of love, joy and happiness in each other.

I was sitting with some friends, a married couple, at the Club. We were waiting for the band to start. She is a petite blonde and he is a neatly dressed, successful businessman, a very nice and normal appearing couple. But they are both divorced, she was molested as a young girl as a result of the divorce of her parents, they both have children and their lives are a horror story rooted in molestation and broken families. Now they face having to raise children together as husband and wife, they face having to raise these children when the parents, themselves, are emotional and psychological cripples. And they are aware of this.

They have sought my counsel but what can I really tell them? The enormity of the damage in their own lives will be a factor in every decision of life that they will make for their children. And those children have no family as such. Who are the other parents, grandparents, aunts and uncles in such cases? Scattered, fractured, a witch's brew of kin and quasi-kinfolk- The American Family?

But this couple, as so many others of similar background who have to live with the heartache of the betrayal of innocence, of the betrayal through divorce and resulting molestation, have become staunch supporters of the amendment. They understand the importance of it, the hope and protection it offers their children that they had to grow up without.

Heaven, to me, will be a place where my own Gidget and I will be able to share our love for each other, a place where we, finally, will have all that the immortality of love promises, a place where we will be fulfilled by living that love for each other. *Corny.* Heaven will have to be a place where Susan will have her tears wiped away, where her love will find fulfillment without fear of betrayal, where her real purity as a woman will be realized for its true value. I know Heaven will have someone for Susan and all the other Susans who have suffered so much in this world. *Corny.*

A very lovely, attractive woman who recently read my Birds book got in touch with me and asked if we could possibly meet over coffee. She told me some of her own story. She was under the care of a psychologist because of her problems with relationships due to her being molested as a child. She shared with me that she had her psychologist, a woman, read the book. The verdict of the psychologist: "This Dr. Heath really loves women!"

What higher praise could any man ask for? Yes, I love women, my daughters, Gidget, Audrey, Susan taught me to love them. It is why I can write of women like Gidget, Audrey and Susan as I do. A woman has a great capacity for love; she does not have to deal with some phony macho syndrome. She can expect of herself, like Gidget, to represent the softness of love and trust. Yet women will betray themselves in the very area of which they are supposed to represent the ideal. With a false message of some kind of ephemeral equality, women have forsaken the very position for which they alone could represent the ideal of that softness and purity of virtue that, alone, can bring out the best in men.

Men, as the responsible parties in the area of seduction, have taken full advantage of this abandonment by women of their position. And the children suffer the consequences. Unlike so many men who have tried to get in touch with their so-called *feminine* side, I don't have one to get in touch with. I never bought into the wimp sermon. I'm proud to be as masculine a man as you will find. But I never became a Neanderthal that had to prove he was a man. Because of the genuine love I knew and was surrounded with as a child, I didn't have to go looking for love in all the wrong places. I had a proper male role model in my grandfather and the best of role models of women in my grandmother and great-grandmother. But the love I had to offer, the love I learned in such an environment, was betrayed by the girls I met who hadn't had such a loving environment.

As a young man, it was easy to blame the girls since I was without understanding. The years and experiences of life were needed for maturity and understanding, and especially for the absolute essential of compassion. I watch Gidget now knowing that that is the way it was supposed to work out in my life. But, as I said, she and I were betrayed by generations that did not take the necessary action to allow us to find each other and be what we were intended to be for each other. Our love was betrayed by those who allowed the Monster, the Beast to rule over us.

Living the life I have has given me impeccable credentials concerning the Beast. I know the enemy as few others know him. I have been plunged into the dark side of the betrayal of love and romance, the betrayal of hope of a future for our children.

But those credentials, to be effective, have to be exposed and few would choose to expose such a life in such personal terms. And it takes a genuine compulsion to do so else I would die of mortification. It takes a compulsion to stand like Luther and say: *Ich Kann nicht anders*! I can do no different. No one in his right mind would purposely set out to look such a fool and suffer such acute embarrassment.

So I write as I do from compulsion, not choice. My choice, as I've said many times, would be to tell the world to go to hell and I'd go fishing, I would choose the critters to a corrupt humanity and live my life by the trout stream in the wilderness. But my daughters, Gidget and Audrey, Susan and so many others will not allow it. Most certainly Polly, Julie and Melissa will never allow it. As a result I'm a condemned man in a sense, condemned to make my own foolishness a public spectacle, telling such embarrassing truths about myself as to evidence no sense of shame of my own thoughts and failures.

The shame, at times, is appearing an egotistical, pompous ass while at the same time calling others by these same epithets. The seeming hypocrisy is not lost on me. I cringe from the very justice of such an accusation. But the compulsion to tell the truth, the whole truth and nothing but the truth is to live with the consequences. That the consequences are appearing, at times, the egotistical, pompous fool and hypocrite comes with the territory of that whole truth.

God knows only those with nothing to lose could possibly take on such a task, even unwillingly like myself. No man with the responsibility of a family to protect should consider such a thing. The Beast is there and will shred you if you have a name he can attack, if you have anything you hold of value, especially your pride, above the things necessary to do battle against him.

The Beast has the power to make even your good to be evil spoken of. He has the power to destroy your reputation and good name no matter how well deserved and earned. The best of men and women do well to consider this before enjoining the battle.

Not being naive, I knew when the compulsion to do battle against the Beast became such that I could no longer refuse it; he would delve deeply into my own life to discredit me as the messenger. My best defense against this is to make my life an open book to all, no matter how foolish I may be made to look in the process. If he can discover any dirty secret in my own closet of shame, he will use it in an attempt to stifle this amendment.

Fortunately, I have never been arrested; I have never done any sordid thing of which others can justly accuse me. While I have made many mistakes in life and suffered many failures even as a husband and father, none of you have to worry about some dark skeleton I have tried to hide.

This has not been the result of any kind of moral perfection in my life. I have lived with thoughts of murder and revenge in my heart, I have the normal capacity of lust common to men when I see a beautiful woman, there are many shameful thoughts that come to my mind that I struggle against.

But the love I knew and was taught as a child, the accident of birth that gave me the music and literature, the good people I knew and know, and most of all my children, were my salvation from becoming the worst of men. That I have remained out of prison, that I have not followed the leading of a treacherous and betraying heart is due more to others than to me.

Far from retreating and living in the past, in attempting an escape into it through the music, art and literature of a softer and gentler time, I have chosen to learn from it; and in learning from it, to fight the battle in the nasty here and now. Confusing to the enemy as well as to my friends is my propensity to mix Montaigne and Gidget. The two would seem to be of two different worlds, the world of the academic and the world of the romantic and poet.

Allow Samuel Johnson to help make the connection. For those familiar with Johnson's life through James Boswell's masterpiece of the biographer's art, it may come as a surprise to some few that the great man himself was an unsurpassed essayist. Called the *Literary Cham* (Khan) a virtual literary dictator of his time, only Shakespeare is more quoted in English literature.

In regard to my own attempt to explain the point of a man like myself, a seeming contradiction in so many ways, trying to get others to strive for success in the face of my own, many failures, I will let Samuel Johnson help me out:

Nothing is more unjust, however common, than to charge with hypocrisy him that expresses zeal for those virtues which he neglects to practice; since he may be sincerely convinced of the advantages of conquering his passions, without having yet obtained the victory, as a man may be confident of a voyage or a journey, without having courage or industry to undertake it, and may honestly recommend to others those attempts which he neglects himself.

The interest which the corrupt part of mankind have in hardening themselves against every motive to amendment, has disposed them to give to these contradictions, when they can be produced against the cause of virtue, that weight which they will not allow them in any other case. They see men act in opposition to their interest, without supposing that they do not know it.

Those who give way to the sudden violence of passion, and forsake the most important pursuits for petty pleasures, are not supposed to have changed their opinions or to approve their own conduct. In moral or religious questions alone they determine the sentiments by the actions, and charge every man with endeavoring to impose upon the world whose writings are not confirmed by his life. They never consider that they themselves neglect or practice something, every day, inconsistently with their own settled judgment; nor discover that the conduct of the advocates for virtue can little increase, or lessen, the obligations of their dictates. Argument is to be invalidated only by argument, and is in itself of the same force, whether or not it convinces him by whom it is proposed.

Yet since this prejudice, however unreasonable, is always likely to have some prevalence, it is the duty of every man to take care lest he should hinder the efficacy of his own instructions. When he desires to gain the belief of others, he should show that he believes himself; and when he teaches the fitness of virtue by his reasonings, he should, by his example, prove its possibility. This much at least may be required of him, that he shall not act worse than others because he writes better, not imagine that, by the merit of his genius, he may claim indulgence beyond mortals of the lower classes, and be excused for want of prudence or neglect of virtue.

It is recorded of Sir Matthew Hale, that he for a long time concealed the consecration of himself to the stricter duties of religion, lest, by some flagitious and shameful action he should bring piety into disgrace. For the same reason it may be prudent for a writer who apprehends that he shall not enforce his own maxims by his domestic character, to conceal his name, that he may not injure them.

From: "An Author's Writing and Conversation Contrasted."

So I let Sam speak for me in order to force critics to find argument with the great Samuel Johnson before taking me on. I strongly suspect they will find Sam too formidable for the task. In this way, Gidget and I will have the last laugh by my refusal to hide behind a *nom de plume*, by refusing to couch the message in more palatable fashion and words designed to spare both myself and the reader from the embarrassment of reading of my actual life and thoughts where I am compelled to tell (or confess) them to make a point. In the words of Jesus, "there is nothing hidden that will not be revealed." So why hide?

The Biblically literate will immediately make the connection between Samuel Johnson's comment and the Apostle Paul: "For what I want to do I do not do, but what I hate I do." Romans 7:15. But in Paul's case, contextually, he is making the point for the necessity of law in a civilized society; hence the absolute necessity of the proposed amendment as essential in a civilized society.

And in making every attempt to avoid non-sequiturs in my own apologetics, I take advantage of a certain skill in being able to discern the fallaciousness and weaknesses of the arguments of those that oppose the amendment, of those who would consign Gidget and me to wearing rose-colored glasses, of a Pollyanna view of life. In my own defense, no one who has read any of my books would even be able to consider me in such a fashion. On the contrary, they will discover how deeply I have plumbed the depths of the depravity to which some of the race called human can lower itself.

I will not joust or play at quoits linguistically in some egotistic orgy of verbiage cleverly designed to conceal my real message. I will call a spade a spade even to my own hurt in many cases. In telling stories on myself it is my hope that any embarrassment falls on me rather than others and others may take heart that if such a fallible human being as myself can undertake to do battle with the Beast, they may also.

There are some who, understandably, have reservations about the success of the amendment. But there has already been a dramatic impact from it in Congress. The mailing of the amendment to President Clinton directly effected the recent votes defeating giving perverts special status in employment and same sex marriages and every governor and senator in the U.S. How do I know this? By a remarkable phone call I received from one senator.

With a promise of anonymity from me, this man told me being informed of the proposed amendment influenced his own vote on these two measures! I am sure he was not the only one so influenced. Here in California, the same sex marriage bill was withdrawn due to the action of congress so the proposed amendment has successfully hurt the Monster, the Beast without its even yet being law! But the Beast knows this is coming and I expect the battle to really start heating up. I take great encouragement by the victories already won. But I have no illusions about the ability of the Beast to do battle. He is firmly entrenched in power and authority and has the forces to bring to bear in waging war against those of us who work to protect our children from him.

The Human Rights Campaign is one of the nation's largest pro-homosexual political groups. The close vote in the Senate gives us a pretty accurate assessment of how many in authority are perverted themselves! This group will continue to lobby for legal sanction of perversion. You can well imagine the kind of response this organization, masquerading under the title of Human Rights would have to the amendment!

But the human right of children to be protected from perverts is not the concern of such a so-called human rights group. On the contrary they will work to protect perverts and in the same breath try to say that just because a person is homosexual does not make him a molester. And I agree. Then let this same group come out publicly in favor of this amendment and quit lying about their concern for human rights! And you can take it for granted they didn't take part in that conference in Stockholm!

I want to take this opportunity to confront politicians, and the Beast, concerning Megan's Law and all its variations from state-to-state. Just what in the hell are these molesters doing running loose in any neighborhood! Why aren't they kept in prison where they obviously belong?

How nice that a concerned parent can go to the local police office and have them punch up the names of all the molesters in their neighborhood. Why the hell are they in any neighborhood? The beast who tortured and murdered little 7-year-old Megan Kanka was already a twice-convicted child molester!

I quote Assemblywoman, Barbara Alby, R-Carmichael, California: "Child molesters are very effective at what they do and will continue to do it as long as they can. Under a cloak of virtual anonymity, they exploit innocence by feigning sincerity in order to prey on children." The State of California Department of Justice presently lists a database of 64,000 registered child molesters. I judge this to be, conservatively, one-fourth of the actual number in the state!

The World Congress Against Commercial Sexual Exploitation of Children in Stockholm, Sweden was the first such conference ever held. 1,000 participants represented 130 countries. Every speaker expressed anger and outrage at things like the torture-murders of little Melissa Russo and Julie Lejeune.

Child-sex pornography is a multi-billion dollar industry worldwide. But King Albert II of Belgium is getting educated to the fact that it is an industry filled with people in authority. His call for action has already resulted in the arrest of 23 people involved with the beast, Marc Dutroux, including 9 high-ranking police officials!

These same police authorities had been asked by the parents of the missing girls for help and pretended to be on the case! And all the time they were cooperating with the animal that had these little girls in a dungeon, raping them, starving them and selling videos of the child-rape to other beasts!

Now, are we going to see any arrests of the judges, psychologists and psychiatrists who determined the monster, Dutroux, should be released for good behavior? How about We the People taking a hard look at just who is responsible for letting monsters like Richard Allen Davis in this country out of prison for good behavior so he could rape, torture and murder Polly Klaas?

How many of the literally hundreds of thousands of child molesters are walking the streets of our neighborhoods, hunting for their innocent little victims, because of judges, police, politicians, church, school and civic leaders, psychologists and psychiatrists saying they are no threat to children! Take a very hard look at those that say the molester is only a poor, sick person in need of understanding and can be cured! As the people of Belgium have discovered to their horror and shame, many of these professionals are a part of the Beast's network!

Nor can we afford to overlook the entertainment media's role in this. This media in support of perversion under cover of espousing tolerance produces the slickest propaganda imaginable. Because of the battle for this amendment, Americans are in for a surprise when they discover, and they will, how many of these professionals are in the business themselves and are looking out for their own perverted interests here in this country!

Some believe we can solve the problem of the Beast by passing laws like chemical castration, Megan's Law, etc. Extremely naive and foolish proving such people know nothing in reality of the nature of the Beast. And I have repeatedly pointed out the fact that most of these proposed state laws are nothing but political posturing by politicians who know, full well, that the A.C.L.U. the homosexual lobby and the Supreme Court will not allow any effective legislation to be upheld.

Do not be deluded by the lip service of politicians. They make good political rhetoric but nothing, and I mean ABSOLUTELY NOTHING short of the proposed amendment has any chance of success in destroying the Beast, in breaking the back of the Molester Mafia! But we are going to have to confront Samuel Johnson's *Suspirius* "The Human Screech-Owls first. Their only care is to crush the rising hope, to damp the kindling transport, and daily allay the golden hours of gaiety with the hateful dross of grief and suspicion. But ... heaven seems to indicate the duty of barren compassion by inclining us to weep for evils which we cannot remedy."

Johnson, like Sam Clemens and so many like them, had little hope of humanity, S.J. calling his own a dark generation.

But Johnson and Clemens, et al. didn't consider Gidget. She does not allow of despair of humanity. Her star gleams brightly throughout. In spite of being surrounded by the Screech Owls most of my life; those who wring their hands and preach apocalyptic sermons saying "Nothing can be done!" In spite of having to confront them every where I go, I have the memory of Gidget and Audrey to give me hope, the memory of Susan, Polly, Melissa and Julie to make me never give up the battle.

As a result I stopped thinking and writing in terms of evils without remedy and began to consider the ultimate causes of such evils. This study took me, literally, into frontiers beyond the scope of Star Trek, frontiers where no man had gone before.

Before I am accused of boasting of such an extraordinary area of exploration, let me point out two curious facts I cover in a couple of my books. One, women are not permitted in the areas of philosophy and theology. Two, the relationship between men and women has been a problem without a solution since the beginnings of recorded history. It was an exploration of these phenomena that led me into areas of inquiry that were so seemingly diverse, even oppositional, that I finally had to conclude they were uncharted territory.

The innumerable talk shows on the subject of relationships, the thousands of books written are immutable proof that these things have defied solution. And, since this is the case, there is something missing in the research, many prejudices, false hypotheses and erroneous assumptions that had to be confronted. Beginning with my own, the hardest task of all.

Because of my publishing my research about these things, a friend (ex), Dr. Gary North, a well-known publisher and theologian consigned me to the eternal flames of hell unless I publicly recanted my heresies. Another acquaintance, Dr. John MacArthur of Grace Community Church, a man well known to the religious community world-wide warned me, graciously and charitably as opposed to Gary, of espousing extremely dangerous doctrines!

You would have to read my books to get the full meaning of the kinds of exploration I have done that made these two worthy men feel compelled to pronounce such dire warnings of my soul's peril. Essentially, the exploration led me to the conclusion that God has made errors of love, that humankind blames and profanes God, scapegoats Him by asking him to do things he cannot, that are the responsibility of humankind, people, and not God.

Including the role of subatomic particle physics in the area of paranormal studies, the possibility of life elsewhere in the universe, the possibility that we are not dealing with actual human beings in the normal use of the term when we encounter the beasts that prey on children, the lack of anything like a true systematic theology in any religion and several other things quite critical of religion and much quasi-science in general have not made life easy for me with the brethren and colleagues in religion and academia.

But study and research into even the most seemingly esoteric phenomena, physics and mathematics has its place in studies of human behavior. As I've said many times, the need to bridge the gap between the arts, social and hard sciences is one of the missions of the poet, his Grand Unification Theory of understanding.

In studies of brain function, a frontier as vast in its way as that of the universe, separate memory systems suggest themselves. This together with proof that the brains of men and women are different in some very fundamental ways raises fantastic speculations about human behavior. I explore many of these things in my HEY, GOD! book.

My own studies of such things have played a prominent roll in my coming to the conclusion that nothing short of the proposed amendment will accomplish what is needed to turn America back to the ideals this nation has historically stood for. The knowledge of the very diversity of such things and how they impinge on each other is essential to understanding both the need of the amendment and its effects that are of an extreme sociological complexity.

In reading the "Declaration and Agenda for action by the World Congress Against Commercial Sexual Exploitation of Children" held in Stockholm, I am impressed by the effort those representatives of the world community have expended in making the seriousness of the Beast known. I most urgently recommend people get a copy of this. It can be ordered directly from UNICEF in New York. Write UNICEF, New York, NY 10017. I suggest including a donation of at least five-dollars when requesting the report.

As I chronicle the effort of getting this amendment passed, it will eventually be a book I am thinking of titling: "The Evolution of a Revolution!" And make no mistake; the amendment will revolutionize America! Since it will take some years to accomplish this, as with most revolutions, it should grow to quite a book.

A part is already being recorded in these essays. To come will be the responses of the various leaders in government, the churches, the media, and well-known personalities. It is already proving to be quite interesting just from the responses I have in hand, the way just making the amendment known is having an impact.

For many who are frustrated with the fact that a constitutional amendment is a very lengthy process, I would point out the necessity of educating people to the very need of the amendment. And this process of education is going to take some time, even years. As a classroom teacher of many years experience, I understand the process and have no illusions that the lesson is going to be an easy one for the majority to comprehend.

For example, the adult is a result of his or her childhood. Adults build their lives on the experiences of childhood. Not especially profound and everyone shakes their head in the affirmative. The molested child as with the child who was raised on a TV diet of inanity, sex and violence, a deficiency in reading and math skills, a broken home, etc. shows up in what is sometimes referred to as the X generation. This generation never knew of the things I experienced in the wilderness and Camelot.

But the X generation can learn if it is given the chance and has the desire to learn. It is my fervent hope that by writing of things like the wilderness and Camelot, of Gidget, people will catch the vision of what is needed and how to accomplish bringing it to pass. An example of this educative process is the fact that far too many people are not aware and have no understanding of how absolutely essential it is to raise children in innocence. The loss or lack of such in their own lives, tragically in too many cases, has clouded the judgment of such people. This leaves them with no basis of understanding, no foundation to build on. It is an extremely arduous undertaking to provide such a foundation of understanding.

Charles Lamb (1775-1834) noted for his warmth and gentility of tone in writing, clearly perceived the problem.

He writes of a picture that haunted him from childhood, one he wished he had never seen. It was that of the Witch of Endor calling up the prophet Samuel. That witch and mantled wraith were his pillow-mates in the dark and made the nights a torment for him.

He wrote: "Parents do not know what they do when they leave the tender babe alone to go to sleep in the dark ... when they wake screaming with no tender voice to sooth them ... That detestable picture gave the fashion to my dreams, if dreams they were!"

My own version, as a child, was the movie, "The Picture of Dorian Gray." No child should have been exposed to such a film and it took a great while before I, like Charles Lamb, was free of the spectral images and hobgoblins such things induce in the mind of a child.

I knew there were dangers in the pictures, music, TV, videos, movies and literature which society allowed, even forced, upon children that would haunt their childhood, things that would tear at the fabric of sleep with horror and dread! The common cry became that children faced a hard world and had to be taught the realities of it, that they should not be grown like hothouse plants. Well, we certainly succeeded beyond all expectations to grow children by the millions like little, tormented devils instead.

I thoroughly enjoyed the old classics of Dracula, Frankenstein, The Mummy and The Werewolf. I still do. But even these now dated classics of horror, like the fun of Halloween, must be carefully monitored according to a child's age. America's preeminent funny man, Bill Cosby, I'm sure would agree. But we all know the horrors of shock and splatter movies and videos, largely pervert generated, to which even the youngest child has been exposed in this generation! And we all know these things have had a dreadful effect on millions of children. I will not watch a movie where women and children are raped, tortured, murdered, used and abused. I deal with enough of the reality of such things that I don't need to watch them represented by so-called *entertainment* media.

I was discussing the Lotus Land, Camelot, of my youth with my eldest son, Daniel, the other night. He still lives in Torrance and has easy access to the area Gidget and I knew so well. Fortunately, I can now share some of the intimate details of my life as a Lotus Eater with my son. Virtually no one who did not live it could believe such a fairyland existed as the old South Bay of the late fifties and early sixties. And as I pointed out to Dan, it was the stuff of dreams that others could only experience vicariously through the music and movies of the time. But it was real, it did exist and I lived it.

The memories of your girl and you being able to park in your convertible at the sea shore to watch a blood-burst sunset while listening to Ebb Tide on the radio; the music of the waves rolling onto the sand in tune with the song was magic. The warmth and softness of the heavenly-scented girl in your arms while the music played; the sight and sound of the ocean with isles of imagination just beyond the horizon of that great, mystical expanse of water promised the immortality of the love that swelled in your heart.

Now I realize it was only the tiniest almost infinitesimal blip on the screen of history, the tiniest of microcosms in time and geography. But it was real. It happened. And I was there. It happened to me, I was a part of it. And that makes Gidget and me unique. I know this. Finally.

But it took the innocence of childhood to evoke the kind of love, the kind of magic in my life while living in such an enchanted fairyland to keep and hold the images for the use of the understanding and appreciation of what Gidget and I had which would come to me years later. It would work itself out in the later experiences of life as I matured in that understanding and appreciation.

Throughout my training in business and industry, my university work, the classrooms of the thousands of teenagers with whom I was entrusted, my own children, the immortality of love I had experienced by living that early fairy tale was always there. In spite of all the tragedy and ugliness of life thereafter, my idyllic life in the wilderness and the old South Bay gave me the essential foundation to appreciate the absolute necessity of innocence in childhood. I saw the evil that was being forced upon children and was helpless to do anything about it. Oh I tried. But a whole society seemed bent on making my warnings the cant of a moralist, a dreamer.

But the reality of the wilderness and South Bay experience insulated me, protected me from the growing ugliness others were accepting as reality. I watched, helplessly, as real love and romance were being traded for this other, demonic reality. For the briefest period of time, I uniquely lived the reality that Gidget represents. And Gidget brought out the best in the man; she was the real responsibility of genuine love and romance.

But the evil that was set on destroying what Gidget represented was hard at work, had been hard at work to make sure there would be little hope for the millions of children of the next generation having a chance to become Gidget or Jeffrey. The Beast was determined to make Susan the rule rather than the exception. Gidget and I were going to be relegated to a fairy tale and reality was going to become If it feels good, do it and to hell with a future, to hell with the consequences! *I want it all right now and I want it all my way*!

In our turn, Gidget and I were to become quaint hobbies for antiquarians. But at what a tragic, dreadful price! Childishly, selfishly, far too many were buying into the idea that there can be real freedom and liberty without responsibility and self-discipline. The chance for being Gidget or Jeffrey, of finding and being able to offer genuine love has a price. It is following the path of virtue, the path of self-discipline and refusal to settle for anything less than real love and romance, the reality of which is evidenced by personal responsibility.

The enemies of innocence are not just found in the ranks of the Beast. They are the millions who know they missed the best of life, who traded their own innocence for that doctrine of I want it all and I want it all now! But in those ranks are those with a conscience, those who have learned the hard way that the price they paid is one children should never have to pay. And among these I will find people who will stand up for the right of children to be raised in innocence, boys who will grow up with a right to expect to find their Gidget, girls who will grow up with a right to expect to find their Jeffrey!

I've sometimes made a point of what the great American Musicals, the last time poets worked in America as Wodehouse pointed out, have meant in my life. I've written about women like Julie Andrews in her role of Maria in The Sound of Music being really in love in order to play the part as convincingly as she looks at Christopher Plummer as she sings. To watch Sandra Dee as James Darren sings to her is to see the look of love. The great tragedy of Hollywood has been its continual betrayal of love. So many who played out their fantasies, so many who gave us our enduring fantasies of love were actually in love or seeking love.

No one will ever forget Marilyn Monroe. Like Susan, to all outward appearances, Marilyn had it all. But she died betrayed by the illusion of a fantasy, betrayed by the assaults on her by men who had treated her as a thing to be used when she was young. But it never lessened her need of love; it never lessened her need to be treated as something other than a sex object.

In Picnic, Kim Novak tells William Holden she is tired of only being thought of as pretty. She meant she was tired of not being taken seriously as a woman, a person instead of a thing! Yes, she was a beautiful woman. She knew this. But, like Gidget, she knew she was a great deal more than that, that she had much more to offer a man than just pretty!

James Darren sings to Gidget the words: "There's no such thing as the next best thing to love." You can see in the eyes of Sandra Dee her belief in this, it is so much more than playing the role of Gidget, it isn't something that even the best of her talent, her training as an actress can pretend, it's real. Sandra knows, like Gidget, what love is. She had to know to make Gidget believable, to call up that look of love in her eyes as Darren sings to her.

But there has to be a worthy object of such love. I write in my Birds book about the tragic irony of an institution, Hollywood, that portrays such marvelous, glamorous pictures of the fulfillment of love, romance and dreams and is filled with so many that are lonely. To hold that girl in your arms and, looking into her eyes, to sing to her, to share that belief in each other's love that the music has to have such expression, such an outlet for it's overwhelming emotion of a full heart is the stuff and the glory of the stars.

The enemies of such beauty of love and romance are many. In a sour grapes voice they cry: Corny! The enemies of these things of real beauty would have us believe Sandra and Julie are only actresses playing a part in a fantasy. They're wrong! The best of talent and professional training cannot put that look in their eyes while the music plays or make them believable without their actually being in love. Those wells and windows of the soul will not allow it!

Women like Gidget are the inspiration, the poetry and music that bring out the best in a man. A man should feel he can hold such a woman in his arms and sing to her. After all, she was created to be the object of his heart's desire, the inspiration for the song and the best he can do as a man. He should feel the whole weight of the responsibility she represents, the responsibility and obligation to be a real man who is sensitive and gentle to her warmth and softness.

Gidget has the right to expect such sensitive gentleness from such a man, together with the needed strength to meet the obstacles and adversities of life and overcome them, protecting her and providing her the things that only a real man can provide a real woman. Knowing such things, having experienced them in my own life, I know the obligation I have to preserve their memory, to work for giving our children a chance at them. This means restoring our children their inviolable right to innocence. Only then can we raise our children in an atmosphere of hope for their future.

Innocence once lost is not to be recovered. But for those of us blessed with the memory of it, it should be the inspiration, like Gidget, to do better for our children, to recover it for them. I have lived my life in association with much violence, and not just the violence of Watts and East San Jose, the ghetto and barrio. But I have also lived my life with the music, the language of love, playing always in the background, the knowledge and love of great art and literature always alive in my soul.

The fact that I could write, that I could make music with clarinet, saxophone and guitar, that I could sing were vital to my heart's need of such things. The tragedy was that I couldn't seem to understand how to make these things of such beauty real and needed to others. I knew others desperately needed such things but they seemed unaware and I didn't know how to preach the sermon.

I know now that my text should have been Gidget and the great Musicals, not the orthodox one approved of an increasingly callous, depraved society. There was nothing wrong with the message of Gidget and the Musicals, it was a corrupt society that kept calling the real and needed message Corny, a fantasy, and all the while the Beast was stealing our children's rightful inheritance of innocence.

I belong to the Columbia House Video Club. I just looked through the Holiday 1996 catalog. There were listings for Action, Comedy, Drama, Family, Foreign, Horror, Musicals, Sci-Fi, Suspense, War and Westerns. Take a look at that list and tell me what category is missing. Romance! Sure, romance is to be found in some of the categories like the Musicals. It just didn't deserve its own category. Horror and War did; something to think about. I do.

The squirrels come to my back door for treats. My furry little companions trust me. It was easy for me to earn their trust and they reward me by their trust. I write a good deal about the relationship between people and animals. I have always loved animals and was raised in an environment where they were my constant companions, even those called wild.

But it is, to me, a heartache to see a wild animal caged. Now I know the zoo serves an important function. Nevertheless, what a sadness it is to know so many children will never know what it is like to experience such creatures in their natural, wild environment.

It would be wonderful if all children could have the experience of living in association with animals, if they could have the experience of growing a vegetable garden. The responsibility of tending animals or vegetable gardens is lessons needed in childhood. The pet cat or dog and the lawn are inadequate substitutes. Yet millions of children don't even have these.

What have we traded for Sir Walter Scott, James Fenimore Cooper, Swiss Family Robinson and Huckleberry Finn? What have we traded for the music that used to be romantic and fun? What have we traded for the fraternity pin of pledged love Gidget wore so proudly? In a word: Innocence!

There are those who are concerned that meeting the evil of the Beast, doing battle with him in the form of this amendment, will result in a battle among good people, that it is not necessary to meet the evil with such seemingly drastic measures. Yet those of us who are so intimately acquainted with such evil know there is nothing else that will avail. The chain of molestation can be broken in no other way. And breaking that chain is the only hope of destroying the Beast!

Had the source of the Black Death been understood, millions would have been saved. I know the source of this Black Death that has robbed our nation of hope for its children. I cannot use ignorance as an excuse for not taking the necessary action.

Lincoln freed the slaves yet we, as a nation, have not a single element of our constitution or its amendments specifically addressed to the particular needs and protection of children. Why not an Emancipation Proclamation directed at freeing children from the slavery of molestation?

Why should it seem a drastic measure to protect our children at the most fundamental level of human rights imaginable? For a nation that beats such a drum as that of human rights, that intrudes itself constantly into the affairs of other nations at this level not to practice what it preaches, is a hypocrisy at which other nations rightly sneer! We will pass federal laws aimed at the protection of animals, aimed at protection of our environment, yet there are those who dare, ignorantly or with malicious purpose, to say this amendment is a drastic measure! Just who is kidding whom?

There are those who claim it is up to the individual states to pass laws about molestation. This is not a state issue; it is a national one, a worldwide one! I strongly advise every governor and state senator to stop their political posturing and support what is a national need! So California governor, Pete Wilson, has legislation for chemical castration. He knew when he signed it that the A.C.L.U. and the homosexual lobby would challenge it. And sure enough, the A.C.L.U. immediately hollered: Barbaric! Of course they haven't called what Mark Allen Davis or Marc Dutroux have done Barbaric! But it will look good on a conservative resume if Pete tries for President again. And I think he will. Several governors have already replied to the proposed amendment. I've yet to hear from Pete. No one is a stauncher believer in state's rights than I. But I am not a propagandist of the statist creed that denies there are areas where we must take action as a nation in concerted agreement!

If America is to lead in the direction the conference in Stockholm points for the world; what better affirmation of our determination to do so than this amendment? I can think of no better affirmation of virtue, removing the stench of national hypocrisy, than for We the People to demand this amendment!

Certainly the Screech Owls are going to continue to be there, and like the song says there are always those who get their kicks stomping on a dream. We are always going to contend with the patrons of virtue as opposed to those who know it is not enough to discern evil but know action is required.

If you think yourself good, then do good, stop being merely a patron of virtue and quit profaning God in your prayers, start doing the things that only you, not God, can do, the things that are your responsibility, not His!

Jesus Loves the Little Children of the World. There are many who profess to represent Jesus. But Jesus isn't here. You are!

Please write or call your elected representatives in government, local, state and federal to tell them of the amendment and your support of it. You can also inform your local radio, TV and newspapers.

CHAPTER TWELVE

It took infidelity to kill Camelot. The blasting of love and trust through the monstrous act of betrayal is a real assassin, it kills the heart. But the dream of Camelot, as I have discovered, lives on. Why? Because, as I further discovered, to know Camelot, to have experienced it is larger than my heart, this small, human heart that cannot hold all the love that exists in spite of the evil of those who try to destroy the Dream. The Mordred's will never understand nor will they ever carry the day against the Arthurs. The Dream, the idea of the Dream cannot be destroyed as long as genuine love exists, as long as the story of Camelot continues to be told.

So, while the loss of innocence is never to be recovered, once known, like genuine love, it is never forgotten. And to have known innocence is to have known love. And to have known love is to have the desire to love others, to make the world a place where such love and innocence have a chance in the lives of our children.

Molestation, like infidelity to which it is akin, is a betrayal and blasting of love and innocence. The one whose love and trust is betrayed never recovers from either. It shouldn't hurt to be a child! Makes a nice slogan and the whole world nods in agreement. Yet children are suffering in greater numbers than ever before in history. Apparently the world doesn't have a handle on the problem or just engages in lip service, as is too often the case: Reminds me of politics.

The recent international conference on molestation in Stockholm, Sweden gives me encouragement and hope that this may change. The replies I am receiving from government leaders concerning the amendment are also encouraging. We have some good people in government, charitable organizations, even the entertainment media who will help once they realize this amendment is going to be pursued with vigor. The responses I have received from President Clinton, governors and senators gives me further encouragement and hope. These leaders know the import of this amendment and are preparing for the battle ahead.

Former federal judge Robert Bork has a book out, "Slouching Towards Gomorrah." He says: America is in decline and the rot is spreading. As cures, he proposes censorship and an amendment that would allow congress to override the Supreme Court. As to the court, not going to happen but I can appreciate his thinking. The checks and balances of our Republican form of government are supposed to allow for us, We the People, to veto the court, the congress and the president through the amendment process. Granted this is a time-consuming and laborious process but it is a right of the people. And we are the government as long as we exercise our rights.

Judge Bork proposes censorship of the "... vilest aspects of our popular culture ... It is the courts that threaten our liberty ... the liberty to govern ourselves ... more profoundly than does any legislature." He further says that "decadence permeates most of American culture ... its popular entertainment, art, religion, activity, science, technology, law and morality."

I've written so much on this theme over the past years. I watched it all happening from a front-row seat in the schools, colleges and universities, in the changes in the music and Hollywood. I watched our young people give up hope of a future as corrupt leadership sold out our nation.

Most of what I have written falls into line with judge Bork's assessment. But he missed the conclusion I reached. Maybe his judicial training caused him to miss it. And maybe he never met Gidget or experienced Camelot as I did.

I have said that if I had been old and wise enough back then when I was preaching, I would have taken my text from Gidget and the great Musicals. Instead, I spent years attacking the symptoms of the disease without realizing what was causing the disease. Also, I was entrenched in a false theological mind-set that God was going to straighten the mess out, that I did not have the responsibility to do battle against the root of the evil all about me. I just had to preach harder. But my preaching missed an essential truth: That God cannot do some things that are our responsibility as adult human beings!

I lay in bed last night wondering why I cared about this amendment, why I am doing what I am and why I cared about what happens to children? I didn't always feel this way, I didn't always care about children or love them; I was a very selfish young man. It is true that I was raised in an environment of love; that I was never in doubt that I was loved and cared for. I never really suffered want or deprivation.

There were elements of my childhood that kept me from being cruel to others, to animals; I had just enough kindness to love; but not unselfishly. I had just enough morality to keep me out of prison but not enough to make me care for others unselfishly; until I fell in love. And, later, was loved. I tell the story in my Birds book. The girl was the one I told my teenage children, Danny and Diana, about. It was that story that led to my daughter, Diana, putting her arms around me and with tears in her eyes say, "Dad, I really love you." And I knew she did. That was the foundation of the later understanding and compassion I did not have as a young man. With the death of Diana, it took years and many other tragedies together with the experience of working with thousands of children in the schools to bring me to the point I finally reached in writing the Birds book and with that foundation, to propose this amendment.

A lovely lady said the other day that I needed someone to protect me. I replied that I really needed a keeper. She was right and I just haven't wanted to deal with the truth of her statement. After all, I'm a man and I don't need anyone to protect me, right? At least that is what the man says. The child within the man, that's an entirely different matter. It's not the man who needs protection; it's that best part of the man, the child within, which is in danger. And I'm increasingly aware of this; it is part of the nightmare I've lived with for so long.

That other guy who writes this material is one with that child. He hears that child's voice and this leads to the softer and gentler writing of the stuff of dreams and enchanted lands, of the glory of the stars and the future we have as we enter that Promised Land, of our relationship with the birds and animals, the whales and dolphins.

This other fellow cherishes Gidget and Camelot, the laughter of a child. He really knows the supreme value that these represent. He knows how great a nation can become by learning to value these things, what they can do for children, for the transformation of an entire civilization.

The child doesn't know anything about danger or evil. He or she simply enjoys the enchantment of nature, the birds, animals and other creatures. But the child does know they shouldn't be harmed, that there is something terribly wrong when people mistreat animals or each other. It might be called the wisdom of childhood.

That child is extremely vulnerable and I know this. What I don't know is how he is to be protected, at least until his task is finished along with mine. But I depend on him and he has to depend on me. What happens to me happens to him as well. So I lie in bed and ask God and myself why I'm doing this, why I care? I think only that other guy and the child have an answer to this. I don't. But if there is anything to being driven by the love of God, there must be a corollary to being driven by the pain of God as well.

It was in a conversation with a friend who used to work in the studios and had his own TV show that I got on this track. My friend used to be very successful in the business. He and his wife were used to the good life, of visiting homes such as that of Charlton Heston. Being a very talented and artistic man, it is easy to share some of my thoughts with him. I gain a lot through his own insights.

Samuel D. G. Heath, Ph. D.

The question we were discussing was whether the pain of God might be driving me, compelling me to do some of the kind of writing I do, that the work for this amendment, might in fact be an unconscious awareness of the pain of God, that what I am doing is trying to find a remedy for that pain in my own life, the kind of pain that results from not loving enough, not showing enough of what love I did have to offer? My conservative, Christian theological background lends itself to often thinking of the love of God (much preached, little practiced) but not the pain of God.

Since I cannot honestly say that I have such a great love for children, for others, since I failed so miserably as a father to show my love to my own children and was so very selfish in many ways, it makes it all the more improbable that I would be the author of the proposed amendment.

Accepting the fact that I usually try to avoid pain, it occurred to me that the pain of those relentless nightmares, images that plague me of children like Polly Klaas, Melissa Russo and Julie Lejeune being so horribly tortured and murdered by beasts in the form of men compels me to deal with the nightmares and pain by this amendment. Am I trying to get away from the pain, trying to find a remedy rather than suffer? Why am I tormented by the image of the countless thousands of unmarked graves across our nation filled with the bodies of little ones, the missing children? I can see nothing in my life, in my heart, which would lead to such a nightmare for me personally.

If anyone should be having the nightmares and leading the fight for this amendment it should be a man like John MacArthur of Grace Community Church and founder of The Master's College in Sun Valley, California.

John MacArthur, of international religious reputation, writes me concerning the amendment:

"Dear Don; Thanks again for informing me about your concern over the wrongful death of children. God will certainly have His day with those who 'cause these little ones to stumble.' May God bless you as you pursue this burden on your heart."

My argument with John and the rest of my brethren in the churches is my contention that fixing this problem is not the responsibility of God. It is our responsibility! And as I have told John and so many others: Jesus loves the little children of the world. But Jesus isn't here. We are!

As to the extreme brevity of John's reply, I cannot help comparing it with the lengthy letter I received from President William Clinton. Just who, do you suppose, would most people expect to be the most sensitive to the needs of children? Surprise! Not to mention the fact that I have heard nothing from James Dobson, Jerry Falwell, Pat Robertson, Bob Dole, Pat Buchanan et al., so much for their much preaching about their concern for children and family values.

256

As to John's mention of God having his day, why doesn't God hear the cry for justice of those thousands of little victims, of the literally millions suffering worldwide? I believe He does. But I don't believe He can do anything about it. I don't believe it is His responsibility. I do believe it is ours. How I wish I could get that point across to so many like John that are preaching the message I used to: God is going to kiss it and make it all better! WRONG!

Knowing that the amendment is absolutely necessary regardless of the motive that drives me is not enough to explain why I would be the one to author it, why a much better man like John MacArthur suited to the purpose has not done so. A strictly philosophical attempt at an explanation might be the pain of God. Maybe good men like John do not feel the pain of God?

Who of us has not wondered why God does not prevent such suffering of children? Why he allows creatures like Richard Davis, Marc Dutroux, Dahmer and Bundie to even exist? Pragmatically, history teaches us that it is useless to blame God (as most of what passes for prayer does) for things that are our responsibility. It may simply be that the amendment is just that, an act of responsibility. But it does seem strange to me that I should be the one to accept this kind of responsibility.

In my defense I am a man. I have always behaved responsibly toward others and fulfilled commitments. I am aware of the responsibilities of manhood for those who are really men. Knowing what I do of these beasts that pass themselves off as men adds impetus to my hatred of such creatures; and the nightmares. Yet the conundrum exists. Why me? Why not the male equivalent of a Mother Theresa?

I get so very lonely for someone to talk to, for someone who cares enough to try to understand what I don't understand myself. Some of my writing is, undoubtedly, a reaching out for that kind of communication, a reaching out crying that I don't know what I'm doing and I need help to do it whatever it is. At times it's as though the child is trying to break through, but being a child, he can't really articulate the wisdom he possesses. The innocence that he knows is so vitally important cannot find expression because he is a child, he doesn't understand why it's so important. Perhaps there is a need for a poet. Perhaps only a poet can communicate with the child.

But children, being innocent of evil, don't know anything about evil or evil people. There is nothing of evil for the child to relate to. When confronted by evil or evil people, how is the child to be protected? Who is responsible to protect the innocence of the child?

I look at those statements and I really have trouble trying to understand them. What is it that the child is trying so hard to communicate? Whatever it is, I know it is uncorrupted. But my own knowledge of evil gets in the way of my understanding. My only hope is that maybe that other guy, the poet, will understand it and make it comprehensible. Then, maybe, he will be able to make it comprehensible to others. I know this is vitally important. Just how important it is makes me dizzy, I go around in a fog trying to sort it out.

The very monumental complexity of it is rooted in the entire history of humankind and the failure to make the world what it was intended to be, for men and women to be what they were intended to be for each other. Paradise Restored. That is too much for my mind to grasp. But a large part of that Paradise is still there in the laughter of children. The laughter of a child is a reminder of Paradise.

Some things are so indelibly imprinted on the mind that there is never any forgetting them. One such memory of mine is the laughter of Laurie. She was only a toddler when we were visiting the grandparents. A sister-in-law had a little toy dog that would hop and squeak. She placed it on the floor in front of Laurie and when the little dog hopped and squeaked, Laurie put her tiny hand to her mouth and gave a little laugh, a magically pure silver tinkling sound like you would imagine the laughter of fairies. It was the first time she had really laughed and it thrilled my heart and soul with an indescribable joy.

In fact, it thrilled everyone in the room; it touched us all with its joyous magic. We were enchanted and transformed, transported by this precious, little child's laughter. The sister-in-law gave the little dog to Laurie.

That best part of a man knows what the word cherish means, he knows what is worthy of cherishing, loving and protecting, he knows real beauty and truth. So I look at Gidget without lust, I know there is a supreme value in what she represents that, as a woman, brings out the best in a man, that best that will not, cannot defile that best in a woman like Gidget but on the contrary cherishes it and will do anything to protect it.

It's the very innocence of Gidget, the best part of her as a woman, that little girl within that has a right to guide the woman, and be protected by her and the man she chooses. This is what makes Gidget Quite a woman! This is what makes her a real responsibility for a man! The innocent ideals of youth are worth everything we can commit to them. A real man recognizes this in a real woman and responds to her, cherishing and protecting her in every way possible. Their shared dream is to pass such a heritage on to their children.

A great truth of the Bible is that the blasting of innocence led to death. This is the point judge Bork missed in his otherwise excellent assessment of what is wrong with our culture. Like the judge, I had followed a lot of leads but couldn't seem to track the Beast to his lair. But thanks to Laurie's laughter, the love I have had for others and those like Diana and Karen who have loved me, I finally cornered the Beast and have the weapon that will slay him.

But first I had to gain enough experience, compassion and wisdom to recognize the ultimate need of innocence and what it represents. That is the story of The Fall that is the lesson God wanted us to learn. With the blasting of innocence, the world becomes a harsh taskmaster.

The Beast roams like a roaring lion seeking whom he may devour! Virtually every parent who truly loves his children has had the feeling that they wished they could keep their little girl or boy a little girl or boy. None of us wanted them to grow up in some ways. That is the preciousness of recognizing, as adults, the wonder of childhood in our children.

The magic of childhood when the world is so full of enchantment and wonder should be, must be, encouraged. There is such a brief time in our lives that constitutes childhood. Yet it is in this all too brief moment of time that the adult is formed for the years ahead.

Our failure to encourage that innocence, our failure to cherish our children has led to Judge Bork's dismal, and accurate, assessment of our nation. But I am ever more, daily, persuaded that this amendment is the answer. Only this amendment addresses the root of the evil in our nation.

It isn't just molestation we are talking about. It is the recognition of the basis of a civilization and its hope of a future as a nation. When Jesus said, "Unless you become as a little child, you cannot enter into the Kingdom of Heaven" he was specifically speaking of that very innocence we are to be the guardians of for our children. More than just guardians, we are to cherish that innocence.

That word, *Cherish*, needs to be understood in the sense of I Corinthians chapter 13 where the ending, "now abides faith, hope and charity, but the greatest of these is charity" makes it clear. The word love was substituted in modern Bibles. This hastened the devolution of the word charity.

The very innocence of the child, the innocent virtue of Gidget is to be cherished, held dear above all else. It is of supreme value, virtually priceless! It is the very thing that the best of men will cherish in a real woman; it is the thing, like Laurie's laughter and the love of Diana and Karen that brings out the best of the tenderest emotions of love and protectiveness in a man. This is what the word Charity means in that Bible passage. Yet, the churches seem oblivious to the obvious message. By a process of blind orthodoxy that insulates even the best intentioned, the message has been obscured and obfuscated to meaningless gibberish clothed in religiosity.

For example, I have some close friends, men of the cloth that are so entrenched in their religion that it keeps their minds closed to the fallacies they believe and preach. We remain friends because we can be open and candid with our mutual criticisms; as the Scripture says "A friend loves at all times," not just when you're in agreement. They exhibit their charitable natures in putting up with me.

But they speak using terms such as hermeneutics and exegesis and will accuse me of being philosophical rather than exegetical. Yet they refuse to acknowledge the extreme narrowness of their own beliefs that could easily be refuted if they, themselves, were honest in their own exegesis. But this would be to admit that their own basis of belief is more substantially a philosophy than anything empirical.

To admit that a truly systematic theology is non-existent in any religion is to admit there are errors in your own. The alternative in too many cases is to force a system that does not hold up to logic or even face its own contradictions and superstitions. We call such people ignorant or prejudiced. But try telling that to the average Catholic, Protestant, Jew or Moslem theologian.

Some wonder at the intrusion of religion in any form concerning the amendment. But the amendment invites such intrusion. Virtually anything concerning the subject of sexuality automatically comes under scrutiny on a religious basis and has to be considered.

The superstitious, Black Calvinism that hunted witches and consigned humor and the enjoyment of all things beautiful to the pit, the Inquisition and Crusades, Holy Wars, Jihads are all rooted in so-called systematic theologies that in action deny the very love of the God they all say they worship and honor by atrocities and hatred of those not of their kind!

Like the song says, children have to be carefully taught to distrust and look with suspicion or hatred on those not of their kind. Humanity should have learned long ago that such teaching of children is the blasting of innocence! Yet who can deny that such evils as racism are entrenched in the peculiar prejudices of most religions! A system that teaches one person or a society is better than another because of some supposed divine favor flies in the face of all humanity!

Any theology that does not begin with love of one another as its foundation is flawed to begin with. Any theology that does not emphasize the necessity of cherishing children as its basis has no right to proselytize! The Biblically literate should be able to quote Jesus on these two immutable tenets of Christianity.

And what of those who preach a gospel of exclusivity that would consign all to hell if not a proper Moslem, Jew or Christian? I can't help wondering about those who preach some kind of decision for Christ or go to hell religion. Are they really interested in the love of God, the love of Christ or selling themselves?

The one thing that should be considered above all other considerations is the fact that irrespective of one's religious beliefs or lack thereof a commonality of all humanity is a father and mother's love for their children. This is true whether that family is Christian, Moslem, Jewish, Buddhist, Hindu, Atheist or Agnostic.

But religious views aside, there is another commonality that is not so easily dealt with. The fact that women, disproportionately, exhibit more concern for children than men seem to. I know this is wrong, that men should be far more responsible and sensitive to the needs of children. But this may have to do with the fact that the mother, historically and biologically, cares for the child in a much closer and bonding relationship than the father. There is nothing more dangerous in nature than a mother bear when she thinks her cubs are threatened. I think women, as the mother bears, have far more concern for little ones than men. Where is that father bear when the cubs are threatened?

While I am somewhat of an aberration in this regard, I am a man and have to face the fact that it will be the women of America who will, disproportionately, carry this amendment. Men, by and large, will make all kinds of excuses for not supporting it. Much like the adult molesters of young girls who refuse to be responsible for the babies they father.

To emphasize a point, I have yet to hear from people like Bob Dole, Pat Robertson, Jerry Falwell or James Dobson concerning the amendment. Yet I received gracious responses from President Clinton and Barbara Boxer who could hardly be called conservatives. These others preach a message of their concern for children, family and family values. But I am not surprised at the lack of response from these conservatives. They are men and lead male-dominated empires.

In my reply to Senator Boxer I made the point that these men like Falwell, Dobson, Robertson, Dole et al. have a mind-set of male dominance. They would never admit that they have not answered me because the amendment empowers women, that women do not have babies to sacrifice them on the altar of the wars men create or national politics, religions and religious empires which are male dominated.

Women have been excluded throughout history in the areas of politics, philosophy and theology. And please don't insult this fact by anecdotal blips on the screen of history. But men will see the threat to them by this amendment. It is men who would like to keep women subjugated to second-class citizenship, which would like to keep young girls a private preserve and hunting ground for their own lust.

But for the first time in our nation's history, this amendment gives women the chance to take the destiny of America in their hands in such a fashion as to give them their rightful value, to protect children, especially little girls who are vastly disproportionately the victims of molest, in a way that men have refused. I know senator Boxer replied as a woman. Irrespective of her personal life, she replied because she is a woman first and a senator second.

There are honorable men, men like Governor Gary Johnson of New Mexico, who have applauded my efforts. There are going to be many others like him who are courageous enough to go against men like those I mentioned. As to my being a man and the author of the amendment I would like to call attention to the point Samuel Johnson made as per my essay of October. Let me make it clear, as Johnson did, that men may espouse a virtue they do not possess without hypocrisy.

Put me under the microscope and you will find one of the most fallible of men. No false humility intended. But few would use Jerry Falwell or Louis Farrakhan as exemplary paragons of virtue under the same microscope. Let us be frank, it wouldn't matter if the amendment was authored by these men, Attila the Hun or Hitler, the basis of the need for such an amendment and its beneficial effects would remain unchanged!

My point, as per S. J., is that there are many who may very well commend a virtue they neither possess nor practice which they may earnestly be trying to cultivate. If the amendment had been authored by any of these men mentioned would it make the amendment itself any less worthy? Of course not!

As the debate over the amendment grows in intensity, I know full well that I will come under the microscope. There will be those who will try to discredit the amendment by trying to make its author and messenger the focus of attention. Like most people, I aspire to higher virtues than I possess. I will even preach such virtues to others and fail of attaining them personally. Yet I will not discredit myself or others who have similar aspirations yet fail of their domestic application. It can be equally said truthfully that works of great artistic genius can be appreciated in spite of the personal lack of qualities in the artist as a person.

I have made my life an open book by my books. There is, as I have pointed out, no moral perfection about me any more than that of Falwell or Farrakhan. While I have no lurid or sordid skeleton in my private closet of shame this does not make me a paragon of moral perfection. But my life has been directed toward hatred of the evil that men do, the kind of evil of the bully, hatred of those who abuse their positions of authority, hatred of those who harm children.

What I learned of the softer and gentler aspects of humanity I learned largely from children. The little girls and women I have known have had an especially profound effect in my life. The experiences of my life, particularly what I learned from my daughters, made me a champion, if you will, of that softer and gentler need men have in order to be real men. To the shame of men, however, I also learned that men in general do indeed think of girls and women as objects of lust to be used, that girls and women have no value apart from their looks and sex. So, to repeat, I do not expect to find men, by and large, enthusiastic supporters of the amendment.

It took having daughters to get me on a different track. It took Gidget and my daughters to teach me what the word cherish really means. Only then did God's use of the word in Scripture make sense and take effect in my life, to make the absolutely essential need of innocence in childhood clearly understood.

A part of the educative process of this amendment is to call attention to an interesting, modern phenomenon in the schools. Forty years ago, high school pupils were children, kids. But the disastrous sexual revolution of the 60's brought many changes in the schools. One of the more devastating was that high school pupils were no longer children, they weren't even adolescents; they were young people.

The entertainment media and much of the music glorified this change aided and abetted by fuzzy-minded, so-called education and psychology *experts*. Now the children were not children any longer. But they were not adults either. Just what were they? Nobody really knew. But they definitely were not allowed to be children and they definitely were not adults. The bottom line was a loss of that part of childhood, an essential transition from childhood adolescence to adulthood, with adult sexuality encouraged but with no adult responsibility attaching. Devastating!

A 21-year-old man and a 15-year-old girl; that girl is not an adult by any definition. But that young man is. But because the girl is not considered a child, thanks in large part to Hollywood and the schools, the mind-set created in the man is that the girl can be molested and no one is going to take it seriously. And he is right!

The girl may even be encouraged, where possible, to marry the man as in cases where Child Protective Services has actually encouraged such marriages! Does any 14 or 15-year-old child have the maturity for marriage? What chance does a child born of a child have in such a marriage? One only has to examine the stark, tragic statistics to know the truth about this. Once the amendment is passed, we will find methods of contraception being practiced on an unprecedented scale leading to far fewer abortions, far fewer babies being born to teenage mothers.

It would be foolish to expect adolescents whom the media and Hollywood, an entire society has taught sexual license to become chaste overnight. But, eventually, chastity will, once more, become something of value, something not to be sneered at. Encouraging and valuing innocence in childhood is the essential foundation of charity, virtue and chastity.

William Hazlitt made an excellent point when he wrote: "Things near us are seen as the size of life: things at a distance are diminished to the size of the understanding. It is only reasonable that the human race, given some thousands of years of experience, should produce some wisdom that will never become superannuated or arcane. Thoreau can say decayed literature makes the richest soil and Joseph Krutch can understand that this is no mere advocating of primitivism. Rather it is understanding that the wisdom of the past teaches one can take a superficial delight in nature; even talk of love without experiencing it. But is it possible to really understand without the poetry of either? No. Only the poet really enters into nature and only the love of a woman or a child can give him understanding and compassion.

Without such experience there is only a didactic knowledge that, by itself, cannot move hearts and minds together to compatible and compassionate action. Unfortunately, as true as this is, it would have been better for humanity if women had been included in this Great Conversation of thousands of year's duration.

There is a great need to expand our understanding of the issues confronting America and the world in order to avoid the parochial mind-set that leads to an ignorant prejudice that only those things close at hand are our responsibility. While molestation is a worldwide problem, I doubt the parents of Polly Klaas, Melissa Russo or Julie Lejeune or, for that matter, even the King and Queen of Belgium gave the subject much serious consideration let alone any effort to confront until tragedy struck home.

Politically it is only natural that the governors of the several states express concern over any law that would seem to further empower the federal government. Yet the need of a federal government and constitution existed and our founding fathers recognized this. The prosecution of a war is a national issue, not a local one. There is a need to declare war on the molester. This is a national issue and must be dealt with on a national basis, not piecemeal, state-to-state.

While Thoreau considered all government evil, even he admitted to the need of some government. I would tell my soul brother the need of some government is rooted in the evil that men do. As the Bible teaches and we all understand, the law, government, is not for the lawful, but the unlawful. As long as lawless people exist, there will be a need for laws and government to enforce those laws.

Judge Bork and others have written extensively about the fact that America is in moral decline. But these worthy writers miss the essential point of our decline. The reason this point is missed is because of the historical mind-set of men concerning women. We all know the double standard of boys will be boys, and as young men, experienced, but girls are to be chaste is a lie from the pit of hell! The continued perpetuation of this hellish lie has resulted in the present moral decay of our nation. There must be an absolute standard that applies equally to boys and girls.

Only maintaining the innocence of our children can accomplish a generation dedicated to the higher standards of morality, chastity and virtue. And this can only be accomplished by the same standard applying to both boys and girls. We lost our moral bearings as a nation when we began to fail to raise children in innocence, when we began to fail to cherish our children. And this failure has its roots in the attitude of men who continued to treat women as second-class citizens, as sexual objects as opposed to persons in their own right in every way as valuable as men to a society, to a civilization.

Women began to fail in the single most important position for which they were created, the primary softness and gentleness children (and men) desperately need when they began to buy into a false equality with men in areas where they were never suited. Ladies, you were never meant to compete with men. This competition with men has degraded you. By reacting to the use and abuse of you by men in attempts to compete in areas like policemen, firemen, etc. you only made a bad situation worse! The family is the basis of all civilizations. The role of father and mother has to be clearly delineated or the result is chaos, the kind of moral chaos we live with today. In attempts to prove you are just as good as men, you have only succeeded in making yourselves as bad as men.

Because men don't listen to women they have the reputation of being far more verbal, even garrulous, than men. The very lack of sensitivity by men to women, however, encourages the verbosity of women and is rooted in that false doctrine that boys do not have to be raised in the innocence that is the very foundation of that sensitivity!

I have written much on the need for men and women to learn to exercise the compatibility of differences rather than competitiveness and combativeness. But a problem of such huge dimensions will never admit of a solution unless we can train our children in such things as learning to value the compatibility of differences properly, to value those differences and give due honor to them. And this cannot be done unless we start with children raised in innocence, an innocence that is open to the ideals of such compatibility.

Here is where the amendment empowers the Momma Bears at the very level where they are the most concerned and effective, where they exercise the best attributes of themselves as women. Ladies, this is where you, far more than men, have the necessary sensitivity to the problem that men lack. Here is where you can be heard, where you must be heard!

Women bear the discomfort, the pain, even the risk of death giving birth. Don't expect men to understand that which is impossible of their understanding. But do that, as women, which you know you must because of your understanding that which men cannot by accepting the responsibility of your greater understanding of this issue.

Men lead and women are forced to follow. In this one area, women must take the leadership position because men in general not only will not, but they lack the qualifications to assume such leadership. Children have no voice or choice. There are many good men who will support this amendment. But it is women who will fight for it because of that greater understanding in this instance; it is women who hear the cry of children much more clearly than men.

Men make war, not women. But in this most singular and monumentally important instance it is women who will sound the battle cry for children and prosecute the war against molesters, it is women who will fight for this chance for our children to be protected and raised in innocence. Despite the dismal failure to abolish slavery the founding fathers gave us a nation conceived in liberty and justice. But it will be the founding mothers, if you will, who will guarantee our children will be able to build on what those founding fathers provided as a foundation to the greater goal of raising children who will be able to make the most of that early heritage.

Japan is facing a moral disaster- Teenage girls, some as young as 13, openly advertising for sex with older men. The girls are making from $300 to a $1,000 per tryst. Why are the girls doing this; because of a breakdown of morality in Japan. Chastity and virtue have given place to materialism, the Bubble as they call it of the 80s and 90s of an affluent society. But Japanese leaders are right in blaming the previous generation, not the kids, for this happening. And as one young girl put it: "If it weren't for the old men willing to pay, none of this would be happening!" Japan needs my proposed amendment.

World events seem almost being orchestrated to prove my basic premise that children must be raised in innocence, that they have an inviolable right to such a childhood. Now that world attention is being focused on the problem of molestation, it is only reasonable for America to take the lead in what I call: Zero tolerance of molesters! Only when this is a fact will children have the chance for Camelot, for true love and romance in their lives, for them to bring to adulthood those virtues that can lead to Paradise Restored.

One of my all-time favorite Musicals is "The Music Man." In one scene Robert Preston looks at Shirley Jones and says: "You pile up enough tomorrows and you'll find you've collected nothing but a lot of empty yesterdays."

As a man without common sense, I've lived a life refusing to pile up tomorrows. The result has been a host of memories filled with eventful yesterdays, filled with the memories of the pain and joy that comes with the territory of risking really living.

Shirley Jones; so beautiful and talented with her matchless, lyrical voice, with triumphs like Oklahoma, Carousel and The Music Man; yet, the love isn't in her eyes as she sings. Maybe it has to do with the personal character of Gordon MacRae and Robert Preston. You can admire the artistry of the artist and still despise the artist as a person. Was this what stifled the love in Shirley's eyes?

I watch Julie Andrews sing to Christopher Plummer and I know Julie is in love as she sings. Her eyes declare it. I watch Jeanne Crain as she sings that masterpiece, "It Might As Well Be Spring" in "State Fair" and I know this beautiful girl is in love. You see it in her eyes.

I feel the tears still forming toward the end of The Music Man. The tears come from a happy ending, the triumph of love and romance. But they also come from the knowledge of the tragedy of what our children have missed; and for Shirley. I wish I could talk to Shirley. I would ask her what happened in her life to rob her of the love she couldn't show with her eyes. Somehow, I suspect she would cry when asked the question. I've known other women who have done so.

Many of the women I write of in the Birds book who suffered the loss of hope of a decent man in their lives gave in to the bitterness and cynicism that are often the natural result of the betrayal of love and trust. And while in most cases they remained decent women, their eyes always told the story of their lost hope of genuine love and romance in their lives.

Shirley's eyes reflect, like those of so many women I have known, the results of the philosophy of Professor Hill in "A Sadder But Wiser Girl For Me." However, confronted with the genuine purity and real love and virtue of Marian, as with Jeffrey confronting the same thing with Gidget the responsibility of such a girl, such a real woman, the tenderest emotions of love, of cherishing and protectiveness is evoked in a real man.

So Professor Harold Hill faces up to this and for the first time in his life this conniving salesman gets his foot caught in the door. That Pearl of Great Price is worth everything to a real man. But he didn't suspect such a man existed in himself until he met Marian.

In the single, most moving part of this great play, Harold tells Winthrop: "I always believe there's a band, kid." Marian knew this about Harold; she recognized it in the magic of what he had done in transforming River City and its inhabitants, what he had done in transforming her and her little brother. In this consummate con man there was the latent goodness of his heart and gifts. But it took a Marian to bring out the best in the man, to transform him, to make him fully aware of the gladly paid price of the responsibility of genuine love, of cherishing.

It is during this exchange between Marian and Harold, this realization of what they have discovered in each other that the emotions rise forcefully in me as The Music Man takes Marian in his arms with the words, "Till there was you."

You have to look beyond the persons as actor and actress to the story. You have to be involved with those characters portrayed, Marian and Harold, to receive the timeless message of love and romance. Yes, there had been love all around, there had been birds and bells, music and roses and moonlight but they didn't have much meaning "Till there was you!"

Marian and Harold give me hope, hope that such magic will not be lost to our children forever. And yes, even hope that it might be found for some of you who have given up such hope. It is that foundational hope that compelled me to write the Birds book.

Our children need the sermons and poetry of the great Musicals far more than the pap they are fed from conventional pulpits. Our boys should grow up to be the kind of real men who find the timeless inspiration and motivation for the best they can do as men in the innocent purity and virtue of the Gidget's and Marian's. You parents should be raising the kind of girls who will be the inspiration of such young men. Watching the great Musicals can help parents teach their children the right kinds of lessons.

An important part of this teaching is the expectation of genuine love and romance that is due those whose ideals remain intact, to those who refuse to sell out their dreams and hold fast to the rewards of virtue. For those familiar with the great Musicals, of which there are very few, I ask you to name the two, most spectacular and beautiful that achieve the real essence of real love and romance where the lovers never kiss or even embrace? You'll have to stop and think about that one. The answer: "Gigi" and "My Fair Lady."

Of the less than a dozen truly great Musicals, these two are so superbly done that one is fully caught up in what is happening as the lovers fall in love, realize that love and play the parts so well that you don't even notice they have never so much as shared a kiss during the entire play! That is the kind of work that qualifies a masterpiece of real art; that is the essence of real romance.

Why am I so sensitive to this? Because I learned what it was to make love to a woman by merely touching her hand or sharing a smile I learned how a woman can make love to a man by merely touching his hair or his arm or by the expression in her eyes. It isn't any wonder to me that women by the millions buy romance novels to feed their impoverished souls when the lesson of Gigi is no longer taught or learned by our children, when adults don't even know the message!

I saw a little girl, only ten-years-old, wearing a T-shirt with the words: "Hello Boys on the front." The mother of this child really loves and cares for her little girl. I know this. So how is it that she doesn't understand the message, an invitation to sexual harassment, and this little girl is conveying about herself as a girl?

A six-year-old boy kisses a six-year-old girl in a North Carolina school and is disciplined for sexual harassment. Was the boy acting out what he had seen on TV or some movie? Can a child of this age really force such unwanted attention on a little girl?

The incident is made a national media event. The school and the families are embarrassed. The children are too young to know the significance of it all. But of this I am certain; this little boy had never been taught the lesson of Gigi.

Yes, little boys can force unwanted attention on little girls. The problem grows more serious as they advance in age to the point where actual sexual harassment is commonplace by the time of junior and senior high school. But if little girl's ten-years-old are already advertising sexuality, what is to be expected of the little boys in return? And if Hollywood and TV continue to encourage and exploit such sexuality of children, a bad situation continues to worsen.

Ask yourself what a six-year-old boy or a ten-year-old girl really understands of sexuality? It is the adults that bear ultimate responsibility for such things as children's attitudes toward sex and regard for one another. But parents are caught in a crossfire; they don't want their children to seem peculiar to their peer group. And, in too many cases, the parents themselves grew up in a sexually permissive environment.

Here again the so-called *experts* that appeared wholesale on the scene in the sexual revolution of the 60s sold gullible parents a bill of goods. Aided and abetted by an immoral entertainment media, by encouraging sexual license under the guise of promoting the natural, healthy curiosity of children concerning sex, these quacks in psychology and the schools destroyed what should be one of the great and innocent mysteries of childhood.

Every parent must face the story of the Birds and the Bees eventually. But what constitutes genuine, natural, healthy curiosity about sex is far removed from the encouragement of sexual license, of the abuse of what should always be something beautiful and pure between a man and a woman. But that takes the necessary maturity to appreciate. It is insane to expect children to exercise such maturity. Not to mention the insanity of a society that actually promotes such a thing as child-sex!

Ah, gentle reader; the sins of the past in our culture have robbed us of the sensitivity to such things. We are a callous and jaded society that has sold out the finer sensibilities of the best we can be for ... for what? It will take a generation of children raised in innocence to be the best that we can be. It will take a return to the message of truly civilized behavior and manners, of boys raised to be gentlemen once more opening the door for girls who were raised to be ladies.

Ask yourself a very simple question. Just what was the inspiration for the great composers and lyricists, the directors and choreographers of the great Musicals? It was Gidget, Jeanne Crain, Julie Andrews, Shirley Jones, Leslie Caron, and Audrey Hepburn.

And why didn't women write the great songs and lyrics; because they are the inspiration of poets. And men are the poets. There folks is the compatibility of differences in sum, where the differences receive their due honor. Ladies, it is the ideal of purity and virtue of which you are capable that brings out the best in real men. Don't expect what has never been and never will be, to have men value what is of little value to you!

One of the problems with retreating and escaping into a nice, comfortable, cozy insanity is not knowing you're nuts. But that nervous breakdown you've worked so hard for and earned has the disadvantage of a still partially functioning brain. Alas, there is no Utopia.

It is profound observations like the above that give me pause at times to consider whether those who accuse me of being a true poet and intellectual might be at least partly right in the allegation. I get into this frame of mind when I try to explain what makes the romance of Gigi so successful without so much as a kiss or embrace between the lovers. Perhaps it has to do with something I wrote in the Birds book.

In the book I describe the beauty of a particular woman as a great work of art. Now great art cannot be explained, it can only be experienced. It draws you into it with its grand subtleties; it makes you want to explore those seemingly limitless dimensions that speak so profoundly to your very soul. You can never quite grasp all of its significance or even understand why it absorbs you as it does. Real love and romance is a great work of art. It is so profound and complex it is not explainable, it has to be experienced.

Gigi and Gidget explain as much as is possible to explain of the Art. As Gaston struggles with this art of the heart at the end of the play, the masterful brush strokes of his poses in front of the fountain with chiaroscuro-shaded silhouettes straight out the best of The New Yorker for sophistication and effect, as he struggles with the tormenting question of what course to follow, a lump rises in your throat. You find yourself cheering him on, pleading: Don't be a fool, don't lose your chance to be the best a man can be, don't miss this Pearl of Great Price; don't lose Gigi!

As he makes the decision to return, we cheer in our hearts. But I wonder how many of the millions who have seen the play notices the very subtle lighting of the cobblestone courtyard as he crosses it? It displays a heart. But so unobtrusively it has to be discovered. That is art. Of all the truly artistic touches of this masterpiece of romance you can never take it all in, there is always something more.

How many times I have watched and listened to Louis Jourdan sing the theme song, "Gigi." And yet I still find the emotions rising within me as he portrays so magnificently and with such feeling his sudden awareness that Gigi isn't a little girl anymore. Lerner and Lowe outdid themselves in the very profundity of the music and lyrics that so move the heart as a man discovers such rare treasure of the soul and heart in the ideal of Gigi.

And no matter how many times I have watched the triumph of virtue, love and romance at the end of the play, I still feel the lump in my throat form again as Gaston says to Gigi's grandmother: "Madam, will you do me the honor, the favor, give me the infinite joy of bestowing on me Gigi's hand in marriage?"

For those who are sensitive to great art, it is of no wonder the picture captured 9 academy awards including Best Picture. And you can only bow humbly to the genius of a director like Vincente Minnelli in making this all work together to form one of the truly great romances. Gigi, as with Gidget and Marian, bring out the best in a man; even a director.

While the play deals with infidelity and mistresses in a so-called civilized way, we are left in no doubt at the end that the old German maxim holds true through the best of life: *Schoenheit vergeht, Tugend besteht*, Beauty fades, Virtue remains! What have our children lost by not being raised in innocence, in being raised to disdain and dishonor virtue? A whole world!

I never won the battle for Gigi personally. But I never piled up a lot of empty yesterdays. As a consequence, by continuing to carry on the fight I have really lived, I have lived the play of life fully. And "The play is the thing!"

There is a flaw, however, in most works of romance, even the great Musicals like Gigi. The infamous double standard that women are to be virtuous, pure and chaste but men are acceptable if they are *experienced*! The notorious history of this lie from the pit of hell has led to a society where women themselves have decided what's sauce for the goose is sauce for the gander.

Rather than fight for the same standard of decency applying to both boys and girls, women degraded themselves to the level of men. Now who led women to think passing themselves around like rutting men should be a part of equality? Men. Once again, ladies, don't expect what has never been and never will be, to expect men to value what you yourselves don't value.

Free love? No such thing; just a euphemism that serves the purpose of so-called men who want their cake and eat it too. Where do you think, ladies, expressions like "Why buy the cow when milk is so cheap" originate? It is for this reason that I find more virtue in a prostitute than in a betraying wife or husband. And I am sure most of you would agree. Jesus most certainly thought so.

This no-win situation that women have bought into has resulted in many tragic changes in a very short time. One is the fact that there has been a 30 per cent increase in just ten, short years of women suffering PMS contemplating suicide. Virtually one in ten women now fall into this depression-engendered frame of mind.

But when a woman's value is strictly young, thin and pretty, when there is no longer any self-esteem engendered by virtue, depression is the natural result as youth and beauty fades. When sex, rather than virtue, rules, the end is easily forecast. Small wonder that depression is forecast to be one of the top killers worldwide in the near future! Ladies, men value virtue, not sex. Believe it or not! But that virtue has to be the real thing.

The Mormons are trying to solve the problem by encouraging women to pick family over career. But they have a most ignoble history of denigrating women to the infamous male mind-set of things like polygamy from which the religion has never recovered.

Who could have imagined the insanity of a girl winning a lawsuit for $500,000 because of sexual harassment in a school and another girl is wearing a T shirt saying: Hello Boys! As to drugs in the schools, a girl is suspended for giving another girl a Midol tablet? *In loco parentis*. But when it comes to the schools, I have been telling parents for almost thirty years: Things aren't as bad as you think. They are far worse!

I have been fighting the battle for many years. There have been wins as well as losses. *So ghet's im leben*, so it goes in life. I have been blessed with much of the romance of the great Musicals. I have danced with and sung to that girl in my arms because she inspired the music. I have never wanted for the memories to call upon for needed inspiration in my writing. The play and the music have always been there for me as musician, singer and writer; and the great literature that has sent my soul soaring beyond the stars! It has never failed me; where I have failed, where others have failed me; the music and the play, the grandness of creation, the greatest of the art of the writers who understood never failed.

In 2010, the movie closes with the message: "All these worlds are yours, use them together, use them in peace...." I have the confidence and hope that people will catch the vision so our children will know peace, will live in peace and be cherished for the real treasure they represent.

My youngest daughter, Karen, is strikingly beautiful; so much so that I could not resist using her for the cover picture of the Birds book. She is, without a doubt, the most beautiful girl in the world. But you don't have to take my word for it. Just look at the picture. It took me a year of nagging her to get that picture. She is shy and doesn't know how beautiful she really is. By now enough people have told her that I hope she is beginning to believe me.

When I write of the great Musicals I am reminded of the time I took my little girl out for our first formal dinner together, just she and I. She was sixteen. As we sat in that fashionable restaurant, I marveled at the treasure she represented. And I wondered to myself: How did a man like me ever have such an extraordinarily beautiful daughter?

And yes, I was saddened as well. I knew full well the curse of beauty in our society. I knew the tremendous responsibility such beauty carries with it, a beauty that requires guidance and maturity to handle, that requires the protection of an entire society, a beauty that parents alone cannot protect in their little girls. I had seen what it had done in the lives of so many girls and women. I had no way of knowing the course of the future, of knowing how many more I was yet to meet who had suffered the worst of the curse of beauty.

Beth Hossfield and so many others are working on the problem: "Girls feel they don't have a chance in a society that stresses being thin and pretty." Movies like Reviving Ophelia and Matilda, publications like New Moon, The Magazine for Girls and Their Dreams and Celebrating Girls: Nurturing and Empowering Our Daughters, none of these get to the heart of the issue.

I applaud the dialogue with the children, the girls who have been taught so well, so devastatingly well, that their only value is their looks and sex. And to make a tragic situation worse, taught to start displaying their wares at the earliest!

The absolute need to raise children in innocence is a hard message to get across to people; especially since it requires facing ourselves as a people, as a nation, with a ruthless honesty about ourselves. Just what, we must ask ourselves do we really want for our children? Are we willing to pay the price for their future? And the hardest question of all we must face: Do we really cherish our children?

I have answered President Clinton's letter and it might be fitting to close with my reply:

September 23, 1996
President William Clinton
The White House

Mr. President:

I have received your reply to my letter advising you of my proposed amendment. It was gracious of you to take the time to write in view of your schedule and the extraordinary, exhausting demands of your office. I take encouragement from your prompt reply that your concern for children, that your comment about the need to make their welfare a national priority is from your heart.

Your outline of the things you have done in support of children is impressive and speaks well of your genuine concern for our posterity, our children.

Having received a number of responses from governors of the several states, they would like to make this issue of child molestation one of state jurisdiction whereas it is one of national concern. As you so well said Children are our nation's most precious responsibility and providing for their well-being must be a national priority.

We will enact national laws protecting animals and our environment yet there is nothing in our Constitution or its articles specifically addressed to the needs of children.

Lincoln freed the slaves yet our children have no such Emancipation Proclamation freeing them from the predator/molester. As good and well-intentioned all efforts like Megan's Law are, they fail to get to the root of this evil. Efforts like Pete Wilson's signing legislation concerning Chemical Castration are little more than Political Posturing since he knows full-well such a thing will never pass a constitutional challenge.

The chain of molestation must be broken. Only this amendment can accomplish this and break the back of the pedophile/molester/pornography Cartel.

The recent meeting in Stockholm, Sweden has focused world attention on this problem. I believe the United States has a responsibility to lead in confronting this Beast that is destroying children worldwide.

I am a writer. I write books about family and children, about the relationships between men and women, about political and theological philosophy.

It has taken years of study and research, experience in the schools, in Social Services, in the pulpit, of living life to reach the point where I was convinced that only this amendment will avail.

Those like yourself, well educated and highly intelligent will recognize the literally revolutionary implications of the amendment. I struggle daily with these implications.

Yet I know this is the only thing that will do the job; that will change the course of immorality our nation is heading and give our children a real chance of a future.

Because I am a writer and publisher and have the necessary contacts to make the amendment known throughout the nation, it will eventually claim national prominence. I foresee it becoming a matter of raging, national debate.

Of this I am confident; the amendment will, eventually, be passed. It only remains to be seen who, of all those of national and inter-national reputation, will join in the battle for the amendment.

Books like mine and former federal judge Robert Bork's make the need of the amendment clear. Our writing together with that of many others will focus attention on the need of such action.

As Thoreau so well said "There are 999 patrons of virtue for every virtuous man." It is my challenge to draw attention to the need to change that disproportionate number.

I am expert in the area of education and human behavior (my academic specialty). I know the need to educate people to the actual meaning of this amendment with its enormously, complex sociological ramifications. You surely know we are not talking just about molestation but the very foundation of our nation and the direction it will go for the future.

Your leadership in pursuing that direction is vital to the future of America. This nation is committed to human rights, even intruding into the affairs of other nations on this basis.

Yet the most fundamental right of humanity, the inviolable right of children to be raised in all innocence, has no viable, national priority. This amendment will force that priority.

The molester must be imprisoned for life to break the chain of molestation. Nothing short of this will avail.

Barring the unforeseen to which all flesh is heir, you will have another four years holding the single, most important office in the world. There will be nothing of the import of this amendment during your tenure. The question will be whether you will be known in history as the Lincoln of our children? I sincerely hope so.

Most respectfully:

Donald G. Heath, Ph. D.

Americans for Constitutional Protection of Children.

CHAPTER THIRTEEN

Mr. Dole: I can more easily overlook your calling the president a Bozo than I can your slight of Barney Fife. Doesn't have anything to do with anything but felt I had to say it.

When my children went through the toddler stage, the little ankle-biters showed an amazing proclivity to rearrange the house. Being responsible parents, their mother and I did our best to do the sensible things like putting protectors in the electrical outlets, the funny plastic ties and stops on cabinet doors, placing cleaning and other hazardous materials in high, secure places.

We knew never to leave a panhandle pointing out over the stove, etc. But it's funny the things even the best of parents overlook. After all it had been a while since we adults had gone through the stage and we forget. But little ones are marvelous teachers. In spite of our best efforts to accommodate the beginning walking stage, the sense of exploration in these little critters is boundless and ingenious. At times, it looked like we were the victims of a raccoon in the house. And for those who have had the experience of how quickly a coon can rearrange the furniture you know what I'm talking about.

Then there is the miraculous capacity to swallow things. Now I never thought a one-year-old could ever swallow a wristwatch or a horny toad intact. None of the children ever performed this neat trick (to the best of my knowledge) but after experiencing some of the things they seemed capable of swallowing, I started worrying if a couch pillow or the resident hamster or parakeet turned up missing. And when they discover the toilet, amazing new worlds of investigation and experimentation are opened to little ones. This device alone opens broad, new vistas on the horizon of imagination.

Most thoughtful and responsible parents are capable of keeping the family M-16, 12-gauge shotgun, 9mm automatics and anti-personnel and in-law grenades out of the reach of little ones. But some things are not quite so obvious to parents.

When I begin to think of things like this it reminds me of the time my brother and I washed our mother's electric mixer, iron, clock, toaster and waffle iron in the bathtub. I think we included some items of lesser consideration like cups, plates and utensils as well. And of course we had to do this chore by climbing into the tub to do it properly. The bubble bath was a nice touch. By God's grace and the intervention of angels, we didn't think to plug any of these items in while washing them. Or maybe none of the cords were long enough to reach the outlet, I don't remember.

Speaking of household hazards and toddlers in an age of such marvelous, timesaving (?) appliances like the garbage disposal and trash compactor, parents really have to have their wits about them at all times; especially when the little one gets to about three-years-old. I have stories ... but I must forbear out of concern for embarrassing my children. But I do recall becoming familiar with the hospital emergency room during those early years.

No one who has raised two or three little ones will fail to make at least a couple of visits to the hospital; or, to a veterinarian. For example, you are blessed with a particularly curious and inventive little genius, a quick learner. But the family cat or pooch disappears. Where do you look? The trash compactor, of course.

Taking your little one in to get a shot; I wonder how many of you have ever had the fairly common experience of a crazed wildcat performing alterations on your shirt or blouse? While wearing same, of course.

Compared to the Addam's Family, I suppose my children were, all in all, fairly normal and typical. I found the usual dried foodstuffs and petrified lizards under beds and in drawers, the bedrooms were usually scenes out of the movie "Twister" and my youngest daughter at age fourteen tried to elude the cops in the family Chevette.

I'll never forget the phone call from the police. At three-o-clock in the morning: "Dr. Heath," an officious voice sounded in my ear, "do you have a daughter named Karen?" I was a little fuzzy at that hour but my unconscious was awake. It immediately advised me to deny knowing anyone named *Karen*. It didn't occur to me at three-o-clock in the morning that my little girl might be slipping out of the house after everyone was asleep to take driving lessons. But silly me, I rubbed my eyes awake, reluctantly told my unconscious to shut up and admitted I had a daughter named Karen.

Now I know most parents have had similar, normal and common experiences with their own little angels. So I won't bore you with any more family stories. With a little luck, children usually grow up, marry and have children of their own. And it is payback time for us as grandparents! That is our reward. Grandparenting is definitely better!

Ok, so children are loads of fun and parents get invaluable lessons in life raising them. And these are lessons that can be learned in no other way. I haven't anything but sympathy or pity for those without children or those who elect not to have children. They miss a huge dimension of life. And people without hope of grandchildren are most to be pitied. But I seldom fail to find humor in the antics of adults as well. Keep the monkeys, people are far funnier, and, in many cases, dumber.

Like most of you, I depend on newspapers for current events and to be informed. Aside from the things of world-wide interest like the usual wars, general mayhem, fires, floods, earthquakes, plagues, famine, pestilence and the O. J. trial, in short the things I need for the occasional chuckle and general merriment, there are the small, side-bar reports of real interest.

For example, recently a guy replaced a blown fuse in his car with a live, .22 caliber cartridge. Now most people know that a fuse blows from an electrical problem that produces excessive heat. Ergo, this rocket scientist installs a live round of ammunition in place of the fuse. The slug struck him in the knee. Could have been worse; since he was driving the car and in a seated position, suppose the round had struck him between the knees; would have ruined his whole day. Reminds me of the guy who while drunk at a party demonstrated the proper way of crimping a dynamite blasting cap with his teeth. Talk about shooting off your mouth!

A science teacher and former colleague of mine had taken his class on a field trip into the desert. A part of his program was warning and demonstrating to his pupils the dangers of this environment such as rattlesnakes and scorpions.

"Now all of you pay attention," he said, "don't ever put your hands into a bush." He demonstrated this hazard by putting his hand into a bush. Fortunately for him, the snake only had one fang. He still came close to having the finger amputated and spent two weeks in the hospital. His pupils were most suitably impressed with the heroic demonstration. Nothing takes the place of practical application in science. Few teachers have such an opportunity to impress their pupils in such a dramatic manner. And he certainly got their attention!

I had some fun asking him if he would be willing to repeat the demonstration for the edification and instruction in the scientific method for the benefit of his fellow teachers? He declined. In fact he declined with some of the most colorful language for emphasis ever heard in or out of his classroom.

Curiously, it was another science teacher I knew who, while clearing some property he had bought, thought it would be a good idea to dispose of a large amount of poison oak by burning it. While recovering in the hospital, he spent some time adding the hazards of burning poison oak and inhaling the smoke in his lesson plans for the next school term. Again, the practical experience of a thing transcends most textbooks.

With over 20 years of school experience, I've got some definite opinions on why the kids are not getting a good education in math and science. These two science/math teachers and so many like them that I have known contribute not a little to my opinions.

Then there was the wood shop teacher I knew who demonstrated the hazards of using a radial arm saw without the proper guard in place. He explained to me how the resulting loss of three fingers on his left hand never interfered with his teaching. Practical experience once more to the fore!

Most safety lectures are dry and boring to pupils. Nothing takes the place of shredded flesh and splattered blood to make an impression and cause the lessons come alive. But to give credit where it is due, who can fail to admire the dedication of teachers who get bitten by snakes, inhale poison oak and amputate fingers for the benefit of their pupils? No sacrifice too great.

Being a pilot myself, a favorite of mine is the story of the airline captain I read of who was fired for a comment he made. He had taxied out and gotten clearance for takeoff at LAX. Dutifully notifying his passengers to buckle up in preparation for the takeoff, he then said to his co-pilot: "Ok, let's see if we can get this over-loaded mother off the ground!" But he had forgotten to switch off his mike to the passenger compartment. The ensuing pandemonium among the passengers can easily be imagined. Now why waste paper and ink on headlines about Madonna having a baby or a militia plan to blow up the White House when you've got things of real interest to readers, real jewels like the above which truly inform and educate?

I love this one too much not to pass it on. Cleveland, Ohio judge Shirley Strickland Saffold gave this advice to one Katie Nemeth to get rid of a boyfriend and get a better one. How? According to the judge men are easy. You can go sit in the bus stop, put on a short skirt, cross your legs and pick up 25. Ten of them will give you their money. If you don't pick up the first 10, then all you got to do is open your legs a little bit and cross them at the bottom.

The judge was right, of course. Men are easy and pretty stupid when it comes to sex. I know if all the women of America could be convinced to cross their legs and keep them crossed for 30 days, Congress would call an emergency session and pass this amendment immediately! You ladies take note.

And since I have your attention, i.e. sex, let's talk about obesity. Ok, let's not talk about obesity.

Seriously, former U.S. Surgeon General C. Everett Koop names obesity the second leading cause of preventable death in the U.S. But in his list of things like heart disease and diabetes that are linked to obesity, he neglects a related real killer: Depression!

Fat people generally do not feel good about themselves; low self esteem. They are subjects of ridicule as children. They seldom find satisfactory relationships in marriage and romance. Thin and pretty or handsome should not be the criteria of a person's value as a human being. But there are some things inherent to all human beings. One of these things is sexual attraction. Obesity is not sexually attractive. Never has been, never will be.

Some of the finest friends I have are overweight. Their weight has nothing to do with their value to me as friends. But for their sakes, I want them to slim down. I know it will do wonders for their health and self esteem. As a friend, I care about this.

However, when virtually one-third of Americans are obese you have to wonder just what is going on here? Whatever the reason, there is no doubt that such a large segment of the society suffering low self esteem has to have a dramatic impact on society in general.

A perfect example of what I am talking about is the recent case of Sharon Lopatka who, being obese, advertised for sex on the Internet. What she really wanted was for someone to kill her. She linked up with Robert Glass who fulfilled her wish. Before the date she wrote her husband: "If my body is never retrieved, don't worry, know that I am at peace." This is an example of *Fat Kills* that the Surgeon General did not take into account. And it is not an easy one to take into account. But it has a lot to do with the general low self esteem of many Americans that has an enormous impact on an entire nation.

You all know of my comments concerning the ineffectiveness of registering sex offenders. Here's a good example of what I'm talking about from Arkansas. This state has at least 1,000 sex offenders behind bars at any one time. But it's the responsibility of the criminal to register! As a result, the Arkansas register only has about 50 names! And some of these give bogus addresses! A perfect example of a well intentioned but largely worthless law.

All good research is a process of slow, thorough, meticulous study. Often involving experimentation, hypotheses and theories evolve as the research suggests ideas and, hopefully, conclusions. When people ask me how I came up with the proposed amendment I don't have any quick and simple answer for them. The proposed Amendment itself is so revolutionary in scope that in itself should tell people no one could come up with such an idea in some flashing moment of insight or inspiration. From some questions asked of me, you would think I got up one morning, looked out my window and decided it would be a nice day to change the world; didn't happen that way.

Now I knew the world needed changing. I've known this for quite some time. But it isn't all that simple to do. In fact it isn't all that simple to come to any conclusion about what those changes should be. There are people who think the changes should start with Shakespeare's advice: First we kill all the lawyers. While the idea might have some merit, we have to admit that a lawyer does serve a useful function on rare occasions. There is even the rare lawyer who does us a service rather than services us. Then there are those who believe we should all be living underground in order to preserve the environment and conserve energy. These mushroom people have some good ideas but would we want the world changed in this manner?

As with most ideas of wide scope and vision, there is a background of a great breadth of research involved. Such ideas are usually the result of many years of study and contemplation of the problem for which a solution is sought. And we accept as axiomatic that defining the problem is the first step toward a solution.

It took many years of study and experience in a wide range of careers and living life, of mixing with people and children in a milieu of circumstances, of asking myself fundamental questions about humanity before the amendment began to suggest itself. It took the writing of six, lengthy books to provide a foundation for even being able to formalize the problem and address a solution.

For example, you have to meet and get involved with so many as I have, some very close to me, who are afraid to hope, dream, trust and love. The pain they have suffered in their lives by hoping, dreaming, trusting and loving only to have these things betrayed has been too much for them. I don't blame them or try to change their minds. I grieve for them.

But I know this amendment offers the hope that evil can be overcome. And I firmly believe we have to start with our children, we have to start by proving we cherish our children and want them to be able to hope, dream, trust and love with the expectation that these things will not be betrayed! And speaking of betrayal, it has a lot to do with the proposed amendment.

Ellie Nesler shot the molester of her young son to death in the courtroom. She knew what she was up against and had the courage to take justice into her own hands.

The perverted justice we face in cases of child molestation allowed the monster that molested her son to sit there in that courtroom smirking at Ellie knowing full-well he probably wouldn't even serve any time. And even if he did, he would soon be free on good behavior. There aren't any little girls or boys in prison. There was even the threat that he would be coming after her and her son once he was set free.

Our perverted laws sent Ellie to prison. She is dying of breast cancer and the family is trying to prevail on Governor Pete Wilson to let her come home to die. I have written the governor on Ellie's behalf as follows:

The Honorable Pete Wilson
Governor of California

State Capitol, Sacramento, CA 95814

Dear Sir;

You have been gracious enough to reply to me in your letter of September 21 that you have sent my proposed amendment to Donald Currier of Criminal Justice Planning. Several other governors have answered in the same fashion and I am grateful. The amendment is enormously complex, revolutionary in fact, in its impact legally and sociologically and it deserves the closest professional examination.

The following is to be included in my December edition of THE AMERICAN POET, the monthly essay I use to disseminate information and progress of the amendment. I sincerely hope you will act in favor of Ellie Nesler. (I included the above remarks concerning Ellie at this point)

Respectfully;

Donald G. Heath, Ph. D.

Americans for Constitutional Protection of Children.

Naturally I hope the governor will act on Ellie's behalf and I will inform my readers accordingly.

The appeal of the noble gunman who rights injustice is something we all applaud. We always applaud the good guy who blows away the bullies. It is intrinsic in good people to want justice, to protect those who cannot protect themselves. Should Ellie Nesler have let the law handle the evil man who molested her son? And what would have happened to Ellie and her son if this animal was released and came after her and her son? Are the victims to stand guard with guns to protect themselves because the law fails to do so, to wait in fear not knowing when the predator will attack?

The weakness of any law falls into two general categories. One, it fails to be just. Two, it is impossible of thorough enforcement. The laws governing child molestation are of the first category. They are not just. And when a law fails to meet out justice, the people have a right to cry out for a just law to take its place.

The leadership, failing to hear the cry of the people, has an ultimate precedent confronting them in our founding fathers. Laws have become so punitive against honest, responsible, law-abiding citizens and so favoring the irresponsible, the bullies and criminals that the leadership better begin listening to the cry of the people.

I doubt any of us would advocate anarchy. And while no reasonable person could fail to sympathize with Ellie Nesler, no reasonable person, for the sake of a civilized society, wants to have to resort to her method of seeing justice served. Then what? The only answer is law that is just, law that we can depend on to be enforced, expeditiously and without an eight to ten year appeal process, law that does not make the victims wait in terror for the criminal to come back to do them further harm. Without a just system of law, there can be no civilization worthy of the name. I want my children and grandchildren to grow up and live in a civilized society, not one where it takes a gun to meet out justice.

This amendment is a good place to start. If it had been the law at the time, Ellie would have known she and her son would be safe. They would never have to live in fear of this animal being released for good behavior and come hunting for them.

It would serve us well to look to some of the wisdom of the past in addressing this issue. There is a solid foundation of historical wisdom from which to draw. How many today, for example, know much of William Penn, the founder of Pennsylvania? Yet his wisdom of religious toleration is still an excellent example to follow in many ways.

Penn wrote a great deal. He had the spirituality of a John Woolman mixed with the common sense of a Benjamin Franklin. Penn's most well known work is "No Cross, No Crown" that he wrote while in prison in the Tower of London for his heterodox, religious views. A devout Quaker, he questioned the orthodox interpretation of the trinity among other things but his preaching and teaching of mankind's responsibility for social ills, the opinion of Benjamin Franklin and others, was especially ill-received by the churches of his time.

An example of his opposition to the pseudo-spirituality of his time (and ours as well) is a statement from his book which fairly represents his (together with Franklin's and my own) view of the relationship between men and God: "True Godliness does not turn men out of the world, but enables them to live better in it, and excites their endeavors to mend it."

Would that those who profess to love and serve God would pay heed to Penn's words in this regard. Particularly those who insist you must belong to their little, exclusive club in order to really be right with God and have His blessing and favor!

From his "Some Fruits of Solitude" we read:

Inquiry is human; blind obedience brutal. Truth never loses by the one, but often suffers by the other.

There are some men like dictionaries; to be looked into on occasions, but have no connection, and are little entertaining.

A wise man makes what he learns his own, another shows he's but a copy, or a collection at most.

It takes a great breadth of reading and study to take advantage of the best of wisdom, to learn the lessons of the past in such a way as to improve the future. By paying too much attention to expediency, to palliatives that do not cure the ills or advance civilization, we have suffered mightily.

Blind obedience, for example, to some superstitious or religious orthodoxy invariably leads to conflict, conflict which, like that between Arab and Jew is in itself a crime against humanity. Consider the divisiveness in our own country of those that promote one form of religious interpretation of Christianity over another. And especially those who preach and teach that their way is the only way of salvation!

It is obvious that such fanatical, superstitious, religious taboos and hatreds such as that of the Moslem Taliban in Afghanistan are repugnant to any civilized society. To beat men, women and children openly in the streets for a failure to adhere to religious dogma is barbaric. But in May of this year one Carlos Santiago was arrested in San Francisco for stabbing his wife more than a dozen times because she refused to read the Bible!

The White House plans to appoint a panel of religious leaders to investigate and defend religious liberty abroad. I applaud this. But those protesting such a panel include James Dobson of Focus on the Family who has never even responded to my proposed amendment!

Would that those like Dobson and so many others who call themselves Christian had as much interest in children and religious liberty as President and Mrs. Clinton. Dobson and the others would do well to listen to William Penn and Benjamin Franklin regarding the duty of men and women before God to one another rather than religious nonsense that make people better Catholics, Baptists and Presbyterians than better citizens!

But, I remind myself, while President Clinton and governors George Bush, David Beasley, Gary Johnson and Pete Wilson recognize the import of the amendment, those like Dobson and Robertson of the Christian Coalition are probably not that enlightened or astute; and are far more interested in their egos and male-dominated, religious empires. Of course, these extreme, religious conservatives are going to have their hands full when the exploration of Mars, Io and new discoveries in astronomy, paleontology and archaeology take their toll on their narrow view of God and His creations.

In the meantime, I have to struggle through without God speaking to me directly and without Robertson's miracles, divine manifestations of angels and an angelic language. I guess Dobson and Robertson would call me spiritually under challenged.

To illustrate the immensely complex dimensions of the problem the amendment addresses, one of the parts has to do with the question of why history has been a story of continual warfare between nations? Another part of the problem is why women have never been included, except in the most cursory and incidental way, in politics, philosophy and theology? The thousands of books on the subject of relations between men and women, between nations, cultures and ideologies give you an appreciation of the complexities involved.

Racial and religious hatreds seem always to have abounded. Prejudices against women are clearly seen in their continual exclusion from the decision-making processes. The very system of laws governing our nation proves how very complex a society can become. Yet most would agree that we are not on course in providing a future for our children, most certainly not the kind of future that life post World War II seemed to promise.

We are being bombarded with bad news on every hand. Books like former judge Robert Bork's hit hard at some of the wrong turns we have made as a nation. But this reminds me of a scene in Schindler's List where an engineer points out the fact that the foundation for a structure is all wrong and must be replaced. She gets shot for her trouble.

Virtually no one would disagree that unless you have a suitable foundation it is worse than useless to expend time, energy and money on the structure. Jesus made this very point. We have done a good job putting paint and filigree on the structure with gingerbread galore. But the foundation is rotten and must be replaced. Now you can have me shot or benefit from the warning.

Foundational to any civilization is its hope of the future. This is predicated on the family unit. And the success of the family unit is predicated on the relationship between a husband and wife. And this relationship predicts the future of children, the hope of a nation's future.

But it takes an entire society working in unity with a priority of encouraging family and protecting children to advance and maintain such hope. Not especially profound and everyone nods their head in agreement. But there is a responsibility factor that must be faced; the failure of this responsibility must be faced.

For example, if babies are born without responsible parents, they become the wards of society that can never do the job of actual parenting. With divorce and illegitimate births so wide spread, the rottenness of the foundation is assured. It is essential that a society faces its failure to be responsible; its failure to prioritize and encourage family and children or the foundation will never be repaired or rebuilt.

Selfishness is the criteria of irresponsibility. Whether that selfishness is evidenced by so-called men who rut like animals and take no responsibility for the babies they father or the selfishness of a man or woman who divorces just because they are tired of their partner with no thought of how this impacts on children, it makes for a rotten foundation.

We need to, as a society, look deeply into the laws, attitudes, mores that have brought us to such irresponsibility as a nation, an irresponsibility that makes it ever more apparent that we care little for our children, for our future as a nation. It certainly does not bode well that a number of surveys prove older people no longer hold on to the values of their parents. It isn't unusual anymore to find the gray generation using vulgar and profane language, lacking in civility and concern for children. The greedy geezers, as they too often are appropriately called, seem increasingly unconcerned for the future of children.

Most certainly making the courts take over the responsibility for children is not any kind of an answer. Yet when half of marriages result in divorce, a major contributing factor in the change in attitude of older people toward children and loss of values, the courts invariably are called upon to try to make up for failed marriages in the disposition of children.

Dependency courts in the juvenile justice system are no answer either. In short, nothing will ever take the place of a father and mother staying together and working for the welfare of their own children; then, as proper grandparents, giving continuing help and support to the young families that so desperately need the love and wisdom of those grandparents. Rather than laws that make divorce as easy as buying a bottle of shampoo with virtually no concern for the impact on children, as a society we need to make it far more difficult to divorce!

Further, as a society, we need to address the painful problem of the values taught and encouraged in our children. An adulterous parent, for example, has forfeited any moral basis of instruction to children. A promiscuous man or woman has forfeited any moral basis of instruction to the young. In other words, there must be a virtuous parent to instruct children in virtue.

It is a failure of a whole society, its homes, churches, schools and government, to produce virtuous parents that lead to the lack of needed innocence and virtue in children. This is the most damning indictment of America! This is the core of the rottenness of our present foundation!

While divorcing at the drop of a hat is a problem of supreme importance to resolve because of the damage to children, the damage done to any sense of moral values, there is the further problem of ingrained prejudices to be faced. To amplify the dimensions of the problem my good friend, Byron, came by the other day and as we were chatting I told him: Suppose we were watching a group of Christian, Jewish and Moslem children playing in my backyard. Now imagine they are all only three-years-old. These children wouldn't have any trouble playing together. But give them a couple of years of indoctrination into their respective religions and by the time they are six-years-old they will have learned to be suspicious of one another, even hatefully prejudiced and resentful of those not of their kind!

The wisdom of childhood is rooted in innocence. Children have to be carefully taught to be suspicious and hateful of others not like them. And who is responsible for such teaching? A society that is dedicated to teaching such hatred.

Yet religions, cultures, are too often dedicated to such prejudicial hatreds. And these hatreds are rooted in a professed love of God, of upholding His honor! The very hypocrisy of such a thing would seem to be obvious. How is it, then, that such hypocrisy is not obvious to its practitioners?

I was such a person myself. But I could never get around what Jesus said about becoming like little children or there was no hope of heaven! Like Nicodemus, I struggled with that seeming impossibility. How could I become like a little child?

Christians make much of something they call the New Birth, being born again. But I never saw such a profession on the part of these people that changed their lives back into childhood. I most certainly didn't see it happening in my own life. I remained prejudiced toward those not of my kind. I had a superior and condescending attitude toward those who were not Christian by my definition of the word. I was anything but a child again in the innocence of childhood, the kind of innocence that encouraged my playing with those other children not of my kind.

If anything, I became ever more distrustful, suspicious and disdainful of those not of my kind. This, I knew, could not be the kind of childhood, new birth Jesus was talking about. But I also knew that a religion that taught superiority over others, even hatred of others, whether Christian, Jewish or Moslem, could not be of God. If there was anything to be learned by the sacrifice of Jesus it was the love of God, a love totally antithetical to the condition of hatred of those not of our kind, of consigning to the pit all those that did not agree with our gospel!

It was just such a hateful, prejudiced religious mind-set that led to the crucifixion! Rather than the wisdom of childhood, the prejudicial hatred of the adult put Jesus on that cross. So I struggled with the true Gospel that Jesus declared was to love God and love one another. Here was the true message that could only be understood by the wisdom of childhood.

But the best of the man, the child within, had a tough time finding other children who would play with him on this basis. If you weren't the right color, if you didn't know the secret password, signal or handshake, if you didn't talk the same language, believe the same legends and fairy tales or wear the right uniform, you couldn't play with the other children. I found the innocence of love and trust, of wanting to play with the other children was stymied by such things. The child just couldn't understand why he wasn't allowed to play with the other children?

But adults were calling the shots. The adults had warned the other children not to play with me. Eventually, the adult in me had to try to make sense of this. The child couldn't understand because there was no suspicion or distrust in him, he knew nothing of evil or evil people. But the man knew, like the gods of Genesis 3:22 the man knew both good and evil.

To maintain a cultural identity is important. But to preach and teach that such an identity makes you superior to others, even a basis to distrust and hate others, to use such a thing as an evidence of God's special favor is wrong ethically, morally and factually!

There is no discounting the advances in science and the arts a particular culture or race might contribute to civilization. Tragically, such advances are not accompanied by advances in compassion and love of others but are usually corrupted to a doctrine of superiority over others.

If my race has the advantage of a science which is able to manufacture the ball and another child of another race that cannot produce a ball wants to play, at what point does a child begin to share that ball or tell the other child, "You can't play with my ball?" But don't we, as parents, tell our children: "It's nice to share." Don't we try to teach our children to be unselfish?

"Give me a child until he is six-years-old and he will be mine forever!" was not original to Hitler. Most nations of antiquity knew this maxim. We will cherish children in innocence or we will raise little devils. That, too, is a maxim. We will raise them in love of one another, of others, or in distrust, suspicion and even hatred of those not of their kind. A nation will reflect the way it trains its children.

If a nation is dedicated to a religious superstition that makes children starve in preference to killing cows that adult superstition must be confronted. If birth control is not practiced by a nation that insists other nations feed its starving which result from irresponsibility, that fact needs to be confronted. Anywhere children and families are made to suffer because of the superstitious ignorance of religion or some fancied superiority of a culture this fact must be confronted for the evil it really is.

The cruel and barbarous practice of sacrificing children for the appeasement or favor of a Moloch or some Baal is not that far removed from making children suffer and starve in appeasement of irresponsibility and selfishness whether on an individual or national basis!

If a child is found filthy and hungry, physically abused, we are quick to condemn the adults responsible and try to help the child. If medical treatment is refused for a child on the basis of a religious superstition, civilized people are right, and even have the duty, to remove that child from such a harmfully selfish superstitious environment.

But what of the children who are being taught to distrust, even hate others? We are quick to defend the parent's right to teach that child such things. We have an article of the Constitution that forbids owning another human being, of treating other human beings as chattel, pieces of property. But where is the same law that protects children in the same manner? Oh, we say, that is the right and responsibility of parents! Well and good, that is the way is should be. But what if the parents will not accept the responsibility of their own child?

Now society steps in with its laws to govern this contingency. Americans are compelled to care for children who are abused or neglected by their parents. And this, also, is as it should be; but how to confront a nation that promotes the abuse and neglect of children? Anyone who reads a newspaper knows of this happening in other countries. And if you still doubt this, get a copy of the report from the international conference on molestation recently held in Stockholm, Sweden. This will make a believer out of anyone!

Responsibility for confronting the cruel treatment of children starts with a nation setting the example for other nations. It is my firm conviction that America, as the most uniquely God-blessed nation in history has the responsibility of setting that example. And I further believe the acceptance of such a responsibility for America rests in this amendment.

There is no way of minimizing the truly revolutionary concept of this amendment. This is why state governors have submitted it to legislative review. These state leaders know it is enormously complex. It calls for a nation to dig deeply into its whole psyche, to ask the supreme question of itself whether it truly values, cherishes its children!

Belgium is in worldwide disgrace because of the evidence of the molester/pornography/pedophile Cartel operating in that nation with the protection of those in high authority. Few know how powerful this organization is that is promoting the murder, torture and selling of children throughout the world. And yes, even some of those beasts such as "The Finders" in America as well!

Most of you know about the protest march by 300,000 people in Belgium concerning the cover-up and protection of those high in authority that are involved in the pedophile Cartel. Carine Russo whose little eight-year-old daughter was repeatedly raped, the rapes being video taped for sale, and starved to death in a dungeon said of the protest: "This is all about our children and about citizens who have realized they need to express themselves as citizens."

Well, Mrs. Russo, the citizens of America have been handed a wake-up call via this amendment. My fervent hope is that once America has led the way in this, other nations such as Belgium will recognize their responsibility to children and take like courses of action to protect them.

That wild, predatory, conscienceless monsters like Marc Dutroux and Richard Davis were imprisoned and released after only two or three years for good behavior only to rape and murder children is one of the most unconscionable, criminal acts against humanity imaginable of any government! It is just such perversion of law and on the part of those in authority that drove Ellie Nesler to do what she did, that cries out for the justice and protection of this amendment for children and their parents!

If people want some shocking insight into the problem of our priorities as a nation, take a look at the codes for your state governing real estate. Then look at the codes concerning molestation. The California State Code Book is an excellent example- Page after page after page concerning real estate. Less than one-half of one page concerning molestation!

Since I first began the battle for this amendment, many interesting things are coming to light. I voiced the thought in the beginning that the fight for this amendment would cause a raging debate in this nation, a debate that is sorely needed in order that Americans will be able to face themselves and determine our priorities as a people.

But many thought the conservative right wing would immediately jump on such a bandwagon. Wrong! This proves my contentions about those people and organizations that pay lip service only in their much preaching about their love for children and families, about their love for God and country.

For example, the Christian Coalition; you wouldn't believe the non-answer I got concerning the amendment from this organization. But as I've written previously, organizations like this and James Dobson's that are male-dominated are not very responsive to things in which women, historically, have had more interest than men. As I've said many times, women, the momma bears, hear the cry of children much more than men. But men have the power. At least until women have had enough and speak up for the children; something that men who make the wars, have never done.

There is another disturbing element relevant to the failure of religious organizations to address this amendment that several people have pointed out and in which I concur. The fact that Robertson, Falwell, Dobson, et al. didn't think of the amendment themselves and can't take credit for it. And it has been my experience of many years of working with and for religious organizations that if they didn't think of it, it can't have any merit and isn't worthy of their support. Of course, such thinking has more to do with the egos involved than anything else. But putting egos before the welfare of children? That is inexcusably shameful!

In this I think of Nathanael's retort concerning Jesus: "Can anything good come out of Nazareth?" John 1:46. Boy, was he ever wrong! The escalating abuse and molestation of children has brought about a much needed and long neglected attention to Pediatric Gynecology. Dr. Thomas Irons, a professor of pediatrics at the East Carolina University School of Medicine recently said: "We brush it aside because nobody wants to deal with it. Culturally we are very sensitive to the idea of examining the private parts of a little girl."

Long quagmires of neglect, together with the risk of being accused of sexual impropriety, doctors have been most reluctant to make such examinations of children. Yet Dr. Susan Pokorny, head of obstetrics and gynecology and past president of the North American Society of Pediatric and Adolescent Gynecology says: "I see mothers bringing in their daughters with symptoms the girl has put up with for two years, problems a grown woman would never put up with for more than two weeks! There is 50% of the childhood population that has never had a very important part of their anatomy examined!"

An important aspect of examination in cases of suspected child molestation is that the child is made as comfortable with the doctor as possible, a point made by Dr. Kenneth Schikler director of adolescent medicine at the University of Louisville School of Medicine in Louisville, Kentucky, and that the child is not made to feel that the examination is a continuation of the molest. We have a long way to go in order to get out of the Stone Age in regard to children, a Stone Age that has not a little to do with why people and nations still behave in Stone Age warfare toward one another!

It wasn't that long ago that cancer was thought to be a localized condition and was treated by simply cutting out the tumor. Look how far we have come in just this one instance as knowledge has increased. Yet how little progress we have made as human beings in our treatment of children. It may well be that we must solve this problem before there can be any hope of a global village where the adults will get along together without prejudice and hatred by meeting on the common ground of love for children.

I just heard that Bill Mauldin has died at 75. Rummaging through my archives of WW II memorabilia, I came up with his Pulitzer Prize-winning book, "UP FRONT" that chronicled that part of the war in Europe in cartoons of Willie and Joe. Like Ernie Pyle in his stories from the front in the Pacific war, Bill made those fighting the war personal and close to those at home.

It is hard to believe that Bill was only in his early 20s while at the front of the European Theater of war, traveling with those dogfaces he immortalized in his cartoons. But, I remind myself; B-17 captain pilots were in their early 20s, a lot of responsibility for those so young. As I thumbed through the old, yellowed paperback, so many memories as a child were evoked. Our heroes were Willie and Joe, MacArthur, Patton and Bradley. But Eisenhower became president.

While our teachers were telling us not to pick up suspicious objects on the playground because they could be bombs left there by Japanese or German spies, I would think of some cartoon of Willie and Joe. It helped take the edge off the dark thoughts of explosive booby traps intended to maim and kill children.

Re-reading UP FRONT I'm transported to that time and I see, once more, the windows of the shacks in Little Oklahoma and the small flags with blue stars hung in them proudly proclaiming a son or husband was fighting the war. And the occasional gold star that proclaimed the ultimate sacrifice of that loved one.

I'm reminded of the late night visit of a naval officer and his handing my mother an envelope containing the personal effects of a sailor, Joe Brown, our stepfather. The only thing I remember well was the fire blackened pocket watch.

I helped grandad flatten tin cans, peel foil from cigarette packs and roll it into a ball for metal drives. We bought war stamps at school and licked and stuck them in little books. When the books were filled, they could be used to purchase war bonds. My brother, Ronnie, and I would put our pennies and nickels into piggy banks with the faces of Hitler and Tojo that would squeal when you deposited a coin for the war effort.

We children would watch the fighters from Minter Field in mock combat overhead and in our childish innocence never could know the deadly earnestness of what was really at stake as those young flyers prepared for mortal combat overseas. And it all makes me wonder when we adults will realize we have to fight for our children, that a far more heinous and deadly enemy than Hitler or Tojo is murdering our children; that virtual war has to be declared against this Beast!

But not even a Bill Mauldin could come up with a cartoon about this war. It's one thing to find dark humor in adults killing one another. The torture and killing of children, of the innocent, is quite different.

It gave me pause recently to learn that Humphrey Bogart was acclaimed the greatest actor ever from a list of 100. Bogy made a lot of films. He certainly matured in his later films and movies like Treasure of the Sierra Madre, The Caine Mutiny and African Queen proved his versatility and talent.

Thinking of some of Bogart's early work led me to mention to my eldest son, Daniel, that for a real look at the America of the 30s and 40s, watch an old Humphrey Bogart movie, especially those in which he worked with Lauren Bacall, Sydney Greenstreet, Peter Lorre and Edward G. Robinson.

When I watch one of those old classics of the 30s and early 40s it is hard for me to believe that life was once so simple for the average American. But, as per Casablanca, how many young people today would believe people could really be so idealistically self-sacrificial, romantic and dedicated to a cause? But we were.

Could any man ever love so much and be as noble as Rick to give up Ingrid Bergman? Can a song like "As Time Goes By" so move the hearts of two people? Yes. And the movie moved the hearts of Americans. It remains, rightfully, a classic of real, idealistic love and romance, that for which all our hearts yearn.

The power of real art, especially that of the theater and cinema, of written expression, to move hearts is well known. The best of such work can never be mechanically contrived. It must come from the heart of the artist in order for heart to speak to heart.

It takes, tragically, to have really loved in order to know the pain of the loss of real love, to understand its profound depth of grief. Some who have known such pain will never take the risk of loving so much again. And some have never even taken the risk the first time. Some like Thoreau and Kierkegaard would write mechanistically of love but lacking wife and children, lacking that kind of commitment to love, could never understand what they had never experienced. They should have had more sense than to offer anything on the subject.

Yet there is always that kind of ego that will even have the bald effrontery to pontificate on subjects of which the pontiff has no real knowledge or experience. Into this category fall those critics of film and literature who could never be successful in either but feel they know all about the subjects.

If someone suggests that I mix a can of creamed corn and a can of spaghetti and meatballs with my vanilla milk shake I think I'll take a pass. Somehow I just don't think the combination is something that would get past my nose, let alone fool my stomach into a Try it; you'll like it.

It just might be ok, though. And I'll never be sure unless I try it. Thus, experience. And some experiences are of that kind where a prejudice may stand in the way. And I'll tell the person: That sounds terrible! But I'll never know unless I taste it. However I won't speak *ex cathedra* on such a concoction because I really don't know how it would actually taste. Very doubtful I ever will.

Critics should confine themselves to the actual reasons they like or don't like something. They should never criticize the artist by telling him how he could have made it better. If they had that kind of expertise and insight, they would be artists instead of critics. At bottom, the critic is someone who is a frustrated wannabe without the talent or the self-discipline of the craft.

For example, simplicity; just who are you to criticize simplicity if you haven't had the complex experiences that justify your applauding or criticizing simplicity? In this I give Thoreau high praise. When he wrote of simplicity in living he knew whereof he spoke. He mixed with the most complex men of his time and his Walden experiment was successful by a valid comparison with the complex.

A reading of Jimmy Breslin's book on Damon Runyon helps to explain that simplicity America once enjoyed, a simplicity that still attracts people and made The Waltons so successful. Runyon made Broadway a household word across America. He made Little Miss Marker and Guys And Dolls a part of America. He made many liars, thieves, murderers, and scoundrels of all sorts kind of lovable in many instances. He was the founder of the Gangster movie. So *Runyonesque* became a part of our language and not long ago one of the twelve most often used literary adjectives (according to Breslin).

I can only pity those who don't know Runyon's history. To be ignorant of such an Icon of his time, of the imprint he made on the story of America during this period and after, is to be inexcusably ignorant. I have met people who thought they knew something of Broadway and Hollywood, of people like Frank Capra, George Raft, Edward G. Robinson, and yet knew nothing of Runyon.

The bald-faced and entertaining treatment of Runyon by Breslin is an insight into the character of both men. Breslin's own views are easily seen in things like his equating crummy little criminals with politicians. Not off the mark to most Americans. And Breslin gives the crummy little criminals better marks than politicians for character and honesty.

For example, according to Breslin, the alliance of builders, bankers and politicians, by stealing tax money wholesale, form the real criminal class in this country. Few would dispute this. The exposing of the embezzlements and adulterous affairs of Bishop James C. Cannon Jr. of the Southern Methodist Church and one of the loudest and most influential voices next to Billy Sunday's in favor of prohibition was one of the achievements of Runyon.

Runyon was able to give us the Madam with a heart of gold right out of Gone With The Wind. But it took others to corrupt his writing of crummy little criminals (and many not so little like Capone) to fabricate a Godfather who wouldn't sell drugs because it was a dirty business and a John D. Rockefeller who would never sell oil for the same reason. To quote Breslin: "Organized Crime in America was born with an English accent, not Sicilian. And that accent was Owney Madden's, born of Irish immigrants and the closest, criminal confidant and friend of Damon Runyon."

A large part of Runyon's success and popularity was predicated on his recognizing the fact that there is just enough larceny in most people to make them suspicious of honesty. For example, in my own experience, I can compare the publishers and editors of a newspaper with preachers. Both first con themselves that they are responsible for a gospel. As a result, both get at the business of conning others to believe this gospel and pay them for the preaching. This is their rice bowl.

Both the publisher/editor and preacher are performing a service of informing. Both are going to save people from ignorance and themselves. The most accomplished cons, those like the legendary Wm. R. Hearst and our contemporary Pat Robertson, wind up with the money; the final criteria of the truth of their gospel. Both come from the same stamp of Pancho Villa who could plunder and murder for his gospel but wouldn't allow children to come near a gaming table. I mean, you simply have to draw the line somewhere just to sleep at night with your mattress and pillow lumpy from all the loot.

The poor, struggling newspaper men and preachers who haven't made it lacking the genius and ruthless courage of a Hearst or Robertson or failing to silence their consciences entirely have to content themselves for eking out a survival based on the alms of those they can con. These are the equivalent of Breslin's crummy little criminals.

To Runyon we owe the line: "All horseplayers die broke." So it is, and for the same reason, most newspapermen and preachers die broke. There is always that one horse that is going to make the big score that will put them right up there with Hearst and Robertson. But most lack the courage to bet the farm. They take the little they can make by any other method than legitimate labor and bet small and often. It makes them just as broke and keeps them begging for more.

Now I know there are a couple of honest publisher/editors and preachers that truly believe they are earning an honest living by their respective callings. These few actually tell the truth as they see it. But let's face it folks, punching up the story, whether by the innuendo of press or some divine revelation that approves a little holy lying, is hard to pass on all the time, especially when your job (and ego) is on the line.

As to preachers and holy begging, I defer to Ben Franklin for the definitive criticism. Franklin was a great admirer and enthusiastic supporter of the great preacher, George Whitefield. The two became fast friends.

Pending one of his visits to Philadelphia from England, Whitefield wrote Franklin that he wasn't sure where he was to lodge. Franklin invited him to stay at his house.

Whitefield wrote that if Franklin made the offer for Christ's sake, he would not fail to be rewarded. Franklin wrote back concerning the offer of his house: "Don't let me be mistaken; it was not for Christ's sake, but for your sake." There isn't a single, holy lying beggar in religion, whether Christian, Jew or Moslem, who would understand Franklin's reply. Or take it to heart.

Runyon gave us much by his genius. But in spite of his genius, I despise the man for his abysmal failure to cherish his family. They paid a heavy price for his success. Again, one can appreciate the art and despise the artist. It was only fitting that his ashes be scattered over *The Great White Way*. This was his home and his life. But the family he had made of crummy little criminals would, at the end, never take the place of the family he disdained and needed at the end of his life from throat cancer. While it is true that a real writer is lost in his thoughts most of the time, that even a commitment some weeks away seems an intrusion and is a distraction from the solitude so necessary to the craft, there is nothing that can take the place of the needed humanity of family.

I think the lack of family, or the attention to family, contributed a great deal to writers and filmmakers (not to mention TV) leading America astray. When I consider some of the greats and look at their failure to love wife and children, I have to wonder if some of the views they successfully impressed on people in the name of realism were not terribly distorted? But the genius of the writer and others carried the day and convinced many, as any successful con, that because of such genius, they had to be right!

Just as Runyon wound up living a life of illusion thereby creating a Broadway that never really existed as he described it in his stories, so many great writers and movie producers gave Americans much that has nothing to do with reality, is, in fact, a distortion of reality. The early gangster stories of Runyon became the gangster films. We now had kids that wanted to be Wiseguys. George Raft once related the story of some kids coming up to him and asking him if there was someone he wanted them to bump off? The power of the film.

Never mind that Capone and Adonis were nothing but bloodthirsty hoodlums, we began to see kids to whom such animals were heroes! The glorification of violence later sophisticated to movies like Shane. I got my first parking ticket ever when I took my brother Ronnie with me to see the film. It was downtown L.A. and in spite of the ticket, I'll never forget this first, Adult Western. It had everything, the good guys and bad guys, the virtue of the noble gunman

The change in America can be seen in a young man watching a pretty girl in a flowing, white gown walking across the greensward with the moon behind her and saying, "She walks in beauty as the night." And his heart being moved to respond to such beauty in such a fashion would be appreciated and understood. Then we began to leave this world behind when the young man began to turn sheepishly to his buddies after such a display of sentiment and say, "Or something corny like that."

When young people began to be made to feel foolish or apologetic for such tender sentiment of the heart, we were on the slide to perdition. And we must look to the schools, the universities, the corruption in leadership and entertainment, the churches, parents and grandparents themselves for the answer to where we went wrong.

But only genuine love and romance without fear of betrayal, with hope of a future, can return us to such sentiment of the heart as She walks in beauty as the night; or a Rick sacrificially giving up Ingrid Bergman.

"Solutions To Domestic Abuse Sought!" So screams many a headline these days, especially when children are continually molested and literally beaten or starved to death! Child Protective Services in Kern County, California allowed a situation where a little 4-year-old boy, Dylan Vincent, was beaten to death by one Francisco "Frank" Jay Alvarez. The mother of the child, Diane Borgsdorf, has been charged with felony child abuse and Alvarez, the live-in boyfriend, with murder. Alvarez was already under suspicion in the death of the 5-month-old baby boy of another girlfriend.

I have worked in CPS. I know how badly the agency is run. It did not surprise me that in spite of the dangerous situation little Dylan was in, a CPS worker had marked the case: Inappropriate for Response! It was my undue interest in the shabby and non-professional way CPS does its work that made me *persona non grata* to the agency. My pointing out the fact that the lack of professionally qualified personnel, not those with idiotic basket weaving courses in social work, was a travesty did not endear me to the administration; or to many social workers. But then I had the same problem with the schools that are so corrupted with nepotism and cronyism and just plain ignorance and thoroughgoing incompetence and chicanery.

As to domestic violence, I have no doubt that the murderer of little Dylan had seen too many movies and videos where women and children are abused and murdered, maybe one too many football games. Let's face it folks, we have been saturated with violence and the glorification of violence, most of it generated by perverts.

You don't listen to so-called *music* that has a theme of sadism, drug abuse, sexual irresponsibility and violence without its having an effect. You don't watch interminable hours of violent movies and TV without its having an effect. You don't have books and films dedicated to violence and the tearing down of civilized behavior and manners without its having an effect. And so on.

It doesn't take an expert in human behavior to determine that when a child sees violence in the home, on TV and in movies and videos and hears it in music that child will react to it. Such exposure teaches the child that violence is acceptable. It further teaches the child that violence is an acceptable solution to problems.

One expert on violence, Dr. Jess Diamond, forensic medical examiner for child abuse puts it succinctly: "Kids are dying!" He says the answer is to ban violence. "That's a hard task," he says, "but if we don't start, are we ever going to change? We should make abuse in society a major health problem. Let's address it like we address polio or measles or any other health problem."

Dr. Diamond is absolutely correct. But to ban violence in a society that is so given over to violence? The first and essential step is the amendment. I have no doubt that if the proposed amendment had been law little Dylan, as with Polly Klaas, would be alive today. Ellie Nesler would never have gone to prison. The amendment will force CPS to become a professional agency; it will force those like the mother of Dylan to act responsibly both sexually and in a choice of boyfriends. It will give parents like Ellie Nesler confidence that justice will be served without taking it into their own hands.

Will we, as a people, say NO! to violence? I believe we must, but there seems faint prospect of it happening. Our first lady, Hillary Clinton, speaks of a global village that is necessary for the welfare of children. And I couldn't agree more. But who has the responsibility of such an example to the rest of the world? We the People of America have that responsibility.

Now that the elections are over, I expect to hear from more of our legislators. Some will be newly elected. I will certainly hear from President and Mrs. Clinton. And I hope to hear from Butrous Ghali of the United Nations. I have written him asking if there is any nation in the world that has anything like the proposed Amendment in its constitution or charter of government? Why? Because I know of none personally; but suppose the United States should be the first nation in the world to give this kind of priority to the cherishing of its children? That would indeed be astounding!

And I ask myself an increasingly rhetorical question: Could this have something to do with the history of the world being a history of conflict between men and women, of distrust, hatreds, prejudices and warfare between nations? Could we be on the right track with this amendment to finding the key, finally, as the human race to Paradise Restored?

CHAPTER FOURTEEN

AMERICANS FOR CONSTITUTIONAL PROTECTION OF CHILDREN

PROPOSED AMENDMENT TO THE U.S. CONSTITUTION

An adult convicted of the molestation of a child will be sentenced to prison for a term of not less than ten years.

If the child dies as a result of the molestation the person(s) convicted of the crime will be sentenced to life in prison without the possibility of parole.

A child as defined by this article shall be one who has not attained their sixteenth birthday.

The Congress shall have power to enforce this article by appropriate legislation.

I have initiated a proposal for an amendment to the U.S. Constitution that would protect children at the most fundamental level, protection from molestation. It is essential that such protection be universal. An amendment would serve this purpose. If child molesters knew they faced federal prosecution and life in prison without parole, it would be the strongest kind of deterrent and save many of the Polly Klaas's.

Article 13 of the Constitution abrogated slavery. We the People declared to the world that Americans believed no human being should be owned by another. Lincoln's Emancipation Proclamation has been applauded by history among the nations of the world. And rightly so.

Yet we have neglected, virtually ignored, the enslavement of our children to the molester by not taking the very same step necessary to ensure their rights as children, as human beings, that Lincoln took in abolishing the evil of slavery. Are our children to continue to be considered chattel, owned and brutalized by taskmasters, overseers far worse than those of the Plantations? How much longer, in any sense of conscience, will we refuse our children their own Emancipation Proclamation, freeing them of the tyranny and slavery of molestation?

People have lost faith in our system of government. And how can the people have faith in a system that cannot even protect their children? An amendment would empower the people by giving them a chance to stand up and take action in a cause that declares our love for our children, for their rights to a childhood free of the tyranny of the molester!

It simply cannot be left to the several states to do this on an individual basis. The laws protecting children from molesters are too ambiguous, voluminous and far from being in accord from state-to-state. For the first time parents, family, a nation can directly address a specific, positive step by which We the People can show we care about children and family values. It is my earnest conviction that this would be a mechanism that could draw our nation together in common cause.

When you consider the fact that over one-half of little girls suffer some form of molestation, this goes a long way in explaining some of the major problems in America. This amendment would serve notice that the people of America intend to protect the rights of children to be children in all innocence, that Americans cherish their young, our posterity, that we are, in fact, a moral nation.

Just the fight for such an amendment will pay vast dividends in making the enemies and predators of children, of family, the enemies of our posterity, declare themselves. I can think of no better way of bringing good people together in common cause. Our children have no voice or choice. It is our duty to speak and act for them.

Such an amendment will reduce prison and welfare populations. In the shorter term, it is well substantiated fact that babies having babies are to blame for an enormous burden on taxpayers. These babies of girls as young as eleven-years-old are invariably doomed to substandard care which increases medical costs. As such children grow, they are far more likely to be anti-social, illiterate and begin early, criminal activities loading our juvenile justice systems, and, eventually, our courts, jails and prisons.

If adult molesters of such girls faced life in prison, I guarantee there would be an immediate impact on this problem which is contributing to so much heartache and fiscal difficulty in our nation. In the longer term, there will be fewer such children growing up to a life of crime, thereby reducing prison populations. Fewer such children being born will have a dramatic effect on our economy by reducing the problems they create for the schools, medical care and other financial burdens to the taxpayer.

A somewhat more subjective, but to me, major factor is what this amendment will do for a lower divorce rate and the strengthening of family in this nation. By reducing the number of stepfathers and other predators who prey on the child victims in homes, people will be much more inclined to consider this in marriage or live-in arrangements.

Unquestionably, when we are dealing with the fact that over one-half of our little girls are molested in one way or another, the trauma carries into their adult relationships, especially marriage. By radically reducing such molestations, we have taken a huge step toward establishing healthy marriages, and, by extension, a healthier society. Consider the boys that are molested and the enormous cost, mentally, socially and fiscally to America. Such boys are far more likely than others to be involved in crime and sociopathic, antisocial behavior.

This amendment will virtually eliminate the inhumanity and national disgrace of child prostitution. By force of law, it will encourage sexual restraint, self discipline and responsibility and greatly reduce the number of abortions. It will also dramatically impact Child Protective Services, forcing that agency to act in a far more humane, responsible and professional manner. There is no doubt in my mind, having worked in this agency myself, that with the power of such law as this amendment, CPS will have to do a better job of identifying, establishing factual case evidence and removing the predators of children. Even if this were not a question of morality, the fiscal impact alone makes it deserving of our best efforts.

My hope for passage of such an amendment is based on several facts. One being that it hits at the heart of all Americans regardless of race, creed or political views. Also, if the fiscal impact can be made clear to Americans, this alone would insure passage.

For my part, I will try to make the message one of empowering the people to take action against an evil on which we all agree, action that We the People can take in spite of the lack of concern for us, the lack of moral and responsible leadership in government! If we can succeed in just this one thing, you know the hope it will give Americans that we really can do something positive for the future of our children, for the future of America!

With success in just this one thing to start, imagine where Americans, inspired with such hope that they can take control and make positive changes for the better, might be able to go from here in correcting some of the other evils that are destroying America!

Few people know the actual laws concerning molestation. Having worked in the schools and CPS, I had to know them. In dealing with the arguments against this amendment, we have to confront much ignorance on the part of those who do not know such laws but have much assumed knowledge about the subject.

One example of such ignorance is the person who said to me: You can be arrested if a child accuses you of molesting him! Incredible as it seems, this man actually believed this. Why? Because he had heard something somewhere! You would think such ignorance impossible. But it's out there and has to be confronted.

No one can be arrested on the basis of a child's accusation. Yes, a report might be taken by the police and/or CPS. But an arrest is predicated on evidence and investigation, not simply an accusation whether by child or adult. In this respect, the laws concerning suspected or alleged molestation are no different than the multitude of other laws governing the actions of police leading to arrest and prosecution for a crime.

Yes, the reputation of a person can suffer simply on the basis of such an accusation. But that is true of any number of other things that can destroy a person's reputation regardless of guilt or innocence. As with any crime of which a person is accused, guilt must be established beyond doubt. The amendment must automatically follow due process, a right already established and guaranteed by the Constitution. What the amendment will accomplish by federal guarantee is prosecution of those who have enough evidence against them to be arrested and charged for the crime, not suspicion of the crime.

The most pervasive argument against the amendment comes from those who believe the amendment is too draconian, from those that believe that the child molester is sick, not a criminal. The crux of this argument is the perception that child molestation is not the result of criminal intent, that it is not serious enough to incarcerate a person for life. I will answer this by saying that first and foremost, a child has a right to be a child, to be raised in a loving environment in all the innocence of childhood.

No one would disagree that molestation emotionally scars a child for the rest of his or her life. Try living with that! The molester has done something to the child that literally imposes a life sentence on the child! The molested child is likely to engage in aberrant, sexual behavior. This perpetuates a vicious chain of victims. I know personally of one case where there were 32 counts of molestation involving eighteen children molested by one person! Out of those eighteen children, some will go on to molest others. Only keeping the molester in prison will break this chain.

As to being sick, this is a sickness that admits of no cure in spite of claims to the contrary. You're a psychologist or psychiatrist who subscribes to the sick theory. Very well, treat the molester in prison where he belongs! I suggest, however, that the molester be kept apart from the general, prison population or that separate facilities be provided for the molester.

The molester is a predator. If a mountain lion leaves its natural habitat and starts preying on pets, even children in another environment, we don't say: The poor lion must be understood and treated for its aberrant behavior. No, we hunt down and shoot the lion if it has attacked a person. Why? Because we know an animal like a lion that behaves in such a manner is not susceptible to treatment to correct such behavior. It will never learn not to attack people. Few of us would have any compunction about shooting a lion or mad dog that threatened a child. That thing is trying to kill the child! you say. Since the molester, in most cases, is not trying to kill the child, we don't consider him a mad dog. But he is.

But in the instance of a molester who makes a child of thirteen pregnant, what happens? Abortion; but if not abortion and she has the baby, what happens? Typically she goes on welfare. And, as happens many times, the baby is born with defects and the hospital and medical costs ($5,000 a week to keep a crack baby breathing!) to the taxpayers are enormous!

If the molester is arrested and imprisoned he gets out to continue his depredations. Will the molester be responsible for the babies he has fathered? You know the answer to that one. The baby, and typically, the child-mother become a life-time cost to the taxpayers. The victims of molesters go far beyond the child molested.

But it will help immeasurably for the victim to know that the mad dog, the predator will never have opportunity to do such a thing to someone else! And it will help immeasurably for the victim and witnesses to know they need never fear this animal coming for them when released from prison, that there will never be another victim of his depredation! And I maintain the victim has this right to that much peace of mind!

Ask yourself why molestation is not taken as such a serious matter in society? You may surprise yourself at some of your answers. The bottom line to this is that we, as a society, have been trained not to think about it so seriously.

Since girls, far more than boys, are the victims of molest, this points out a problem of tremendous magnitude concerning a society's attitude toward molestation. Girls and women are there to be used by men! Girls and women do not have the value of men! And this fact of history has a direct impact on child molestation, especially the molestation/rape of young girls.

My books: Hey, God! and Birds With Broken Wings address the truth, the facts of this problem. But you would have to read these books to gain an appreciation of the monstrous magnitude of the problem, its history and dimensions, its impact on the whole history of the human race and how it affects virtually everyone today!

Suffice it here to say that the problem of the relationship between men and women is the most difficult, intractable problem with which the human race has to deal, a problem of such complexity and intractability that it has never admitted of a solution! Yet look at its importance. As goes the relationship between the sexes, so goes a nation. But, I ask in the book, why are women totally excluded from philosophy and theology? I answer: Because they have no value! The natural, historical resentment of women is thus easily understood.

Molesters act on this premise. They know girls, women, have no value and as a result society, led typically of men, will not act against the molester effectively. Women don't realize how treating the molester leniently has led to their victimization as adults.

Rape victims are made by the police and the courts to feel they are to blame for being attacked! Sexual harassment, even being stalked by men, is not treated seriously in our society. Our lenient attitude toward the molester is at the basis of this lack of sensitivity to female victims.

We keep boys and girls in school until they are 17 or 18 years old. But do we consider such teenagers children? No. That is the reason for the amendment dealing with children under 16. It isn't because 17 and 18 year olds are adults. But our society treats them as such sexually. These children are marrying in our society. Our entertainment media encourages, extols their sexuality. We have taught such children that they should be sexually active or there is something wrong with them!

It would be naive indeed to think that children as young as six and seven aren't getting this message as well and responding to it. And just as children are now raping and killing children thanks to the messages received primarily through the sex and violence of TV, videos and movies, the so-called music they are exposed to, the pornographers, pedophiles and molesters have taken advantage of an amoral climate to increase their activities to the most dreadful detriment of our future as a nation!

I can think of nothing as effective to changing our direction as a nation, to tell our children that we do love them and care about their future as this amendment. Draconian? Only in respect to what we, as a society, have been taught to accept and live with.

But who have been our teachers? The psychologists and university professors who have multitudes of theories but do not contribute anything in the way of substantive solutions? The entertainment media that is selling the sex and violence as normal?

Or are they those homosexuals and molesters in the Congress and judiciary who like little boys and teenage girls? Nothing you can name will so expose and call down the wrath of the enemies and predators of children, and our nation, as this amendment!

But parents, people who love children and America, who know the future of our nation rests on our children will be in favor of the amendment. This is not to say that some honest people won't have difficulty with it. And that is their right as Americans.

I ask these, however, to examine the amendment and its ramifications as objectively as possible. This, I fully realize, is asking a lot, especially in view of how we, as a society, have been so successfully propagandized and brain washed in viewing molesters as poor people who need treatment for their sickness. But unless the chain is broken, it will continue to grow worse and worse with no end in sight.

While I anticipate that there will be good people in the churches who will help in its passage, this amendment is not a church issue, it is a We the People issue. Further, I think it reasonable to accept as a fact that a Hindu, Buddhist, Moslem, Jew, Republican or Democrat loves their child as much as any calling themselves Christian.

The historical importance of this amendment cannot be overemphasized. We have the opportunity to turn this nation around by empowering the people to take action in the most fundamental cause of liberty, the liberty of children, and the posterity of this nation, to grow up without fear of being preyed on by adults.

Let us resolve to give our children their needed Emancipation Proclamation, freeing them to be children, granting them their right to the innocence of childhood without fear through this amendment!

Donald G. Heath, Ph. D.

About the Author

Samuel D. G. Heath, Ph. D.

Other books in print by the author:

BIRDS WITH BROKEN WINGS
DONNIE AND JEAN, an angel's story
TO KILL A MOCKINGBIRD, a critique on behalf of children
HEY, GOD! What went wrong and when are You going to fix it?
THE AMERICAN POET WEEDPATCH GAZETTE for 2008
THE AMERICAN POET WEEDPATCH GAZETTE for 2007
THE AMERICAN POET WEEDPATCH GAZETTE for 2006
THE AMERICAN POET WEEDPATCH GAZETTE for 2005
THE AMERICAN POET WEEDPATCH GAZETTE for 2004
THE AMERICAN POET WEEDPATCH GAZETTE for 2003
THE AMERICAN POET WEEDPATCH GAZETTE for 2002
THE AMERICAN POET WEEDPATCH GAZETTE for 2001
THE AMERICAN POET WEEDPATCH GAZETTE for 2000
THE AMERICAN POET WEEDPATCH GAZETTE for 1999
THE AMERICAN POET WEEDPATCH GAZETTE for 1998
THE AMERICAN POET WEEDPATCH GAZETTE for 1997

Presently out of print:
IT SHOULDN'T HURT TO BE A CHILD!
WOMEN, BACHELORS, IGUANA RANCHING, AND RELIGION
THE MISSING HALF OF HUMANKIND: WOMEN!
THE MISSING HALF OF PHILOSOPHY: WOMEN!
THE LORD AND THE WEEDPATCHER
CONFESSIONS AND REFLECTIONS OF AN OKIE INTELLECTUAL
or Where the heck is Weedpatch?
MORE CONFESSIONS AND REFLECTIONS OF AN OKIE
INTELLECTUAL

Dr. Heath was born in Weedpatch, California. He has worked as a manual
laborer, mechanic, machinist, peace officer, engineer, pastor, builder and

developer, educator, social services practitioner (CPS), professional musician and singer. He is also a private pilot and a columnist.

Awarded American Legion Scholarship and is an award winning author.

He has two surviving children: Daniel and Michael. His daughters Diana and Karen have passed away.

Academic Degrees:

Ph. D. – U.S.I.U., San Diego, CA.

M. A. – Chapman University, Orange, CA.

M. S. (Eqv.) — U.C. Extension at UCLA. Los Angeles, CA.

B. V. E. – C.S. University. Long Beach, CA.

A. A. – Cerritos College. Cerritos, CA.

Other Colleges and Universities attended:
Santa Monica Technical College, Biola University, and C.S. University, Northridge.

Dr. Heath holds life credentials in the following areas:
Psychology, Professional Education, Library Science, English, German, History, Administration (K-12), Administration and Supervision of Vocational Education and Vocational Education-Trade and Industry.

In addition to his work in public education, Dr. Heath started three private schools, K-12, two in California and one in Colorado. His teaching and administrative experience covers every grade level and graduate school.

COMMENTS BY SOME WHO HAVE READ THE AUTHOR'S WORKS

Your writing is very important. You are having an impact on lives! Never lose your precious gift of humor. V. T.

You raise a number of issues in your material ... The Church has languished at times under leaders whose theology was more historically systematic than Biblical ... (But) The questions you raise serve as very dangerous doctrines. John MacArthur, a contemporary of the author at Biola/Talbot and pastor of Grace Community Church in Sun Valley.

You have my eternal gratitude for relieving me from the tyranny of religion. D. R.

Before reading your wonderful writings, I had given up hope. Now I believe and anticipate that just maybe things can change for the better. J. D.

I started reading your book, The Lord and the Weedpatcher, and found I couldn't put it down. Uproariously funny, I laughed the whole way through. Thank you so much for lighting up my life! M.G.

Doctor Heath, every man with daughters owes you a debt of gratitude! I have had all three of my girls read your Birds With Broken Wings book. D. W.

I am truly moved by your art! While reading your writing I found a true treasure: Clarity! I felt as if I was truly on fire with the inspiration you invoked! L. B.

You really love women! Thank you for the most precious gift of all, the gift of love. Keep on being you! D. B.

Your writing complements coffee-cup-and-music. I've gotten a sense of your values, as well as a provocativeness that suggests a man both distinguished and truly sensual. Do keep up such vibrant work! E. R.

Some men are merely handsome. You are a beautiful man! One of these days some wise, discerning, smart woman is going to snag you. Make sure she is truly worthy of you. Desirable men like you (very rare indeed) who write so sensitively, compellingly and beautifully are sitting ducks for every designing woman! M. G.

Now, poet, musician, teacher, philosopher, friend, counselor and whatever else you have done in your life, I am finally realizing all the things you say people don't understand about a poet. They see, feel, write and talk differently than the rest of the world. Their glasses seem to be rose colored at times and other times they are blue. There seems to be no black or white in the things they see only soft pastel hues. Others see things as darker colors, but these are not the romantic poets you speak of. C. M.

You are the only man I have ever met who truly understands women! B. J.

Dr. Heath;
You are one of the best writers I've had the privilege to run across. You have been specially gifted for putting your thoughts, ideas, and inspirations to paper (or keyboard), no matter the topic.
Even when in dire straits, your words are strong and true. I look forward to reading many more of your unique writings. T. S.